Escapees

Escapees
The History of Jews Who Fled Nazi Deportation Trains in France, Belgium and the Netherlands

Tanja von Fransecky

Translated by Benjamin Liebelt

berghahn
NEW YORK • OXFORD
www.berghahnbooks.com

Published in 2019 by
Berghahn Books
www.berghahnbooks.com

English-language edition © 2019, 2023 Berghahn Books
First paperback edition published in 2023

Originally published in German as *Flucht von Juden aus Deportationszügen in Frankreich, Belgien und den Niederlanden*
Original German-language edition © 2014 Metropol Verlag

The translation of this work was funded by Geisteswissenschaften International – Translation Funding for Humanities and Social Sciences from Germany, a joint initiative of the Fritz Thyssen Foundation, the German Federal Foreign Office, the collecting society VG WORT and the Börsenverein des Deutschen Buchhandels (German Publishers & Booksellers Association).

All rights reserved. Except for the quotation of short passages for the purposes of criticism and review, no part of this book may be reproduced in any form or by any means, electronic or mechanical, including photocopying, recording, or any information storage and retrieval system now known or to be invented, without written permission of the publisher.

Library of Congress Cataloging-in-Publication Data

A C.I.P. cataloging record is available from the Library of Congress

Library of Congress Cataloging in Publication Control Number: 2019022983

British Library Cataloguing in Publication Data

A catalogue record for this book is available from the British Library

ISBN 978-1-78533-886-1 hardback
ISBN 978-1-80073-923-9 paperback
ISBN 978-1-78533-887-8 ebook

https://doi.org/10.3167/9781785338861

Contents

Acknowledgements	vi
List of Abbreviations	viii
Introduction	1
1. Deportations from Western Europe	17
2. Escapes by Jews from Deportation Trains in France	39
3. Escapes by Jews from Deportation Trains in Belgium	133
4. Escapes by Jews from Deportation Trains in the Netherlands	203
5. Summary	252
Concluding Observations	263
Sources and Bibliography	266
Indexes	287

Acknowledgements

Extensive research work requires support, for which I would like to thank many people.

I am especially grateful to the witnesses who spoke to me in interviews and conversations: Jacques Altmann (Paris), Simon Gronowski (Brussels), the late Rolf Joseph (Berlin), the late Louis Handschuh (Paris), the late Philippe Kohn (Paris), the late Régine Krochmal (Brussels), the late Jacques Lazarus (Paris), Claire Prowizur-Szyper (Tel Aviv), Fanny Rozelaar (Jerusalem), the late Shaul Sagiv (Yakum), the late Sonja Wagenaar-Van Dam (Groningen) and Frida Wattenberg (Paris).

Sincere thanks to Prof. Dr Wolfgang Benz and Prof. Dr Johannes Tuchel. I am indebted to many colleagues and friends for their support, critique and suggestions: Guido Abuys, Susanne Beer, Johannes Blum, the late Robert Cajgfinger, Katja Happe, Ljiljana Heise, Christina Herkommer, Tanja Kinzel, Beate and Serge Klarsfeld, Stefan Klemp, Cordula Lissner, Insa Meinen, Ahlrich Meyer, Jörg Meyer, Arthur Peys, Jule Pomierski, Judith Poppe, Andrea Rudorff, Lieven Saerens, Barbara Schäuble, Laurence Schram, Ellen van der Spiegel Cohen, Elly Peijs-Stoppelman, Stephan Stracke, Klaus Viehmann, Annemarie de Vries, Hans de Vries and Michael Weiss.

Thanks to Luke Haywood, Bärbel Jänicke, Catalina Körner, Birgit Kolboske, Benjamin Liebelt, Kristof Meers, Nadine Schröder, Lilly Sparnay and Naomi Wiener for translating interviews and texts.

It was very helpful for the research process to present and discuss the results of my study at various workshops and conferences, and I wish to thank the DGB-Bildungswerk Thüringen, the Deutsch-Israelische Gesellschaft and the Begegnungsstätte Kleine Synagoge in Erfurt for inviting me to speak at the series of events on the deportation of Jews from Erfurt, and Clark University in Worcester (USA) for the opportunity to speak at the 'Second International Graduate Student Conference for Holocaust and Genocide Studies'. I am also grateful for the chance to discuss

Acknowledgements

my research results during the research colloquium at the Zentrum für Antisemitismusforschung of the Technische Universität Berlin, as well as at an event by the Zeitgeschichtliche Forschungsstelle in Marburg Town Hall.

Thanks to the Hans-Böckler-Stiftung for funding this study with a PhD scholarship. Thanks again to the Hans-Böckler-Stiftung, the Stiftung Erinnerung in Lindau and the Ursula Lachnit-Fixson Stiftung for covering the printing costs of the German publication. Also my sincere thanks for receiving the 2013 Herbert-Steiner-Förderpreis, an award by the Documentation Centre of the Austrian Resistance and the International Conference of Labour and Social History, which was a great honour.

Finally, thanks to the publishers Friedrich Veitl and Nicole Warmbold at Metropol in Berlin, and Chris Chappell and Amanda Horn at Berghahn Books, New York for all their hard work and support.

Tanja von Fransecky
Berlin, 2019

Abbreviations

Abbreviation	Full name	English description
AEL	Arbeitserziehungslager	Punitive, disciplinary labour camp
AJ	Armée Juive	'Jewish Army', Zionist Resistance movement
AJB/JVB	Association des Juifs en Belgique/ Jodenvereeniging in België	Jewish association founded in Belgium by the German occupiers
BArch	Bundesarchiv	German Federal Archives
BBC	British Broadcasting Corporation	British Broadcasting Corporation
BdO	Befehlshaber der Ordnungspolizei	Overall commander of the Ordnungspolizei
BdS	Befehlshaber der Sicherheitspolizei und des SD	Overall commander of the Sicherheitspolizei and the SD
CDJ	Comité de defense des Juifs	Jewish Belgian Resistance organization
CDJC	Centre de documentation juive contemporaine	Centre of Contemporary Jewish Documentation
Cegesoma	Centre d'Études et de Documentation Guerre et Sociétés contemporaines/Studie- en Documentatiecentrum Oorlog en Hedendaagse Maatschappij	Centre for Historical Research and Documentation on War and Contemporary Society

Abbreviations

DeVlag	Duitsch-Vlaamsche Arbeidsgemeenschap	'German/Flemish Working Group', a pro-Nazi organization in Flanders
DÖW	Dokumentationsarchiv des Österreichischen Widerstands	Documentation Centre of Austrian Resistance
EIF	Eclaireurs israélites de France	'Jewish Guides and Scouts of France'
FFI	Forces françaises de l'intérieur	'French Forces of the Interior', French Resistance fighters late in the war
FS	Fernschreiben	Form of telegraph or teleprinter
FTP	Francs-tireurs et partisans	French Resistance organization
FTP-MOI	Francs-tireurs et partisans-Main-d'œuvre immigrée	French Resistance organization, immigrant subgroup of the FTP
FTPF	Francs-tireurs et partisans français	French Communist armed Resistance organization
GFP	Geheime Feldpolizei	'Secret Field Police', the secret military police of the Wehrmacht
HSSPF	Höherer SS- und Polizeiführer	Higher SS and Police Officer
IKL	Inspektion der Konzentrationslager	Concentration Camps Inspectorate, central concentration camp organizing authority
ITS	International Tracing Service	International Tracing Service
JMDV	Joods Museum van Deportatie en Verzet	Jewish Museum of Deportation and Resistance
LAV NRW W	Landesarchiv Nordrhein-Westfalen, Abteilung Westfalen	State Archive of North Rhine-Westphalia, Westphalia Dept.

LAV NRW R	Landesarchiv Nordrhein-Westfalen, Abteilung Rheinland	State Archive of North Rhine-Westphalia, Rhineland Dept.
MBB	Militärbefehlshaber von Belgien und Nordfrankreich	Military Commander in Belgium and Northern France
MBF	Militärbefehlshaber in Frankreich	Military Commander in France
MJS	Mouvement de la jeunesse sioniste	French Zionist Youth Resistance movement
MOE	Main-d'œuvre étrangère	Communist organization of foreign labourers in France
MOI	Main-d'œuvre immigrée	Renamed MOE
MP	Maschinenpistole	Submachine gun
NGFB	Archiv Breendonk Memorial	Foort Breendonk Memorial Archive
NIOD	Instituut voor Oorlogs-, Holocaust- en Genocidestudies (formerly: Nederlands Instituut voor Oorlogsdocumentatie)	Institute for War, Holocaust and Genocide Studies, the Netherlands
NSB	Nationaal Socialistische Beweging	National Socialist movement in the Netherlands
OD	Ordnungsdienst	'Jewish Police' in the camps, also used by Germans to secure deportations
OJC	Organisation juive de combat	French Jewish Resistance movement
OS	Organisation Spéciale	Clandestine Resistance structure of the French Communist Party
OT	Organisation Todt	Civil and military engineering group named after Fritz Todt
PA AA	Politisches Archiv des Auswärtigen Amts	German Foreign Office Political Archive
PB	Polizeibataillon	Police Battalion

PCB	Parti communiste de Belgique	Belgian Communist Party
PCF	Parti Communiste français	French Communist Party
RFSS	Reichsführer SS	Commander of the SS
RSHA	Reichssicherheits-hauptamt	Reich Main Security Office, a major office of the SS
SD	Sicherheitsdienst	Security Service, intelligence agency of the SS
Sipo	Sicherheitspolizei	Security Police
Stapo	Staatspolizei	State Police
SS	Schutzstaffel	Major German paramilitary party organization
SSO	SS-Offiziere	SS officers
TA	Travail allemand	Communist Resistance movement in France and Belgium
SVG	Direction générale Victimes de la Guerre/ Directie-generaal Oorlogsslachtoffers (Service des victimes de la guerre)	Belgian war victims' service
UGIF	Union générale des Israélites de France	'General Union of the Israelites of France', Vichy government organization pooling all Jewish organizations into a single unit
VNV	Vlaamsch Nationaal Verbond	Flemish nationalist party
WA	Weer Afdeling	National Socialist paramilitary arm in the Netherlands

Introduction

In April 1943, the eleven-year-old Simon Gronowski was helped by his mother as he jumped from the 20th deportation train to leave Belgium. The train was intended to take them from the Mechelen assembly camp to Auschwitz. Well in advance, Simon had practised jumping from the train together with other children, often leaping from their bunk beds in Mechelen.[1] By the time the 20th deportation train had reached the German border, a total of 232 prisoners had managed to escape by breaking open the freight railway carriages with smuggled knives and tools.[2]

I met Simon Gronowski in 2006 and heard the story of his escape. According to his account, many Jewish prisoners fled from this moving deportation train, acting exactly as they had planned in advance. In the following months, I attempted to discover whether this mass escape was an outstanding, isolated incident, or whether such escapes were a widespread phenomenon and therefore a hitherto unresearched chapter of the Holocaust.

During the initial investigation process, it quickly became clear that throughout Europe, countless persecuted Jews had attempted to flee from deportation trains.[3] They usually made their escapes while still in their home countries and it was rare that they tried to flee once they were inside the German Reich. That was regarded as too dangerous since the German population was presumed to be hostile.[4] However, in other European countries occupied by Germany, fleeing from a deportation train also involved risking one's life. Many who dared to jump from the carriages were then hit by the train or crushed, while others were seriously injured. Most escapees died because teams of guards shot at them and many of those who managed to flee were recaptured later on.

The State of Research

Jewish prisoners fleeing from deportation trains are occasionally mentioned in research literature (such as in the standard works by H. G. Adler and Raul Hilberg), but they have not been categorized as an autonomous phenomenon.[5] For instance, in his book *Sonderzüge nach Auschwitz* (1981), Raul Hilberg reproduced a document on a mass escape from a transportation train heading to Bełżec, without discussing it further in the text.[6] Nevertheless, the above-named publications form the underlying basis of this study.[7] Only the work by Reuben Ainsztein in 1974, which examined armed Jewish resistance in Eastern Europe, described, albeit briefly, escapes from trains as a relatively common phenomenon, in the chapter 'Flucht als Widerstand' ('Flight as Resistance'), defining it as a form of Jewish resistance.[8] Ainsztein wrote: 'Escape attempts were so common that the train lines to the death factories were covered with the bodies of those who were mown down by the machine guns of the Ukrainian and German guards'.[9] In a rather brief report on an escape, Yehuda Bauer also described the act as a form of resistance.[10] Finally, Saul Friedländer touched on the theme of this study in his publication *Die Jahre der Vernichtung. Das Dritte Reich und die Juden 1939–1945*, assessing it as follows: 'With respect to the "freight" itself, it caused no notable problems. Naturally there were the usual suicides and a number of attempted escapes before boarding the trains and sometimes during the transportation'.[11]

The theme has not been studied in France, with the exception of an essay written in 1974 by Adam Rutkowski.[12] There is, however, a pioneering study by Ahlrich Meyer entitled *Täter im Verhör*, in which selected cases of escapes from deportation trains in France are presented in one chapter.[13]

The attack by Resistance fighters on the 20th deportation train on 19 April 1943, which was unique throughout Europe and resulted in seventeen prisoners escaping from their wagons, was described in an essay by Lucien Steinberg in 1968.[14] Before the criminal proceedings against the former 'Judenreferent' (officer for Jewish affairs) Kurt Asche, Maxime Steinberg researched significant documents and presented them in his *Dossier Bruxelles-Auschwitz. La police SS et l'extermination des Juifs de Belgique*, published in 1980.[15] It devotes an entire chapter to the raid on the 20th deportation train and the subsequent escapes. In 1982, Steinberg and Serge Klarsfeld published a volume of further research evidence in preparation for the Asche trial. For the first time, it quantified escapes from trains. Klarsfeld and Steinberg counted 343 escapes at the time.[16] In 1984, Konrad Kwiet and Helmut Eschwege pointed out the large number of escapes in Belgium.[17] Between 1984 and 1986, Steinberg published a three-volume paper on the extermination of the Jews in Belgium, focusing on Jewish resistance.[18] In this work, which is still relevant today, Steinberg meticulously reconstructed the escapes from the 20th deportation train.[19]

Introduction 3

The 2009 study by Insa Meinen on the persecution of Jews in Belgium includes a chapter that examines the lives, strategies for avoiding deportation and eventual fates of the prisoners on the 21st transportation train. Escapes from that deportation are described as one of several individual survival strategies.[20] In 2002, Marion Schreiber, the then *Spiegel* Brussels correspondent, described the raid on the 20th deportation train in her book *Stille Rebellen. Der Überfall auf den 20. Deportationszug nach Auschwitz.*[21]

Underlying research by the historian Laurence Schram on deportations in Belgium should also be noted. Thanks to her work, I was able to draw from a list of all Belgian train escapees. Research by Schram produced, among other works, a four-volume edition on the deportation of Jews in Belgium entitled *Mecheln-Auschwitz 1942–1944. De vernietiging van de Joden en zigeuners van België. La destruction des Juifs et des Tsiganes de Belgique. The destruction of the Jews and Gypsies from Belgium*, co-written with Maxime Steinberg.[22] It was possible to draw from a number of references to escapes in the book. In 1965, Jacques Presser laid the academic foundations for the theme of Jewish extermination in the Netherlands with his study *Ondergang*, but mentioned escapes from deportation trains in only one sentence. He presumed that only few prisoners fled, since it would have jeopardized the 'wagon elders' responsible for the arrival of all prisoners.[23] The volume *Een gat in het prikkeldraad* ('A Hole in the Barbed Wire') was published more recently by *Westerbork Cahiers*. It describes escapes from the Westerbork camp and includes portraits of two train escapees.[24] The situation in the wagons during the deportation journey was analysed extensively for the first time in 2009 by Simone Gigliotti in her study *The Train Journey. Transit, Captivity, and Witnessing the Holocaust*, which also includes a short chapter on the phenomenon of escapes from the wagons.[25]

Although the extermination of European Jews is a prominent theme of contemporary history, there has not yet been a focus on escapes from deportation trains. Their relevance, however, is obvious, not least with respect to debate on Jewish resistance. This study aims to close that gap in Holocaust research.

Questions and Methods

To reach meaningful results, the field of study had to be limited sensibly, providing a comparison between the countries of France, Belgium and the Netherlands. In choosing these countries, I followed the Most Similar Systems Design approach,[26] which involves the comparative study of one aspect on the basis of similar research subjects. There are several similarities between the study's three Western European countries. For instance, the Wehrmacht occupied them simultaneously, anti-Jewish policy was implemented in similar steps, the deportation systems had comparable structures and the deportation journeys were roughly of the same distance, all crossing the German Reich.

During the study, I chose two questions as leading research factors: firstly the question of overriding structural factors that enabled or hindered escapes regardless of the situation, and secondly the key incidental factors inside the wagons with respect to the decision whether or not to attempt an escape.

The first question arises from clear findings early on in the research process that the number of identifiable escapes in the three countries does not correlate with the respective share of Jewish deportees compared to the overall size of the Jewish population. Based on that fact, I studied the factors in the three Western European countries that aided or hindered escapes from the wagons.

In social sciences, comparisons are made either to examine the general applicability of one's own research results using an additional comparative group (control group) or to derive the typical, relevant, identical or different aspects of two or more cases with respect to a previously defined question. Depending on how the research is designed, a decision is made either in favour of cases that contrast strongly (Most Different Systems Design) or in favour of cases that are similar (Most Similar Systems Design).[27] This study uses the latter approach, since individual factors can be studied comparatively in most similar systems – in this case the three Western European countries. The individual factors are those that influenced the decision whether or not to attempt an escape. The factors must be selected with respect to significance and operative practicability, and limited in terms of their numbers, since no significant statements are possible if there are too many factors. In a second research step, the factors are compared to establish differences and common aspects. Since the study is designed as a three-stage process (description, classification, comparative analysis), the actual comparison is presented at the end.[28]

During the course of my research, I identified factors that aided or hindered escapes. In this respect, Helen Fein's study *Accounting for Genocide. National Responses and Jewish Victimization during the Holocaust* proved very helpful. In it, Fein addresses the question as to which factors influenced the different chances of survival of the persecuted Jews in the different countries. The key factors she identified included:

- The size and identifiability of the Jewish population and its residence status

- The nature and state of a country before its German invasion with respect to the religion of the majority, the existence of a nationally defined solidarity and the success of anti-Semitic movements
- The type of occupation regime, the time when the occupation and deportations began, increasing awareness of annihilation
- The level of state cooperation in anti-Jewish measures including deportation and the respective willingness to collaborate
- The reactions to occupation, Jewish persecution and deportation, acceptance of different degrees and levels of resistance
- Jewish reaction to the persecution, opportunities to go into hiding, the actions of the *Judenrat* and the self-defence movement
- The local conditions such as open escape corridors out of ghettos or across national borders.[29]

This list of factors is also important for this study. To be able to answer the question of structural factors for the significantly different numbers of escapes in France, Belgium and the Netherlands, the concluding observations first name the factors that emerged as relevant after reconstructing escape cases, before comparing their effectiveness in the respective countries. The factors can be classified on three different levels: the micro-level, on which the motives and actions of the people involved became effective; the structural and organizational meso-level; and the macro-level, including factors that became virulent in a greater social context.

The starting point for the second question is the situation of the wagon. What occurred in the wagons when the intention to flee became apparent? Which incidental factors aided or hindered the escapes? Since the deportees in the wagons often interpreted their situation very differently, there were conflicts as individuals expressed their intention to escape. One extremely effective measure was the regularly announced threat when deportees boarded the trains that if anyone was missing at the point of arrival, all others would be shot dead as punishment. The theme is present in almost every escape story. Very often, it is reported that in view of the threat to execute deportees, panic broke out and serious conflicts erupted in the wagons if someone intended to flee. Those who decided to escape despite the threatened consequences therefore found themselves in a moral dilemma. Based on this insight, I investigated the following two questions: What happened in the wagons when it became clear that deportees intended to escape? Which strategies were pursued to prevent escapes or to enable them?

Recurring patterns of action have been categorized into several motivational situations and strategies.

Structure

Chapter 1 provides a general overview of deportations of Jews from France, Belgium and the Netherlands. The focus lies on the respective circumstances, the invasion and occupation, deportation bureaucracy, the function of the Jewish transportation administration and the official language used to conceal the actual aim of the deportations. The chapter also contributes to underlying research on Nazi criminals through its investigation of the deportation train guards, since the as yet only poorly researched complicity of the teams of guards, who mainly consisted of members of the Schutzpolizei, is studied with respect to the Holocaust.[30] The existing sources are analysed on the basis of the following questions: What did the teams of guards know of the situation in the wagons? What did they know about the fate of the people they were guarding? What characterized the actions of the accompanying guards? The chapter ends with an outlook on the later judicial and social handling of the former Schutzpolizei officers.

Chapters 2 to 4 are each dedicated to one country: France, Belgium and the Netherlands respectively. The chapters have three parts. They begin with the initial situation, the underlying conditions and the actions of the persecutors and persecuted.[31] Among other aspects, the study then deals with the agents of Jewish persecution in each country and the resistance groups relevant to the escapes described later on. This is followed by a reconstruction of the 'method of deportation',[32] which includes the presentation of the camps, the actual process of deportation, the situation before boarding the trains, the function of the wagon elders, the type and condition of the wagons used, the situation of the prisoners in the wagons, the composition and actions of the accompanying guards and a count of the deportations. For each country, this introduction is followed by a section on Jewish prisoners' escapes from deportation trains.

In Chapter 5, the summary, the structural supra-incidental escape factors are identified and analysed on a micro-, meso- and macro-level. The question with respect to incidental factors inside the wagon is also answered. The concluding observations chapter considers why the phenomenon of escapes has remained unresearched to date, including an outlook on possible further research.

This study focuses on escapes by Jewish prisoners from wagons of deportation trains leaving the major assembly camps in France, Belgium and Netherlands, heading for the extermination camps and centres. Attempted escapes from feeder trains or buses bound for the central assembly camps are not included in the study,[33] because such transfers within one country were not regarded to be as threatening or as final as deportations to destinations outside the country. Escapes by non-Jewish deportees, for instance political prisoners or civilians displaced to perform forced labour, are also excluded from this study, although they included a number of people who were Jews as defined by National Socialist doctrine but were not recognized as such and were not treated accordingly.[34]

Sources

This study is based on the premise that written history is always the subjective reconstruction of the past using sources that have been passed on to us.[35] As researchers, we must attempt to break down the site-dependency of our perspective by posing the question of other possible interpretations.

The validity and applicability of sources used must be assessed by an academic process of historical research. Sources do not reflect the past without bias or in an unadulterated way and are instead artefacts created by people. They therefore require an interpretation and must be questioned critically. In doing so, the intentions with which they were or may have been produced should also be examined. One key criterion for examining the reliability of a source is the question of whether its author may have given false evidence or omitted relevant material. A second important factor is plausibility. How plausible is a source if one relates it to other sources or the current state of research?

Different types of sources were relevant to this study: contemporary sources, judicial sources from investigative proceedings or criminal court cases after the war, compensation files and individual testimonies by survivors, which may have been produced in different ways, such as an oral history review or a written autobiography.

Contemporary Sources

For the purposes of the study in France, reports by officers in charge of the transports and correspondence between Schutzpolizei officers, the Paris Jewish Department of the Commander of the Security Police and the Security Service SD (Befehlshaber der Sicherheitspolizei und des Sicherheitsdienstes, BdS), and the Reich Main Security Office (Reichssicherheitshauptamt, RSHA), which were archived in the Centre de documentation juive contemporaine (CDJC) in Paris, proved to be especially informative. It was possible to find individual evidence of escapes along the train route in France in regional archives.

Almost no documents of the BdS in Belgium, especially files from the Jewish Department of the RSHA branch in Brussels, exist today. Some documents from this institution could be found in the Reich Main Security Office or the office of the Commander of the Security Police and the Security Service in Paris. However, a large number of documents on Jewish persecution in Belgium do exist, produced by the authority of the Military Commander in Belgium and Northern France (Militärbefehlshaber in Belgien und Nordfrankreich, MBB).

There are some documents that provide information on the victims, for instance deportation lists and the 'Family and Personal Archives' in the Joods Museum van Deportatie en Verzet (JMDV) in Mechelen, containing documents that Jews carried with them when they entered the Mechelen camp. In some cases, files of the Aliens Police (Ausländerpolizei) proved useful in retracing the paths of persecuted Jews.

In the Netherlands, there are deportation lists compiled by the camp administration of Westerbork, while the central file of the Jewish Council and the file of the 'youth transit camp' in the Vught concentration camp are also fully extant.[36] The Instituut voor Oorlogs-, Holocaust- en Genocidestudies (NIOD) in Amsterdam stores, among other things, files of the General Commission for Security Matters, Higher SS and Police Officer North West (Generalkommissariat für das Sicherheitswesen, Höherer SS- und Polizeiführer Nord-West) and the list of prisoners in the Westerbork youth transit camp, which provided great insight into this research theme. The archive of the Westerbork Memorial Center owns a number of transcribed interviews and a database of individuals containing, among other documents, digitized index cards of the *Jüdische Rat*, which also furthered this study. Countless documents from various camp administrations providing information on the subsequent fate of deportation train escapees could be found in the archives of concentration camp memorial centres or in the archive of the International Tracing Service (ITS) in Bad Arolsen.

Underground publications are archived in the Paris CDJC, the Brussels Centre d'Études et de Documentation Guerre et Sociétés contemporaines/ Studieen Documentatiecentrum Oorlog en Hedendaagse Maatschappij (Cegesoma) and in the Amsterdam NIOD.

In contemporary sources, aside from simple copy errors, for instance in the production of deportation lists, other sources of errors are conceivable. It may be that some escapes were never reported because the officer in charge of the deportation did not wish to undertake the time-consuming process of an investigation or suffer possible negative consequences for his career. It is especially plausible that reports to superior officers were aimed at making the authors appear in a good light.

Compensation Files

To study escapes in Belgium, personal dossiers proved helpful. These were produced by the Brussels War Victims Office in the Ministry of Health, the Direction générale Victimes de la Guerre/Directie-generaal Oorlogsslachtoffers (SVG), following the country's liberation. The War Victims Office had several functions. People for whom a dossier was produced had been persecuted by the National Socialists as Jews and/or as political opponents. The SVG acted as a search service, and therefore collected information on the fate and the whereabouts of those persecuted. Secondly, compensation applications could be submitted there. Relevant correspondence, witness testimonies, arrest confirmations and so on are filed in the personal dossiers.

This evidence is particularly relevant to the reconstruction of escapes by Jewish deportees in Belgium. It includes copies of the index cards of the register of Jews by the Security Police and Security Service (Sipo-SD), as well as search service documents of the International Red Cross in Arolsen, birth, marriage and death certificates, copies from the concentration camp administration and proof of forced labour by a number of Belgian Jews at construction sites for the Atlantic Wall, working for a company contracted by the Organisation Todt.

When analysing these personal dossiers, the possible drawbacks lie in the purpose for which they were produced. The War Victims Office used the official classification of 'Politically Persecuted', which was relevant for compensation. One condition for such classification was patriotically motivated resistance to the German occupiers. It is easy to recognize that this requirement led to an initial structuring effect on the cognitive interest of employees at the War Victims Office. From the perspective of Jews applying for compensation, this requirement influenced some statements justifying their respective applications.

Testimonies and Interviews with Witnesses

Of the total of eleven interviews I carried out for this study, nine were guideline-structured interviews with former train escapees held in France, Belgium, the Netherlands, Israel and Germany. Two further interviews and five conversations with witnesses were carried out in the relevant countries with resistance fighters and Holocaust survivors. I found further sources in, among others, the archive of Yad Vashem, the archive of the JMDV, the Wiener Library, the collection of interviews by David Boders entitled 'Voices of the Holocaust', the Visual History Archive (VHA) and the CDJC. Documentary films in which contemporary witnesses make statements were also used.

For a long time, 'self-testimonies' by survivors were received with great reservation by Holocaust researchers. All sources of this kind have the common aspect that they were produced retrospectively. They reflect their author's subjective perspective and interpretation of the described events. That is their strength.

Such sources must be critically questioned with respect to the following sources of errors. The motivation behind the testimony may lie in an intention to serve a present purpose. This can have effects on the choice of theme and the way in which something is presented. The time at which testimony is given also has an influence on the narrative. It is significant how long ago the testified event took place or to what extent a specific orientation towards the fierce political debate (on commemoration) and metanarratives on the Holocaust can be detected. Another problem must also be considered: according to Michael Pollak, in accounts by concentration camp survivors, self-censorship due to conventional moral persuasions and the fear of appearing to be implausible are possible motives for highly selective accounts.[37] Omissions can also be caused by trauma, as a result of which survivors may no longer have access to some of their memory and are therefore unable to describe their experiences fully.[38] Furthermore, with respect to self-testimony, it must be taken into account that grasping one's life history coherently is essential for one's own identity. Coherence is achieved by connecting events in a meaningful way.[39] Events that are extremely harmful to one's own sense of shame, dignity and integrity, making it impossible to structure them meaningfully into a continuum, are therefore problematic for one's own identity.[40] Coherence is sometimes achieved at the price of suppressing painful events, breaks that cannot be integrated or contradictions. This may lie behind the rather brief or completely absent description of the situation in deportation trains in many testimonies by survivors. There are often statements that the experience can hardly be described in words. For instance, the survivor Heinz Salvator Kounio writes: 'The journey took eight days. It is impossible to describe the life we experienced in those wagons'.[41] H. G. Adler calls the deportation an 'inextinguishable trauma'.[42]

It should also be noted that the plausibility test for the past defined by Theodor Lessing as 'logificatio post festum' applies not only to the 'great' writing of history, but also to subjective historical accounts. Since history is made by people, one is always reliant on 'guessing the so-called motives', as Lessing put it.[43] The usual, yet unrealistic reduction to a monocausal explanation always merely 'reflects the rough approximation of the underlying processes'.[44]

Judicial Sources

Various types of documents from judicial bodies proved helpful for this study. In addition to witness testimonies, indictments, investigation results and prosecution withdrawal orders, statements by former officers of the Schutzpolizei, who had guarded Jews on trains to prevent their escape, were especially interesting. These papers can be found in the files of law enforcement authorities, which are archived in the branch of the Federal Archive in Ludwigsburg. The context of a witness testimony, for instance, in connection with an investigation or a criminal or civil court case, strongly determines the result in advance and therefore has consequences for its usability in an academic historical study.[45]

The former Schutzpolizei officers were not questioned as the accused, but as witnesses, and they will have had no interest in changing that position. This fact had consequences for their statement behaviour. Andreas Kunz addresses the problem of many witnesses who had been close to crimes or those accused in Nazi trials:

> They lied, denied, played down, distorted, glossed over. Formulaic and at times detectably dishonest statement behaviour characterizes most of the questioning records. Often, specific defence and exoneration strategies were used by placing responsibility onto perpetrators who had already died, by referring to 'orders from above' or claiming that one had no choice but to carry out such orders. The gravest consequences came from simply suppressing a fact.[46]

Some of the named strategies can also be found in the complex investigations that were relevant to this study. For instance, there was the strategy of admitting to crimes that were classified as less severe and could no longer be prosecuted since the limitation period had passed. This reduces the plausibility of the guarding Schutzpolizei officer at the time and the statements' value as a source. In this constellation, a further problem was that policemen often questioned their own colleagues, who were either still in service or retired. Solidarity within the force repeatedly had the effect that witnesses were questioned in an unmotivated manner. Kunz comments as follows:

> A particular problem was the existence of insider relationships and conspiratorial cartels between police officers who had been involved in the crimes and found their way back into police duty after 1945. In many places, the police apparatus confronted the investigations with insecurity, antipathy and passivity; it was the exception to openly address the investigation, support it and cooperate.[47]

When assessing the written recordings of witness questioning in investigation processes, it should also be noted that three authors contribute to the production of this type of source: the witness himself with his statement, the questioning investigation officer, who guides the dialogue with his questions, and the person producing the protocol, thereby filtering out all linguistic characteristics such as dialect, pauses and so on, and shortening or clarifying statements.[48] In countless reports, the statements are combined into a continuous text. However, despite all critical reservations concerning sources, passages in a statement that may appear harmless can nevertheless be useful in reconstructing events.

Judicial witness statements by survivors at Belgian military courts and German law enforcement agencies flowed into this study to a far lesser extent. Generally, a judge's questioning in a criminal court case follows the logic of proof, while defence lawyers attempt to undermine its plausibility. Only the circumstances of the case are assessed in terms of their legally relevant facts, within the rigid framework of a court proceeding with its own aim and its own rules, so that any number of connections remain unaddressed. Witness testimonies placed a great emotional strain on survivors.[49]

In reconstructing escapes from deportation trains in the three countries, it was possible to draw from three different source types, depending on the country. The samples also differ from each other. In the case of France, where I was able to make a reasonable estimate of the number of escapes at the beginning of my research, I have documented as far as possible all escapes from trains by Jewish deportees. Due to the large number of escapes, I then made a selection of cases that reflected the different factors. In view of the many escapes in Belgium, from an academic perspective it was neither manageable nor sensible to study all cases. Thus, I formed a sample from the outset according to two criteria: firstly minimum and maximum differences and secondly the degree to which they represented their group. With respect to the minimum and maximum contrasting of people, I included those who stood out for instance due to their age, gender, economic or social status, and supplemented them with members of special groups (e.g. families) and strongly represented groups such as former prisoners of the Gurs camp, Polish and Austrian Jews, as well as Jewish forced labourers for the Organisation Todt (OT). The source situation was ultimately decisive in composing the sample. In the chapter on escapes from deportation trains in the Netherlands (Chapter 4), the small number of cases led me to present all escapes that I was able to document.

In order not only to classify the escapes, but also to appreciate the fates of those fleeing from trains, I have gone further than simply describing the escapes and have instead focused on the fleeing prisoners themselves, as well as the experiences and situations that motivated them to escape. Wherever possible, I have also documented their subsequent fate after their escape.

A few final notes: the racist ideological construct of a Jewish 'anti-race' is reflected in the use of terms such as 'Judenberater', 'Judenbeauftragter', 'Judenstern', 'Judenregister' and 'Mischling 1. Grades'. Since it is evident that these concepts belong to National Socialist discourse, they do not require any stressing. Clear typing errors in the sources were corrected without comment. Other errors and outdated spellings following the German spelling reform were retained. Unless otherwise indicated, the French and Dutch quotes have been translated by the author. English spoken passages in which interviewed persons only spoke English that was difficult to understand are retained in the original. All quotes that were originally German have been translated into English for this book.

Notes

1. Interview with surviving witness Simon Gronowski in Wuppertal on 27 January 2006; see also Simon Gronowski, *Le petit évadé. L'Enfant du 20e Convoi*, Brussels n.d.
2. Maxime Steinberg, *L'Étoile et le fusil. La traque des Juifs 1942-1944*, Vol. II, Brussels 1986, p. 63 ff.; Maxime Steinberg and Laurence Schram, *Transport XX. Malines-Auschwitz*, Brussels 2008; Marion Schreiber, *Stille Rebellen. Der Überfall auf den 20. Deportationszug nach Auschwitz*, Berlin 2000.
3. For example, Rudolf Vrba and Alan Bestic, *Ich kann nicht vergeben*, Munich 1964, p. 296; Fabian Herbst et al., *Ich muss weitermachen. Die Geschichte des Herrn Joseph*, Berlin 2008; Zwi Fenster, Bericht über die Vernichtung (Juli 1941–April 1944), 2 August 1968, 1.2.7.8, ID 82188140, ITS Digitales Archiv; Ruth Altbeker Cyprys, *A Jump for Life. A Survivor's Journal from Nazi-Occupied Poland*, London 1997, p. 99 ff.; Jäcklein, Betrifft: Umsiedlung von Kolomea nach Belzec, 14 September 1942, cited in: Ernst Klee, Willi Dreßen and Volker Rieß, *'Schöne Zeiten'. Judenmord aus der Sicht der Täter und Gaffer*, Frankfurt am Main 1998, p. 212.
4. Louis J. Micheels, *Doctor #117641. A Holocaust Memoir*, New Haven/London 1989, p. 64; Claire Prowizur-Szyper, *Instantanés d'ici et d'ailleurs*, Brussels 1982, p. 89 f.
5. H. G. Adler, *Theresienstadt. Das Antlitz einer Zwangsgemeinschaft*, 2nd ed., Tübingen 1960, p. 52 f.; Raul Hilberg, *Die Vernichtung der europäischen Juden*, Vol. 2, Frankfurt am Main 1997, pp. 520, 522 f.
6. Document printed in: Raul Hilberg, *Sonderzüge nach Auschwitz*, Mainz 1981, pp. 194–97.
7. They include H. G. Adler, *Der verwaltete Mensch. Studien zur Deportation der Juden aus Deutschland*, Tübingen 1974.
8. Reuben Ainsztein, *Jüdischer Widerstand im deutschbesetzten Osteuropa während des Zweiten Weltkrieges*, Oldenburg 1993 [1st ed. 1974], p. 80.
9. Ibid.
10. Yehuda Bauer, 'Forms of Jewish Resistance during the Holocaust', in: Michael R. Marrus (Ed.), *Jewish Resistance to the Holocaust*, London 1989, pp. 34–48, here p. 47.
11. Saul Friedländer, *Die Jahre der Vernichtung. Das Dritte Reich und die Juden 1939–1945*, Munich 2006, p. 520 f.
12. Adam Rutkowski, 'Les évasions des Juifs de trains de déportation de France', in: *Le Monde Juif. La Revue du Centre de Documentation juive contemporaine*, January–March 1974.
13. Ahlrich Meyer, *Täter im Verhör. Die 'Endlösung der Judenfrage' in Frankreich 1940–1944*, Darmstadt 2005, pp. 247–69.
14. Lucien Steinberg, 'Un aspect peu connu de la résistance juive: le sauvetage à main armée', in: *Le Monde Juif* 52 (1968).
15. Maxime Steinberg, *Dossier Bruxelles-Auschwitz. La police SS et l'extermination des Juifs de Belgique*, Brussels 1980.
16. Serge Klarsfeld and Maxime Steinberg, *Mémorial de la Déportation des Juifs de Belgique*, Brussels 1982, p. 57.

17. Konrad Kwiet and Helmut Eschwege, *Selbstbehauptung und Widerstand. Deutsche Juden im Kampf um Existenz und Menschenwürde 1933–1945*, Hamburg 1984 (*Hamburger Beiträge zur Sozial- und Zeitgeschichte*, Vol. 19), p. 144.
18. Maxime Steinberg, *1942. Les cent jours de la Déportation des Juifs de Belgique*, Brussels 1984; idem, *L'Étoile et le fusil. La traque des Juifs 1942–1944*, Vol. I, Brussels 1986; idem, *L'Étoile et le fusil*, Vol. II.
19. Steinberg, *L'Étoile et le fusil*, Vol. II, pp. 67–103.
20. Insa Meinen, *Die Shoah in Belgien*, Darmstadt 2009, p. 144 ff.
21. Schreiber, *Stille Rebellen*.
22. Ward Adriaens et al., *Mecheln-Auschwitz 1942–1944. De vernietiging van de Joden en zigeuners van België. La destruction des Juifs et des Tsiganes de Belgique. The Destruction of the Jews and Gypsies from Belgium*, Vol. 1–4, Brussels 2009.
23. Jacques Presser, *Ashes in the Wind. The Destruction of Dutch Jewry*, Detroit 1988, p. 481 (English translation of: *Ondergang. De vervolging en verdelging van het Nederlandse jodendom 1940–1945*, Gravenhage 1965).
24. Guido Abuys and Dirk Mulder, 'Een gat in het prikkeldraad. Kamp Westerbork – ontsnappingen en verzet', in: *Westerbork Cahiers* 10 (2003).
25. Simone Gigliotti, *The Train Journey. Transit, Captivity, and Witnessing the Holocaust*, New York/Oxford 2009.
26. Carsten Anckar, 'On the Applicability of the Most Similar Systems Design and the Most Different Systems Design in Comparative Research', in: *International Journal of Social Research* 11 (2008) 5, pp. 389–401, here p. 390.
27. Adam Przeworski and Henry Teune, *The Logic of Comparative Social Inquiry*, New York et al. 1970, p. 32 f.
28. Ibid., p. 59.
29. Helen Fein, *Accounting for Genocide. National Responses and Jewish Victimization during the Holocaust*, New York 1979, p. 48 f.
30. Apart from the study in France by Ahlrich Meyer, the composition of the accompanying guards and their complicity in the Holocaust remain largely unresearched. Recently, a study of the Bremen Police Battalion 105 by Karl Schneider showed that it repeatedly provided the accompanying guards from the Westerbork assembly camp. Meyer, *Täter im Verhör*, pp. 247–69; Karl Schneider, *Auswärts eingesetzt. Bremer Polizeibataillone und der Holocaust*, Essen 2011.
31. Reinhart Koselleck, 'Vom Sinn und Unsinn der Geschichte', in: Klaus E. Müller and Jörn Rüsen (Eds), *Historische Sinnbildung. Problemstellungen, Zeitkonzepte, Wahrnehmungshorizonte, Darstellungsstrategien*, Reinbek 1997, pp. 79–97, here p. 87; Dieter Pohl, 'Vernichtungskrieg. Der Feldzug gegen die Sowjetunion 1941-1944 im globalen Kontext', in: *Einsicht. Bulletin des Fritz Bauer Instituts* (2011) 6, pp. 16–31, here p. 20.
32. The term refers to the chapter of the same name in H. G. Adler's underlying study on the deportation of Jews from Germany: 'Der verwaltete Mensch' (Tübingen 1974).
33. Brunner and Knochen, Merkblatt, 14 April 1944, CDJC, CDXXXIV-10, cited in: Serge Klarsfeld (Ed.), *Die Endlösung der Judenfrage in Frankreich. Deutsche Dokumente. Dokumentationszentrum für Jüdische Zeitgeschichte CDJC Paris. 1941–1944*, Paris 1977, p. 227; written statement by Laure Danon on the escape of Robert Danon made to the author, 23 July 2009; Elie Rotnemer, Interview Code 32165, VHA, USC Shoah Foundation Institute; Josef Gottesmann, *Von Wien über Deutschland und Belgien nach Frankreich 1938–1942*, June 1958, Tel Aviv, Cegesoma, mic 122.
34. For example the written statement by Marc Monpeurt to the author, 25 June 2009; Déposition de Monsieur Lévi sur sa déportation et son évasion, CDJC, CCXVIII-12.
35. On the subjectivity of interpretation of sources, see Christopher R. Browning, *Ganz normale Männer. Das Reserve-Polizeibataillon 101 und die 'Endlösung' in Polen*, Reinbek 1999, p. 15.

36. Gerhard Hirschfeld, 'Die Verfolgung und Vernichtung der Juden in den Niederlanden', in: Joachim Castan (Ed.), *Hans Calmeyer und die Judenrettung in den Niederlanden*, Osnabrück 2003, pp. 102–15, here p. 110.
37. Michael Pollak, *Die Grenzen des Sagbaren. Lebensgeschichten von KZ-Überlebenden als Augenzeugenberichte und als Identitätsarbeit*, Frankfurt am Main/New York 1988, p. 94.
38. Dori Laub, 'Zeugnis ablegen oder Die Schwierigkeiten des Zuhörens', in: Ulrich Baer (Ed.), *'Niemand zeugt für den Zeugen'. Erinnerungskultur nach der Shoah*, Frankfurt am Main 2000, pp. 68–83, here p. 68; Cathy Caruth, 'Trauma als historische Erfahrung: Die Vergangenheit einholen', in: Baer, *'Niemand zeugt für den Zeugen'*, pp. 84–98, here p. 85.
39. Pollak, *Die Grenzen des Sagbaren*, p. 80 f.
40. Ibid., pp. 13, 88 ff.
41. Heinz Salvator Kounio, cited in: Tullia Santin, *Der Holocaust in den Zeugnissen griechischer Jüdinnen und Juden*, Berlin 2003, p. 134.
42. Adler, *Theresienstadt*, p. 267.
43. Theodor Lessing, *Geschichte als Sinngebung des Sinnlosen. Oder die Geburt der Geschichte aus dem Mythos*, Hamburg 1962, p. 212.
44. Ibid., p. 213.
45. Raul Hilberg, *Die Quellen des Holocaust: Entschlüsseln und interpretieren*, Frankfurt am Main 2002, p. 51.
46. Andreas Kunz, 'Justizakten aus NSG-Verfahren. Eine quellenkundliche Handreichung für Archivbenutzer', in: *Die Außenstelle Ludwigsburg, Mitteilungen aus dem Bundesarchiv* 16 (2008), pp. 37–58, here p. 46 f.
47. Ibid., p. 48.
48. Jürgen Finger and Sven Keller, 'Täter und Opfer – Gedanken zu Quellenkritik und Aussagekontext', in: Jürgen Finger, Sven Keller and Andreas Wirsching (Eds), *Vom Recht zur Geschichte. Akten aus NS-Prozessen als Quellen der Zeitgeschichte*, Göttingen 2009, pp. 114–31, here p. 117.
49. Pollak, *Die Grenzen des Sagbaren*, p. 99.

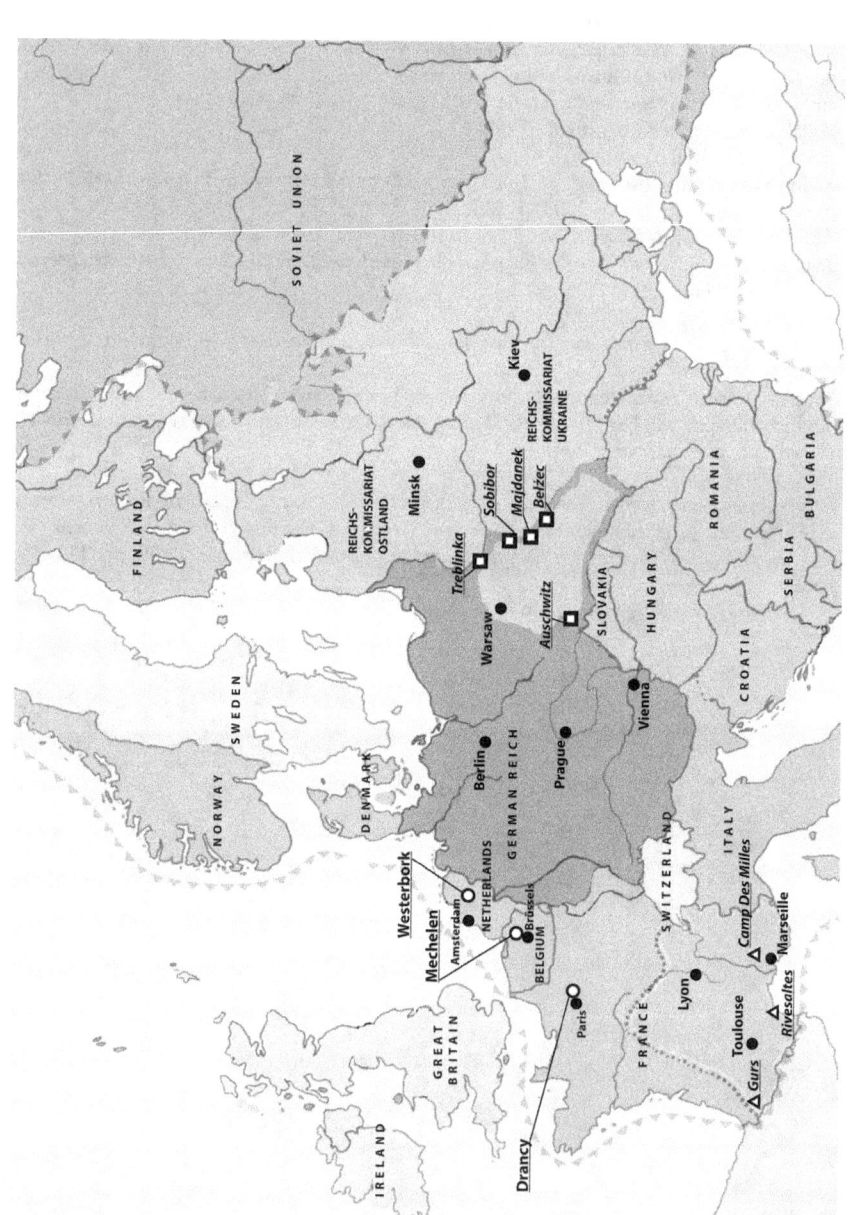

Europe in 1942

CHAPTER 1

Deportations from Western Europe

Organization and Procedure of Deportations from Western Europe

There are a number of similarities between the organization and procedure of deportations from France, Belgium and the Netherlands. It was not only the deportation bureaucracy and processes that were similar; in all three countries, deception strategies were staged to conceal the actual goal of the deportations. Nevertheless, information did manage to trickle through regarding the deportees' planned extermination at their destination.

The RSHA began deporting Jews from Western Europe immediately after the Wannsee Conference on 20 January 1942. In all three countries, the Jewish population had already been defined, identified and registered by the end of 1941.[1] The National Socialist persecutors applied their worldview of 'racial biology' in classifying people as members of the Jewish 'race'.

The Reich's Transport Ministry provided trains following a request by the Jewish Department of the RSHA.[2] For capacity reasons, freight wagons were mostly used in Western Europe. At the time, it was not uncommon for such wagons to transport people and they were standard means of transport for prisoners of war and German army soldiers. Generally, the freight wagons were equipped with simple wooden benches for forty people per wagon. The key difference lies in the conditions during transportation.

The historian Harm-Hinrich Brandt writes:

> In fact the conditions were worse than for mass livestock transportation, since the deportees were not only living beings degraded to the status of mere material assets, but living beings without any value, whose death was readily accepted.

In such conditions, widespread sickness and death actually occurred during the transportation.³

Fifty to sixty people were planned for each wagon, with a total of one thousand per deportation train.⁴ The otherwise completely empty freight wagons contained just two buckets, of which one was filled with water and the other was intended for excreta. Straw was sometimes spread out on the floor. After their arrival in Auschwitz, the wagons were usually cleaned in a 'decontamination unit' since they were heavily soiled by human faeces.⁵

During the deportations, there were frequent forced stoppages, for instance because other trains were given priority or because personnel or locomotives were replaced. Generally, the wagon doors were not opened during these periods, although some deportation survivors from the Netherlands report open wagon doors during stoppages in stations.

Between August and November 1942, numerous deportation trains from the Netherlands, Belgium and France stopped in Cosel, Upper Silesia (today's Koźle), about 80 km from Auschwitz. There was an enormous camp complex there known as the Schmelt Camps, which exclusively used Jews as forced labourers. Due to increasing labour demands in 1942, Albrecht Schmelt, who was responsible for the camp's organization, had received permission from Himmler to select able-bodied, deported Jews from Western Europe for forced labour. Between eight and ten thousand were taken to the Schmelt Camps as a result.⁶

Before boarding the deportation trains, prisoners were warned that if anyone was found to be missing at their destination, all others would be shot dead as punishment. The threat often led to conflicts between prisoners in the wagons. Collective punishment was a typical method of control used by the National Socialists: the victims were pitted against each other by making an entire group responsible for the actions of individuals.⁷ Deportees could not have known that the threatened shootings were never carried out.

The Function of the Jewish Transport Leaders

Another strategy used to burden the prisoners themselves with responsibility for the smooth organization of the deportations was to appoint a Jewish 'Transportleiter' who had to ensure order, calm and cleanliness.⁸ The first concrete evidence of using Jewish Transportleiter is provided in a note written in November 1939 by Theodor Dannecker, an employee of the Jewish Department of the SD headquarters, on the deportation of male Jews from Ostrau (today's Ostrava) in Moravia to Lublin.⁹ The function of such a wagon elder was described by Dannecker in detail in 1942: 'One Jew should be appointed in every wagon to ensure order during the journey and clean the wagon after arrival. That Jew must also carry sanitary material with him'.[10]

H. G. Adler, a historian and survivor of Nazi persecution, describes the selection of the transport wardens for deportations as follows: 'A "Transportleiter" and several "wardens" were chosen from among the victims to ensure calm and order during roll calls, boarding and the journey itself. These people usually received yellow armbands'.[11] The wagon elders are also mentioned in many survivors' reports. Some reports state that those selected had to speak German, so that they could understand the orders of their German guards.[12] The wagon elders often played a key role in conflicts that arose when people intended to escape. They often attempted to prevent prisoners from fleeing, mostly due to the responsibility they had been given and also out of a sense of duty towards the welfare of prisoners left behind.[13]

In addition to wagon elders, further prisoners, Jewish doctors and nurses, were forced to assume functional responsibility for the period of the deportation (as so-called 'Funktionshäftlinge' or 'functional prisoners'). Like the wagon elders, they too received armbands.[14] Early orders required the deployment of Jewish 'Krankenbehandler' (the Nazi term for Jewish doctors who were only authorized to treat other Jewish patients, literally 'treaters of the sick'), who were permitted to take instruments and medicine on board with them.[15] Responsible doctors were named as a formality for deportations from Western Europe, but they received no medicine or medical equipment to fulfil their tasks.

Deportation Bureaucracy

The deportation bureaucracy was developed in stages and continually optimized. It is likely that Franz Novak, the RSHA expert for transportation, developed the procedure for the train's departure and arrival reports in January 1942, the month in which the systematic organization of the genocide of European Jews, which had already begun, was discussed at the Wannsee Conference. Directly after the departure, the following data had to be telegraphed to the RSHA Department IV B 4 for Jewish affairs, the Inspectorate of Concentration Camps (Inspektion der Konzentrationslager, IKL) and the Camp Commander of the camp receiving the deportees: date and time, transport number, number of deportees, name and rank of the transport's commanding officer (Transportführer), distributed provisions, and total means of payment carried by the Transportführer. The arrival was also standardized, requiring the following information:

place of departure, train number, time, any delay, place of arrival, number of persons, provisions on board, means of payment, incidents and problems.[16] The Transportführer received two copies of the transport list.[17] It generally contained data on the deportees: surname, first name and occupation; in France, it appears that in some cases these were listed by wagon.[18]

Pery Broad, a member of the Auschwitz concentration camp's Political Department, which was responsible, among other tasks, for registering prisoners in a central file, wrote that in Auschwitz, the Transportführer always presented the lists to the 'Reception' Department. According to Broad, only those who were intended for labour were recorded by the Political Department. As a result, the total number of prisoners in the relevant transport train was subtracted to calculate the number of those who were murdered immediately after arriving. Older transport lists were destroyed.[19]

Concealment of the Destination and Purpose of Deportations: Note on the Language

Officially, it was forbidden to speak of 'deportation' and euphemisms were used instead, such as 'evacuation' ('Evakuierung'), 'labour assignment' ('Arbeitseinsatz'), 'migration' ('Abwanderung') and, in the case of deportations to Theresienstadt, 'change of residence' ('Wohnsitzverlegung').[20] There were several reasons for such deception tactics, including the need for deportations to be carried out smoothly. For instance, it was necessary for as many Jews as possible to obey their induction orders for forced labour and arrive at the collection camps by themselves (albeit involuntarily), board the wagons without resistance and behave calmly during the journey.

If foreign diplomats enquired, they were to be told that Jews from occupied France were being taken to southern Poland.[21] It was also prohibited to use the words 'to the East' and 'deportation' in official statements in the Netherlands. Instead, the term 'consignment to forced labour' was to be used.[22] Apparently, the camp and deportation train guards did not always use the defined vocabulary, as the following RSHA behavioural reprimand shows. To ensure the smooth reception of arriving deportees, the Auschwitz camp made the following request:

> to make no disconcerting revelations to the evacuated Jews of any kind prior to the transportation with respect to their destination and imminent use. . . . Above all, I ask you to regularly instruct the accompanying guards to ensure that during the journey, they do not make any implied comments to the Jews or speak of as-

sumptions on the type of their accommodation etc. that could lead to particular resistance.[23]

Deportees' Level of Awareness of the Destination and Purpose of the Deportations

It is difficult to determine what was known regarding the extermination that took place at the transports' destination and how plausible the constantly arriving news of the destruction of the Jewish population in Western Europe would have seemed.[24] The fact that underground newspapers wrote about it and the BBC reported on it is not an indication of how widespread the news was. Furthermore, to hear or read about the unthinkable does not mean one believes it. Countless deportees were convinced that they were about to be forced into a labour assignment.[25] Perhaps some people's unawareness was based on a form of denial that served as self-protection. Optimism and hope are powerful survival resources. Others presumed that the National Socialists intended to displace Jews from Europe once and for all and therefore deported them eastwards in families on the premise of a limited spell of forced labour.[26]

From the autumn of 1942 onwards, underground newspapers and radio broadcasts reported on the extermination of Jews. In late 1942, the clandestine newspaper *En Avant* reported that two million Jews had been murdered by the National Socialists in Eastern Europe up to that point.[27] The term 'gas chamber' is first used in *J'accuse* dated 25 December 1942.[28] From then on, the Jewish underground press attempted above all to receive and spread valid information so that as many persecuted people as possible would realize that they had to save themselves from the Nazis' intended genocide.[29]

At the same time, counter-propaganda was spread – by, among others, the weekly magazine *La Gerbe*, which was published by French collaborators. It published an article on the apparent settlement of deported Jews in the East for the purposes of forced labour, including photos of tidy buildings and smiling people. A French Jew recalls the calming effect of the report.[30] Presumably in January 1943, three postcards with postmarks from 'Birkenau' arrived in Drancy, all with almost identical content. The former Drancy prisoner Georges Wellers commented on Birkenau in the Jerusalem Eichmann trial: 'It was a name that we heard for the first time and meant absolutely nothing to us, neither to me nor to anyone else in the camp. . . . These people wrote that they were well, content and that they were good labourers'.[31] When the judge asked whether they were not aware that they would be deported for extermination, Wellers replied: 'No, I knew nothing about it; we knew nothing about it; although we had heard from the London radio that people were talking about gas chambers, but we didn't take it seriously. . . . We had good reasons for not believing it', because Alois Brunner 'had been so very German in the way . . . he developed his deception measures':

> for instance people who were standing in front of the train were talked into handing over their money because they were promised that as soon as they reached their destination, they would receive the equivalent in Złotys from the council of elders after presenting the receipt they had been given. We therefore presumed we were being sent to Poland, that it would be possible to buy something at a place like that, that despite the perhaps difficult, unsettling conditions, we would still at least remain alive there. None of us realized that we were heading for extermination. . . . . When I was sent to Auschwitz in 1944, I still believed it even after three years' experience in the French camp.[32]

Fania Fénelon was also deported from Drancy in 1944 and describes the speculation that arose in her wagon during the deportation. Someone spread the story that they were heading for a labour camp in Bavaria, with 'those cosy little German houses, clean and tidy with a little garden for families and children',[33] while another woman claimed to know that they would all be 'machine gunned' in the wagons, and yet another was sure that they would be killed using electricity.[34]

This shows that even until the last transports in 1944, there was diverging speculation, but no knowledge of the intention to exterminate the deportees. This is confirmed by testimony of the Sobibór survivor Abraham Margulies: 'The transports from Holland, the CSR and France were received politely. . . . The transports from eastern countries, which already knew what to expect, were driven forward'.[35]

From the summer of 1942 onwards, the BBC radio station, which was transmitted in the Netherlands, and Radio Oranje, which broadcast on a BBC frequency, reported on information from the Polish government in exile on mass killings of Jews and the use of poison gas.[36] It stated that before the first deportations, people were told they were being taken to work in Upper Silesia, while in Westerbork, the destination of Auschwitz had been known since the winter of 1942/43, but not its function.[37] Elie A. Cohen, a former inmate of Westerbork, writes in a witness testimony on his assessment of the situation in June 1943: 'We did not know what lay beyond Westerbork. But we had a vague feeling it wouldn't be pleasant'.[38]

Etty Hillesum saw the situation differently in August 1943: 'Of course we know that we are leaving those among us who are sick and defenceless, exposed to hunger and the cold, abandoned, unprotected and left to be exterminated; and we even clothe them and take them to the bare livestock wagons'.[39] Immediately before being deported, one girl said how difficult it is to go to one's death.[40] The Berlin-born Hans Margulies worked in Westerbork as a 'Funktionshäftling' in the camp's internal Jewish Police ('Ordnungsdienst', OD). He states that they had known the names of the three destinations of Theresienstadt, Bergen-Belsen and Auschwitz, but not about the extermination. Occasionally, members of the OD had asked returning guards about the conditions in Auschwitz. They answered that there was a labour camp there, in which most people probably worked for the German industry, and that the words 'Arbeit macht frei' were written above the entrance.[41]

The political scientist Ahlrich Meyer managed to reconstruct the situation: the security police threatened that anyone disobeying the labour order could expect to be taken to a concentration camp in the German Reich. As a result, people in the Netherlands believed that a labour assignment was not as severe as being imprisoned in a concentration camp such as Mauthausen, which they knew usually ended in death.[42] Another effective deception manoeuvre in the Netherlands was the system of exemption. Initially, members of the Judenrat and various professional groups, for instance Jews working in the arms or diamond industry, were exempt from deportations. Many Jews criticized the policy of the Judenrat. Anyone who had money or connections to its members as a result of their bourgeois background could buy an exemption stamp ('Sperrstempel') that prevented them from being deported in the short term. Thus, the Judenrat was willing to sacrifice poorer proletarian Jews for their own purposes.[43] A large number of exemption lists, which became ever shorter, were in circulation. The hope of exemption meant that many Jews did not go underground because they felt relatively secure. Hope and the competition for the prized exemptions also divided the Jewish community.[44]

When deportations began in Belgium, the local Judenrat (Association des Juifs en Belgique/Jodenvereeniging in België [AJB/JVB]) informed those selected for deportation in writing that according to the responsible authorities, the measure was not a deportation but a labour assignment.[45] The mass displacement of Belgian labourers to Germany during World War I was still very present in their collective memory.[46] This firstly led to a low level of willingness to cooperate with the German occupiers.[47] Secondly, the order to work in Germany appeared to be plausible, especially since in 1942 Jewish men actually were being used for forced labour along the Atlantic Wall in northern France. The objects listed in the labour assignment orders, such as a pair of sturdy boots, made it seem plausible that the announcement was a labour assignment.[48] However, the fact that children and people who were unfit to work were also required to report for forced labour strengthened the suspicion that the measure was aimed at permanently driving all Jews out of Belgium.[49]

Soon after deportations began, the first indications of the Jewish deportees' fate trickled back.[50] In August 1942, the Flemish underground paper *De Vrijschutter* reported on people being gassed and shot.[51] The illegal Belgian newspaper *Radio Moscou* also reported in December 1942 that 'Jews are being shot en masse and exterminated with gas'.[52]

Léopold Goldwurm and William Herskovic, both from Antwerpen, were deported from Drancy on 26 August 1942 and 12 September 1942 respectively, and were selected for forced labour in Cosel. Together, they managed to escape from the Pyskowice camp. Back in Belgium, they reported, among other things, that the camp doctor's diagnosis of 'less than two weeks' fitness for work' meant that the patient would be burned alive in 'Oschwitz' two weeks later. Their report was printed several times in the underground press from June 1943 onwards.[53] In November 1943, *Le Flambeau* wrote: 'For more than two years, Jews have been undergoing eradication from Belgium. The truth has far exceeded what one could imagine of the horror of the Nazi barbarians'.[54]

Ahlrich Meyer stresses that the camp personnel in Mechelen made insinuations towards prisoners and warned them of their deaths on countless occasions.[55] Above all, the Deputy Camp Commander Max Boden, an alcoholic who was often drunk, lied about the purpose of deportations when sober, but when drunk he threatened prisoners that they would all die in any case.[56] Two survivors of the 12th transport made witness statements before the military tribunal in Brussels that Karl Meinshausen, who was posted in Mechelen at the time of their arrival, promised them a beautiful life in Germany, for instance that their children would go to school. Nobody knew that deportation to Auschwitz was tantamount to a death sentence.[57]

Retrospectively, many survivors stated in trials against the former camp personnel that they did not believe Boden's words and only grasped what he had said after arriving in Auschwitz.[58] The survivor F. Nuchim stated: 'Had we known our fate, we would certainly have tried to escape'.[59]

Schutzpolizei Guard Teams

The so-called 'Begleitkommandos' that guarded Jewish prisoners during the deportations were usually provided by the Ordnungspolizei, of which the Schutzpolizei was a part. While the Ordnungspolizei's role in the war of annihilation against the Jews in Eastern Europe has been demonstrated by various authors in recent years, the active participation of the Ordnungspolizei in the Holocaust in occupied Western Europe has only been researched to a limited degree to date.[60] Undoubtedly, the reason for this is that, unlike Eastern Europe, no mass murders were carried out by shooting people into pits. By contrast, Jürgen Matthäus presumes that in Eastern Europe, a considerable proportion of the 1.3 million people that Raul Hilberg records as the minimum number of Jews executed in the open air were murdered by Ordnungspolizei firing squads.[61]

The primary responsibilities of the Ordnungspolizei and its subordinate Schutzpolizei with respect to Jewish persecution were arrests and the guarding of deportation trains. This complicity in the Holocaust has hardly been a subject of interest so far, neither as a field of perpetrator research nor by the general public.

The Schutzpolizei Used as Guard Teams for Deportation Trains

Only a few days after the Reichsführer SS (RFSS) Heinrich Himmler was also appointed Head of the German Police on 17 June 1936, he ordered the establishment of two police headquarters with the aim of merging the SS and the police. Firstly, the Ordnungspolizei headquarters were to be led by by SS Obergruppenführer Kurt Daluege. The Schutzpolizei, Verwaltungspolizei, Gendarmerie and the Gemeindepolizei all fell under the jurisdiction of the Ordnungspolizei.[62] Secondly, he established the Sicherheitspolizei headquarters led by SS-Gruppenführer Reinhard Heydrich, which was created by merging the Kriminalpolizei and the State Secret Police (Geheime Staatspolizei).[63] The number of Ordnungspolizei officers increased considerably in 1938/39, as they were exempt from conscription, which was introduced in 1935. Thus, according to Browning, many potential recruits were motivated to join the Ordnungspolizei in view of the imminent threat of war.[64] At the start of World War II, the existing police units, so-called 'Hundertschaften', were converted into police battalions (Polizeibataillone, PB) with an average of five hundred to six hundred men, which reported to the Wehrmacht. The police battalions were subdivided into four and later three companies and were primarily responsible for securing conquered territories behind the army.[65]

The Schutzpolizei was generally used to guard Jewish deportations.[66] In all three countries, deployment as guards for deportation trains was a popular assignment, since it offered various material and immaterial benefits, including unofficial home leave on the return journey from Auschwitz.[67] The accompanying guards consisted almost exclusively of Schutzpolizei teams that had been deployed locally or who had been seconded if necessary from western German cities near the border. They generally took over command of the deportation train immediately before its departure.[68]

In each deportation train, a guard team with a ratio of 1:15, meaning one police officer or non-commissioned officer, the so-called Transportführer, and fifteen ordinary policemen, were to guard the one thousand Jewish prisoners during the journey. This applied both to the German Reich and to territories occupied by the Reich, although in practice these guidelines were rarely observed. Guard teams were generally posted in separate passenger wagons at the front, in the middle and at the end of the train and were strictly separated from the deportees.

Differences between Guard Teams in France, Belgium and the Netherlands

There were a number of differences in the composition of guard teams in France, Belgium and the Netherlands. The guards in the Netherlands were always deployed from the Schutzpolizei in Police Battalions 66 (later PB58), 68 and 105, which were posted in the Netherlands. These accompanied the deportation trains without being relieved until their arrival at the final destination. In Belgium, however, the Schutzpolizei teams, which were always seconded from western German cities, initially guarded the trains to the border or a nearby city, where another Schutzpolizei team replaced them. As a result of the attack on the 20th deportation train from Belgium, with the escape of 232 prisoners on board, the Schutzpolizei teams were reinforced by members of the Judenreferat under the auspices of the BdS and by a company of SS guards. In France, the Feldgendarmerie, which was part of the German army, was responsible for guarding the trains up to the border until early 1943. From there, Schutzpolizei teams posted near the border initially replaced them. From the onset of deportations, the respective German command also had authority over a large body of the French Gendarmerie. In the spring of 1943, the Vichy government withdrew them from guarding deportation trains in protest against the planned deportation of Jews with French nationality. The resulting lack of personnel led to inconsistent practices. Some deportations no longer had any change of guard; teams of guards were requested from Stuttgart, Münster and elsewhere; and more members of the Paris BdS unit were used for guard duty.

What Battalion 105 Guard Teams Knew about the Fate of Deportees

During the prosecution process initiated in 1964 against Hans Helwes, the Schutzpolizei major and Commander of the Bremen Reserve Police Battalion 105, 226 former members of the battalion gave statements, also with respect to guarding Jews on deportation trains.[69] Of those, 120 admitted that they had been deployed as guards on deportation trains.[70] The former battalion member Julius Aschermann reports: 'I believe the guard teams knew where the transports were heading. I deliberately refrained from making enquiries because I did not want to be burdened by these things'.[71] This is confirmed by his former colleague Johann Alberts:

> At first we had no idea where the Jews would be taken. Only those who returned told us that they had to present the relevant transport at the camp gate in Auschwitz. After that we gradually became aware of the actual intention. That fact made it increasingly difficult to assemble teams of guards.[72]

The former Westerbork prisoner Aad van As describes how he asked the commander of the transports several times about the situation in the East. The Transportführer gave no answer. When he approached a policeman in the guard team, he only replied, 'Shit'. That did not bode well.[73] The former Schutzpolizei officer Theodor Krämer stated that he knew what would happen to the Jews:

> We knew, I mean I knew what would happen to the Jews in Auschwitz. I had heard English radio on several occasions and also deduced from the way the Jews were treated in the camps that they would be killed; there were also rumours about it within the battalion.[74]

Another former guard stated that the Auschwitz camp personnel's treatment of the Jews after their arrival 'was an eye-opener, so I could imagine that these Jews would be killed'.[75] Pery Broad, a former member of the Political Department in Auschwitz, confirmed that the accompanying guards must have known what would happen to the Jews, since the transports were taken by the teams of Ordnungspolizei guards and the accompanying railway personnel to the 'unloading' ramp. Thus, they must have been able to observe the 'process to select who was to be gassed':

> the arrivals had lost all their belongings and could deduce from the circumstances that their property would never be returned to them. Furthermore, they could see how the majority of arrivals were separated into a group that was then loaded onto a lorry by brutal force. 8–10 such lorries drove towards the visible incineration sites before returning after some time.[76]

Broad's statement is also confirmed by other Transportführer reports.[77] A former Schutzpolizei officer stated that he had heard from a train driver who often drove deportation trains that the Jews were being murdered. The train driver 'was afraid, however, to talk about it and told me . . . I should not tell anyone else'.[78]

Other former guards reported meeting residents who approached the train near Auschwitz and tried to take food from the Jews, since they knew that the Jews would not live for much longer.[79] While the wagons were being unloaded, one Schutzpolizei officer in the team of guards spoke to a young member of the SS in the cordon: 'This man told me that in a few hours, not one of the deportees would still be alive'.[80]

During a witness hearing, two members of the battalion, Hermann Gansel and Theodor Krämer, willingly admitted that they were aware of the Jewish deportees' fate. Both stated that after making the discovery, they nevertheless guarded one further deportation train.[81] As a result, the Bremen Public Prosecution launched an investigation, suspecting them of being accessories to murder.[82] Only two months later, the investigation was terminated for the following reason, among others:

> To prove that the accused were accessories to murder, however, it must first be objectively determined whether prisoners of the second transport from Gansel were killed in Auschwitz. No such proof can be provided.[83]

It was not sufficient that it was considered likely.

As the *nolle prosequi* for the prosecution of former Battalion Commander Helwes states, it was also impossible to prove that Helwes knew of the fate of the deported Jews.[84] This is not least astounding in view of the numerous statements by former members of the battalion, who admitted that they knew of the fate of the Jews in the trains they were guarding. Furthermore, in view of the fact that members of Battalion 105 had been deployed in the Soviet Union from July 1941 to July 1942 and are proven to have shot Soviet prisoners of war, Jews and Communists, it is evident that both Commander Helwes and members of the battalion knew of the mass murder of European Jews and the fate of those deported.[85]

Overview of the Judicial and Social Handling of Former Members of the Schutzpolizei: Two Case Studies

Prosecution Proceedings against Hans Helwes

Although the police battalions in the Netherlands assumed numerous tasks connected to the persecution of Jews, this participation in Jewish persecution by members of the Ordnungspolizei has almost never been the subject of public prosecution proceedings.[86] One exception was the investigation against Hans Helwes, the former Schutzpolizei major and Commander of the Bremen Reserve Police Battalion 105, which Bremen's public prosecutor initiated in 1964, on suspicion of murdering civilians and prisoners of war in the Soviet Union and participation in the deportation of Jews.[87] The proceedings were prompted by the charge against Hans Helwes made by a former member of his battalion, Hans Hespe.

The special committee was explicitly instructed to investigate the battalion's participation in the deportation of Jews, to document it separately and assess its criminal relevance.[88]

Numerous former policemen from the battalion were not even investigated as witnesses although this would certainly have been easy in some cases.[89] The witness statements by former PB 105 policemen were so redundant in terms of their content that one must assume tactical collusion between the former battalion members. During the course of the investigation process, the statement behaviour also shows collective trends, for instance with respect to the sudden increase in the number of people exercising their right to remain silent in accordance with Paragraph 55 of the German Criminal Proceeding Code. The interrogations appear to have mainly used a standardized, superficial guideline. The protocol mainly records unmotivated interviewers. Hardly anything had to be explained to the interrogating police officers and there were very few queries. It is likely that the similar nature of the witness statements is the result both of detailed collusion and of the fact that the investigating policemen did not want to cause problems for their active and former colleagues.[90]

Thus, the witnesses made few or no statements on the first three charges referring to executions while posted in the East. By contrast, they were all able to comment on the fourth charge, namely 'Participation of Police Battalion 105 in the transportation of Jews from the Netherlands to Auschwitz', which was referred to within the battalion as the 'Judenkommando'.[91] Presumably, the fourth charge was considered to be the least relevant to criminal proceedings, so witness statements were made as tactical concessions. Stefan Klemp makes the same assumption: 'During their investigations against members of the police battalions, West German public prosecutors almost always presumed that their deployments in the West were not relevant to criminal proceedings'.[92]

The longer an investigation proceeded, the more former battalion members refused to make statements. Those who had initially given statements became extremely reticent later on. The former members of the Schutzpolizei declared in formulaic uniformity that during the journey, the Jews had had enough to eat, a supply of water and that the journeys were always executed without any problems. Hans Helwes, the former Commander of PB 105, stated that his team had only guarded the trains three to five times.[93] This is clearly implausible since among the investigated and interrogated former battalion members, 120 stated that they had participated in a guard team. The investigation was terminated in 1968 on the grounds that it could not be proven that Helwes had known the fate of the deported Jews.

Impunity for Murder

On 22 March 1943, a Jewish prisoner escaped from a deportation train in France. Walter Kantim, a member of the Schutzpolizei, pursued the fleeing prisoner and killed him by the bank of the River Marne with a targeted shot from his service gun.[94] Immediately after the deportation, Kantim's superior officer, Transportführer Hermann Uhlemann, wrote a report on the events of the deportation, describing in detail Kantim's pursuit and shooting of the escapee.[95] The document was found by Thomas Harlan seventeen years later in the Paris archive CDJC while seeking evidence against Ernst Achenbach, a former embassy employee and promoter of Jewish deportations in Paris.[96] The same year, Harlan provided the names of seven suspects to Public Prosecutor Vogel at the Frankfurt am Main district court, including Hermann Uhlemann, a former Transportführer and author of the above report on the deadly escape attempt. Uhlemann, an Oberleutnant of the Ordnungspolizei and SS Hauptsturmführer,[97] was additionally included as the Transportführer among 110 suspects in List 'IV B4 of Jewish Deportations France' that was presumably produced by the Central Office of the State Judiciary Administrations for Prosecuting National Socialist Crimes (Zentrale Stelle der Landesjustizverwaltungen zur Aufklärung nationalsozialistischer Verbrechen, Zentrale Stelle) in Ludwigsburg.[98] In the presence of Chief Public Prosecutor Fritz Bauer, Harlan also made charges against ninety-six members of the Paris SS and police force on 5 October 1960.[99] He indicated that the evidence against these men could be found in the Paris CDJC. As a result, systematic preliminary investigations were ordered by the Central Office for the so-called 'France Complex' ('Frankreich-Komplex') against former members of the Sicherheitspolizei and Military Command.[100] It appears that no investigations were carried out against the former members of the Ordnungspolizei included in the Harlan list. Thus, Hermann Uhlemann was procedurally included in the Central Office's list of persons, but no search was made for him. He would have been easy to find: after returning from Soviet captivity in 1953, he was active on police duty in Berlin-Kreuzberg, by then a Police Chief Inspector (Oberkommissar).[101] Nor was Uhlemann sought during investigations on the events in the Sobibór extermination camp, although Public Prosecutor Zeug from the Central Office in Ludwigsburg had proposed this in 1961 to determine the extent to which Uhlemann was aware of the operations in the Sobibór camp.[102]

Furthermore, no search was carried out for Walter Kantim, the man mentioned in the report by Uhlemann as having killed an escaping prisoner. There is conclusive evidence that no later than 1971, the Central Office in Ludwigsburg was aware of this report by Uhlemann, because during that year, the Schutzpolizei member Franz-Ludwig Daigfuss, who was also mentioned in the report, was confronted with passages from the report during his interrogation.[103] Nevertheless, no proceedings were initiated against Walter Kantim, although it was the duty of the investigating public prosecutor and policemen to do so. There was evidence of qualified murder, 'base motives' such as 'racism' and 'murder for the purpose of displacing or destroying members of a foreign ethnic group'. However, since the deadly pursuit by Walter Kantim was not prosecuted at the time due to the applicable 'Gehilfenrechtsprechung' ('case law on complicity'), Kantim did not have to fear that his actions would become the subject of an investigation.[104]

After a brief period as a prisoner of war, Kantim returned to active police duty in the autumn of 1945 and became an Oberwachtmeister for the Bottrop Kriminalpolizei. He had no difficulties in passing through the denazification process and did not even have to lie, since in the declaration he signed personally, he stated that he had been in SS Police Regiment 4 at the time of the crime.[105] In another statement for the purposes of calculating how long he served as a policeman, he declared that he had been a member of Police Battalion 323 since 16 November 1940 and prior to that in Police Battalion 65 established in Recklinghausen.[106] He was classified in Category V, Persons Exonerated. The Special Committee for Examining the Police recommended his continued employment in the police force: 'No political reservations. No party member. No activist'.[107] One assessment includes the following: 'He is tireless in his duty and shows motivation and love for his work'.[108] In July 1949, Walter Kantim was appointed a permanent civil servant.[109]

Impunity for the Teams of Guards

No officer or guard assigned to deportation trains has ever been prosecuted in West or East Germany. From a legal perspective, it was apparently unclear which measures against Jews in occupied territories can be described as participation in or implementation of 'Final Solution' measures. The Cologne investigation on the 'Final Solution of the Jewish Question in France' did not regard anti-Semitic measures as 'Final Solution' measures; the same applies to the registration of Jews and their branding with Jewish badges.[110] If one follows this logic, only the mass murders in extermination centres in the East are criminally relevant. This approach was not changed when it came to light that there had been fatal persecutions of fleeing Jews and even, as in Kantim's case, that the perpetrators were known by name. Thus, Kantim's deed was recorded in the files of the Cologne investigation on the 'Final Solution of the Jewish Question in France', but had no consequences.[111]

The reasons for such a lack of interest in the prosecution of National Socialist crimes, combined with the highly effective amnesty campaigns for condemned Nazi criminals, has been analysed and presented in recent years by Ulrich Herbert and Norbert Frei, among others.[112] In an essay on the treatment of Schutzpolizei members with a National Socialist past during the 1950s and 1960s, Klaus Weinhauer shows how strongly the police force was characterized by the male bond of *esprit de corps* and how they resisted the investigation of Nazi crimes perpetrated within their own ranks.[113] Public Prosecutor Barbara Just-Dahlmann, working at the Central Office in Ludwigsburg, highlighted this situation in a speech in Loccum in November 1961, which caused great indignation: 'Normally, the Public Prosecutor orders an interrogation by Police Station X. Now it appears that the police station is filled with people who should be arrested themselves by the Central Office'.[114] The few police officers who were willing to investigate their colleagues' active participation in such crimes were met with an effective cartel of silence. They were also accused of fouling their own nest.[115]

Notes

1. Michael R. Marrus and Robert O. Paxton, 'The Nazis and the Jews in Occupied Western Europe 1940–44', in: *Journal of Modern History* 54 (1982) 4, pp. 687–714, here p. 696.
2. This led to investigations against Albert Ganzenmüller, the former State Secretary at the Reichsverkehrsministerium. The trial was terminated due to long-term inability to stand trial. See Dr Hedding et al. (Landgericht, V. Strafkammer), Beschluss, 17 December 1970, proceedings against Dr Ganzenmüller, 45 Js/62, No. 3137, LAV NRW R.
3. Harm-Hinrich Brandt, 'Nationalsozialismus und Bürokratie. Überlegungen zur Rolle der Eisenbahn bei der Vernichtung der europäischen Juden', in: Eisenbahnjahr Ausstellungsgesellschaft mbH Nürnberg (Ed.), *Zug der Zeit – Zeit der Züge*, Vol. 2, Berlin 1985, pp. 692–701, here p. 695.
4. Dannecker, 'Richtlinien für die Evakuierung von Juden', 26 June 1942, printed in: Gerhard Schoenberner, *Zeugen sagen aus. Berichte und Dokumente über die Judenverfolgung im 'Dritten Reich'*, Berlin 1998, p. 220 f. (Original in CDJC, XXVI-32); statement by Nowak quoted in the indictment against Dr A. Ganzenmüller, 1970, YVA TR-10 835, p. 123; *Richtlinien zur technischen Durchführung der Evakuierung von Juden in das Generalgouvernement* (Trawniki bei Lublin), no date, RW Mikrofilm, A 28-2, *Deportationen der Stapo Leitstelle Düsseldorf*, LAV NRW R.
5. Indictment text, trial of Dr A. Ganzenmüller, 1970, YVA TR-10 835, p. 168.
6. Andrea Rudorff, 'Das Lagersystem der "Organisation Schmelt" in Schlesien', in: Wolfgang Benz and Barbara Distel (Eds), *Der Ort des Terrors. Geschichte der nationalsozialistischen Konzentrationslager*, Vol. 9, Munich 2009, pp. 155–160.
7. Wolfgang Sofsky, *Die Ordnung des Terrors: Das Konzentrationslager*, Frankfurt am Main 1997, p. 137 ff.
8. RSHA IV B 4 to all Security Police units in the 'old Reich' and in Vienna, guidelines on the technical implementation of deportations to Trawniki near Lublin, 31 January 1942, printed in: Kurt Pätzold and Erika Schwarz, *'Auschwitz war für mich nur ein Bahnhof'. Franz Novak –*

der Transportoffizier Adolf Eichmanns, Berlin 1994, p. 122; cf. Adler, *Der verwaltete Mensch*, pp. 433, 451; idem, *Theresienstadt*, p. 70 f.; Schreiber, *Stille Rebellen*, p. 237; Hauptwachtmeister der Schutzpolizei Salat, Betr.: Gestellung von Transportkommandos, 24 October 1941, 1.1.0.4, ID 82292612, ITS Digitales Archiv.
9. Theodor Dannecker, 11 October 1939, cited in: Hilberg, *Sonderzüge nach Auschwitz*, p. 121.
10. Dannecker, Richtlinien für die Evakuierung von Juden, 26 June 1942, BArch 162/20403.
11. Adler, *Theresienstadt*, p. 70 f.
12. Goldsteinas, Plusieurs témoins (20ème convoi), Cegesoma, AA 1593 M251.
13. Maurice Rajsfus, *Drancy. Un camp de concentration très ordinaire*, Paris 1996, p. 319.
14. Adler, *Theresienstadt*, p. 70 f.
15. Günther to the SD headquarters, Merkblatt Umschichtung von Juden, 23 October 1939, cited in: Hilberg, *Sonderzüge nach Auschwitz*, p. 129; RSHA IV B 4 to all Stapo central offices in the Old Reich and in Vienna, Betreff: Evakuierung der Juden, 31 January 1942, cited in: Pätzold and Schwarz, *'Auschwitz war für mich nur ein Bahnhof'*, p. 122; Schutzpolizei Hauptwachtmeister Salat, Betr.: Gestellung von Transportkommandos, 24 October 1941, 1.1.0.4, ID 82292612, ITS Digitales Archiv.
16. Printed in: Pätzold and Schwarz, *'Auschwitz war für mich nur ein Bahnhof'*, p. 117.
17. Aus der Fünten to the BdS, Theresienstadt, 22 April 1943, NIOD, 77/1290.
18. Statement by Max Hermann Boden, 19 February 1968, BArch B 162/4405.
19. Pery Broad, report, in: Staatliches Auschwitz-Museum, *Auschwitz in den Augen der SS. Rudolf Höß, Pery Broad, Johann Paul Kremer*, Warsaw 1992, pp. 125, 134.
20. Adler, *Theresienstadt*, p. 61.
21. Hagen, Betr.: Sprachregelung zum Abtransport der Juden aus dem unbesetzten Gebiet nach Osten, 4 September 1942, CDJC, DLXVI-9.
22. Der Militärbefehlshaber, 13 May 1942, BArch R 70 Niederlande.
23. Günther to Zoepf, Knochen, Ehlers and later to the BdS branch in Metz, Betr.: Evakuierung von Juden, 9 April 1943, CDJC, XXVc-240.
24. See the fundamental study: Ahlrich Meyer, *Das Wissen um Auschwitz. Täter und Opfer der 'Endlösung' in Westeuropa*, Paderborn 2010.
25. For example, Robert Levy's statement in: Serge Klarsfeld, *Le Calendrier de la Persécution des Juifs en France 1940–1944*, Paris 1993, p. 881.
26. For example, André Warlin's statement in: *Le tunnel de Drancy*, documentary film by Claudine Drame, 1993.
27. Adam Rayski, 'Le combat contre le grand secret', in: Stéphane Courtois and Adam Rayski, *Qui savait quoi? L'extermination des Juifs, 1941-1945*, Paris 1987, p. 160.
28. Stéphane Courtois, 'Que savait la presse communiste?', in: Courtois and Rayski, *Qui savait quoi?*, p. 109 f.
29. Ibid., p. 110.
30. Henri Szwarc, 'Souvenirs. L'Étoile jaune', 1993, CDJC, CMLXVII-(2)-12.
31. Georges Wellers, cited in: Dov B. Schmorak, *Sieben sagen aus. Zeugen im Eichmann-Prozeß*, Berlin 1962, p. 70.
32. Ibid., p. 90; regarding the effectiveness of this deception tactic, see also the statement by Eugène Handschuh, in: *Mit dem Mut der Verzweifelten. Jüdischer Widerstand im zweiten Weltkrieg*, documentary film by Rena and Thomas Giefer, 2006; Hans Safrian, *Eichmann und seine Gehilfen*, Frankfurt am Main 1997, p. 264; Leo Bretholz, Interview Code 8503, VHA, USC Shoah Foundation Institute.
33. Fania Fénelon, *Das Mädchenorchester in Auschwitz*, Munich 1981, p. 15.
34. Ibid., p. 18.
35. Witness statement by Abraham Margulies to the Landgericht, 16 November 1965, LAV NRW W, Staatsanwaltschaft Dortmund, Zentralstelle für NS-Verbrechen, No. 4476.
36. Meyer, *Wissen um Auschwitz*, p. 53.
37. Fred Schwarz, *Züge auf falschem Gleis*, Vienna 1996, pp. 138, 149.

38. Elie A. Cohen, *The Abyss. A Confession*, New York 1973, p. 39.
39. Etty Hillesum, 'Die Nacht vor dem Transport', in Gerhard Schoenberner (Ed.), *Wir haben es gesehen. Augenzeugenberichte über die Judenverfolgung im Dritten Reich*, Wiesbaden 1981, pp. 222-231, here p. 223.
40. Ibid.
41. Hans Margulies, in: Willy Lindwer, *Kamp van hoop en wanhoop. Getuigen van Westerbork 1939-1945*, Amsterdam 1990, p. 137.
42. Meyer, *Wissen um Auschwitz*, p. 67 ff.
43. Vom Ringen des holländischen Hechaluz, NIOD, 614 A, doc II.
44. Meyer, *Wissen um Auschwitz*, p. 69; Ron Zeller and Pim Griffioen, 'Judenverfolgung in den Niederlanden und in Belgien während des Zweiten Weltkriegs: eine vergleichende Analyse', Part I, in: *1999. Zeitschrift für Sozialgeschichte des 20. und 21. Jahrhunderts* 3 (1996) 1, pp. 30–54, here p. 51; statement Aus der Fünten Proces Verbaal, Verhoor van getuigen inzake contra W. Harster, W. Zöpf en G. Slottke, 15 March 1966, NIOD, 270g, 4.4.
45. Such an announcement is recorded in Antwerp and printed as a facsimile in: Adriaens et al., *Mecheln-Auschwitz 1942–1944, Vol. 1*, p. 208.
46. Jens Thiel, *Menschenbassin Belgien. Anwerbung, Deportation und Zwangsarbeit im Ersten Weltkrieg*, Essen 2007.
47. J. C. H. Blom, 'The Persecution of the Jews in the Netherlands in a Comparative International Perspective', in: Jozeph Michman (Ed.), *Dutch Jewish History. Proceedings of the Fourth Symposium on the History of the Jews in the Netherlands 7-10 December - Tel Aviv - Jerusalem, 1986, Volume II*, Jerusalem 1989, p. 343.
48. Ehlers, Arbeitseinsatzbefehl, 8 August 1942, cited in: Serge Klarsfeld and Maxime Steinberg (Eds), *Die Endlösung der Judenfrage in Belgien. Dokumente*, New York 1980, p. 39.
49. Chaim Pereilman, Plusieurs témoins (20ème convoi), Cegesoma, AA 1593 M250.
50. See the underlying study by Steinberg, *L'Étoile et le fusil, Vol. II*, p. 231 ff.
51. *Ve Vrijschutter*, August 1942; also the *Bulletin Interieur du Front de l'Independance*, 17 October 1942, partially printed as a facsimile in: Joods Museum van deportatie en verzet, *De Belgische tentoonstelling in Auschwitz. Het book. L'exposition belge à Auschwitz*, Le livre 2006, p. 120; cf. Steinberg, *L'Étoile le fusil, Vol. I*, p. 241.
52. *Radio Moscou*, No. 90, 27 December 1942, cited in: Klarsfeld and Steinberg, *Endlösung*, p. 57; see also *Le Flambeau*, 10 May 1943, cited in: ibid., p. 65.
53. Klarsfeld and Steinberg, *Endlösung*, p. 66 ff.; Steinberg, *L'Étoile et le fusil, Vol. I*, p. 250 ff.
54. *Le Flambeau*, Die Liste der jüdischen Märtyrer in Belgien, November 1943, No. 4, cited in: Klarsfeld and Steinberg, *Endlösung*, p. 84.
55. Meyer, *Wissen um Auschwitz*, p. 128 ff.
56. Ibid., p. 133 ff.; witness statement by Eva Fastag, 7 April 1948, Collège des Procureurs, Conseil de Guerre Bruxelles, Sipo Brüssel, Vol. 10.
57. Witness statement by Szlama Sagal, 16 March 1949, Collège des Procureurs, Conseil de Guerre Bruxelles, Sipo Brüssel, Vol. 10; witness statement by Herz Adler, 19 March 1948, Collège des Procureurs, Conseil de Guerre Bruxelles, Sipo Brüssel, Vol. 10; witness statement by Lejb Lajzerowicz, 6 May 1949, Collège des Procureurs, Conseil de Guerre Bruxelles, Sipo Brüssel, Vol. 10.
58. Meyer, *Wissen um Auschwitz*, p. 133.
59. F. Nuchim, cited in: Meyer, *Wissen um Auschwitz*, p. 103.
60. For Eastern Europe, see, for instance, Browning, *Ganz normale Männer*; Stefan Klemp, '*Nicht ermittelt'. Polizeibataillone und die Nachkriegsjustiz. Ein Handbuch*, Essen 2005, p. 10; Klaus-Michael Mallmann, 'Vom Fußvolk der "Endlösung". Ordnungspolizei, Ostkrieg und Judenmord', in: *Tel Aviver Jahrbuch für deutsche Geschichte* 26 (1997), pp. 355–391; Wolfgang Curilla, *Die deutsche Ordnungspolizei und der Holocaust im Baltikum und in Weißrußland 1941–1944*, Paderborn 2006; idem, *Der Judenmord in Polen und die deutsche Ordnungspolizei 1939-1945*, Paderborn 2011. For Western Europe, see Johannes Houwink ten Cate and

Alfons Kenkmann (Eds), *Deutsche und holländische Polizei in den niederländischen Gebieten. Dokumentation einer Arbeitstagung*, Münster 2002.
61. Jürgen Matthäus, 'An vorderster Front. Voraussetzungen für die Beteiligung der Ordnungspolizei an der Shoah', in: Gerhard Paul (Ed.), *Die Täter der Shoah. Fanatische Nationalsozialisten oder ganz normale Deutsche?*, Göttingen 2002, pp. 137–167, here p. 139.
62. Hans Buchheim et al., *Anatomie des SS-Staates*, Munich 1994, p. 56; Florian Dierl, 'Das Hauptamt Ordnungspolizei 1936 bis 1945. Führungsspitze und die Befehlshaber in den Wehrkreisen', in: Alfons Kenkmann and Christoph Spieker (Eds), *Im Auftrag. Polizei, Verwaltung und Verantwortung*, Essen 2001, pp. 159–175, here p. 159.
63. Johannes Tuchel and Reinold Schattenfroh, *Zentrale des Terrors. Prinz-Albrecht-Straße 8: Hauptquartier der Gestapo*, Berlin 1987, pp. 91 f., 98 ff.; Buchheim, *Anatomie des SS-Staates*, p. 56.
64. Browning, *Ganz normale Männer*, p. 24 f.
65. Ibid., p. 26.
66. Ibid., p. 47; Hilberg, *Sonderzüge nach Auschwitz*, p. 78; Klemp, 'Nicht ermittelt', p. 221.
67. For example, witness statement by Julius Aschermann, 8 July 1966, BArch L 162/4100; witness hearing, Johann Albers, 4 July 1966, BArch B 162/4100; witness hearing, Herbert Arnold, 7 July 1966, BArch B 162/4100.
68. Witness hearing, Gottlob Busch, 27 April 1972, BArch B 162/4406.
69. Klemp, 'Nicht ermittelt', p. 221.
70. Schneider, *Auswärts eingesetzt*, p. 352.
71. Witness hearing, Julius Aschermann, 8 July 1966, BArch B 162/4100.
72. Witness hearing, Johann Alberts, 4 July 1966, BArch B 162/4100.
73. Aad van As, in: Lindwer, *Kamp van hoop en wanhoop*, p. 251.
74. Witness hearing, Theodor Krämer, 11 December 1967, BArch B 162/4103.
75. Witness hearing, Ernst Rautenhaus, 12 December 1967, BArch B 162/4103.
76. Pery Broad, cited in: Schoenberner, *Wir haben es gesehen*, p. 278.
77. Fischmann, Erfahrungsbericht Transportkommando für den Judentransport Wien-Aspangbahnhof nach Sobibor am 14. 6. 1942, 20 June 1942, printed in: Browning, *Ganz normale Männer*, p. 49 ff.; Jäcklein, Betr.: von Kolomea nach Belzec, 14 September 1942, cited in: Ernst Klee, Willi Dreßen, and Volker Rieß, *'Schöne Zeiten'. Judenmord aus der Sicht der Täter und Gaffer*, Frankfurt am Main 1998, p. 216. The former 'functional prisoner' in Sobibór, Icek Lachman, reported that the guard teams were not permitted to enter the camp. Witness statement to the main committee investigating Nazi crimes in Poland, Icek Lachman, 9 December 1975, LAV NRW W, Staatsanwaltschaft Dortmund, Zentralstelle für NS-Verbrechen, No. 4476.
78. Witness statement by Meinolph Derenthal, 10 July 1967, BArch B 162/4102.
79. Witness statement by Johann Eickworth, 11 July 1967, BArch B 162/4101.
80. Ibid.
81. Landeskriminalamt SK, Schlußbericht, investigation proceedings, Bremen public prosecutor re. the former Commander of Police Battalion 105, Major Hans Helwes, 8 February 1968, BArch B 162/4104.
82. Höffler (Senior Public Prosecutor, district court), Verfügung, 16 April 1968, BArch B 162/4106.
83. Senior Public Prosecutor, district court, Verfügung, 24 June 1968, BArch B 162/4106.
84. Höffler (Senior Public Prosecutor, district court), Verfügung, 16 April 1968, BArch B 162/4104.
85. Hans Hespe, who was seconded to PB 105, described shootings in their company (witness statement, October 1964, BArch B 162/4100), as did his former colleague Karl Roelle (witness statement, 26 April 1966, BArch B 162/4100); see also Landeskriminalamt SK, Schlußbericht. Investigation proceedings by the Bremen public prosecutor re. the former Commander of Police Battalion 105, Major Hans Helwes, 8 February 1968, BArch B 162/4104; Schneider, *Auswärts eingesetzt*, p. 198 ff.

86. Stefan Klemp and Herbert Reinke, 'Kölner Polizeibataillone in den Niederlanden während des Zweiten Weltkrieges', in: Harald Buhlan and Werner Jung (Eds), *Wessen Freund und wessen Helfer? Die Kölner Polizei im Nationalsozialismus*, Cologne 2000, pp. 263–276, here p. 263.
87. Stefan Klemp, 'Einsatz im Westen – Deutsche Polizeibataillone in Holland 1940 bis 1945', in: Houwink ten Cate and Kenkmann, *Deutsche und holländische Polizei*, pp. 29–66, here p. 33; Schneider, *Auswärts eingesetzt*, p. 336.
88. Schneider, *Auswärts eingesetzt*, p. 337.
89. Ibid., p. 338 f.
90. Regarding this phenomenon, see also Klemp, *'Nicht ermittelt'*, p. 19; Jürgen Matthäus/Georg Heuser, 'Routinier des sicherheitspolizeilichen Osteinsatzes', in: Klaus-Michael Mallmann and Gerhard Paul (Eds), *Karrieren der Gewalt. Nationalsozialistische Täterbiographien*, Darmstadt 2011, pp. 115–125, here p. 118 ff.
91. Witness statement by Heinrich Bass, 30 September 1966, BArch B 162/4101; witness statement by Ludwig Walter Coors, 11 May 1967, BArch B 162/4101.
92. Klemp and Reinke, *Kölner Polizeibataillone*, p. 267.
93. Schneider, *Auswärts eingesetzt*, p. 283.
94. See the report in the ARD television programme *Monitor* on the results of my research on Schutzpolizei guard teams on deportation trains based on the case of Walter Kantim, 'Polizei: Die unerforschten Nazi-Verbrechen deutscher Beamter', 13 August 2009.
95. Hermann Uhlemann, 24 March 1943, CDJC, XXVb-75.
96. Bernhard Brunner, *Der Frankreich-Komplex. Die nationalsozialistischen Verbrechen in Frankreich und die Justiz der Bundesrepublik Deutschland*, Göttingen 2004, p. 196 ff.
97. SS-Stammkarte Hermann Uhlemann, BArch ZA VI 0643, Bl. 162; Karteikarte Hermann Uhlemann, NSDAP-Zentralkartei, BArch B (formerly BDC), SSO; BArch Personenregister.
98. Harlan, (IV B4) Judendeportationen Frankreich, BArch B 162/3395; Harlan to Vogel, Beglaubigte Abschrift, 28 September 1960, BArch B 162/3395.
99. Danker, Verfügung [prosecution extract], 18 October 1960, BArch B 162/3395; cf. Brunner, *Frankreich-Komplex*, p. 196.
100. Brunner, *Frankreich-Komplex*, p. 197 ff.; Annette Weinke, *Eine Gesellschaft ermittelt gegen sich selbst. Die Geschichte der Zentralen Stelle Ludwigsburg 1958–2008*, Darmstadt 2008, p. 145.
101. BArch Karteikarte Personenregister.
102. Zeug to Dr Wenzky (Landeskriminalamt Nordrhein-Westfalen), Ermittlungsverfahren 45 Js 27/61 StA Dortmund (Vernichtungslager Sobibor/Polen), 13 December 1961, BArch B 162/4429.
103. Witness statement by Franz-Ludwig Daigfuss, 9 November 1971, BArch B 162/4405.
104. Regarding the 'Gehilfenrechtsprechung', see: Marc von Miquel, *Ahnden oder amnestieren? Westdeutsche Justiz und Vergangenheitspolitik in den sechziger Jahren*, Göttingen 2004, p. 186 ff.; Michael Greve, *Der justitielle und rechtspolitische Umgang mit den NS-Gewaltverbrechen in den sechziger Jahren*, Frankfurt am Main et al. 2001, p. 145 ff.
105. Statement by Walter Kantim, 27 June 1946, Entnazifizierungsakte (denazification file) Walter Kantim, LAV NRW R, NW 1039-K Nr. 5533.
106. Dienstliche Erklärung über abgeleistete Zeiten zum Zwecke der Aufstellung einer Dienstzeitberechnung, 13 December 1948, Kreispolizeibehörde Recklinghausen, Personalakten, Unterordner A; regarding Police Battalions 65 and 323, see Klemp, *'Nicht ermittelt'*, pp. 166, 294 ff.
107. Entnazifizierungsakte (denazification file) Walter Kantim, LAV NRW R, NW 1039-K Nr. 5533.
108. Kriminalabteilung Bottrop, Beurteilungsnotiz, 15 December 1946, Kreispolizeibehörde Recklinghausen, Personalakten, Unterordner A.

109. Die Polizeibehörde des RB Münster, Der Polizeiausschuß, 20 July 1949, Kreispolizeibehörde Recklinghausen, Personalakten, Unterordner A.
110. Bericht über das Ergebnis der bisherigen Ermittlungen im Ermittlungsverfahren der Staatsanwaltschaft Köln zu Aktenzeichen 130 (24) Js 1/66 (Z) - Komplex: Endlösung der Judenfrage in Frankreich, 10 July 1974, LAV NRW R, HstAD, Rep. 158/1674.
111. [Commented, presentation table of all documents viewed to date by the investigation proceedings], LAV NRW R, HStAD, 158/1676.
112. Ulrich Herbert, *Best. Biographische Studien über Radikalismus, Weltanschauung und Vernunft 1903-1989*, Bonn 2001; Norbert Frei, *Vergangenheitspolitik. Die Anfänge der Bundesrepublik und die NS-Vergangenheit*, Munich 1999.
113. Cf. Klaus Weinhauer, 'NS-Vergangenheit und struktureller Wandel der Schutzpolizei der 1950/60er Jahre', in: Wolfgang Schulte (Ed.), *Die Polizei im NS-Staat. Beiträge eines internationalen Symposiums an der Deutschen Hochschule der Polizei in Münster*, Frankfurt am Main 2009, pp. 139–158.
114. Barbara Just-Dahlmann, cited in: Weinke, *Gesellschaft*, p. 45.
115. Cf. Weinhauer, 'NS-Vergangenheit', p. 143 ff.

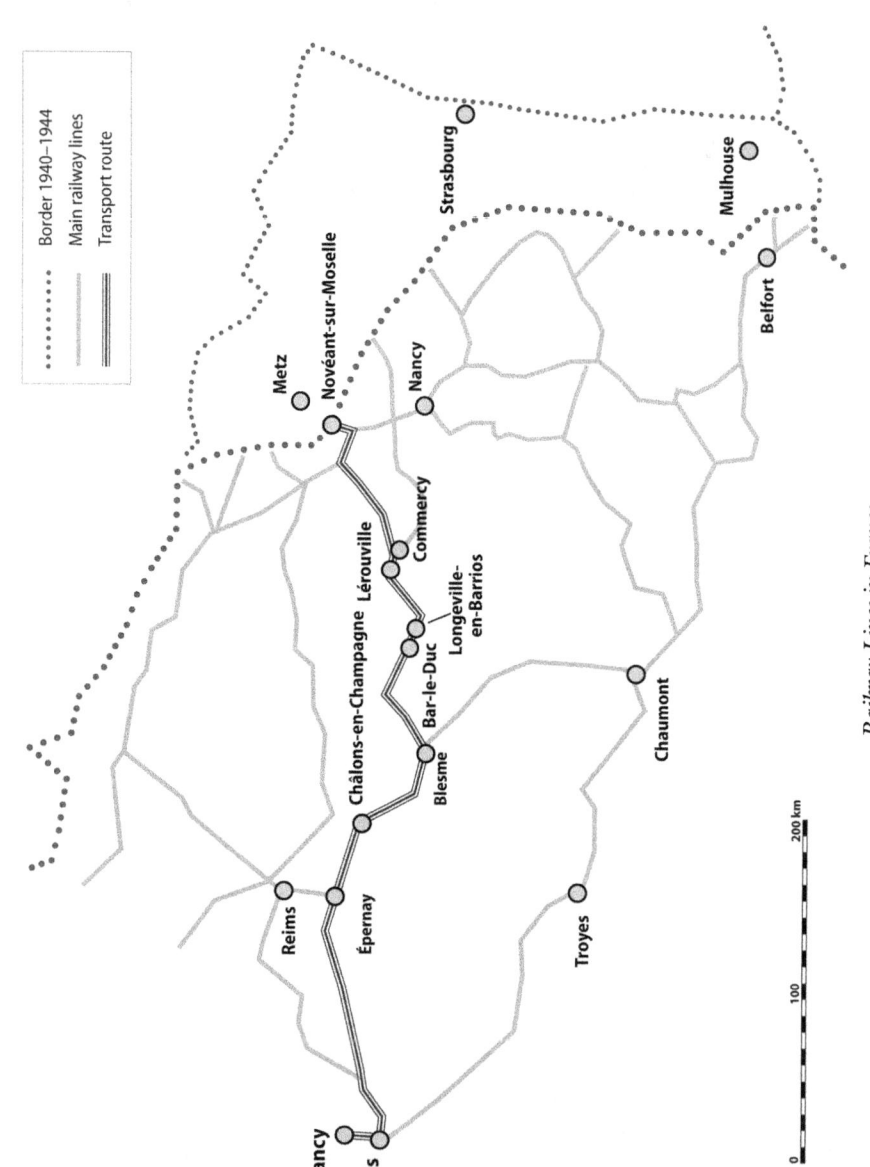

Railway Lines in France

CHAPTER 2

Escapes by Jews from Deportation Trains in France

Initial Situation in France

Composition and Status of the Jewish Population before German Occupation

Between the French Revolution and 1861, the number of Jews in France doubled to eighty thousand.[1] Between 1880 and 1925, one hundred thousand Jews migrated to France from Central and Eastern Europe. The reasons for leaving their countries of origin included anti-Semitic pogroms and discrimination.[2] Due to the demographic shortfall created by the deaths during World War I, France considerably increased its immigration quotas.[3] Polish Jews in particular came to France as a result of increasing anti-Semitism following the foundation of the Polish state, but also to escape poverty. Most Eastern European Jews settled in Paris.[4] Many of these migrants were united in wanting to maintain their eastern Jewish identity, mainly expressed in the speaking of Yiddish, which in the 1930s was spoken by 80 per cent of all Parisian Jews born outside the country.[5] Many of these immigrants earned a living as labourers or craftsmen, above all in the tailoring sector, and a Jewish lower class developed.[6]

In 1927, a law was passed that made it easier for immigrants to become French citizens.[7] Four years later, immigration reached its highest level as France became the country with the highest proportion of immigrants worldwide.[8] The same year, due to the effects of the worldwide financial crisis and xenophobic sentiments, all applications by foreign labourers were rejected. In 1932, the employment of foreigners was restrictively curtailed.[9] In 1939, around 300,000 Jews lived in France, of which

110,000 were French citizens, 70,000 had been recently naturalized, and 120,000 were foreign citizens or stateless persons.[10]

In the 1920s, the French Communist Party (PCF) was the only organization that was open to immigrants, including Jews. To prevent new foundations outside the PCF and to recruit new members, the PCF founded the organization MOE (Main-d'œuvre étrangère – foreign labourers) in 1923 and renamed it the MOI (Main-d'œuvre immigrée – immigrated labourers) in 1932.[11] It was organized into language groups. For instance, in Paris there were Romanian, Armenian, Italian and Yiddish-speaking sections, the latter consisting mainly of Polish immigrants.

In the mid 1930s, political tensions developed between the PCF and the MOI, for various reasons. The PCF pursued the aim of integrating the language groups of the MOI, which acted with relative autonomy, into the PCF. However, the groups regarded themselves as representatives of the respective language groups, related strongly to their countries of origin and criticized the locally nationalist tone of the PCF.[12] The division widened with the Hitler-Stalin Pact, which Jewish Communists largely rejected.[13] After the invasion of Poland by the German army, the pact and the silence of the Comintern paralysed the PCF and the Jewish MOI section.[14] On 26 September 1939, the French government outlawed the PCF. The MOI officially disbanded, but both organizations continued to exist underground.[15]

As a result of the German invasion of Poland, the French authorities interned eighteen to twenty thousand Germans and Austrians in camps, most of whom were Jewish emigrants, as so-called enemy foreigners.[16] Atrocious hygiene conditions, malnutrition and a lack of medical care led to the deaths of many internees.[17]

The Wehrmacht Invasion and Early Mass Deportations in June 1942

On 10 May 1940, the German army marched into France. The ceasefire agreement signed twelve days later planned the division of France into different zones. The North, including the Channel and Atlantic coasts, was placed under the authority of the German Military Commander ('Militärbefehlshaber', MBF) in France. Exceptions were the two northern departments of Nord and Pas-de-Calais, which, for strategic military reasons, were placed under the auspices of the Military Commander of the simultaneously occupied Belgium, as well as Alsace and Lorraine, which were de facto annexed and co-administrated by the neighbouring 'Gaue' of Saar-Palatinate and Baden.[18] The south of France initially remained unoccupied, but was occupied by the Wehrmacht and a small contingency of Italian troops on 11 November 1942 in reaction to the landing of Allied forces on the North African coast. One day after the ceasefire in Italy on 8 September 1943, German troops marched into Italy and into the French departments that had previously been occupied by Italy.

The German rulers did not have a united concept of the role France should play in a Europe ruled by the German Reich. The three key tiers of the German occupying machine in the occupied North were the MBF, the Führungsgruppe SS and the German embassy. Unlike in many other occupied countries, Himmler was unable to install a Higher SS and Police Officer (Höherer SS- und Polizeiführer, HSSPF). The targeted prevention of the appointment of an HSSPF, which would have entailed a powerful status for the SS, can be seen as a reaction by the Wehrmacht to the excesses of brutal violence and murder by the SS in Poland.[19] Instead, the sole executive authority remained with the Wehrmacht even after the end of military hostilities. The highest occupation authority was therefore Military Commander General Otto von Stülpnagel.

From late June 1940 onwards, the SS was represented only by a twenty-man Sipo-SD unit led by SS-Sturmbannführer Dr Helmut Knochen, the Commander of the Sicherheitspolizei and the SD (BdS) in the field of the Military Commander (MBF) in France. Although subordinate to him, Knochen engaged in constant competition with the MBF for power and influence. His unit was only responsible for tasks relating to intelligence, and members of the unit were forbidden to contact the Reichssicherheitshauptamt (RSHA) directly.[20] The Head of the RSHA, Reinhard Heydrich, and Knochen were unhappy with this situation. To increase its scope of influence, the 28-year-old SS-Obersturmführer Theodor Dannecker was sent by the RSHA to Paris as a consultant on the Jews in early September 1940. In effect, he reported directly to Adolf Eichmann, the Head of the RSHA Judenreferat.[21]

Vichy, in the unoccupied southern region of the country, became the seat of the newly formed, merely formally independent government of all of France. The administrative organization and government led by Philippe Pétain operated under the observation of the German occupiers. The Vichy regime was an autocratic response to the 'Popular Front' government led by Léon Blum and was aimed at establishing an antidemocratic reorganization of French society according to the motto 'Work, Family, Fatherland'. Laws passed by the French government also applied in the occupied North, as long as they did not contradict orders by the occupiers. The German occupiers relied on the collaboration of the French government, above all in its role as a legislator, to increase acceptance of anti-Jewish laws and measures among the non-Jewish population.[22] It was also essential to use the support of the French police force, due to personnel shortages, among other reasons.[23]

In mid August 1940, members of the military administration and the German embassy initiated the persecution of Jews living in France.[24] The embassy even had an expert on the Jews in the Legation Councillor Dr Carltheo Zeitschel, who regularly conferred with the Sipo-SD's consultant on the Jews. German Ambassador Otto Abetz and Werner Best, Head of the Department for Administration in the Administrative Staff of the MBF and since 1935 responsible in the German Reich for the formulation and implementation of anti-Jewish measures, proposed measures against the Jews that were still orientated towards the Madagascar Plan discussed at the time.[25] After the Wehrmacht leadership had agreed, Best decreed the Erste Judenverordnung ('First Jewish Regulation') on 27 September 1940, followed a week later by the 'Statut des Juifs' passed by the Vichy government. For the first time, it included descriptions of the Jews as a 'race' and prevented them from holding public office and liberal professions. Jewish entrepreneurs were expropriated and their businesses were 'Aryanized'.[26] Furthermore, Jews were forbidden to travel to the occupied zone. The decree was accompanied by the production of a comprehensive Jewish register by the Jewish Department established in the Paris Police Prefecture.[27]

The French government also decreed the internment of French and foreign Communists, as well as other enemy foreigners in the already existent camps.[28] This mainly affected Jews who had immigrated to France from Eastern Europe in the 1920s and Jews and/or political refugees from Germany and Austria, Spanish refugees fleeing from Franco and former members of the International Brigades.[29] From a German perspective, the concentration of political opponents and Jews in camps proved to be useful for the deportations that began later.[30] The deprivation of the rights of Jews in the occupied zone and their expropriation was largely completed by the end of 1940. The procedure had progressed further than any other Western European country at the time.[31]

The French government also provided assistance by establishing the General Commissariat for Jewish Questions (Commissariat Général aux Questions Juives) on 28 March 1941, headed by the Judenkommissar Xavier Vallat. Theodor Dannecker and Helmut Knochen hoped that the newly founded Commissariat would make it possible to instruct a French authority to carry out the deportation of all Jews living in France. After the plan failed because the Commander of the Generalkommissariat refused to participate in the persecution of Jews with French citizenship, embassy staff members Otto Abetz, Ernst Achenbach and Carltheo Zeitschel joined forces with Dannecker in late February 1941 to put pressure on the MBF to transfer its authority to imprison all Jews to the SD.[32] Otto von Stülpnagel, who regarded this as an attack on his executive power, refused. Instead, as the historian Ulrich Herbert writes, he instructed his employee Werner Best to 'further accelerate the speed of Jewish policy to prevent the BdS from having any angle of attack for its own ambitions'.[33] In March 1941, Best therefore instructed the Vichy government to set up the two camps in Pithiviers and Beaune-la-Rolande for the purpose of imprisoning foreign Jews and Communists on occupied French territory.[34] On 14 May 1941, based on the French police's Jewish register, Best ordered them to arrest 3,747 Polish, Czech and Austrian Jews as a 'punitive measure' and imprison them in the two camps. Some of them were shot as hostages in retaliation for assassination attacks on German soldiers.[35]

Until the summer of 1941, German occupation of France ran smoothly without any major problems or resistance from local citizens. The French public accepted the anti-Semitic policy of the occupiers with a great deal of indifference.[36] The German spread targeted anti-Semitic propaganda.[37] The film *Jud Süß* was watched by a large audience and the anti-Semitic exhibition 'Le Juif et la France' in Paris attracted two hundred thousand paying visitors.[38]

Only the German attack on the Soviet Union on 22 June 1941 led to outcries among Communists. The Comintern called upon all Communists to take up arms in resistance against the National Socialists. Even before then, in April 1941, the Jewish section of the MOI, which was by then clandestine, had decided to fight the occupiers from underground and was preparing to do so.[39] Immediately after the invasion of the Soviet Union, the Jewish MOI section successfully sounded out the possibility of cooperating with the Comité Amelot, an umbrella association of various Jewish organizations, camouflaged as a charity organization, which brought together mainly Zionists and Bundists from Eastern and Central Europe who had generally been exposed to violence and persecution in their countries of origin.[40]

From late July 1941 onwards, there were several demonstrations and strikes in Paris, as well as assassination attempts on Wehrmacht soldiers, while the number of acts of sabotage also increased.[41] In August 1941, the MOI took up armed resistance and carried out attacks on German logistics and infrastructure; there were targeted assassinations of Wehrmacht soldiers. Von Stülpnagel reacted with an order to punish 'Communist machinations' with the death sentence. In this way, Stülpnagel discovered a way of getting hold of French Jews protected by the Vichy government: they were declared Communist ringleaders who were subjected to punitive measures in retaliation for anti-German acts of resistance. Following further assassination attacks in August 1941, von Stülpnagel ordered the French police to carry out mass arrests of Jews on that basis. During the resulting raids, 4,300 people, including French citizens, were taken to the Drancy camp.[42] In connection with the debate on the hostage shootings by Germans, this measure in fact seemed lenient and was widely ignored by the general public. Thus, the MBF managed to imprison French Jews without any protest by the Vichy government.[43]

In view of the Madagascar Plan, which had failed in the meantime, and to make more space for more Jewish internments, Embassy Councillor Otto Abetz proposed in September 1941 to deport the ten thousand already interned Jews to the East. Himmler approved on condition that there were capacities to do so, but the authority to take the decision rested with the MBF.[44] According to Ulrich Herbert, from the perspective of the MBF, 'due to the turbulent events as a result of assassinations and hostage shootings, Jewish policy continued to be a less important problem and was regarded more as an instrument than as an autonomous goal of occupying policy'.[45]

Dissatisfied with MBF policy, Knochen and Dannecker attempted to add momentum to the persecution, recommended themselves for sole responsibility in 'Jewish matters' and stoked the fires of anti-Semitism among the French population.[46] During the night from 2 to 3 October 1941, Knochen staged bomb attacks on several Paris synagogues for this purpose, with the support of the anti-Semitic group Deloncle. When it was revealed that Knochen, rather than anti-Semitic Parisians, was the instigator of the explosions, Otto von Stülpnagel demanded his dismissal as his presence damaged the reputation of the Wehrmacht and the Reich. Heydrich strictly rejected the demand, assumed responsibility for the attacks and accused von Stülpnagel of a lack of determination in combating the enemy. A power struggle ignited, resulting in a split between the MBF and the BdS.[47]

Following two murders of high-ranking Wehrmacht officers on 20/21 October 1941, all internees held on German orders or by Germans were declared possible hostages for retaliation measures, bringing an end to a relatively calm period. There was pressure on the MBF in France from the Führer's headquarters to regularly shoot a large number of hostages in retaliation.[48]

Werner Best believed that such large-scale hostage shootings would undermine the willingness among the French population to collaborate. Since Best was responsible for the police custody camps and the internment camps and was instructed to select the hostages to be shot, he proposed that instead of retaliating for future attacks by shooting hostages, other measures be used, including the deportation of Jews and Communists, also adding the argument that the camps were overcrowded.[49] Implementation of his proposals marks the beginning of Jewish deportations in France. The two retaliation measures – hostage shootings and the deportation of Jews – were linked.[50]

Otto von Stülpnagel resigned on 15 February 1942. He no longer wished to be responsible for mass shootings of hostages and he had been unable to convince Hitler of his proposal for the alternative retaliation measure of deporting one thousand Jews to the East for each attack.[51] The power vacuum caused by his resignation, and the fact that Stülpnagel's successor, namely his cousin Carl-Heinrich Stülpnagel, only took office in June 1942, was used by the Reichsführung SS to strengthen its influence at the expense of the military administration.[52] With the appointment of an HSSPF in March 1942, the SS and police force, which had hitherto acted informally and was not systematically integrated into the occupying rule, consolidated its activity as an agent of Jewish persecution in France. The SS Brigadenführer and Generalmajor of the Police Carl Albrecht Oberg was named HSSPF. He had been a longstanding member of the National Socialist Party and the SS and had coordinated murders in connection with the 'Night of the Long Knives' ('Röhm-Aktion') together with Best.[53] He had authority over the BdS and the Geheime Feldpolizei (GFP); the latter meant that the Sipo-SD could therefore carry out executive functions.[54] Immediately, so-called retaliation measures – hostage shootings and deportations – began, and the SS and police force also gained the right to monitor the French police.[55]

Formally, Oberg had to report to the MBF, but in fact the MBF had lost considerable power due to the new executive positions and the transfer of the authority to repress the population. The SS and police force used the transferred repression authority, especially with respect to the 'retaliation measures against criminals, Jews and Communists',[56] as an opportunity to implement the deportation of Jews in France.

On 27 March 1942, the first train was sent to Auschwitz, before an enforced interruption of two months. Presumably the preparations for the summer offensive against the Soviet Union led to a lack of usable wagons.[57] The HSSPF machinery received additional personnel. Further anti-Jewish measures were passed, such as the requirement to wear a star, which was introduced in June, and a curfew for Jews at night.[58]

The Resistance Becomes Organized

After the invasion of the Wehrmacht, the PCF was initially reluctant to organize clandestine groups of fighters, but ultimately founded the 'Organisation Spéciale' (OS) consisting of members, anti-Fascist migrants and former fighters in Spain.[59] In the spring of 1942, the OS was transformed into a unit of the Francs-tireurs et partisans français (FTPF). Unlike the organization's name suggests, the FTPF consisted mainly of migrants. The MOI, which was the first group in Paris that decided to enter into armed combat, formed its own underground group, the FTP-MOI (Francs-tireurs et partisans-Main-d'œuvre immigrée).[60] This organization was the most militant and effective resistance group.[61] The four Paris MOI departments also represented the most active core of the Resistance. One of these four departments consisted of Jewish migrants.

Jewish armed resistance organizations were also founded in the unoccupied zone, such as the Armée Juive (AJ) in Toulouse. It carried out attacks on denouncers and 'Jew hunters', members of the Gestapo and people who benefited from the occupation, as well as organizing escapes from the camps in unoccupied France. Members of the AJ established contacts with Switzerland and Spain and forged high-quality ID papers on a large scale.[62] New fellow combatants were only recruited from members' close circles of friends. The AJ worked together with various other resistance groups, including Le movement de la jeunesse sioniste (MJS), an umbrella organization of Zionist youth groups founded in Montpellier in May 1942.[63] The AJ and the Jewish scouts in France, the Eclaireurs Israélites de France (EIF), which was the only organized group within the MJS to form an armed unit, amalgamated in June 1944 to form the Organisation juive de combat (OJC), in order to be integrated into the Allied forces as a fighting unit.[64]

From the Beginning of Mass Deportations in June 1942 to Liberation

The departure of the first deportation train on 27 March 1942 was initially followed by a period of interruption lasting over two months. On 2 June 1942, the deportations were recommenced and subsequently carried out in quick succession. The hunt for Jews began. At the end of June 1942, the General Secretary of the French police, René Bousquet, agreed to deliver ten thousand foreign or stateless Jews from the unoccupied territory to the Germans. Among the first three thousand Jews to be handed over were many expatriated Jews from the German Reich. They were to be taken to Drancy and deported from there to the East from early September 1942.[65] On 16/17 July 1942, a notorious raid was carried out by the French police, in which more than 12,884 children, men and women were arrested and then held for days without water, food or sanitary facilities in the Paris Vélodrome d'Hiver (Winter Velodrome). From there, they were taken to the camps in Pithiviers and Beaune-la-Rolande. In late August 1942, the RSHA ordered that the number of deportations should be considerably increased within a short time, since 'the current evacuation programme (deportation of stateless Jews) should be completed by the end of this year'.[66] Heinz Röthke, who replaced Dannecker as Head of the

Sipo-SD Judenreferat in Paris in July 1942, was dissatisfied with the progress up to that point and presumed that the French had not been working intensively enough on the internment and deportation measures.[67]

The Foreign Office Judenreferent, Zeitschel, regretted that although daily trains, each with a capacity of one thousand, had been available to deport Jews in September and October 1942, Jews had disappeared into the unoccupied territory due to the intervention by the Christian Church, the American representation in Paris and the British radio.[68] The French police were therefore unable to achieve the originally intended 'catch rate'. This was said to be particularly regrettable since the RSHA had already announced that from 15 November 1942 until the spring of 1943, no trains at all could be provided. Indeed, many people did attempt to evade the deportations by assuming false identities, hiding or attempting to escape to a neighbouring country.

Ambassador Abetz proposed to deport Jews with foreign nationality first, since, 'as in Germany at the time, where [there had been an] influx of Eastern and other foreign Jews', the immigration had led to an increase in anti-Semitism in France, which could be used to their advantage. The deportation of foreign Jews could incite anti-Semitism among the French population and lead to acceptance of the deportation of French Jews.[69]

When German and Italian troops occupied southern France in November 1942, the situation of the Jewish population deteriorated dramatically. For instance, the already difficult and risky escape over the Pyrenees to Spain became considerably harder, as the border was not only strictly guarded by the French Gendarmerie and customs officers, but also by German mountain troops since the complete occupation of France.[70] Between the late summer of 1939 and the liberation in August 1944, approximately eighty to one hundred thousand people fled over the Pyrenees, most of them Jews.

Röthke attempted to accelerate the deportations and expand them to include French Jews. In January 1943, he enquired of Eichmann whether Jews of French nationality could be deported if they lived in a state of intermarriage ('Mischehe'), had not adhered to the Jewish regulations ('Juden-Anordnungen') or had committed a different criminal offence. Röthke requested instructions on how to handle French Jews who had been interned during raids in late 1941 and 1942.[71]

In the spring of 1944, the Commander of the Sicherheitspolizei and the SD (BdS) in the field of the Military Commander in France, Helmut Knochen, issued a leaflet with instructions on the complete deportation of all Jews in France. Efficiency was to be the guiding principle of actions: 'For reasons of saving work and petrol, the arrest measures must be prepared in a way so that not only one Jew is arrested, but an appropriate area is cleansed in a single operation (in rural areas the entire village or housing block)'.[72]

The Jews in the French internment camps or OT work camps, as well as patients in hospitals and prison inmates, were not to be forgotten. The Jewish spouse of a so-called 'Mischehe' sealed after July 1939 immediately lost exemption from deportation and the marriage was annulled. Knochen explicitly pointed out that the deportation of arrested Jews had to take place in a manner that was 'completely secure against escapes': '1–2 Jews are missing from most transports on arriving at the Drancy camp. If no other means of securing them is available, they should be tied together by the hands using a long rope'.[73]

On 6 June 1944, Allied troops landed in Normandy. Eight days before the liberation of Paris, on 17 August 1944, the last wagon with Jewish prisoners travelled eastwards to Buchenwald concentration camp. By early September 1944, all of France was liberated.

Deportations from France

Summary of Deportations

Out of a total of 300,000 Jews who lived in France before German occupation, around 76,000 lost their lives as a result of persecution; 24,700 of those murdered were French citizens, 51,300 were foreign citizens or stateless persons.[74] A further three thousand Jews died in French internment camps and one thousand were murdered as hostages or as resistance fighters.[75]

The deportations began in France on 27 March 1942 with a transport from Drancy via Compiègne to Auschwitz. There was then an interruption in deportations until June 1942. By the end of 1942, 42,129 Jews had been deported for extermination. This represents more than half of all Jews deported from France.[76] Most of them – around 67,000 of the 76,000 – were deported from the Drancy assembly camp in sixty-two transports from the Drancy-Le Bourget and Bobigny stations. The remaining eleven deportation trains departed from Pithiviers, Beaune-la-Rolande, Angers and Lyon, generally destined for Auschwitz. Only five trains arrived in Majdanek, Sobibór, Kaunas (Kovno) and Reval (Tallinn).

The Drancy Assembly Camp

The assembly camp in Drancy to the northeast of Paris was set up in a building that had originally been planned as a residential complex for social housing. Its ground plan resembles a horseshoe.[77] On 14 June 1940, the Wehrmacht confiscated the as yet unfinished housing complex and converted it into a prisoner of war camp. The building was fenced off with barbed wire and watchtowers were erected. In September of the same year, Theodor Dannecker assumed responsibility for the facility and turned the prisoner of war camp into a camp for the internment of Jews. Dannecker defined the camp regulations and handed over the management, administration and guarding of the camp to the French Gendarmerie in August 1941.[78]

The internal camp administration operated according to the principle of a concentration camp. Inmates were used as 'functional prisoners' ('Funktionshäftlinge'), generally of French nationality. The 'camp elder' was their leader. Similar to the function of the 'block elder' and due to the architectural conditions, each of the twenty-two stairwells was allocated one 'chef d'escalier' ('staircase elder') and in each dormitory leading from them, a 'chef de chambrée' ('room elder') was appointed.[79] Stairwells 1 to 10 were allocated for foreign citizens who were not protected by foreign policy commitments and those for whom no provisions were made, for instance due to an 'Aryan' spouse. Unlike the French Jews, they could be deported at any time.[80]

In Drancy, numerous workshops were set up where inmates worked, but there was virtually no infrastructure for the prisoners themselves.[81] There were neither beds nor mattresses, only meagre food supplies and initially no medical care. The rooms were insufficiently heated.[82] Infectious diseases spread quickly, also due to the poor hygiene standards. Even in the summer of 1943, Drancy was still in a makeshift condition.[83] Until it was 'cleared' in May 1944, prisoners with serious illnesses were taken to a guarded part of the Jewish hospital, L'Hôpital de la Fondation Rothschild.[84]

In the first year, only men were interned at Drancy. Most of them were among the five thousand arrested during the raids in August 1941. After only a few weeks, many of them suffered from malnutrition and some starved to death.[85] In early November 1941, as the situation seemed to be running out of control, eight hundred prisoners who had almost starved to death were released. From then on, inmates were permitted to receive food parcels.[86]

Repeatedly, hostages were selected from among the internees in Drancy and Compiègne; they were shot in retaliation measures ordered by the Military Commander. As a result of the raids agreed upon by the Sipo-SD and the Vichy government, and carried out throughout France in early July 1942, leading to the arrest of thirteen thousand stateless and foreign Jews, the camp was also filled with children and women.

In early July 1943, the deportation expert SS-Hauptsturmführer Alois Brunner took over command of the camp from Heinz Röthke. Brunner had been sent to Paris with his special Viennese troops, which had experience in Jewish persecution and deportation. The occasion provided the opportunity for an expatriation law passed by the Vichy government that removed the citizenship of foreigners, of whom the majority were Jews, who had been naturalized since 1927. The aim was to remove the citizenship of a large number of French Jews who would otherwise have been protected from deportation. Knochen estimated that one hundred thousand people would be affected.[87] This would allow deportations to increase and the Sipo-SD Judenreferent Heinz Röthke would require the assistance of Brunner's special troops.[88] On the one hand, Brunner aimed to improve conditions in the camp and carry out deceptive measures to calm down the internees, but on the other hand he used extreme brutality with his SS troops against prisoners on several occasions.[89] Brunner remained the Camp Commander until its liberation on 17 August 1944.

In addition to Drancy, the occupied zone included the assembly camps in Compiègne, Beaune-la-Rolande and Pithiviers. In Compiègne, political prisoners, prisoners of war and Jewish prisoners were accommodated separately. The living conditions for the Jewish prisoners were especially poor, and some starved to death.[90] Like Compiègne, the camps in Pithiviers and Beaune-la-Rolande (until August 1943) were mainly used as transit camps, primarily as 'reserve capacity' for the by then highly overcrowded Drancy.

Despatching and Departure

The administrative procedure of the deportations, including items to be taken on board as equipment, was roughly outlined by Adolf Eichmann in an official order. It permitted each person to carry one item of baggage, a suitcase or rucksack.[91] Each deported person was to take: 'provisions for 14 days, 1 pair of sturdy work boots, 2 pairs of socks, 2 shirts, 2 pairs of underwear, 1 working overall, 2 woollen blankets, 2 sets of bedding (covers and sheets), 1 eating bowl, 1 drinking mug, 1 spoon and 1 jumper'.[92] The list made it seem plausible that they were travelling to a labour assignment. However, many internees hardly had any more belongings as by then they had already been completely robbed and expropriated. The required objects had to be provided by the Union générale des Israélites de France (UGIF), a compulsory merger of Jewish organizations in France.[93] However, the enormous volume of food also sent by the UGIF was actually intended for the local SS personnel. The deportees only received a few provisions for the journey. The equipment sent with the deportees was distributed from Auschwitz to relocated ethnic Germans or to the Winterhilfswerk.[94]

Before boarding the deportation train, Jews in the Drancy camp had to undergo a series of formalities and body searches. They were searched for weapons, ammunition, explosives, poison, money, knives and jewellery, among other things.[95] Items forbidden on the train included 'forks, scissors and other sharp objects'.[96] In Drancy, it was in any case forbidden to own objects such as knives, scissors, pliers or torches.[97] Clearly, Röthke considered the body searches by French policemen to be inadequate, since 'Jews attempted to smuggle out forbidden objects despite their explicit prohibition'.[98] Tools or tool-like objects were repeatedly used during the deportation to cut open the wagon wall and floor in order to escape. Röthke ordered that deportees should be inspected more thoroughly. In addition to body searches for forbidden objects, another strategy to prevent escapes was to partially or completely undress the deportees. Such 'naked transports'[99] are reported to have been ordered by the SD.[100]

The BdS in Paris had to report the departure of a deportation train immediately by urgent telegraph to the RSHA IV B 4, the Concentration Camp Inspectorate (Inspektion der Konzentrationslager, IKL) in Oranienburg and the destination, naming the Transportführer and the number of deportees.[101] From October 1943, Brunner regularly added to his standard report on the departure of a train a request to be informed by telegraph if the number of arriving deportees differed from the number on departure.[102]

The deportation trains were numbered, occasionally inconsistently, by the Judenreferat in Paris.[103] The itinerary planned several stops, for instance in Épernay and Châlons-sur-Marne, and the train was only permitted to travel at a maximum speed of 75 km/h.[104] Depending on the timetable, the more than 300-km journey from Drancy to the German border at Neuburg an der Mosel (today's Novéant-sur-Moselle) lasted between nine and eleven hours.[105]

The Wagon Elder

Before the departure of a deportation train, two German-speaking wagon elders ('Waggonälteste') were selected for each wagon, one head and one deputy. Their tasks included producing a list on the evening before the deportation with the names and prisoner numbers of the fifty or more people allocated to them, who had to spend their last night in the camp in a dormitory in a separate wing of the building.[106] The next morning, the groups were transported by bus to the station, where they boarded a wagon of the waiting deportation train, guarded by the SD.[107] The wagon elders had to identify themselves by wearing white armbands.

The Wagons Used for Deportations

Only the first deportation train consisted exclusively of passenger wagons. Dannecker proposed that the transports should comprise twenty freight wagons and three passenger wagons for the guard team.[108] Later, Röthke regularly ordered twenty-three freight wagons and three passenger wagons, which were to be provided the day before the deportation to allow them to be cleaned and secured with barbed wire.[109] The wagons were ordered by the RSHA via the Reich Ministry of Transport and provided by the French railways company SNCF.[110] The sliding doors of the freight wagons were secured with a padlock and bars were attached to the lateral upper ventilation hatches.[111] Brunner asked the Paris Judenreferat whether it was possible to use lead seals on the wagons. The answer was as follows: 'Sealing wagons occupied with Jews is not possible for purely guarding purposes and also useless against escapes'.[112] In one case, however, which occurred before the arrival of Brunner in Drancy, the Transportführer does report the use of lead seals on the wagon doors.[113]

In July 1942, the Judenreferent Heinz Röthke received a message from the main transport authority (Hauptverkehrsdirektion) that in future, Jewish transports must use passenger wagons because freight wagons were urgently required for other purposes. He explained to Eichmann that in that case, guards would be required for every compartment and it would be impossible to deploy two hundred guards per deportation train. Thus, Röthke (successfully) asked Eichmann to ensure that freight wagons continued to be available.[114]

In January 1943, Röthke reported to the Judenreferat of the RSHA that the Drancy camp was overcrowded.[115] He therefore requested one or two deportation trains to Auschwitz. Despite the winter weather, he argued in favour of using freight wagons: 'Please inform me whether transports in freight wagons can still take place in the case of severe frost. Transportation with passenger wagons is not possible due to a lack of sufficient guard personnel'.[116]

Friedrich Köhnlein, who himself admitted to guarding four or five transports in his capacity as Transportführer in the winter of 1943/44, stated that 'the wagons were connected to heating pipes from the steam locomotive to heat the freight wagons'.[117] This is contradicted by other statements, for instance the instructions by the BdS-Judenreferat employee Karl Wannenmacher, to preheat the wagon intended for the team of guards behind the locomotive.[118] Köhnlein's former subordinate Gottlob Busch stated: 'It should be noted that the transportation trains were used during the winter period and the wagons were not heated. Even the wagons that were provided for us were not heated'.[119] Survivors' testimonies indicated that no provisions were made for heating in winter or cooling in summer.

The Situation in the Wagons

It was extremely crowded inside the wagons. The instructions that each wagon should be filled with fifty people must often have been ignored. Many descriptions by survivors mention numbers higher than fifty, often seventy-five and even 100 or 120 people in the wagons.[120] It was often so cramped that nobody could move, let alone sit or lie down. Reports state that it was impossible to change the position in which one stood.[121] Another survivor reports that at night, they practically lay piled on top of each other.[122] The survivor Rolf Weinstock, who described the deportation as a 'journey of destruction',[123] recalls the transport that left Drancy for Auschwitz on 10 August 1942 as follows: 'We stood packed tight beside each other. We could not move. One eye stared at another's. Our faces had the expression of lunatics'.[124]

A single bucket served as a toilet for all prisoners, and sometimes overflowed, spreading urine and faeces on the wagon floor.[125] If the bucket was full or inaccessible due to the cramped conditions, people were forced to relieve themselves where they stood.[126] The situation caused disgust and shame, as well as creating a nauseating stench.[127] There was a constant struggle for spaces near the ventilation hatches.[128] Severe heat or cold also plagued the prisoners. Transportführer Urban reported that to ensure the smooth operation of one transport, it was necessary to open the sliding doors of the wagons by a hand's breadth, because even before the departure 'it was so hot that the Jews became very restless in the lead-sealed wagons and were screaming'.[129] Above all there was a lack of water, causing torturous thirst and hunger.[130] Many deportees stated that they begged in vain for water. Weinstock wrote that after two days, the train stopped in Frankfurt am Main and he spoke to an older guard through the ventilation hatch, asking him for a little water. The guard shouted back: 'Get back, you wretch, or I'll shoot! Die without any water, that's smarter!' ('Geh zurück, Du Sauhund, oder ich schieße! Verreckt ohne Wasser, das ist gescheiter!')[131] Some guards extorted the last valuables the deportees possessed in exchange for a little water.[132]

Some state that the atmosphere was very tense and nervous, with many arguments, hysterical attacks and fits of crying, and that it was generally very loud.[133] The journey was an 'indescribable nightmare'.[134] One survivor wrote about his experience travelling to Auschwitz on the 67th deportation train as follows: 'Three days. Three nights. Hunger. Thirst.

Madness. Urine. Excrement. Madness. Blows. Screams of people gone mad'.[135] One deportee on the penultimate train from France reported that they all had only one desire: to finally arrive.[136] The days passed with arguments, screams and hysterical fits of crying. Many became mad.[137] During the journey, many died due to the gruesome conditions or by suicide.[138] Weinstock described the conditions during the transport:

> There were already two bodies beneath us. We had to leave them sitting there as they had died. There was no space to lie the bodies flat. . . . On the fourth day, we had to endure a further six deaths, two of whom as a result of heat stroke, while three others suffered from asthma and literally 'suffocated'. One young man had severe pains in his appendix. He too died after an hour of terrible torment. . . . Eight bodies sat among us living people. Silent and rigid, they stared at us with reproachful looks – their lips closed. We decided to pile the dead on top of each other. We cleared a part of the wagon for that purpose. A mad woman screamed and constantly interfered with blows. So we were forced to bind her by her hands and feet.[139]

The Guard Teams

There was apparently a difference of opinion regarding the deployment of guard teams, since neither the Feldgendarmerie nor the Ordnungspolizei believed it had sufficient personnel for the task. Initially, the Deputy BdS, SS-Obersturmbannführer Kurt Lischka, asked the MBF to provide guards for the deportation of Jews.[140] The MBF decided to use the Feldgendarmerie, which was primarily intended for Military Police tasks within the Wehrmacht. In late June 1942, Dannecker wrote: 'The deployment of guard teams at a ratio of at least 1:40 men up to the Reich frontier must be arranged locally with the Feldgendarmerie'.[141]

In fact, the number of guards in the Feldgendarmerie teams was reduced to one officer and eight men, since it also had authority over a team of thirty French Gendarmerie officers.[142] This German-French group of guards initially accompanied the deportation trains to the border of the Reich, which had moved westwards as far as Neuburg an der Mosel in Lorraine due to the de facto annexation of Alsace and Lorraine.[143] There they were replaced by a Schutzpolizei team.

Only a month later, the Kommandant of Greater Paris indicated that he intended to withdraw the Feldgendarmerie from this task since they were overstretched. He proposed that the Ordnungspolizei could instead assume the task of guarding deportation trains.[144] The Ordnungspolizei stated that this task was not part of its portfolio.[145]

It took until early 1943 for the Schutzpolizei, which was part of the Ordnungspolizei, to replace the Feldgendarmerie.[146] The French continued to provide most of the guards. The Schutzpolizei guard teams were provided by, among others, the 2nd Police Guard Battalion in Mülhausen and the 2nd Battalion of SS Police Regiment 4, which was posted in Paris until June 1943.[147]

In the spring of 1943, the Vichy government prohibited the French Gendarmerie from participating in accompanying guard teams. This represented a protest against the planned deportation of French Jews, who had previously been exempt from deportation. Thus, the Schutzpolizei were required to guard the trains without the support of their French colleagues. From the late summer of 1943 onwards, this practice changed again, perhaps because the Ordnungspolizei units in Western Europe that had previously guarded the trains were relocated to the eastern front.[148]

Thus, it appears that there were personnel shortages. On 2 September 1943, Alois Brunner, SS-Obersturmführer Karl Wannenmacher of the Paris Judenreferat and five Unterführer from the BdS Paris accompanied a transport to the Reich frontier, where a Schutzpolizei team took over the guard duties.[149] A team of guards from the Stuttgart Schutzpolizei was recruited for the transport on 7 October 1943. The guards led by Meister der Schutzpolizei Schramm guarded the train throughout its journey from Paris to Auschwitz, an exception that was in no way to become the rule.[150] In fact, the guards for the next transport, on 23 October 1943, were requested from Münster.[151] The following transport, on 28 October 1943, was again guarded from Paris by the Stuttgart police officer Schramm and twenty members of the Schutzpolizei from Metz, presumably all the way to Auschwitz.[152] There appears to have been no available Schutzpolizei team available to guard the deportation train on 7 December 1943 to the border of the Reich, so guards from the Sipo-SD led by Wannenmacher fulfilled the task.[153]

To summarize, the composition of the guard teams changed several times from the onset of deportations, initially due to the switch from the Feldgendarmerie to the Schutzpolizei, then due to the withdrawal of French guards and later due to a lack of personnel in the Ordnungspolizei. No sources are available on the composition of guard teams for the thirteen deportation trains in 1944.[154]

The former Schutzpolizei officer Gottlob Busch was one of those who described how the prisoners were received and guarded during the journey. When questioned as a witness, he stated that after staying overnight in a hotel or barracks, they were driven to Drancy station in the morning and took over the 'Judentransport'. Generally, the train was already waiting, 'loaded' and ready to depart ('abmarschbereit'). Occasionally, the trains were still being 'loaded' when they arrived, which was supervised by members of the local SD.[155] Before the departure, the Transportführer received all keys to the wagon locks and two copies of a list of all deportees, which was sorted by wagon and was to be handed over at the destination.[156] Gottlob Busch, who stated that he was a member of the guard team eight times, described the instructed procedure in the case of an escape:

> Before the deportation began, we were instructed by the respective Transportführer ... to shoot in the case of attempts to escape. In response to questioning, I cannot state with certainty whether guards were instructed to aim and shoot in the case of escape attempts, or to shoot warning shots first. Jews were also told before the journey that they were required to report attempted escapes since others would otherwise suffer. Those instructions were generally given by the SD, occasionally also by our Transportführer.[157]

In 1971, Gustav Zuschneid,[158] the Commander of the 2nd Battalion of SS Police Regiment 4 (formerly PB 323), who was posted as a Transportführer, stated that since they were guarding prisoners, attempted escapes were to be prevented by using firearms if necessary.[159] The former Transportführer Willi Nowak produced two reports on the procedure of the deportations, in which he also described the order to shoot and measures he undertook to prevent escapes. While being questioned in 1971, he was 'emphatically reproached' for his report, to which he responded by saying the Jews were handed over to him as prisoners who had to be passed on to the subsequent team of guards without any losses. Thus, he and others warned the Jews that escaping prisoners would be shot. Furthermore, he stated that attempted escapes had to be reported immediately or otherwise they would be punished.[160] Another order in the case of an escape was to activate the emergency brake and pursue the escaping prisoner. The train driver was also instructed to maintain as fast a speed as possible to prevent people jumping from the train.[161] In some cases, guards were repositioned, for instance in the elevated brakeman's cab situated at the front of some older wagons or directly inside the wagons to ensure better guarding.

As is confirmed by witness testimonies, the guard teams were aware of the inhumane and life-threatening conditions in the wagons.[162] According to statements by former colleagues at the time, guards said that the transports were carried out in 'gruesome conditions',[163] and that after unloading the wagons there was a 'terrible stench'.[164] Gottlob Busch stated that the transports were taken over by members of the SS outside the actual camp grounds. He also reported that after the Transportführer handed over the lists, their 'mission was completed'.[165] They returned to Strasbourg on a regular passenger train. Busch's colleague Otto Gehring stated that returning guards had the impression that 'the people in Auschwitz were being incinerated'.[166]

France: Escapes and Attempted Escapes

On 27 March 1942, the first deportation train left France with 1,112 male prisoners, travelling from Drancy via Compiègne to Auschwitz. The logistical planning was carried out by Theodor Dannecker. On 20 March 1942, Dannecker was informed by telephone by SS-Obersturmführer Franz Novak, Transport Officer of RSHA Department IV B 4, of the timetable for the deportation train as determined by the Reich Transport Ministry. However, passenger wagons rather than freight wagons would be provided. Dannecker noted that he had explicitly pointed out the problems this entailed in terms of guarding the train.[167]

On 25 March 1942, Eichmann's deputy, SS-Sturmbannführer Rolf Günther, confirmed 'the provision of the required special train (passenger wagons) for 27. 3. 42 from Paris-Nord'.[168] After the Military Commander had initially refused to take over guard duties, he agreed to provide sixty members of the Feldgendarmerie shortly before the departure.[169] Dannecker instructed the Deputy Director of the Department for Jewish Affairs at the Paris Police Prefecture, André Tulard, to make ten city buses available on 27 March 1942 at 14:00 in front of the Drancy assembly camp. Dannecker ordered the Head of the French anti-Jewish Police, Director Jacques Schweblin, to separate the Jews selected for transportation in Drancy and to examine them very thoroughly, above all to prevent 'any metal objects, with the exception of a table spoon'[170] and any money being taken with them. Each prisoner was only permitted to take one item of luggage. Dannecker also noted that Schweblin was to ensure that the French Gendarmerie prevent people from gathering in front of the camp, on the way to the station and at the station.

After the first stage, the train was due to stop at the station in Reims from 22:25 to the next morning at 9:10. The Reims Feldgendarmerie was responsible for guarding the standing train.[171] On the following day, the train was due to arrive at the border station in Neuburg an der Mosel at 14:00. Guards would be changed, as a team from the Ordnungspolizei took over under the supervision of the BdS Metz.[172]

The transport counts referred to all of France and not to assembly camps or stations from where the trains departed.

Georges Rueff – Escape from the 1st Transport on 27 March 1942

On 26 March 1942, a roll call was ordered in Drancy in which all internees had to take part. Dannecker announced that the 'residents' of the blocks beside the kitchen would be transferred to Germany for labour assignments.[173] Georges Rueff (born in Blotzheim/Alsace in 1916), who had been interned in Drancy since September or October 1941 as a result of being denounced, lived in a different block, but was desperate to leave Drancy as the conditions were so terrible.[174] Since he understood German, he spoke to Dannecker and asked whether he could join his comrades, as he did not wish to sit around and do nothing. Dannecker agreed. All those selected for deportation were required to shave their heads on the same day.[175]

The next morning, they were taken to the station and loaded onto a third-class, open-plan wagon with wooden benches and a central aisle. Two German guards were posted in each wagon. The prisoners were told that any attempts to escape would be punished by shooting all the occupants of the wagon.[176] The deportation train travelled to Compiègne, where more prisoners boarded. On the way, German nurses distributed water to the German guards. The deportees received nothing.[177]

When Georges Rueff noticed that the train was travelling at a slower speed, he believed it would be possible to escape. He had already reached the door and touched the door handle when other deportees began to cry out to draw the guards' attention to the attempted escape.[178] One soldier asked what the matter was. Georges Rueff quickly replied in German that all was well and it was just a minor dispute.

When the train began to slow down again around fifteen minutes later, Georges Rueff quickly jumped through the wagon door of the moving train. When he realized that he was in the middle of Reims station, he left the building as quickly as possible because both German and French policemen were carrying out inspections there.[179] Rueff knew his way around Reims and went to a hotel. He was able to pay for the room with money he had hidden in a sock. He did not leave the hotel during the night and took a train to Paris the next day.[180] In early April 1942, he crossed the demarcation line into southern France with the help of a paid trafficker, managed to reach Lyon and finally received false papers in Nice.[181]

In an account written in 1966, Rueff closes his report with the conclusion that nobody in the deportation train was shot due to his escape. He learnt this after a chance meeting with his former comrade Bercovici, who had been in the same compartment as Rueff.[182] The escape of one deportee from this transport, albeit shortly before Reims, was confirmed by Simon Gutmann, who had apparently been transported in the same wagon as Georges Rueff.[183]

Bertha Goldwasser – Escape from a Transport on an Unknown Date

Bertha Goldwasser (born around 1912 in occupied Poland) left Poland in 1936 to study chemistry in Paris. As she lacked money and language skills, she began teaching Polish. Her husband Kuba was arrested in 1941 and interned in Drancy. While attempting to give him food through the camp fence, Bertha Goldwasser was arrested and held there herself for a short period. Perhaps because she had her nine-month-old daughter with her, or because only men were interned in Drancy at that time, she was released shortly afterwards.

Bertha Goldwasser then took measures to prevent her and her child from being deported. She placed her child in the care of others (it is unknown for how long) and did not wear a star. As a result of raids in Paris on 16/17 July 1942, she was nevertheless interned in Drancy together with her daughter. During her deportation, she saw through the wagon hatch that the train was approaching higher ground. She broke a board out of the wall and jumped out of the wagon with her baby in her arms. The train was travelling near Colmar at the time.

In a 1946 interview in Paris with David Boder, which was carried out in German, Bertha Goldwasser described the horrific end of the escape: 'well, I already knew where the deportation was heading and I jumped off the train with my child in my arms. Alas, my child was killed while I jumped down'.[184] Boder asks when she decided to jump:

> Bertha Goldwasser: No, no, I had been . . . considering the idea the whole time. I told myself: 'Once and for all and I am travelling to my death and so I may be able to save my life'.
>
> David Boder: Really?
>
> Bertha Goldwasser: And the child. But unfortunately I lost the child while jumping down. And with the hands . . . with my hands I had to take the child together . . . I left extra parts of the body in the forest.
>
> David Boder: What does that mean, extra parts?
>
> Bertha Goldwasser: A foot, a hand, I . . .
>
> David Boder: Collected them together?
>
> Bertha Goldwasser: Yes, when I jumped down, the train quickly went . . . went up the hill.[185]

She herself was also severely injured. She buried her dead child, and when she was found by two passers by some time later, she did not dare to tell them the truth and instead said she was a Christian who had been brought there by the Germans and left behind. Bertha Goldwasser was fortunate that the two men were active in the Resistance and she was nursed back to health over a period of nine months. After her recovery, she also joined the Resistance, for instance taking British, Canadian and American airmen who had been shot down to the Spanish border. During the battle to liberate Paris, she was a lieutenant in the armed FFI (Forces françaises de l'intérieur), an organization of fighting units from various resistance groups.

Bertha Goldwasser may have been deported under a different name as she is not recorded in the deportation lists.

Adolphe Fuchs – Attempted Escape from the 35th Transport on 21 September 1942

Adolphe Fuchs, aka Addy (born in Paris in 1926), had Polish parents.[186] He was arrested by the Gestapo on 26 July 1942 together with his relatives. Equipped with false ID papers by the MOI, the small group had attempted to cross the demarcation line.[187] In Pithiviers, Adolphe Fuchs was taken to Shed 17, in which a group of young people were accommodated.[188] On 20 September 1942, they were driven from Pithiviers to Auschwitz for the deportation planned the following day.[189] The young men were intent on fleeing from the train, including Addy Fuchs, who was, according to his own statements, rather small and looked more like a twelve- or thirteen-year-old. The older youths entrusted him with a suitcase containing tools; they hoped that in view of his childlike appearance he would not be searched before entering the wagon. The plan succeeded and the tools were distributed among the friends. The Germans checked the wagons regularly, and to prevent any form of escape, they threatened to execute everyone in the wagon if someone fled.

Six boys, including Adolphe Fuchs, equipped with a butcher's knife, tried to use the toilet bucket to strike a hole into the floor of the wagon, so they could let themselves down onto the track bed. They had seen this method in a film. Alarmed by the noise, an old, traditionally clothed Jew approached them and said: 'You want to flee, that is clear. But you will have our deaths on your conscience. Have you considered the babies, pregnant women and old people? What will you do? The German will kill us all'.[190] Adolphe Fuchs and his friends gave up their attempt to escape and used the hole that already existed to empty the toilet bucket.

During the selection process in Cosel, Adolphe Fuchs was allocated to the group of men who were fit to work, and survived the camps in Blechhammer, Groß-Rosen, Buchenwald and Langenstein.[191]

Hans and Theo Catz – Escape from the 40th Transport on 3 November 1942

The brothers Hans (born in Rotterdam in 1917) and Theo Catz (born in Rotterdam in 1921) left their hiding place in the Dutch region of Noord Brabant in September 1942, since it no longer appeared safe, with the intention of making their way to Switzerland.[192] Shortly before reaching the unoccupied zone in France, they were arrested by Germans in a bus to Besançon.[193] For two weeks they were imprisoned in Besançon, where they shared a cell with Heinrich Rosenthal, who reported on his escape from the 26th deportation train from Drancy. Then, escorted by the Gendarmerie, they were taken by regional train to Drancy. Hans and Theo Catz planned to escape from the train.

On changing trains in Dijon, Hans noticed that his brother had moved away from the train unnoticed. Hans did the same and hid in a freight train.[194] It was five minutes to midnight. He had to survive another twenty-five minutes before the train would continue to Paris with his parents. A quarter of an hour later, he heard his father call his name: 'Hans, I beseech you, help us, come back, Theo has also come back'.[195] Hans saw that his father, who was constantly calling his name, was handcuffed by a member of the Gendarmerie. He wanted to give himself up, but instinctively jumped out of the wagon as a Gendarme discovered him. He was caught, handcuffed and returned to the wagon. The French Gendarmes reproached the two brothers, saying they themselves would spend two months in prison and be demoted for the brothers' escape attempt. Most of those in the wagon also accused Hans Catz of irresponsibly risking the lives of everyone.[196]

On 16 October 1942, they were interned in Drancy.[197] The deportation was planned for 3 November 1942. The two brothers both failed in their attempts to smuggle a passport photo into the wagon in preparation for obtaining false papers.[198] They had agreed with another pair of brothers, Henri and Jacques Marcel De Metz from Antwerp, to attack the two French policemen who usually escorted the buses on the journey to the station and to flee. They were unable to carry out their plan, however, as they were in an unfavourable position on the bus, there were three escorting policemen and there was an additional Gendarme patrolling the convoy on a motorcycle.[199]

Inside the wagon, they focused intensively on the hatches, two elongated openings at a height of around 1.5 m. They believed it would not be too difficult to escape through them.[200] Along the outside of the wagons, there were metal bars on which one could put one's feet and jump down. Furthermore, there was the chance of working one's way forward towards the ladder that led to the brakeman's cab at the front of the wagon.[201] They believed they could wait in the brakeman's cab for a good opportunity to jump. The brothers quickly took their place at the hatch.

The train stood in the station for nineteen hours before departing the next day. Their parents could at least sit on their suitcases while the two brothers had to stand the entire night for lack of space.[202] Theo and Hans ate their entire three-day rations. They were convinced that their escape from the wagon during the journey would be successful.[203] That night, Theo emptied a can that had been converted into a toilet around sixty times out of the hatch. Repeatedly, the contents got spilt and it began to stink terribly. The situation in the wagon was hardly bearable.[204]

The next morning, people tried to find space for everyone in the wagon. Accompanied by disputes and discussions, luggage was stowed in a space-saving way or converted into seating. At 10:00 the train departed. Since they wanted to jump from the train under protection of darkness, Hans and Theo Catz were very concerned that the train would reach the German border before nightfall. They hoped to find assistance in the annexed Lorraine from the local anti-German population after their escape. If they were forced to escape within the territory of the old German Reich ('Altreich'), they had an address near Saarbrücken where they could find refuge. However, that meant risking an illegal border crossing back into France.

Every time the train stopped, the French Gendarmes got out of the passenger wagons. A number of German guards were also present. They carried out patrols along the train. When the train set off again, they looked out of their windows to see whether anyone had attempted to escape. One of the German guards told them that their journey was taking them to Poland.

Hans Catz describes in detail the great dilemma facing the brothers. They would have preferred it if their parents had also decided to escape, but they were unsure whether their mother would have been physically able to do so, and their father would only flee together with his wife. The brothers' parents told them they should do what they thought was best. Most of the other deportees in the wagon advised against fleeing. The brothers were torn both ways, asking themselves whether they were cowards for leaving their parents to fend for themselves in order to egoistically spare themselves an unknown future in Poland. The considerations tormented them both in the wagon and for many years afterwards. They ultimately decided to flee.

The two De Metz brothers also intended to flee and shared the 400 Francs they had managed to smuggle past the checks in Drancy in equal parts with the Catz brothers. If after jumping they came across each other anywhere, they would pretend not to know each other.

First, Theo climbed out of the hatch, clambered along the outside wall of the wagon up to the ladder leading to the brakeman's cab and waited there for Hans to follow. The train was travelling too quickly to jump from it. From the brakeman's cab, they told the De Metz brothers that they would wait for a little while and told their parents that the first stage of their escape plan had been successful. After half an hour, the De Metz brothers appeared and they squashed together in the brakeman's cab. When the train stopped, they decided to jump down as it set off again. They would lie flat on the ground until the train had passed. The De Metz brothers were to jump to the left and then walk straight ahead. The Catz brothers would jump to the right and walk back in the direction from where they had come. During the stop, a Gendarme on patrol checked the train at their level with a torch, but failed to discover the four men in the brakeman's cab. They jumped as the train set off. The Gendarmes in the rear section of the train shed light on the track beside the train. Hans feared that he and Theo would be discovered, so he quickly moved a few metres away from the train, stood straight with his hands in his pockets and tried to look like a railway worker. The ploy worked. The guards shone their torches at him but the train continued to move on. When the train's rear lights disappeared, they found the De Metz brothers, wished each other good luck and escaped in different directions.

One day after jumping from the train to Auschwitz, they were stopped by French Gendarmes in Longwy, close to the Belgian border. After a while, they were released on condition that they were to cross the border into Belgium immediately.[205] They reached Liège on 6 November 1942 and remained there, hidden in an attic, until April 1943. Theo Catz then fled to southern France, but was arrested there, fled again, this time from the Gurs camp, and escaped via Spain, Portugal and Great Britain to the USA, where he trained as a pilot and flew missions for the US Air Force.

Hans Catz managed to flee to Switzerland, where he was received in a refugee camp. Together with his cousin and a friend, Hans Catz decided to travel to the Allied troops that had landed in Italy in September 1943 in order to join them. However, the German Reich suddenly occupied large parts of Italy and the Allies only managed to advance slowly. The three men were immediately arrested after crossing the border, imprisoned and sentenced to death. They managed to jump from a travelling prisoner transport and survived for two months in the Apennines and Umbria as they made their way south towards the front. There, they were again arrested by Germans as they attempted to pass the Gustav Line, but again managed to escape. A few days later, when they were stopped again, they presented themselves as South African sergeants, of whom a number served in North Africa in the British Army and were captured there as prisoners of war and interned in Italy. The Germans apparently believed the story and initially arrested them in Spoleto, from where they were to be sent to the Moosburg camp near Munich. Hans, who was not in the same wagon as his cousin and friend, used a penknife to cut a hole in the wooden roof of the wagon and jump from the train near Bolzano. He aimed to escape to Switzerland, but was again arrested by Germans, who presumed he was the South African Sergeant Coenen and incarcerated him in the prison in Trento. In January 1944, he was taken to the Emsland prisoner of war camp. There, it was noticed that he should actually have been transported to Moosburg, which then occurred. He met his cousin and friend there. In April 1945, the Moosburg prisoners of war were to be evacuated to Austria. During the evacuation march, Hans and his cousin managed to escape and hide for a week in a field on the bank of the River Danube. They were discovered when German soldiers posted artillery positions there, and fled again before meeting the American army a few days before German capitulation.

Leo Bretholz and Manfred Silberwasser – Escape from the 42nd Transport on 6 November 1942

Two successful escapes are known to have occurred during the 42nd transport, which left Drancy for Auschwitz on 6 November 1942. Leo Bretholz (born in Vienna in 1921) and Manfred Silberwasser (born in Vienna in 1923) jumped from the moving train.

In October 1938, as the situation for Jews in Austria became increasingly unbearable, the seventeen-year-old Leo Bretholz left Austria, mainly due to his mother's insistent encouragement. The escape, which was supported by the Jewish organization Ezra, initially took Leo Bretholz to Trier.[206] He swam across the River Sauer, which marked the border with Luxemburg. A few days after his arrival, following an inspection by Luxembourg Gendarmes, he was deported across the border to France. Leo Bretholz returned to Luxemburg without being discovered and fled from there to Belgium in early November 1938. After the Wehrmacht invaded Belgium in May 1940, Leo Bretholz was arrested as an enemy foreigner and taken to the St. Cyprien internment camp in southern France. In August 1940, he managed to escape beneath the camp fence and hide with friends in France.

Bretholz and his friends regularly listened to forbidden Allied radio stations. In June 1941, the BBC reported four thousand killings during a pogrom in the Lithuanian city of Kaunas (Kovno) and they also learnt of other atrocities such as that in Lemberg (Lviv). In the winter of 1941/42, the horrific news became more frequent. Bretholz recalls:

> On the . . . radio we heard reports on German troops committing atrocities that were hitherto unimaginable . . . and we attempted to listen to the sum of daily murders; in Lithuania, troops had murdered thirty-two thousand Jews in only a

few days; more than a quarter of a million Jews were murdered in the Baltic States in the first six months of German occupation.[207]

During the early months of 1942, Leo Bretholz first heard of frightening rumours about death camps where terrible things happened to Jews. It was also known that people were being deported from Drancy to those camps in the East.[208] Leo Bretholz had a fairly clear idea that deportation would end in death. After his failed attempt to flee to Switzerland in October 1942, he was deported to France and interned in the Rivesaltes camp.[209] While there, he 'almost incessantly thought of fleeing'.[210] On 20 October, twelve days after arriving in Rivesaltes, Leo Bretholz learnt that he would be deported to Drancy.[211] Once there, the conditions in the camp only strengthened his resolve to escape: 'You instinctively thought of fleeing, or you imagined a wonderful end to the war within the next thirty seconds, or you simply resigned to your fate and became accustomed to the idea of death. "Yes", I told myself. "Escape."'[212]

Leo Bretholz was in Drancy at a time when the camp was extremely overcrowded. On 31 October 1942, Röthke, the Head of the Sipo-SD Judenreferat in Paris, enquired whether further transports would be possible on 4, 6 and 9 November 1942, since there were already 2,600 prisoners in the 'Drancy Jews' Camp'[213] and he expected the figure to increase to three thousand the following week. Röthke stated that enough wagons were available.

In Drancy, Leo Bretholz met Manfred Silberwasser, a former neighbour in Vienna from his childhood, who was arrested during a raid and deported to Drancy via Rivesaltes. Together, they decided to jump from the train if they were deported, regarding it as their last chance.

After two weeks, Leo Bretholz and Manfred Silberwasser were told they were to be deported. On 5 November 1942, they were driven to the station by armed French Gendarmes, who shouted at the prisoners as they rammed their rifles into their backs, before forcing them onto cramped buses and military trucks.[214]

After their arrival at Drancy station in the early evening, the deportees were counted and allocated to wagons in groups of fifty.[215] Some of the oldest had to be transported on a stretcher, while many children who had lost their parents cried in despair. Newborn babies were transported in cardboard boxes and covered with dirty rags as makeshift blankets. Leo Bretholz was sure that everyone was doomed to death. He writes:

> There was more sadness than I could bear. . . . I was powerless and hated myself as a result. . . . I swore to myself that I would never be helpless again. I would run and run and run. Nothing would stop me – neither the guards, nor the people I

loved, not the war. My eyes filled with tears, . . . and [I] asked myself when my opportunity to escape would come.[216]

It was very cramped in the wagon, with hardly enough space for everyone. An empty bucket was provided for people to relieve themselves. Leo Bretholz reports:

> After one or two hours, the bucket overflowed. There was no way of emptying them and then you could hear the sounds of helpless people relieving themselves on the floor. The stench in the wagon was almost unbearable and we struggled not to vomit, though some failed. The vomit stuck to people's clothes and also fouled the air.[217]

The wagon stood on a siding for a whole night and only departed the following morning. At that time, the wagon was already flooded with urine. Manfred Silberwasser and Leo Bretholz intended to attempt an escape through one of the two hatches before the train reached the German border. Both hatches were secured with horizontal iron bars. When Manfred and Leo spoke of their plan to escape the next night in the shelter of darkness, a discussion unfolded between a number of prisoners on whether such an escape attempt was at all possible and, if so, whether it was not far too dangerous. Leo Bretholz recalls: 'There were stories of men who had attempted to jump from trains and died while jumping because they were struck by a passing train, or captured by the guards and tortured. Why should our fate be different?'[218]

One man feared that those left behind would have to pay for the two men's escape. Another said that they would all be killed anyway. Finally, an older woman said that if the two men jumped, they would be able to tell the story of the people cramped inside the wagon. Those words encouraged Leo Bretholz to carry out his escape plan. Albert Hershkowitz, with whom he had already attempted to escape to Switzerland, was also in the wagon and pointed encouragingly at the hatch above them. Albert Hershkowitz had a much bigger build than Leo Bretholz and believed he would not fit through the iron bars. Leo Bretholz suspected that it was not just Albert's sturdy figure that prevented him from attempting an escape. He presumed that Albert was generally too exhausted and had already given up. Together, Leo Bretholz and Manfred Silberwasser tugged and pushed at the iron bars in front of the hatch to bend them, but they did not move. Someone told them it was senseless. Another gave them the idea of using jumpers to pull at the iron bars, but that made no difference, nor did belts. To increase the friction, they made the jumpers wet. Leo Bretholz recounts:

The water we needed was on the floor: the collected excretions of our fellow deportees, which swilled back and forth with the movement of the train. Manfred called 'Go!' I hesitated a moment. . . . Struggling against the revulsion, I bent over and dipped my jumper into the urine. Pieces of faeces floated in it. I felt humiliated. It was the most disgusting thing I had ever done. To save my life, I first had to defile it in a way that went beyond all imagination in my former existence.[219]

Manfred Silberwasser and Leo Bretholz took turns in tugging at the jumper soaked in urine, which gripped better than before. Leo Bretholz regarded it as the last chance to save his life. For five hours, perhaps longer, they worked on the iron bars. Other wagon inmates repeatedly advised them to desist. Finally, the bars gave way a little and could be bent downwards and upwards, creating a gap about 30 cm wide. Leo and Manfred bid their farewells to their friends and other acquaintances. Leo put his cap in his pocket. He stacked a number of luggage items on top of each other to reach the opening more easily. Manfred and Albert helped him climb up. Leo Bretholz describes the situation:

> My midriff was now at the level of the window. I grasped through it to grip an edge at the place where the side wall of the wagon was connected to the bottom of the roof. Leaning my head out, I felt the cold wind strike my shaved head. I pulled up with both arms, while at the same time twisting my body back and forth and pulling my stomach in. From inside the train, Manfred and Albert pushed up, allowing me to slowly squeeze through the train window, centimetre by centimetre.[220]

Once he was outside, he held onto the ledge above the hatch and shuffled with his right leg towards the end of the wagon and to the coupling. He was afraid he would be heard or caught by spotlights. At the same time, he was euphoric at having managed to get so far. Manfred Silberwasser followed him, also with the help of Albert Hershkowitz.[221] They stood on the coupling, held onto the wobbling ladder leading to the wagon roof, held onto each other to prevent falling between the wheels and waited for a good moment to jump.[222] They intended to wait until the train travelled more slowly around a bend and the lights could not shine on them due to the curve in the train. After a few minutes, between Bar-le-Duc and Nancy, there was a bend in the track and the train slowed down. Manfred Silberwasser jumped first into the darkness, followed by Leo Bretholz.[223]

They immediately heard shrill whistles and shots. Their escape attempt had clearly been noticed.[224] Leo Bretholz remained as close to the ground as possible. The train stopped and guards spread out to search for the escapees. After a few minutes, there was silence. Leo then heard the creaking of the train as it set off again. Manfred Silberwasser and Leo Bretholz found each other, removed the yellow stars from their clothing and continued on foot. They arrived at a village near Mussy, where they asked for the priest. He hid them for a night and then sent them to a colleague in the neighbouring village. From there they continued their escape to Paris.[225]

From then on, Leo Bretholz was forced to endure a terrible odyssey through French prisons and camps. Time and again, he was captured and managed to flee – a total of seven times. Eventually he joined the Resistance group 'La Sixième'.[226] Manfred Silberwasser, who arranged new ID papers for Leo Bretholz some time after their joint escape, was able to flee from persecution and later lived in Belgium.[227]

In his autobiographical book *Flucht in die Dunkelheit*, Leo Bretholz repeatedly stresses the difference between people's ability to act if they were tied to others, compared to those who were independent and could act without taking others into account. He was able to attempt so many escapes due to his independence.

In accordance with procedure, SS Obersturmführer Röthke reported the departure of the 42nd deportation train with one thousand Jews on board to Eichmann at the RSHA, to the IKL and Rudolf Höss, the Commander of Auschwitz, on 6 November 1942. The transport included 221 children and youths under the age of eighteen. Only four men from this transport survived the Shoah.[228]

Escapes from the 46th Deportation Train on 9 February 1943

The 46th transport deported one thousand Jews from Drancy-Le Bourget station. Before the train was boarded, the French police were instructed to 'thoroughly search all prisoners for transportation and their luggage for tools and similar objects that they are forbidden to take with them'.[229] A guard team led by Willi Nowak, lieutenant in the Reserve Schutzpolizei and Ordonnanz-Offizier in the 2nd Battalion of Police Regiment 4, guarded the train as far as Neuburg an der Mosel.[230] In his report on the deportation, Nowak states that the train was already ready and waiting in Drancy-Le Bourget station when the guard team arrived at 07:00 on 9 February 1943. A large contingency of Paris policemen and the guard team from the French Gendarmerie were present at the station. The buses, carrying a total of one thousand Jews, mainly women and children, arrived after a delay of more than an hour. Of the twenty-five waiting freight wagons, he chose the best twenty for the transport, each with fifty deportees, while the guards' luggage and provisions were stored in the remaining five wagons. Due to the very cold conditions, women and children were permitted to keep their luggage, which contained blankets and warm clothing. The commanding officer of the SD assured him that everything had been thoroughly checked. Three passenger wagons were arranged at the front, in the middle and at the end of the train. Both guard teams were evenly distributed among the three wagons. The brakeman's cabs were occupied by members of the Schutzpolizei.

Due to the short ramp, loading had to take place in two stages, which led to a departure delay of two and a half hours in Drancy. Nowak gave an order that whenever the train stopped, all guards had to form a chain around the train. Any damage to the wagons caused by prisoners during the journey had to be reported to him. In the case of attempted escapes, he ordered the immediate use of firearms. The report continues:

> The journey progressed smoothly until Chalons s. M. [Châlons-sur-Marne], where we arrived around 16:00. When the train slowly entered the station, 11 prisoners jumped from one wagon. As it was later discovered, they had apparently created a large hole in the front wall of the wagon using jigsaws. The escapees were immediately pursued. I could not permit the use of firearms in the station, since it was very busy with civilians, but outside the station grounds 4 shots were fired by an officer of the French Gendarmerie. We managed to recapture 7 men and 1 woman. 3 prisoners escaped. The French Gendarmerie in Chalons s. M. [Châlons-sur-Marne] was immediately informed. I ordered the damaged wagon to be evacuated and the prisoners were distributed in the other wagons. I ordered the recaptured prisoners to be specially guarded by 3 men. After 40 minutes, the train was able to continue its journey. While travelling normally beyond Chalons s. M. [Châlons-sur-Marne], one Jew jumped from the moving train. The leader of the French Gendarmerie guard, who was situated in the last wagon, immediately pulled the emergency brake and the train stopped after about 200 m. 6 rifle shots were fired at the prisoner from the moving train and one man who pursued him fired 2 shots with his pistol. As a result, the Jew stood still and allowed himself to be recaptured.[231]

The former station master at Châlons-sur-Marne, Raoul Pageot, stated that twice in March 1943 he saw on Platform 2 'how Israelite deportees attempted to flee, but were then massacred, either by shots or brutally with rifle butts'.[232] One of these cases must have involved this train, which, according to Gustav Zuschneid, the Battalion Commander of II/SS Police Regiment 4 (formerly PB 323),[233] made an unscheduled stop at the station.[234]

The continuing journey to Neuburg an der Mosel, where the transport was handed over to a different guard team, passed without incident, according to Willi Nowak's report. Collaboration with the French Gendarmes was apparently good. They had shown unconditional commitment 'in recapturing the escapees'.[235] Since the Gendarmerie had reported the arrest of two escaped Jews in Châlons-sur-Marne, only one fugitive Jew remained. The two arrested Jews were handed over to the German Command in Châlons-sur-Marne.

It seems that the escapes had raised questions concerning the Gendarmes' loyalty, which required a clarifying statement. The Deputy Director of the Gendarmerie and Chief of the Gendarmerie in the occupied territories, Serignan, defended the behaviour of the Gendarmes on 9 February 1943. The inspection of the prisoners before departure was a task for the French police, not the Gendarmerie. The number of escorting Gendarmes was determined by the German authorities, as was the distribution in the wagons during the journey. During the journey, the brakeman's cabs had been occupied by German members of the Schutzpolizei. When the train stopped, the Gendarmes had formed a chain of guards along the entire length of the deportation train. When the eleven Jews fled from one wagon, the Gendarmes immediately sounded the alarm and pulled the emergency brake. Only their fast, considered actions had led to the recapture of eight fugitives. Two further fugitives were arrested by the French police, who had been informed of the escapes by telephone by the accompanying Gendarmerie officer. When one prisoner escaped through a hatch at around 18:00, he had been recaptured by the Gendarme. Thus, of the twelve fugitives, only one had managed to escape. It was noted that the escapes were only possible due to the knives the prisoners had managed to keep with them and the poor condition of the wagons. Although it was not their field of responsibility, the Gendarmes raised the alarm and captured almost all of the fugitives. Serignan stressed that the Gendarmes had behaved in a remarkable way under the circumstances and should only be congratulated. This was confirmed by the German non-commissioned officer who thanked them warmly several times for their commitment.[236] Röthke, the Head of the Sipo-SD Judenreferat in Paris, thanked Serignan for the report and wrote: 'The behaviour of the French Gendarmerie on the occasion of the transport on 9 February 1943 clearly deserves full recognition'.[237]

Attempted Escapes from the 47th Transport on 11 February 1943

On 21 February 1943, Transportführer Walter Kassel, Oberleutnant of the Schutzpolizei, wrote a report on the transport dated 11 February 1943. In the morning, the French Gendarmerie had received the transport of camp internees from Drancy to the station and taken over the 'loading of the Jews'.[238] Towards the evening, the train repeatedly came to a standstill due to a lack of steam or progressed very slowly. Kassel reports: 'One male and one female Jew took advantage of the latter situation to jump through a wagon opening while the train was moving. They were recaptured by the French Gendarmerie after a brief pursuit'.[239] To prevent further escapes from slow-moving trains, Kassel issued the following instructions: 'The

French train driver was strictly ordered either to drive quickly or to stop the train'.[240] Nevertheless, a further escape was attempted: 'When later the train stopped again, another Jew tried to flee through a hole sawn into the front side of the wagon. He was also immediately recaptured and two French policemen were ordered to guard that wagon for the rest of the journey'.[241]

The continuing journey to Neuburg an der Mosel passed without incident. Kassel complained that some of the train wagons had been of a very poor quality and 'covered with apertures through which the prisoners could escape without great difficulty'. He also proposed that members of the guard team should be equipped with torches to make it easier to guard the transport in darkness. Kassel's conclusion was as follows:

> The train should at all cost refrain from travelling at low speeds. Wagons should be examined at every stop to check for fresh damage. Constant observation while moving and checks at every stop reduce the escape options of the deportees to a minimum.[242]

Escape from the 48th Transport on 13 February 1943

This deportation planned to transport to Auschwitz 661 Jews with French citizenship 'who are interned in Drancy due to their crimes',[243] with the authorization of Eichmann. Their crimes consisted of breaking anti-Jewish laws imposed by the German occupiers.[244] The French government refused to participate in the deportation of French citizens as long as there were no appropriate provisions for them.[245] Thus, it did not provide a team of French Gendarmes for this deportation train.[246] The Sipo-SD Judenreferent Röthke was annoyed by this stance, as Jews with French citizenship who had broken the anti-Jewish laws had been deported since 1942. A guard team from the Gendarmerie comprising one officer and thirty-three men arrived for duty after all, though the reasons for this are unknown.

Röthke, who a day before the deportation had assumed that a thirty-man team from the Schutzpolizei would be guarding the train, sent a request to the BdO (overall commander of the Ordnungspolizei): 'I request that the team of guards is instructed that in the case of prisoners attempting to escape, firearms should be used immediately without calling out to them'.[247] According to Röthke, luggage inspection should take place in the camp the day before the deportation. To guard the transport, Bataillonskommandeur Zuschneid ordered that on the next day, the 5th Company should provide a fifteen-man guard team commanded by Nowak, the Reserve Schutzpolizei Lieutenant, for the 'Judentransport' from Drancy to Neuburg an der Mosel.[248]

To prevent escape attempts from the outset, Zuschneid sent the following order to Nowak, whom he named Transportführer: 'The provided loading wagons must be checked in detail with respect to their suitability for use. If necessary, luggage should be loaded onto damaged wagons. The French train personnel should receive a warning in case of conspicuous speed reduction at night and near the German border'.[249]

One half of the Schutzpolizei guards were to be equipped with two machine guns and pistols, while the other half were to receive rifles and sixty rounds of ammunition each. The Schutzpolizei team was distributed evenly throughout the three passenger wagons. At every stop, they had orders to secure the train immediately with a chain of guards and examine each individual wagon for damage by the prisoners.[250] After the transport was implemented, Nowak reported: 'I also had the brakeman's cab occupied by men equipped with submachine guns. All men received the orders that if anyone tried to escape, they should use their firearms without warning. The prisoners were also informed of these instructions'.[251]

According to Nowak, 'the loading of 998 Jews of both sexes'[252] at Drancy-Le Bourget station took five hours, since due to previous experience, an attempt was made to make it 'impossible for prisoners to break out'.[253] To prevent attempted escapes, the 455 men were packed separately into eleven wagons without any luggage. Nowak also reported:

> Furthermore, I distributed the French Gendarmerie in those wagons so that 2–3 Gendarmes were in every wagon. I had previously told them to keep an eye on each individual prisoner. That was best achieved if all prisoners were forced to lie down or sit in the freight wagons. Only in this way were the guards able to observe any actions and work on the freight train walls by the prisoners.[254]

Until the last section of the route, the journey was satisfactory from Nowak's perspective. When the train stopped shortly before entering Neuburg station, the guards noticed a wagon with an approximately 40 x 40 cm sawn-open hole. Nowak wrote:

> When I asked what was going on, the 3 French Gendarmes in the damaged wagon replied that they had not noticed anything. An immediate count showed that 8 Jews were missing. I am completely at a loss how it was possible for the Jews to escape with those guards. The relevant guards must have behaved carelessly or been in league with the French Jews, whom they clearly still regarded as their fellow citizens.[255]

In a telegraph to the BdS, presumably from the KdS (Commander of the Sicherheitspolizei) in Nancy, the reported number of fugitives is given as ten:

On 13 February 1943 around 23:00, 10 Jews jumped from a moving deportation train with Jewish prisoners between the stations Tronville [Tronville-en-Barrois]-Nancois [Nançois-sur-Ornain] and Ermecourt [Ernecourt near Erneville-aux-Bois]-Loxeville (Meuse) and fled. 1 Jew was discovered with a broken leg and taken to the hospital in Commercy (Meuse). The search for the remaining fugitives has been taken up by Feldgendarmerie and the French Gendarmerie and police. To this hour, we have no information on further recaptured fugitives.[256]

Röthke requested a report from the General Director of the French police, as he wanted to know the circumstances of the escapes.[257] He had previously also requested a report from the BdO, so as to be able 'to take any measures against the French Gendarmerie'.[258] Based on the witness accounts by the Transportführer of the last three deportation trains, Bataillonskommandeur Zuschneid produced a written statement defining problems and proposed solutions for future guarding. It was repeatedly observed that the trains travelled without interruptions up to the region of Chaumont and Bar-le-Duc, but then reduced their speed or, as on 9 February, stopped at Châlons-sur-Marne station. In this way, fugitive prisoners could mingle with travellers and 'make it impossible to use firearms'.[259] Furthermore, it was 'striking that these train stops (apparently due to a lack of steam etc.) became more frequent after dark'.[260]

Zuschneid also criticized the fact that escapes had been possible due to the dilapidated wagons and because the SD failed to remove penknives from the Jews while inspecting them and that these had been converted into small saws. Due to previous experience, 'to prevent damage to the wagons from inside for the purpose of escaping',[261] he had ordered that the Gendarmes for the transport on 13 February were posted inside the wagons. Zuschneid continues: 'At the same time, male Jews (without luggage) were to sit or lie down so that they could be seen more clearly. (Standing groups only provide protective environments)'.[262] Transport Officer Nowak also gave such orders, but the Gendarmes had not fulfilled the instructions. No culpable behaviour was apparent among the German transport officers.

Deputy BdO Niemann proposed a meeting with the relevant department of the BdS, the BdO and the Commander of PB II/Pol. 4 to discuss ways of preventing escapes, since 'similar problems have been evident in prisoner transports from Compiègne to Neuburg/Mosel on 23 January and 24 January 1943'.[263] The RSHA reacted to the escapes with the following guideline:

> To secure the transports, each transportation train must be allocated an appropriately equipped accompanying team of guards (generally Ordnungspolizei in a ratio of 1 leader and 15 men), who must be informed in detail on their tasks with

reference to the constant attempts to escape and measures to be taken in the case of attempted escapes.[264]

On 21 April 1943, Röthke again received a report from Serignan, who wrote that the wagon from which the escape took place had ventilation shafts and four sliding doors. Three had been sealed with lead and one could be locked from the outside. Fifty men with luggage and blankets had been inside the wagon. They were all required to sit down. Serignan attached a hand-drawn sketch showing that one longitudinal side with the two sealed sliding doors was unguarded because all three Gendarmes had posted themselves along the other longitudinal side: one directly beside the front, sealed, forward-facing door, one directly beside the locked sliding door and a third facing forwards at the rear, guarding the ventilation shaft. Between 19:00 and their arrival at 21:00, a number of prisoners had been able to saw an opening into the unguarded side wall under the cover of darkness and aided by the noise, apparently using a penknife that had been converted into a saw. The opening had a size of around 50 x 40 cm. Eight prisoners had escaped in this way. To conceal their escape, they had formed human contours with their blankets.

The three guards – Gendarmes considered to be reliable – were punished with arrest. Serignan noted that one must take into account that they were working under difficult conditions and there were without doubt other aggravating circumstances, for which others had been responsible. The escape had only been possible because the deported Jews had cutting tools with them. The inspection of Jews before they boarded the train was the responsibility of the Police Prefecture. Furthermore, the thirty-three Gendarmes had been distributed in the eleven wagons for the entire period of the journey. Without relief, the Gendarmes had to carry out their duty for twelve hours in difficult conditions, dealing with vibrations, noise and stench. The wagons were also in a poor state; in fact, two needed to be replaced along the route. The lighting was inadequate to discover the escapes, and there was no alarm signal that would have enabled the Gendarmes to stop the train in case of an incident.

To conclude, Serignan stated that mistakes made by his personnel in carrying out their duty would be sanctioned, but equally that the Direktion Générale de la Gendarmerie expected the working conditions to improve and normalize.[265] Röthke hand-wrote on the report: '3 Gendarmes fail to notice when 8 Jews saw a hole and escape!!!'[266]

Jakob Silber – Escape from the 50th Transport on 4 March 1943

The 50th deportation train departed Drancy on 4 March 1943 carrying one thousand prisoners who had mostly been transported to Drancy from the southern French camp of Gurs. The Sipo-SD Judenreferent Röthke called the destination 'Cholm'.[267] Cholm was the Russian name of the city of Chełm, a town with a station around 70 km to the east of Lublin in the direct vicinity of the camp of the 'Aktion Reinhardt'. Accordingly, the standardized departure report was addressed to Eichmann's Judenreferat at the RSHA in Berlin, but not as otherwise to the IKL in Oranienburg and the camp commander at Auschwitz, but instead to the BdS Krakau (Cracow) and the BdS Lublin in the General Government. The destination was therefore the extermination camp of 'Aktion Reinhardt'. It appears that the train travelled to the Sobibór extermination camp approximately 55 km to the north of Chełm.[268]

The Transportführer to Neuburg an der Mosel was Leutnant der Ordnungspolizei Ott, who received two copies of the list of named deportees.[269] On the way from the Drancy camp to the train, one prisoner had already managed to escape and another, the unmarried furrier Jakob Silber (born in Tarnow/occupied Poland in 1893), fled from the moving train.[270] He was captured shortly afterwards. SS Sturmscharführer Küver from the BdS Lothringen-Saarpfalz in Metz reported the arrest to the BdS in Paris as follows:

> Silber was arrested on 5 March 1943 in Metz. He states that he left Lyon on 4 March 1943 at approximately 22:00 and travelled to Metz on the express train to visit his friend Meyer there. On the journey near Metz, he fell out of the train, whereby he injured his head. S. does not own papers with which to cross the border. S. denies being a Jew. It must be presumed that S. jumped from the Jewish transport from France on the night of 4/5 March 1943 and injured himself. As has since been discovered, one Jew was missing from that Jewish transport.[271]

The telegram ends with the request to investigate the situation and report the results. SS Obersturmführer Röthke replied on 11 March 1943:

> The above-named Jew was placed onto a Jewish transport from the Jewish camp in Drancy near Paris to the East on 4 March 1943. The assumption there that he jumped from the Jews' train is correct. Please deport the Jew from there to Auschwitz/O. S. or connect him from Metz to one of the local Jewish transports that will be deployed from here in late March.[272]

The last evidence of the later fate of Jakob Silber can be deduced from a telegraph from Küver to the BdS in Paris. In it, Küver states that he 'connected' Jakob Silber with the 'ongoing Jews' transport' on 23 March 1943.[273] As Röthke had ordered, Jakob Silber was locked into a wagon of the 52nd transport in Metz. The later fate of Jakob Silber is unknown. Serge Klarsfeld writes that none of those in transport no. 52 lived to see the liberation of Auschwitz.[274]

Four Escapes from the 51st Transport on 6 March 1943

As was the case with the 50th transport, most of the deportees on the 51st train were taken from the Gurs camp in southern France on 6 March 1943. The 51st transport left Drancy in the direction of Chełm (again wrongly described as 'Cholm') in the district of Lublin. The Transportführer was the Ordnungspolizei Oberleutnant Walter Kassel, who carried two copies of the list of deportees' names with him.[275]

Sal de Leeuwe (born in Amsterdam in 1923) and Albert Matarasso (born in Thessaloniki in 1911) were able to escape from the 51st transport. Both had previously been interned in Gurs and were set to be transported back to Majdanek.[276] Sal de Leeuwe was recaptured only a day after escaping. Ten days later, Küver telegraphed from Metz to the BdS in Paris: 'The above-mentioned escaped from the Paris–Cholm Jewish transportation train on 6 March 1943. He was recaptured here on 7 March 1943. According to his own statements, he had been interned in Drancy near Paris. I will have him returned there'.[277] In his reply, SS Obersturmführer Röthke requested:

> that the above-mentioned Jew is not returned to Paris and should instead join the Jewish transport departing from here on 23 March 1943 at 8:55 with the destination Cholm. The transport will arrive in Neuburg on the evening of 23 March around 20:00. I would be grateful if the Jew is then included in the provided transport list and that I am briefly informed afterward.[278]

A telegraph by Küver dated 25 March 1943 includes a reference to the escape by Albert Matarasso. It states the following:

> I have seen to it that the following Jews, who escaped from earlier transports of Jews to Cholm, joined the Jewish transport on 23 March 1943 from Le Bourget Drancy to Cholm/General Government, namely:
>
> Sal de Leeuwe, born in Amsterdam on 4 March 1923, Dutch citizen, mechanic, single;
>
> Jakob Silber, born in Tarnow on 13 November 1893, Polish, furrier, single;
>
> Albert Matarasso, born in Saloniki on 13 August 1911, Greek, glover, married.
>
> The guard team was handed an appropriate letter with which to inform the receiving camp in Cholm.[279]

All three were deported with the next transport, the 52nd, via Chełm to Sobibór. Nothing more is known of their fate.

Kurt Asser (born in Hamburg in 1907) was also deported on the 51st train and recounted his escape in a letter he wrote to Beate and Serge Klarsfeld in 1978.[280] Kurt Asser, who at the time was a resident of Marseille, was arrested as a Jew on 26 January 1943 by the French police.[281]

He was interned in Gurs and then transferred to Drancy and deported in the 51st transport.[282] In his letter, he describes the situation in the wagon:

> In fact with the help of a comrade, I managed to push the iron bars in front of the hatch to the side. Since I had a sporty, slim figure and managed to get outside through the hatch I had carefully planned the jump to minimize the risk of breaking any bones. That meant jumping in a bend, where the train had to brake and then leaping into the bushes that grew along the railway track.[283]

According to his own statements, he jumped before the train's arrival in Majdanek. Three weeks after the escape, he was arrested at a station in Silesia, where his parents lived, during a raid while the police were seeking forty-one English officers who had escaped from a camp. He was sent to the 'Bräts disciplinary camp'.[284] This is clearly the Brätz reception camp in the city of the same name, in what was then the western Prussian rural district of Meseritz.[285]

The camp was set up according to a request to the RSHA by the responsible Stapo unit in Frankfurt (Oder) for use as a punitive labour camp ('Arbeitserziehungslager', AEL), but was described as a reception camp.[286] The Gestapo was able to convert the Brätz camp into an extended police prison in April 1943 by using a trick that also applied to AELs, whereby it was able to bypass the AEL regulations concerning the period of detention there (up to a maximum of fifty-six days) and with respect to prisoner groups (no political or 'race' prisoners).[287] The Brätz camp was occupied by an average of three hundred prisoners. It was situated in the direct vicinity of the annexed Warthegau. In this region, many Polish and Soviet forced labourers, who had fled from their deployment locations in the Third Reich and tried to return home, were arrested and interned in Brätz.[288]

On 29 July 1943, after four months' imprisonment in Brätz, Kurt Asser was classified by the Stapo in Frankfurt (Oder) as a first-degree 'Mischling' and sent to Buchenwald concentration camp. His personal prisoner's card includes the term 'Fluchtpunkt', which referred to previous escapes.[289] In April 1945, Kurt Asser was liberated from Buchenwald.[290]

Thus, the statement by the Ordnungspolizei, that the 'transport of Jews on 4 and 6 March 1943 from Drancy to Neuburg a. d. Mosel was carried out without incident. No escape attempts were made',[291] does not conform to the facts.

Escape from the 52nd Transport and Deadly Pursuit on 23 March 1943

On 22 and 23 January 1943, the Wehrmacht, supported by French police forces in Marseille, followed Himmler's orders in carrying out mass raids known as the 'Aktion Tiger' in an attempt to crush the Resistance. A major raid took place in Marseille's harbour quarter, where there was an especially large number of people who had fled from their German persecutors. Heavily armed SS police units sealed off the harbour quarter. Wehrmacht pioneer units demolished almost all of it in February 1943. Twenty thousand residents were evacuated and mostly transferred to the internment camp in Fréjus, from where many of the internees were moved to the Sachsenhausen concentration camp. Of those arrested, 1,642, consisting mainly of French and foreign Jews, North Africans and emigrants with residence permits, were taken in freight wagons to Compiègne. Seven hundred and eighty Jews from Marseille were to be deported from Compiègne in the 52nd and 53rd transports via Drancy to Sobibór.[292] Everything for the two deportations had been prepared by the Jewish Department of Röthke's Sipo-SD.[293] Eichmann had agreed and the Reich's Ministry of Transport was instructed to provide trains and integrate them into the timetable.[294] The Ordnungspolizei was ordered to provide a guard team of the usual size, namely one officer and fifteen men.[295]

Röthke planned to deport 780 Jews in the train, including 570 French citizens, who had been arrested 'during the cleansing of the Marseille harbour quarter'.[296] However, unexpected difficulties arose the evening before the planned departure of the 52nd transport train. Prefect Jean Leguay visited Röthke and informed him that Pétain had expressed his concern at the fact that French Jews were being transported, especially since there were so many other Jews in France. The General Secretary of the French police, Bousquet, whose deputy was Leguay, had therefore ordered that the French police should not help with the loading and guarding of the deportees, as they otherwise did. This was a decision by the French government, which intended to solve the problem with the French Jews itself. Röthke could not understand why the French government did not release the group for deportation, as he noted a day later:

> These Jews are *downright criminal vermin*, as the French police has stated to me several times without being asked. . . . Once the Marseille Jews were transported from Compiègne to Drancy, they were first required to undergo a special cleansing measure because they were so riddled with lice and so filthy that the French camp leadership decided that it was necessary to prevent an epidemic. Director Francois and the French policemen in the Drancy camp themselves had *asked* the undersigned and SS Untersturmführer Ahnert several times to deport these Jews to the East soon since they were not only visibly dishevelled, but also almost exclusively consisted of criminal types.[297]

Since the transport was to depart under any circumstances, Oberg immediately ordered the exclusive use of German policemen.[298] Thus, the

Ordnungspolizei was ordered to be present in Drancy at short notice with a team of guards consisting of one officer and thirty men. Since the Ordnungspolizei could not initially provide enough guards, it was agreed that the Feldgendarmerie would provide nine additional uniformed men. The Ordnungspolizei team was sent to the Drancy camp, while the Feldgendarmerie units were deployed at Drancy-Le Bourget station.²⁹⁹

Although the French police had withdrawn their support, around forty members of the French police force arrived on the morning of the departure to assist as usual, as Röthke describes:

> The French police helped in loading the Jews into the buses and accompanying them to the station, without being asked to do so. . . . At 7:30, the leader of the French Gendarmerie unit declared to the undersigned that the French Gendarmerie would travel as the train's guard team to the border of the Reich with a unit of 1/30 as usual.³⁰⁰

Thus, Röthke sent the Feldgendarmes back to their barracks and allowed the Oberleutnant of the Ordnungspolizei to also leave fifteen men behind, since the usual number of guards ('standard cover: 1 officer and 15 men from the Ordnungspolizei, 1 officer and 30 men from the French Gendarmerie')³⁰¹ had already been achieved.

At 8:00, Director Jean François from the Paris Police Prefecture arrived. He expressed his surprise at the presence of French Gendarmes and managed to prevent the French Gendarmerie from accompanying the deportation after all. Röthke praised the subsequent behaviour of the Gendarmes:

> However, the French Gendarmerie units remained at the loading station until the train's departure at 9:42, without being explicitly instructed to do so, and continued to help load the Jews onto the wagons in an exemplary way. It seems they had received precise orders that they were merely not permitted to act as guards accompanying the trains themselves.³⁰²

The guard team was ultimately provided by Transportführer Oberleutnant Uhlemann from the Ordnungspolizei and thirty men.³⁰³ A four-page report on the deportation by Uhlemann has survived. He noted:

> The 997 deported Jews – predominantly men – consist of the vermin from the Marseille harbour quarter and of Algerians with typical criminal faces. I therefore instructed a Paris police officer to inform units that they should shoot without warning at the slightest escape attempt.³⁰⁴

The Jews were separated by gender and loaded onto twenty-three freight wagons. Nine members of the thirty-strong guard teams occupied the brakeman's cabs, while the remaining guards were distributed among the three passenger wagons in the middle and at the end of the train. The men were instructed to form a chain of guards whenever the train stopped and to examine the freight wagons for 'damage caused during the journey – loose or removed boards etc'.[305] If anyone attempted to escape, they were ordered 'to shoot immediately without warning and to take the strongest measures against illegal actions'.[306] The guards ruthlessly carried out these instructions.

The following report by Transportführer Uhlemann documents the persecutional zeal with which one of his men, namely Walter Kantim, who was mentioned in Chapter 1 as an example of impunity, pursued a fleeing Jew. The deadly chase shows the great will of Walter Kantim to kill the fleeing prisoner. He used self-initiative on several occasions to continue his pursuit:

> Shortly before 12:00 Schutzpolizei guard Kantim, 7th Company, noticed a Jew in a blue labour uniform crouching on the running board of the passenger wagon at the end of the train. When he saw Kantim, the Jew leapt from the train, which was travelling at speed. Kantim shot a number of rounds from his submachine gun, which however missed the target. He pulled the emergency brake, whereupon the train stopped after about 600 metres. Kantim ran with a number of men to the place where the prisoner had jumped; labourers working on the track showed them the direction in which the Jew had fled. Kantim borrowed a bicycle from a woman who by chance had approached along the path and cycled after the Jew. He appears to have been seeking a place from where to swim or wade across the Marne and was running between the bushes on the banks of the Marne. While Kantim put aside his bicycle to approach the Jew on foot, the Jew was no longer to be seen. In reaction to several calls, which the Jew presumably believed were coming from civilians, he put his head out for a view of the river bank. Kantim alertly took advantage of the opportunity and shot several rounds at the Jew, who immediately disappeared again. When Kantim arrived at the place where the Jew had looked along the river bank, he saw the Jew's body already lying at some distance from the bank, surrounded by a large amount of blood. His head and feet had disappeared beneath the water. The incident occurred near the town of Changis [Changis-sur-Marne]. It was not possible to inform the Mayor or Gendarmerie to recover the body since there was no telephone connection.[307]

Following the deadly pursuit, it was discovered that a further three Jews had escaped from the same freight wagon. Immediately after the train had stopped, they had hidden themselves in the brakeman's cab outside the wagon and intended to use the moment of surprise to escape when the guard returned. Since the three Jews refused to leave the brakeman's cab and resisted, they were pulled down by force and loaded back onto the wagon. After a short period of travel, around 13:40, an Oberwachtmeister again pulled the emergency brake, since, according to Uhlemann:

Two Jews had used a small axe to cut a hole at the level of the latch securing the door and pushed the latch upwards. One of the Jews was in the process of sliding open the door to flee. Obw. König in the brakeman's cab shot several rounds from his pistol, which however missed their target due to the vibrations while travelling. When the Jews realized they had been discovered, they threw the axe out of the wagon hatch. Since the two Jews attempted to attack guards while being interrogated, I ordered their resistance to be broken, whereby one rifle butt was broken.[308]

The journey continued without incident until Bar-le-Duc. Shortly after leaving the station at around 18:30, another Jew managed to escape. Oberwachtmeister Woll fired three shots at him. The Jew was recaptured without being injured. Uhlemann describes the situation: 'Since the Jew became reluctant the closer he came to the train and the guard leading him, Zugw. Wiegand, who could not shoot without endangering his comrades standing by the train, struck the Jew several times with his submachine gun, whereby the butt broke off'.[309]

As an immediately ordered search of the wagon showed, one prisoner had broken off a board at the front of the wagon during the journey and let it fall onto the track. Interrogations of the remaining deportees in the wagon had not provided additional information on the escape. The final attempted escape occurred around 20:00, shortly before Neuburg. Oberwachtmeister Daigfuss fired his rifle at a fugitive, but did not hit him due to the darkness. The Jew was recaptured by encirclement and returned to the train by force.[310]

Uhlemann ends his report with improvement proposals for future deportations. His experience showed that a team of 1:30 was sufficient. It had been helpful to post guards in the brakeman's cabs during the journey. It was advantageous from the outset to use specific guards for recapturing escaped prisoners and to accommodate them in passenger wagons. In this way, they could shoot at prisoners who had jumped even before the train stopped, or at least see the direction in which the fugitive fled, in order to begin a pursuit immediately. These guards should be equipped with submachine guns. As the escape attempts had shown, allowing luggage on the wagons was not expedient, despite previous checks. Thus, one of Uhlemann's improvement proposals was that deportees should only be permitted to take one fork, one spoon and one blanket onto the wagons. The remaining luggage was to be transported in separate wagons. Furthermore, the ventilation hatches should be secured with barbed wire. This would prevent escape attempts through the hatches as well as attempts to use sticks to open the latch securing the doors and thereby unlock them. Uhlemann concludes:

Only the harshest measures ensure the secure implementation of such transports. These include not hesitating to use blows, even when prisoners do not resist as such, but do show rebellious behaviour towards guards or rebellious behaviour in general that may endanger the secure implementation of the transport.[311]

At a police witness hearing in 1971, Franz-Ludwig Daigfuss, who had been an Oberwachtmeister at the time of the deportation and is mentioned in the report, initially denied having taken part in the 'measures against the Jews'.[312] After being shown the report, he admitted that he had been part of the guard team.

The report largely conformed to his memory of the events during the journey and the attempted escape. Speaking about the event in which he is said to have fired shots, he stated that while he was looking out of the compartment window, he by chance saw a man running away from the railway embankment. 'I had my rifle standing beside me at the window. I immediately took it and fired a warning shot into the sky.'[313] He did not aim at the fugitive. The man escaped and he did not know whether it was a Jew escaping from the deportation train. When he was confronted with the fact that the Jewish fugitive had been recaptured and returned to the train by force, Daigfuss stated that he could not remember the event.[314]

The 52nd deportation train travelled via Chełm to Sobibór. No-one from the train was still alive in 1945.[315]

Escapes and Attempted Escapes from the 53rd Transport near Épernay and Frankfurt Am Main on 25 March 1943

As was standard practice, prisoners intended for this transport from Drancy were taken by Paris city buses to the deportation station Drancy-Le Bourget. The one thousand deportees included 580 French citizens, 114 Polish citizens, 56 Hungarians and 29 Germans; 49 came from the Soviet Union.[316] The transport left Drancy on 25 March 1943 and travelled to Sobibór. On the way, seventeen prisoners in the wagons fled, five of whom while still in French territory.

The team of guards led by Schutzpolizei Oberleutnant Walter Kassel was provided by II/SS Police Regiment 4.[317] One day later, Kassel reported that during the bus journey from Drancy camp to the station, two Jews had already escaped.

Before loading, the train had to be rearranged in a time-consuming process due to the insufficient number and poor condition of the wagons. The journey progressed slowly, which Kassel reported as the reason for the subsequent flight:

The long duration of the journey was made use of in a rear wagon to cut a hole in the front wall of the wagon using a knife and a saw. When the trained decelerated as it approached Epinay [Épernay], 5 men jumped off and fled to the right and left, as well as backwards. The fugitive to the left was shot dead as he fled. One of those who escaped to the right was immediately captured, while the two others were hit by gunfire and arrested after a brief pursuit. The Jew fleeing to the rear was also shot at, but mingled with French railway workers and used the helpful terrain to continue his escape. The train was stopped using the emergency brake as a result of the incident. Since the route had to be cleared, the dead man and the wounded were taken on board the train to Châlons-sur-Marne. During the journey, one of the wounded died; the two bodies were handed over to the Deputy Station Officer in Châlons-sur-Marne and the people in the damaged wagon were moved to a spare wagon.[318]

Of the five fugitives mentioned above, only two are known by name: Joseph Brudasch (born in Vienna in 1912) and Salomon Samuel Perelsztejn (born in Lublin in 1925).[319] Each of their death certificates, produced by the city of Châlons-sur-Marne, state that the body was found at the station.[320] They were buried on 26 March 1943 at the Cimetière de L'Est in Châlons-sur-Marne and exhumed in 1947/48.[321]

On the second day of the deportation, one escape occurred on German territory. Twelve men fled from the train between Darmstadt and Frankfurt am Main. One of them, Sylvain Kaufmann (born in Metz in 1914), described the escape in his memoirs.[322] Kaufmann had grown up in Metz, which was part of the German Reich, and he therefore spoke German. In 1940, he managed to escape from a prisoner of war camp in Moosburg, Bavaria. When the French police arrested him as a Jew in late March 1942, he denied being a Jew and was freed on condition of producing proof of being Aryan within three days. He fled the same evening and reached the unoccupied zone. Two months later, he returned to Paris to collect a large sum of money from an acquaintance who had kept it safe for him. Instead of giving him the money, however, his acquaintance denounced him. Kaufmann was interned in Drancy on 24 June 1942.

In the camp, Kaufmann 'adopted' a fifteen-year-old boy called Hugues Steiner (born in Paris in 1926). Steiner's mother had already been deported to Sobibór and his father lived illegally. Hugues Steiner was collected by the police and interrogated about his father's hiding place, without success.[323] In early July 1942, Hugues Steiner was interned in Drancy. In the autumn, Kaufmann learnt of the atrocities against Jews in camps in Poland while he was listening to an illegal radio in Drancy.

In early March 1943, when it became clear that the Germans would soon deport more French Jews, the Jewish camp elder in Drancy, Robert Kohn, managed to have a number of Jews who were especially at risk, including Sylvain Kaufmann, Hugues Steiner and the brothers Paul (born in Paris in 1923) and Robert Fogel (born in Paris in 1917), transferred to the camp in Beaune-la-Rolande. They jointly decided to flee from the train guarded by Gendarmes that would take them from Drancy to Beaune-la-Rolande. Kaufmann acquired a saw from the camp carpentry and took it with him onto the wagon. After more than 30 km, before they reached Juvisy-sur-Orge, he was able to cut a board out of the wagon wall, slip through and find a hold on the buffer. He wanted to lower himself onto the track between the wagons by clinging onto the buffer and trying to move his foot towards the ground to reach the brake cable, before clinging onto it and letting himself fall. But he was unable to do so. He therefore climbed back into the wagon and returned the board he had cut out to its place. They arrived at the camp in Beaune-la-Rolande without attempting a further escape.

On 22 March 1943, a list was announced in the Beaune-la-Rolande camp containing the names of those who would be transferred to Drancy the next day. Dannecker had planned two further transports from Drancy for late March and these were to be filled by people who were actually exempt from deportation. Kaufmann and the others again attempted and failed to break out of the wagon. Their escape attempt was noticed and prevented by Gendarmes.

In Drancy, Kaufmann sought out the carpenter Arditi[324] in the camp's carpentry, since he kept foxtail saws for people who were willing to escape. However, the Algerian had already given all his available saws to some of his countrymen who had been deported the day before. Hugues Steiner confirmed the plans to flee and reports that they had decided to escape on French territory if at all possible.[325]

Each wagon contained sixty children, men and women; their luggage was at their feet and they held a bundle in their hands. The SS Obersturmführer who guarded the boarding procedure explained to them that they would be travelling to a labour assignment in Germany. By this time, Kaufmann had already heard that there had been successful escapes thanks to French Gendarmes, the population and above all railway workers. It is surprising how positively Kaufmann describes the French Gendarmes in this context after having experienced exactly the opposite while being transferred back to Drancy: instead of turning a blind eye, they actively prevented his escape.

Before the wagon doors were locked, the people inside were told that guards would immediately shoot at anyone attempting to escape. When they were all in the wagon, the hatches secured by barbed wire were nailed shut with boards, making it completely dark inside. The train departed at 10:30. Kaufmann noticed that this time the usual guards escorting the train had been replaced by the French Gendarmerie. He had managed to smuggle two knives that were converted into saws into the wagon. Since a guard was posted in the brakeman's cab, they were unable to work on the side walls and had to saw at the thick planks of the rear wall or the floor. Kaufmann presumed that others also intended to flee and wanted to wait and see how they fared.

Around 15:00, they arrived at Épernay station, where the train stopped opposite a factory. An alarm signal was sounded and the prisoners in the wagon sprung to the hatch. After a few seconds, shots were heard. Unlike Transportführer Kassel, Kaufmann reports that three men were shot dead while fleeing. The Transportführer ordered the three bodies to be loaded onto a wagon. The others were threatened with merciless consequences if they repeated their attempt. After the deadly shots, no-one believed anyone would attempt a further escape. However, Kaufmann and a number of others who were intent on fleeing began to remove two boards from the floor, allowing a man to pass through, although easily replaceable in the case of an alarm. This proved to be complicated and time-consuming. Only three or four men took turns at sawing, while others were afraid and hesitated. The regular floodlights along the outside of the train heightened their fear. According to Kaufmann's report, most of the wagon inmates behaved passively, but had a favourable attitude to their escape plans. Only one young man demanded that they stop sawing and threatened to tell the guards. Gagged and tied, he was hidden beneath the luggage before he could sound the alarm.

After leaving Metz behind them, their chances of escaping on French territory diminished. The first board had been loosened, but the second caused problems. The hole in the floor allowed air to pour in and allowed people to relieve themselves. Many adults and children were plagued by stomach cramps and diarrhoea and they wrapped their arms around their painful stomachs. The stench was terrible. All that could be heard was an occasional sigh or scream from the other wagons. Otherwise, there was total silence. They redoubled their efforts to loosen the board. To hide the noise of their work, they sang the 'Marseillaise'. The guards, who are wrongly described by Kaufmann as members of the SS, shouted at them to shut up. The board began to loosen as the train stopped. To be on the safe side, they replaced the loosened floorboards and covered them with luggage. The wagon door was opened and a Feldgendarmerie guard shone a torch inside. Kaufmann was able to recognize that they were in Metz-Sablon. He gave Hugues Steiner and the brothers Paul and Robert Fogel the address of a female friend of his mother's in Metz, who had assisted him in escaping from the prisoner of war camp in Bavaria back in 1940. They could go to her after fleeing. All four men had managed not to have their heads shaven and had smuggled some money into the wagon. The train stood for about an hour. Only one guard was visible. It began to rain, which was another advantage for the fugitives. Sylvain Kaufmann removed one of the two loose floorboards. It was impossible to slide out of the holes, however, since the brake cable ran beneath them. There was murmuring in the wagon; the consequences threatened in Épernay were having an effect. One man, who presented himself as Simon Badinter, addressed them: he was in favour of releasing the tied and gagged boy and tried to calm down people in the wagon. He said that freedom belonged to those who wanted to grasp it. He then turned back to Kaufmann, who released the boy from his bonds and gags, and asked him to take the boy under his wing.

The atmosphere in the wagon relaxed. Sylvain Kaufmann continued to seek a way through the wagon floor and renewed his efforts. The night was completely dark, which made the work harder. The train only brightened up for a moment when it passed through a station. They passed Kaiserslautern and Ludwigshafen, then the River Rhine. Almost everyone slept or at least tried to.

At 3:30 in the morning, the board finally gave way. Kaufmann quickly filled a bag with some food. He removed the loose boards from the wagon floor, pulled up his collar and protected his neck with a towel, which he stuck into his collar. To protect his head, he wore a beret. He waited for a good moment to drop from the train. Kaufmann shook hands with all of his friends and encouraged them to escape soon so that they could use the cover of darkness. He would wait for them along the track. Kaufmann had no problem sliding his legs and then his upper body through the hole. He wrapped his hands around his bent knees and let himself fall. The impact was heavy.

When he raised his head, he immediately lay flat again as he saw a pair of boots belonging to an armed signalman. As the signalman was distracted by an approaching train, Kaufmann crawled away from the track bed and rolled down the embankment. He wanted to find his comrades quickly. Hugues Steiner was meant to follow him, followed by the Fogel brothers and then the others. As agreed, he followed the railway line on its right side, moving in the direction of the train.

After he found nobody, he wondered whether they had jumped at all. Perhaps they had thought of the deadly shots fired at the fugitives in Épernay station. Or perhaps they were afraid that they were in German territory and could expect denunciation rather than support from the enemy population; furthermore, they could not speak the language. The plan based on an escape in Metz seemed senseless after crossing the German border. Sylvain Kaufmann began to reproach himself for the great hope that his younger companions had placed in him. Suddenly he realized that one of his comrades may be lying injured on the track. He saw the bag of food that a comrade had thrown after him. He sat at the foot of the embankment and waited in the cold. His nose hurt from the fall and bled heavily. At 5:15, he decided to wait one more hour and then seek a hiding place in the forest during the day. After two hours had passed and he had met none of the others, he began to regret the escape.

Sylvain Kaufmann opted for the same tactics he had used after fleeing from the Bavarian prisoner of war camp in October 1940. If anyone asked, he would say he was a French forced labourer who had escaped from his train. He had his ID papers, which had no 'J' stamp, with him. He walked to the town of Dornheim, 4 km to the south of Gross-Gerau, and entered the station there. When by chance he looked at the mirrored backboard of an empty sweets machine and saw his face, he realized he would not remain unnoticed. His nose was injured and swollen; smears of blood ran across his pale face. He was exhausted by lack of sleep and was terribly afraid that he had made an irreparable mistake. And indeed he was immediately arrested.

Hugues Steiner also leapt from the train. Since he only spoke a little German and had neither money nor ID papers, he wanted to wait for a freight train heading for France after jumping, but was captured by an armed signalman. He was taken to the police station in Kasselbach, then to Darmstadt and on to Frankfurt am Main.[326] Two more fugitives were captured immediately after the escape.

On 26 March 1943, the Head of the Staatspolizei station in Frankfurt am Main, SS Obersturmbannführer and Regierungsrat Oswald Poche,[327] reported by telegraph to the BdS in Paris that two fugitive Jews, Paul Guérin and Peter Braunschweig, had escaped early in the morning as the train had stopped at Frankfurt-Süd station. They were arrested around 9:00. Poche wrote:

> They stated that other Jews had loosened the floorboards of a transport wagon. Around 15 Jews escaped from the opening created in this way. They were unable to state the names of these Jews or the exact number of the fugitives. Apparently, the wagon had been filled with 50 Jews. It is not certain beyond doubt where the individual Jews left the wagons. Measures to search the local districts have been initiated.[328]

Poche also reported that the RSHA would be informed and requested instructions on the further procedure for the prisoners.

A day later, the Deputy Head, SS Sturmbannführer and Kriminalrat Heinz Hellenbroich, informed the BdS in Paris of the arrest of six fugitives. According to Hellenbroich, they were Lucian Dubost (born in Algiers in

1924), Alfred Bardian (born in Algiers in 1907), Sylvain Kaufmann, Jak Reman (correct spelling: Jacob Reymann)[329] (born in Paris in 1922), Gilbert Koffman (born in Paris in 1918) and Leon Fouckmann (born in Paris in 1913). Hellenbroich wrote:

> The above-named all stated that they jumped from a moving train transporting Jews from Paris to the East. They had used force to break open the floor of the wagon and let themselves drop onto the track as the train was travelling slowly. Presumably, there are more Jews who escaped in the same way.[330]

Indeed, Bernard Rozenberg (born in Ozarow/Poland in 1928), a thin fourteen-year-old who had already fled from the interim camp Vel' d'Hiv' following the major raid in Paris, and Jean Kotz (born in Paris in 1912) had fled. Kotz was arrested by the French police in mid January 1943, as he had broken regulations by not wearing a yellow star.[331]

To Kaufmann's great dismay, the Gestapo found a yellow star sewn onto an overcoat in the bottom of his bag while searching through his clothes. He was therefore transferred from Gross-Gerau to the Darmstadt Gestapo, where Hellenbroich interrogated him.[332] He wanted to know who had fled with him. Kaufmann said he had jumped alone and denied being a Jew. After a few days, he was taken to a different cell. There he met three men from his wagon. They had been captured after escaping and transferred to a prison in Frankfurt am Main. There, they had stated that they had woken up during the journey and discovered the hole in the bottom of the wagon. They were unable to resist the temptation to slip through it. From then on, the four men had to conceal the fact that they had known each other previously and planned the escape together.

The next day, Kaufmann learnt from Pierre Braunschweig that Hugues Steiner and the Fogel brothers had also jumped, but had been captured and were being kept in a neighbouring cell. Kaufmann had a message sent to them that he would assume responsibility for the escape plan and its implementation. They should only admit to having seen the hole and fled as a result. Braunschweig told them that he had fled and been arrested with the young man whom Kaufmann had had bound and gagged – the young man being Paul Guérin, who was in fact Ludwig Breslerman (born in Leipzig in 1929), originally from Germany and who spoke French with a strong German accent.[333]

Hugues Steiner reported that he met up with the twelve comrades who fled with him in the Frankfurt jail. They were found guilty of sabotaging German property and escaping custody and sentenced to death. Some had been brutally tortured.[334] During the interrogations, in which Kaufmann was used as an interpreter, the others did not reveal that they knew each other. After two weeks, Hellenbroich told Kaufmann that he had requested of Himmler that his and the other fugitives' death sentences be lifted and he hoped for a positive response from Berlin. Hellenbroich showed him a copy of the letter. It stated that Kaufmann was a pro-German, Aryan protestant originally from Lorraine. Hellenbroich added that a Jew would be unable to carry out such an escape.

On 29 March 1943 the Sipo-SD Judenreferent SS Obersturmführer Röthke wrote to the Staatspolizei station in Frankfurt am Main, instructing the 'fugitive Jews Paul Guerin [in fact: Ludwig Breslerman] and Peter Braunschweig to be taken to the Jews' camp in Auschwitz/O. S'.[335] Should the 'remaining escaped Jews' have been captured, Röthke was to be informed. On 7 April, Hellenbroich reported to the BdS in Paris that

> in my field of responsibility, eleven fugitive French Jews who had escaped from the evacuation train that travelled through here on 24 March 1943 have been captured. Following the instructions of the RSHA, the Jews and two other Jews arrested by the Staatspolizei station in Frankfurt/Main have been transported in the proper transportation process to Auschwitz concentration camp.[336]

On 14 April, they were transferred from Darmstadt to a prison in Frankfurt. As an 'Aryan', Kaufmann was separated from the others. Since his military papers identified him as having defended the Maginot Line, he was no longer considered pro-German and was now classified as a traitor. From Frankfurt am Main, they were all taken to a prison in Kassel, from where they continued via Weimar, Plauen and Dresden to Auschwitz, where they arrived on 30 April.

A telegram from the Frankfurt Gestapo still exists, naming a further fugitive from the train, although he was captured after jumping. On 23 April 1943, the Frankfurt Gestapo reported that Alfred Nabet (born in Algiers in 1909), who had escaped from the special train on 26 March 1943, was arrested and transported to Auschwitz with the next collected transport.[337]

Shortly after their arrival in Auschwitz, Jean Kotz was selected by Josef Mengele for medical experiments. According to the surgery diary, an operation was carried out on 4 May 1943 in the prisoners' infirmary due to a supposed case of appendicitis.[338] On 30 July, Jean Kotz was deported to the Natzweiler-Struthof concentration camp and murdered there in the gas chamber on 17 or 19 August. His body and those of eighty-five other Jews were to serve as skeletons for the Anatomical Institute of the University of Strasbourg for anthropological research purposes.[339]

Ludwig Breslerman was transported under the name of Paul Guérin to Dachau on 6 August 1944, from where he was moved to the Karlsfeld subcamp on 1 September 1944 and then transferred to the Mühldorf subcamp on 24 February 1945. He must have lost his life there.[340] Sylvain

Kaufmann was also taken as a Jewish prisoner to Dachau on 6 August 1944. He witnessed the liberation of the Mühldorf subcamp on 29 April 1945.[341]

Hugues Steiner was taken from the main Auschwitz camp to the Jaworzno subcamp.[342] During the evacuation of the camp in the second half of January 1945, after stopping in the Blechhammer subcamp, he was able to hide unnoticed in a ditch by the road while on a night march. His health was extremely poor, but he managed to survive the winter and lived to be liberated by the Soviet army.[343]

Paul and Robert Fogel were taken to the Mauthausen concentration camp on 29 January 1945.[344] From there, they were taken to the Gusen II concentration camp on 16 February 1945.[345] Robert Fogel survived imprisonment in the camp, but contracted tuberculosis and presumably died of the effects of the disease or the camp imprisonment at the age of just twenty-eight on 6 July 1945.[346]

Of the twelve fugitives from the 53rd transport, only three survived Nazi persecution: Hugues Steiner, Sylvain Kaufmann and Paul Fogel.[347]

The Paris Judenreferat's Reaction to the Escapes

It appears that Judenreferent Röthke demanded an additional statement from Zuschneid concerning the high number of escapes and attempted escapes. Zuschneid sent a statement with the reports by Transportführer Uhlemann (52nd deportation train) and Kassel (53rd deportation train). He himself explained that the security measures described in his report dated 15 February 1943 had largely been applied. However, the weaknesses it described also remained: the French police's body searches for all kinds of cutting tools clearly continued to be deficient. It was unclear whether the transport officers provided by the 2nd Company of SS Police Regiment 4 could rely on the support of the French police during the transport. Thus, the guard teams should be reinforced with additional German guards from the outset, or appropriate pressure should be put on the French police. Zuschneid continued that is was essential for pursuit guards to be named from among the guards since in view of the dilapidated wagons, repeated attempts to break out were to be expected. He argued that the proper attitude of the German guards could be seen in the 'shooting of three Jews escaping from the train'.[348]

Escapes from the 55th Transport on 23 June 1943

A copy of the report by Transportführer and Meister der Schutzpolizei Urban survives for this transport, which took 1,018 Jews to Auschwitz. It presents the events of the deportation from Drancy to Neuburg an der

Mosel. Due to the great heat, the prisoners became restless and began to scream. Thus, the responsible SD 'loading officer'[349] decided that, to ensure the smooth handling of the transport, the wagon doors should be opened by a hand's breadth. The escape subsequently occurred while the train was in motion. Urban wrote:

> Around 50 km before Epernay [Épernay] at 13.25, after striking the wagon elder down, three men leapt from the train while it was travelling at a speed of 50–60 km/h. Since the emergency brake failed, it was impossible to stop the train and pursue or shoot at the fugitives, since they were able to flee unnoticed due to shelter of the embankment.[350]

It is very likely that it was this escape on which the former co-inmate Henri Moschkovitch reported. After travelling for a few hours, three young men indicated that they had managed to remove the bars from the ventilation hatch. With a little agility and acrobatic skill, it was possible to escape through the hatch. The wagon elder, a German-speaking Jew aged around fifty who was marked with a white armband, attempted to prevent the escape. When he failed, he began to panic out of fear of having to bear the consequences of their escape. Henri Moschkovitch said to him, 'Give me the armband',[351] and assumed his role and therefore responsibility. The three young men jumped out at a bend in the track, where the train was forced to slow down. Shortly afterwards, shots were heard and the train was stopped. A handwritten note is presumed to have been thrown out of precisely that wagon, describing the unbearable conditions on the train and the escape: 'Three people saved themselves by fleeing from the train as it travelled at 50 to 60 km/h. We do not know whether they are safe and sound'.[352]

Around 19:00, another prisoner managed to escape through the hatch shortly before Lérouville. The escape was noticed and the train was stopped. Since he had jumped in a forested area with poor visibility and the fugitive had had a head start of several hundred metres, the pursuit failed. At 20:35, shortly before Neuburg, a further prisoner attempted to escape. The train was stopped and shots forced the fugitive to throw himself to the ground, allowing the guards to recapture him.

Before the train continued its journey, it was discovered that not all the ventilation hatches were barred. Attempts to convince the French station master to provide wagons with barred ventilation hatches or to fix bars in front of the hatches failed; he insisted that the train should continue according to the timetable. Urban concluded his report with the following proposals:

> To exclude the possibility of escaping in general, I believe it is essential that only wagons with iron bars in front of the ventilation hatches are used for such trans-

ports, and also that at the departure of the train, all wagon doors have lead seals regardless of the prisoners. In view of the train's length (25–30 wagons), 1/20 guard teams for the transport are too weak. I propose increasing them to 1/35 to 1/40.[353]

Judging by the handwriting, it was Röthke who spitefully commented: 'If the policemen don't sleep, 1:20 is enough'.[354]

Escape by the Tunnel Diggers of Drancy and Others from the 62nd Transport on 20 November 1943

At 12:10 on 20 November 1943, a deportation train carrying 1,200 Jews left Bobigny station on its way to Auschwitz. No doubt due to the experience of earlier transports, Röthke telegraphed a message on the train's departure to the Auschwitz concentration camp, among others: 'Should the guard team not hand over the exact number of 1,200 Jews, I request a telegraph from the Auschwitz concentration camp'.[355] It is not known whether Röthke presumed that upon arrival, the Transportführer provided information on the number of escapes during the transport, or whether he wrongly presumed that the prisoners were counted on arrival.

One escape occurred while the train was still in French territory. The commanding officer of the guard team, Meister der Schutzpolizei Friedrich Köhnlein, telegraphed to Röthke from the border control station in Neuburg an der Mosel: 'On the journey from Paris to Neuburg, on the climb before Lérouville, 19 prisoners escaped from wagon 6'.[356] The flight was made possible due to torn-off struts covering the ventilation hatch, which was discovered when the wagons were inspected at 20:30 shortly before Lérouville, as Transportführer Köhnlein stated in an extensive report written a few days later. The wagon elder and a further eighteen prisoners were reported to have escaped. Apparently, due to the climb as the train approached Lérouville, the train was forced to decelerate and the prisoners took the opportunity to flee. Due to the heavy fog and darkness, the escapes went unnoticed. The prisoners escaped although the men in the last guard wagon had fired several warning shots while the train travelled slowly towards Lérouville. After discovering the escapes, Köhnlein drew the following consequences:

> I immediately ordered all male prisoners, except for the sick and aged, to remove their shoes, which were brought to an empty wagon and only handed out again in Auschwitz. As a result, the journey continued without further incident. ... I wish to point out that the escaped prisoners are mainly the tunnel diggers from the Drancy camp. Had they been loaded separately and without clothing, as discussed before the departure, they would certainly not have escaped.[357]

The Drancy Tunnel

Köhnlein was referring to a group of around forty Jewish men who had planned a mass escape from the Drancy internment camp and had dug a tunnel that was to lead to freedom. It would have given all prisoners in Drancy the chance to flee. Many tunnel diggers had been active members of Resistance groups before their arrest and internment, above all in the mainly Communist-migrant FTP-MOI.[358] They included Oscar Handschuh and his sons Louis and Eugène. Oscar Handschuh had emigrated from Hungary to France in 1929 for economic reasons, his wife, Viktoria, and two sons following a year later. When the Germans invaded in May 1940, they immediately decided that they would take part in the fight against the occupying forces, as the Handschuh brothers stated. They were active in the FTP-MOI and 'extremely politicized'.[359] They distributed flyers and sabotaged the logistics of the German occupation. Eugène Handschuh described their resistance as follows: 'In 1941 we took action against the Germans. For instance we blew up a cinema for soldiers, the Rex. And we threw hand grenades into a restaurant that was directly opposite the Rex and was reserved for Germans. Measures like that'.[360]

Looking back, they stressed that they had been arrested as members of the Resistance and not because they were Jews.[361] They were subsequently taken to the Compiègne internment camp. There they met some of the later tunnel diggers and also considered digging a tunnel to freedom in that camp.[362]

Together with their father, the two brothers were transferred from Compiègne to Drancy on 26 May 1943, in a sealed freight wagon that was guarded by French Gendarmes.[363] At the time, Viktoria Handschuh had already been deported to Sobibór on the 53rd deportation train.[364] In Drancy, Oscar Handschuh worked as a tailor, the trade he had learnt, while the brothers Eugène and Louis were used as drivers for the camp kitchen.[365]

Maurice Kalifat was also interned in Drancy and had a good overview of the structural conditions due to his task as camp plumber. He developed the idea to dig a tunnel to freedom that started in the cellar in staircase 21 beneath the office of the Jewish elder Robert Blum. The tunnel was to lead outside the fencing around the U-shaped camp building to Avenue Jean Jaurès. To establish the most appropriate direction for the tunnel, they climbed on the roof with a compass.

After being interned in the Drancy assembly camp, Serge Bouder also joined the tunnel group. His family had emigrated from Russia to France in 1914 due to anti-Semitic pogroms. As an activist in the Resistance group 'Combat', he was interrogated and tortured in Cannes after his arrest.[366] As Serge Bouder stressed, the consensus was that all internees should have the chance to flee: 'The key aspect was that the tunnel was intended for the flight of the entire camp. It was not a private matter. Otherwise we would not have dug a hole that was 1.20 metres high and 80 or 90 cm wide over a distance of 40 metres. We wanted to get the whole camp out of there'.[367]

The mass escape was planned for the evening of 30 November 1943. It had been arranged with the local Resistance that they should provide shelter and help. For instance, trucks were to be provided to transport the aged, sick, women and children.[368] The tunnel construction had to be carried out with great secrecy and was extremely tiring. Roger Schandalow, who had been interned in Drancy since 1942 and worked as a 'functional prisoner' (Funktionshäftling, responsible for various staircases including the dormitories connected to them), immediately agreed to join the tunnel diggers when he was asked in mid September 1943.[369] He remembers almost always working on the tunnel at night. The camp elder Robert Blum warned them to be careful: he could hear the noisy digging in his office.[370] The Handschuh brothers and Serge Bouder stated that only political comrades were involved in the tunnel digging. Bouder recalls: 'We knew who we were dealing with. We knew each other. Knew the reputation of the individual people. We knew who was here because of the Resistance and who was just here for being a Jew'.[371]

The work began in September of 1943. One great difficulty was removing the excavated earth as inconspicuously as possible. It was decided to distribute the earth in the cellar, a decision that raised the cellar's floor level by about half a metre. However, that was not the only challenge with which the tunnel diggers were confronted: there was little air to breathe and the measurements of the tunnel forced the prisoners to kneel down in a very constricted space. Furthermore there was the danger that the tunnel might collapse or that the diggers would be discovered.[372] When the tunnel was indeed discovered in November 1943, shortly before its completion, it was already 38.5 metres long, with only 1.5 metres left to dig. In the deserted tunnel, the Germans found a piece of clothing belonging to the tunnel digger Henri Schwartz, including his prisoner number. Schwartz was tortured into revealing the names of those with whom he had worked on his shift.[373] As a result, fourteen people were arrested and locked in the prison established in the cellar in Drancy: Claude Aron (born in Paris in 1911), Jacques Possicelsky (born in Paris in 1910), Serge Bouder (born in Paris in 1921), Jean Cahen-Salvador (born in Paris in 1906), Robert Dreyfus (born in Paris in 1915), Roger Gerschel (born in the Alsace in 1911), Georges Gerschel (born in the Alsace in 1903), Oscar Handschuh (born in Budapest in 1896), Louis Handschuh (born in Budapest in 1920), Eugène Handschuh (born in Budapest in 1923), Maurice Kalifat (born in Algiers in 1910), Roger Schandalow (born in

Paris in 1915), Henri Schwartz (born in 1902) and Raymond Trèves (born in 1914).[374]

Eugène Handschuh, whose name was also mentioned, stated that he was subsequently severely mistreated and threatened with being shot.[375] Roger Schandalow also reported being interrogated by several Germans. A German nicknamed 'Boxer' was always present, torturing and strangling him.[376] 'Boxer' was the name the prisoners gave Ernst Brückler, who was especially feared for his brutality.[377] Brückler's boss for many years, Alois Brunner, also led some interrogations. He questioned Georges Gerschel, who had been captured along with his brother as a tunnel digger. During the interrogation, Brunner fired a shot into Georges Gerschel's leg.[378] Despite severe torture, nobody revealed any information.[379]

According to reports by the tunnel diggers, the Germans not only attempted to force them into revealing the names of others involved in the escape attempt, but also asked them about their professions. The structural condition of the tunnel, which remained steadfast even after demolition attempts using explosives, did not fit into their anti-Semitic worldview.[380] Bouder and others were made to wall in the tunnel.[381] Alois Brunner then visited them in their prison cell and told them that they had worked well for Jews and since the Führer loved good workers, they would not be shot and would instead be deported.[382]

Escape from the 62nd Deportation Train

The fourteen captured tunnel diggers remained locked in their cells until their deportation and were therefore unable to acquire tools for their joint escape from the wagon, which they had long decided upon. On the morning of the deportation, they were secretly handed tools by the soup distributor, help that Eugène Handschuh stated was not uncommon: 'It was usual for the person who brought the soup to also bring the tools'.[383] Serge Bouder reports that the Jewish camp police who had provided straw, a bucket of water and a bucket to be used as a toilet had hidden a screwdriver and a sawblade in their wagon.[384] To be able to flee together, the fourteen tunnel diggers made every effort to be loaded onto the same wagon, and they were successful. There were a total of fifty men in the wagon. Shortly before it was locked, they were told that the wagon would be checked during the journey. If anything indicated an escape, the guards would shoot those left behind. However, Serge Bouder knew from his experience on the transport from Nice to Paris that these threats were not carried out: there had been escapes from that train, but they had not been punished.

The hatch was blocked by iron bars and nailed down with wooden boards. Shortly after the departure, Serge Bouder and Eugène Handschuh attempted to unscrew the window grid or saw it open to open the hatch.

The aim was to wait for darkness and then let all those willing to escape take advantage of the train's slow speed around a bend and jump off.[385] Initially, Bouder reports, other prisoners tried to stop them from escaping. He replied by telling them of his experience in the Nice transport and encouraged others to flee as well, but the other wagon prisoners were almost mad with fear and wanted to prevent the escapes. The tunnel diggers were a strong group, however, and could impose their will on the others. This was their good fortune.[386]

The efforts by Serge Bouder and Eugène Handschuh to remove the grid from the hatch were not seeing much progress. The large, powerful Gerschel brothers – rugby players and members of the Friends of Nature – soon grew impatient, according to Eugène Handschuh: 'When they saw that we were not achieving anything with the screwdrivers, they grasped the grid with both hands, pushed against it with their feet and tore everything apart. Then they jumped'.[387]

Oscar Handschuh also tried to encourage other people to flee, without success.[388] When it was the Handschuhs' turn to flee, the father jumped first, then the two sons. Serge Bouder jumped too. He ran for hours through the night until he reached a village, where he asked the local priest for help. According to Serge Bouder, the priest was old and began to tremble when he told him that he was a fugitive Jew. The priest let him in, bandaged the head wound he had sustained from jumping from the train and described the way to the station. There, railway workers, who immediately recognized the situation without asking, bought him a ticket for the next train but one to Paris. Since this was in use mainly to transport French prisoners of war, his dishevelled appearance and shaved head did not look unusual. In the train, he saw Maurice Kalifat, who was injured by the jump and was accompanied to Paris by two helpers. For security reasons, they did not reveal that they knew each other. After arriving at Gare de l'Est, Bouder observed that two Feldgendarmes at the end of the platform were checking the passengers. To avoid being checked, he offered to help an elderly lady carrying two suitcases and asked her to take his arm. Deep in conversation, the two passed the end of the platform without being checked.[389]

The Handschuh brothers failed to find their father after jumping, so Louis Handschuh opened the seam of his jacket, into which he had sewn a banknote following his arrest. The next morning, the brothers used it to buy tickets from Bar-le-Duc to Paris. They knew that false papers were waiting for them there. After arriving in Paris, they rented an apartment and tried to be inconspicuous.[390]

Their father, who had been lifted through the hatch by his sons, seems to have injured himself on the head through his fall and fell unconscious.

He awoke in the night, walked to the next village and knocked on the door of the first house he came to. The locals cared for him, as they had several times before with fugitives from the train. Their sons heard this news eight days after the escape, as they were about to return to the location of their flight in search of their father. Oscar Handschuh was able to hide until the liberation.[391]

The Gerschel brothers were also separated by their jump. Roger Gerschel climbed out of the train first and clung onto the wagon from the outside to wait for his brother. When his brother's legs protruded from the wagon, he let himself fall to give his brother space for his jump. Inside the wagon, Serge Bouder helped Georges, who had been shot at during his interrogation in Drancy, to climb out of the hatch.[392] Roger Gerschel walked along the track in search of his brother. After around 100 metres, he found him, close to two guards who had been patrolling the bridge. As soon as he realized they were German, he withdrew and only dared to walk along the lines again several hours later. French Gendarmes stationed along the canal noticed him and pursued him. He came across the railway worker René Bernard, who knew of the escapes and spoke to him. Bernard took Gerschel with him on his bicycle to his home in Longeville-en-Barrois, a village on the railway line, 6 km southeast of Bar-le-Duc in Lorraine. Bernard told him that another fugitive who had also jumped and been hit by the train was already in his care. Roger Gerschel hoped it would be his brother and presumed that he had not been too seriously wounded by the jump. In fact it was Charles Mager, whom he did not know. The local photographer and Resistance leader Arthur Althusser photographed Gerschel to produce false documents for him. With these, Roger Gerschel was able to return to his family in Chalon-sur-Saône.[393] The fate of Georges Gerschel remains unknown.

Further Escapes from the 62nd Transport
Apart from the twelve tunnel diggers, seven other prisoners in wagon 6 dared to jump. Four of them are known by name: Joseph Cajfinger (born in Radom in 1896), Félix Goldschmidt (born in 1898), Charles Mager (born in 1902) and Léon Strubel (born in 1905). Cajfinger and Strubel, both born in Poland and tailors by profession, jumped from the train in Longeville-en-Barrois at a lock where the railway line crosses the canal. Cajfinger was hidden by the 'people-smuggling' Domice couple.[394] Strubel, who was severely injured after his jump and required help, knocked on the door of a remote station. Anne and Ernest Schoellen provided him with shelter. Due to their connections with the Resistance, the couple also managed to organize false papers for the entire Strubel family and thereby ensure their survival.[395]

Charles Mager, who had migrated to France from Poland in 1930, let chance decide whether he would dare to jump from the train or not. He drew a playing card and decided to flee. At the time, according to his statements, eighteen prisoners had already jumped from the train.[396] He describes his flight in stark images. When he jumped from the train, he failed to pull one leg close enough to his body: it was run over by the train's wheels and severed. He carried his leg under his arm, bound his other leg, which also had injuries as a result of the fall, and cried for help. A French Gendarme found him and took him to the hospital in Bar-le-Duc, where he remained as an in-patient until the end of the war.[397] The escape of Charles Mager has been described in the Département monthly gazette,[398] so the support provided by the Gendarme was not kept secret. Presumably, the Gendarme recognized Charles Mager due to his clothing, perhaps his yellow star, his shaved head and his severe injuries. The local Gendarmerie was also informed of escapes in their area of jurisdiction to allow them to search for the fugitives. Nothing is known about the situation or motives of the unnamed Gendarme. Without doubt, however, his behaviour was fundamentally different from the Gendarmes who had pursued Roger Gerschel. These examples show that it was possible to use one's scope for action to help the fugitive Jews.

According to his own statements, Félix Goldschmidt (born in Paris in 1898) had been selected as the wagon elder for wagon 6. He too jumped from the wagon. Before his arrest, he had participated in, among other things, procuring false papers for Jews.[399] However, Goldschmidt is not named in the accounts by the tunnel diggers, although he describes himself as having played a very active role in implementing the escape plans in the wagon. Furthermore, Goldschmidt does not name the tunnel diggers as a group. The escape descriptions cannot therefore be related, and the reconstruction presented in this text therefore presents the two perspectives in parallel without combining them.

Félix Goldschmidt described his escape in a note he secretly sent to his wife. He jumped in a village shortly before the train stopped. The Philbert family who gave him shelter took him in like a son. Once his foot had recovered from the injury sustained by the jump, Goldschmidt received false papers from the Philberts. He asked his wife to send money and some personal items. She and her daughter, who had apparently not yet been interned in Drancy, should hide to prevent being captured in his stead.[400]

Félix Goldschmidt had learnt from a British secret agent called Jim, with whom he shared a cell in Limoges, that it was essential in planning escapes from moving trains to know the speed of the train. Jim explained that it was easy to calculate. Each piece of railway track was eleven metres long and was connected to a new piece, resulting in the familiar click-clack sound. All one needed to do was count the number of clicks in, for instance, one minute and one could calculate the speed. Jim also advised him to jump on a bend, since the train had to slow down to a speed of around 50 km/h. If the train was moving at less than 45 km/h, it could be that the Germans would shoot at fugitives. But the most important factor was to anticipate the direction of travel in the alignment of the jump. He and Jim had practised the jump and rolling over countless times.[401]

At night, when the train travelled a little slower, Félix Goldschmidt stood with his watch by the hatch. His comrades fastened their jackets and people who wore glasses tucked them away. He told them how to jump and lifted one after the other through the hatch. As he did so, people cried and screamed in the wagon, clung to the clothes of those trying to escape and begged them not to jump. Eighteen had jumped when Félix Goldschmidt followed. In his own words, the captain was the last to leave the ship.[402] He remembers the last moment before the jump as follows: 'The last of those who chose freedom. I looked into the wagon for a last time, at the aged, the adults and the young ones, who lacked the courage to flee'.[403] He sprang from the train. 'In the darkness, I saw the red rear lights of the train moving ever further and finally disappearing. That was the most beautiful moment of my life.'[404]

Abraham Weichselbaum (born in Frankfurt am Main in 1922) was deported on the same train, but in a different wagon. He already had a long history of resistance and flight behind him: in France, he had joined the Resistance and was involved in acquiring false papers and food. He had smuggled Jewish children into Switzerland, pretended to be a French volunteer in the Waffen-SS and thereby saved nine Jews from arrest. Soon, Abraham Weichselbaum was leading a group of fifty Maquisards. In September 1943, he was arrested with false papers and so severely tortured in the prison in Annemasse that he admitted to being a Jew after a few days and that he had intended to flee to Switzerland. He hoped to be executed after this admission, but he was transferred to Drancy for deportation.

> From there, the journey continued in livestock wagons. On the way, some of us, including myself, attempted to open a hole in the planks of the wagon in order to flee. The wagon elder, also a Jewish prisoner, reported this to the SS guard team, since he was afraid that all prisoners would be shot if someone successfully escaped. Those of us whom he meant were kicked out of the train together with other young Jews from several wagons and packed into an empty wagon. They took our shoes, braces and trousers.[405]

The measure of removing clothing to prevent escapes is documented several times in France following the increased number of attempted escapes, including during deportations of people persecuted as political opponents.[406]

Weichselbaum also reports that they arrived in Auschwitz without having received anything to eat or drink.[407] The camp commander in Auschwitz, Arthur Liebehenschel, confirmed the arrival of 1,181 Jews rather than the 1,200 that Röthke had announced.[408] Transportführer Köhnlein must have reported nineteen escapees when handing over the transport, as arrivals in Auschwitz were not counted. Following the selection process, some of the newly arrived deportees were immediately sent to the gas chambers, while the rest were interned in Auschwitz concentration camp and registered there.

Nathan Eck – Escape from the 72nd Transport on 29 April 1944

To fill the final deportation trains, the commander of the Sicherheitspolizei and the SD (BdS) under the jurisdiction of the Military Commander in France, Helmut Knochen, ordered that all children's and old people's homes, hospitals, prisons and labour camps were to be searched for Jews, who were to be transferred to Drancy for the purpose of deportation.[409] Of the 1,004 Jews deported on 29 April 1944 with the 72nd transport from Drancy to Auschwitz, 250 came from the Vittel camp as a result of Brunner's efforts, where countless Jews were interned, mostly with passports they had received from South American countries.[410] They included Nathan Eck and the poet Jizchak Katzenelson, author of the later world-famous cycle 'Dos lied vunem ojsgehargetn jidischn volk' ('The song of the murdered Jewish people'), which he had written in Vittel.[411] Before the German invasion, Nathan Eck had worked as a publisher and Headmaster of the Jewish high school in Łódź and was a leading member of the left-wing Zionist 'Hitachdut' organization. After the occupation by the National Socialists, he worked in the Warsaw Ghetto as editor of the journal *Slowo Mlodych* and was the Head of the illegal ghetto high school, where Katzenelson worked as a teacher.[412] Both men were provided with Latin American passports from the Resistance and thereby avoided being sent to the ghetto. As an 'enemy foreigner', that is, a citizen of an enemy state, Eck was initially sent to the internment camp in Tittmoning-Laufen, Bavaria, imprisoned in Vittel.[413] Katzenelson was also interned there with his son and was able to bury the cycle manuscript on the camp grounds with the help of another prisoner, Miriam Novitch.[414] Katzenelson had detailed information on the extermination of the Jews. He wrote about the more than six million murdered Jews and gas chambers in Treblinka, Bełżec, as well as the first gas chamber killings in Chełmno.[415] In Drancy, he is reported to have told other camp prisoners what he knew about the genocide committed against European Jews.[416] Eck was made to promise that if Katzenelson did not survive the Nazi persecution, he (Eck) would publish the manuscript. Nathan Eck managed to flee from the wagon and return to Paris. Novitch, who had also survived, dug up the manuscript after the camp's liberation and gave it to Nathan Eck, who edited it and published it in Paris in 1945 in the original Yiddish language.[417]

Escapes from Alois Brunner's Hostage Transport, 79th Transport on 17 August 1944

The train described as the 79th transport was not a deportation train, but a military transport of the German Luftwaffe to evacuate the Flak cannons.[418] The train included wagons carrying the Flak guns, one accomodating members of the Ordnungspolizei, and one for Alois Brunner and Gestapo officers.[419] Another wagon was a freight wagon containing fifty-one Jewish prisoners selected by Brunner.[420] They included members of various Jewish resistance groups, as well as prominent prisoners from Drancy, who were presumably to serve as hostages for Brunner on his retreat.[421]

The reconstruction of the escapes from this transport encountered particular problems. The existing witness accounts, of which there were many compared to other escapes, are partially contradictory. The main differences lie in the reports from survivors of two resistance groups, the Armée Juive (AJ) and the Westerweel Group. The following account attempts to reconstruct the escape as far as possible; at the same time, it investigates the question of how the reports by survivors could be so divergent from each other.

The Way to Drancy by Some of the Hostages
Some of the fifty-one hostages belonged to the Communist-orientated FTP (Francs-tireurs et partisans, a French Resistance organization) and the Zionist group AJ. The AJ members Henry Pohoryles (born in Strasbourg in 1920),[422] Jacques Lazarus (born in Payerne/Switzerland in 1916)[423] and Sami Kapelovitz (later René Kapel) (born in Paris in 1907)[424] had received the order to participate in a secret meeting with the British Intelligence Service in Paris on 18 July 1944, to receive deliveries for their organization. It would also address the formation of an armed Jewish unit and its equipment.[425] However, the meeting with the apparent British secret service in Paris was in fact an ambush by the German counterintelligence.[426] Kapel and Lazarus believed they would be smuggled to England to build up a fighting unit among the Allies, but they were arrested in Paris.[427] It is likely that German counterintelligence agents tailed Henry Pohoryles, because on the same day, a raid on a secret meeting in a Paris apartment next to Pohoryles also led to the arrest of AJ members André

Amar (born in Saloniki in 1908), Ernest Appenzeller (born in Vienna in 1926),[428] César Chamay (born in Alexandria in 1910)[429] and Maurice Loebenberg (born in Zurich in 1916) as well as Max Windmüller (born in Emden in 1920) from the Westerweel Group.[430] They were interrogated, tortured and transported to the prison in Fresnes, with the exception of Maurice Loebenberg, who was unable to travel due to the severe torture he suffered and was murdered by members of the Gestapo in Paris. Kapel and Lazarus were also taken to the Fresnes prison.[431]

They occasionally saw each other on their walks in the yard, as did members of the Westerweel Group, who had also been arrested and some of whom had been severely tortured: Paula Kaufmann (born in Dąbrowa/Poland in 1920), Ernst Hirsch (born in Aachen in 1916), Kurt Reilinger (born in Stuttgart in 1917), Alfred Fraenkel (born in Breslau in 1920), Susi Hermann and Lolly Ekart.[432] They were known as the 'Dutch' to the AJ, although none of them actually came from there.[433] They made discreet signs to indicate that it was better to pretend not to know each other.

Digression: The 'Dutch' in the Westerweel Group

The Westerweel Group was founded in the summer of 1941. Its members were Socialist Jewish Zionists from the Hechaluz movement[434] who had come to Germany, Austria and the Netherlands, as well as non-Jewish Dutch citizens representing a variety of political ideals. Their aim was to resist the persecution of Jews by the German occupiers. The group was named retrospectively in honour of its founder Johan Gerard ('Joop') Westerweel and his wife Wilhelmina.

Joop Westerweel was a left-wing anti-militarist who worked as the Headmaster of the Montessori primary school in Rotterdam. He had contacts with Palestine pioneers in the Hechaluz movement, who prepared for emigration to Palestine at training camps in Loosdrecht and Gouda. There, they were to acquire agricultural knowledge and practical experience, as well as learning Hebrew. Together with the leader, Menachem Pinkhof (born in Amsterdam in 1920), and Joachim Simon (born in Berlin in 1919),[435] who was taken to Buchenwald concentration camp during the Reichspogromnacht and detained there for several weeks, fleeing from Germany after being released, Westerweel established a network with the aim of saving Jews from deportation.[436] It became one of the most successful efforts to rescue Jews in the Netherlands, saving around three hundred Jews.[437]

One of the reasons the Westerweel Group was more efficient and faster in providing help to persecuted people was because it had come together and grown before the German invasion. It consisted mainly of Jews from Germany and Austria who had fled to the Netherlands in the 1930s. Jews and non-Jews worked together in groups and applied different rescue strategies with great consistency.[438] Members of the group found possible hideouts in the Netherlands, helped internees in the Westerbork camp to flee, planned escapes from the Netherlands to neighbouring countries and themselves guided fugitives across the border along previously investigated routes.[439] Many pioneers dreamed of making their way to Palestine, but that was almost impossible. However, a sophisticated strategy was developed within the Westerweel Group to overcome the heavily secured border to Belgium and France, in order to continue from there to Spain and Palestine. Some members volunteered to use false papers and apply as non-Jewish Dutch workers to build the Atlantic Wall in southern France. The construction of the Atlantic Wall was managed by the Organisation Todt (OT), which had an enormous demand for labourers. By volunteering to work on OT building sites, members of the Westerweel Group received the entry papers they needed to cross the border. They even managed to get blank copies of the sought-after document, with which the otherwise closed borders could be crossed without any problem or cost in wagons reserved for the Wehrmacht.[440] Other sophisticated escape routes with various other blank documents were set up and used with great success.[441] From southern France, some pioneers intended to reach Palestine by crossing the border with Spain over the Pyrenees. Joachim Simon made his way to southern France for that purpose in the autumn of 1942 to investigate the options of escaping to Spain.

This is how the cooperation between the Westerweel Group and the AJ began in 1943.[442] Frida Wattenberg of the AJ reports that her two-room apartment in Toulouse, which was specifically rented for the purpose, was packed full to the ceiling with hiking equipment for crossing the Pyrenees.[443] Despite a number of language problems, Kurt Reilinger, Alfred Fraenkel, Max Windmüller, Ernst Hirsch and Lolly Ekart worked very closely together, so much so that the former AJ members spoke of the 'Dutch group' within the AJ, as the witness accounts report.[444] Some of the 'Dutch' received military training from Jacques Lazarus in the southern French region of Tarn, before setting out on their illegal journey via Spain to Palestine, with the help of the AJ.[445] In return, the AJ received information on the OT and on the German occupation authorities that had been infiltrated by German-speaking members of the Westerweel Group.[446] For instance, Paula Kaufmann was a German native speaker, and in 1944 managed to use a false identity to gain a position in the Gestapo headquarters in Avenue Foch, Paris. From there, she transferred important information to the Resistance, such as the German defence plan for Paris.[447]

From May 1943 onwards, a total of 150 young people are reported to have managed the escape from the Netherlands via Belgium to France.[448]

From February 1944, around eighty of them succeeded in reaching Spain via the Pyrenees and went on to Palestine, which was under British jurisdiction.[449] The figures in some sources are approximately twice as high.[450]

From Fresnes to Drancy

In mid August 1944, all prisoners in Fresnes were released due to the steadily advancing Allies, apart from Jews, who were taken by bus to Drancy.[451] They had actually intended to flee during this journey, but gave their plan up because Appenzeller and Chamay were handcuffed together.[452] Lazarus recalls that the men in Drancy were initially imprisoned naked in the camp cell.[453] Brückler told them that they, the terrorists, would be deported from among the two thousand remaining Drancy prisoners.[454] The guard team arrived in Drancy on 16 August.[455] Either Alois Brunner himself or his right-hand man, Ernst Brückler, announced to the prisoners before they boarded the train that should they flee, they would be shot dead in the open countryside.[456]

On the walk from the Drancy camp to Bobigny station, Kapel and Maurice (actually Moritz) Margulies (born in Czernowitz in 1910)[457] looked for an opportunity to escape.[458] The two had met in 1940 in the St. Cyprien camp where the Austrian Margulies was interned and the Rabbi Kapel had acted as a spiritual carer. Despite their different political beliefs – Kapel was a Zionist and Margulies a Communist – they respected each other.[459] However, the march was escorted by a thirty-strong Ordnungspolizei cordon with machine guns.[460] According to Henry Pohoryles, Resistance fighters had hidden themselves at a junction to liberate them. When they saw the guards, they withdrew immediately; it would have ended in a massacre in view of the guards' superior fire power.[461]

At Bobigny station, a truck stopped beside the wagon intended for the prisoners. Other hostages were loaded onto the wagon, including Paula Kaufmann, the Kohn family, the Russian Princess Olga Galitzine, the aeroplane constructor Marcel Bloch and the German-born camp elder Georges Schmidt with his wife Simone.[462] On boarding, Georges Schmidt claimed the role of wagon elder since he was after all the camp elder, but he was rebuffed.[463]

Armand Kohn was the head of the well-known Jewish Rothschild Hospital in Paris,[464] which served as a prison during the occupation period. It accommodated sick prisoners from Drancy, but it also served as an old people's home.[465] The Jewish camp administration tried to transfer as many prisoners as possible to the hospital to prevent them from being deported. Alois Brunner had accused Armand Kohn of having concealed Jews in the hospital several times before.[466] According to a denunciation statement by the 'Aryan' hospital personnel to the 'German camp commander', a number of Jewish patients manged to escape from the hospital with the help of the Jewish personnel.[467] On 17 July 1944, the Kohn family – Armand and his wife Suzanne, his mother Marie-Jeanne and the four children Antoinette (twenty-two years old), Rose-Marie (eighteen), Philippe (nineteen) and Georges-André (twelve) – were arrested.

As he boarded the train, one of the Kohn sons made the rebuking remark: 'They're deporting us with this rabble!'[468] It seems that, to him, Resistance fighters were precisely what the SS had written on the outside of the wagon: Jewish terrorists. Some reports state that the social situation on the train was strongly characterized by this class conflict. Inside the wagon, there was immediately a social barrier between the political and the bourgeois prisoners. This barrier is also expressed by the spatial separation between the two groups.[469]

Escape by a Number of Hostages during the 79th Transport

The train left Drancy on 17 August 1944 at 19:00, one day before the liberation. Maurice Margulies was named by the prisoners as the wagon elder.[470] The contradicting reports make it impossible to say whether he was chosen by the other prisoners based on Brückler's instructions or whether Brunner appointed him because he knew Margulies from Vienna and is said to have had many violent conflicts with him before the 'Anschluss'.[471]

Philippe Kohn reports on the terrible situation with which his family was confronted inside the wagon. Everything was new for them: being mistreated, being involved with Resistance fighters and being loaded onto a freight wagon. The youngest son, Georges-André, cried and the sisters Antoinette and Rose-Marie were devastated.[472]

According to the historian Anat Gueta, there were various plans by the Resistance to liberate the hostages during the journey, which was often interrupted, but none were attempted.[473] The Resistance fighters in the wagon had decided to do everything they could to escape.[474] This is also confirmed by Alfred Fraenkel from the Westerweel Group, who reports that it was evident that they wanted to flee.[475] César Chamay had already leapt from the 64th deportation train in December 1943. He is the only deportee in France who escaped twice from a train and he already knew that it was possible to jump from a moving train.[476] Henry Pohoryles also knew what their fate would be at the destination. He had spoken to Ignac Honig and Chaïm Salomon,[477] two Jewish prisoners who had escaped from Auschwitz.[478] He urged them to flee.

Tools to work on the wagons had been smuggled onto the wagon in various ways. Since their wagon was directly behind the guards, they only had the option of sawing a hole into the side walls or the floor.[479] Appenzeller and Jean Frydman sawed a hole in the wagon wall.[480] When the train stopped near Tergnier, the guards discovered the hole and nailed it shut.[481]

Chamay remembers that the Kohn daughters naively offered valuable jewellery to a young guard in exchange for letting them go. Fortunately, the guard kept it to himself; had there been a search, not only the jewellery but also the smuggled tools would have been discovered.[482]

The train made very slow progress. The Resistance and Allied air strikes had damaged the track.[483] Every time the train stopped, the guards immediately lined up around the train. On the first morning, the train arrived at Dammartin-en-Goële station. It was fired at by Allied forces there. They missed the wagons, but hit the locomotive. Brunner had it replaced with one that was working.[484] On the third day, 19 August, the train again made very little progress. The following day, the train entered Margival tunnel as protection from Allied air strikes.[485] From there, it continued to Laon, a railway hub, where it was immediately bombarded by Allied warplanes. The locomotive was damaged again. Due to the position of the train, it was only possible to position the new locomotive at the other end of the train, which meant that Brunner's hostages were at the end of the train.[486] The escape was planned for the next night, between 20 and 21 August. Frydman recounts that Bloch, the industrial boss, shouted at the escapees that they were insane. Had not the Germans said that they would shoot everyone else? Frydman answered that it was a risk that had to be taken. In any case, he did not intend to go to Buchenwald, which was the destination Brückler had named.[487] There was a good chance that their plan would succeed. Bloch countered that it was idiotic. The war would soon be over and nobody was shot anymore in Buchenwald. He was ensured protection by a group of German Communists.[488] During the German occupation, a complicit relationship had developed between Bloch and the PCF, which would be an advantage after the liberation. In reply, Frydman pushed Bloch against the wall and warned him to stay still while the others jumped, and ideally to pretend to be asleep.[489]

The escape plans were aided by the fact that they were hit by a powerful storm. The guards closed the wagon doors, which were usually kept open for guarding purposes. By then, they were approaching St. Quentin.[490] Maurice Margulies and César Chamay renewed their escape plans and urged them to flee while they were still in French territory.[491] Around twenty voted to flee the next night.[492]

It seems clear that the order in which they jumped was clarified in advance. It may have been according to family status (husband, number of children), or perhaps they alternated between one member of the FTP and one member of the AJ.[493] Since he was especially at risk of severe consequences from the Germans in his capacity as wagon elder, Margulies was to jump first, followed by Appenzeller and Frydman. Chamay and Kapel concur in stating that all members of the AJ and the FTP had received numbers. Fraenkel from the Westerweel Group states that everyone in the wagon pulled a number and that he had received number twenty-three.[494] Frydman said he was given number twenty-two.[495]

From among the prominent prisoners, Olga Galitzine and Rose-Marie and Philippe Kohn decided to jump. It is impossible to reconstruct how agreement was reached between the two camps in the wagon. Armand Kohn was against fleeing and said that if they fled, the family drama would be forever embedded in their memory, but the sisters prevailed.[496] They wanted to take their twelve-year-old brother, Georges-André, but the mother was afraid that he would break his legs as he was still so young.[497] Antoinette, the eldest sister, decided to stay in the wagon to support her parents and grandmother.[498] Pohoryles reports that when urged to flee, Marcel Bloch replied that he would endure this French way of the cross to the end.[499] Kapel, together with Chamay and Amar, distributed the 1,500 Francs he had smuggled into the wagon inside his trousers.[500] To find each other after their jump, they decided to discreetly signal to each other by hitting two stones together. Frydman and Appenzeller were unable to slide back the door, but finally they managed to unscrew the bars from a hatch.[501] The train then suddenly stopped and the Schutzpolizei guards began shining their torches at the wagon. They noticed nothing. It was four in the morning; nobody was sleeping.[502] When the train set off again at a speed of about 15–20 km/h, Margulies said 'Now or never' and jumped out through the hatch. Ignoring the agreed order, Frydman followed him immediately.[503] Lazarus recounts that due to the heavy storm and the darkness, the guards were unable to see anything despite the slow speed of the train. Lazarus describes the moment of flight: 'The moment had come. One person after another pulled up through the opening, we let ourselves glide outside, we let go . . . it is impossible to forget that escape and the sight of those red rear lights on the train at night'.[504]

Rose-Marie Kohn also jumped, injuring herself on the sleeper. Philippe fell uninjured sixty metres further along and ran to his sister. Years later, Philippe Kohn recalls: 'I saw the wagon moving away. I shiver even today when I see the rear lights of a train, because that night, the train drove away with my entire family. It was a separation for ever. For I knew I would never see them again'.[505]

Alfred Fraenkel and Paula Kaufmann, the only survivors of the 'Dutch' group, describe the situation completely differently. Kaufmann states that when the train set off, she sat together with the Resistance fighters and other people. Together, they initially decided to jump from the train, but then the decision was overturned with the argument that the defeat of Germany was only a few weeks away. They would manage that and it would be better than being responsible for the deaths of the old people in the wagon. There were differences of opinion, but after a long discussion, they again decided to jump. Due to the language problems, they went in pairs, always with one French person, and agreed on an order based on drawing numbers. Those who would be punished most by the escape were to jump first. However, out of a sense of responsibility towards the others, they then decided not to jump and laid down to sleep. When Paula Kaufmann awoke, there was suddenly a great deal of space in the wagon, which had been so cramped before. She saw that all the French had gone, except for one, and she regarded it as a betrayal. Those who fled had presumably thought that the people left in the wagons would not survive and would be unable to tell others of the betrayal.[506] Alfred Fraenkel conforms to other accounts in stating: 'We thought of an order, first one French person, then one Dutch and so on. Then the French disappeared in the night and left us behind. . . . When the Dutch wanted to jump, the train had stopped and we had missed our chance'.[507]

After Jumping

In search of his comrades, Kapel fell into a barbed wire fence and tore his trousers. He was also unshaven. Looking like that he would attract attention from the occupiers and their collaborators. The idea of finding each other in the darkness by striking two stones together worked well;[508] they grouped together and walked in the pouring rain for half an hour until they came across a remote farmhouse. There they were given breakfast. A comrade from the FTP, a tailor from Poland, repaired Kapel's trousers. They continued walking until they were rebuked by passers by: how careless they were – did they not know that the Germans were retreating and liquidated all suspects they met? Thus, all those intending to head for Paris split up into small groups. Kapel would have preferred to go with his familiar comrades, but Maurice Margulies, who spoke French with a strong accent and was known to the French police and the German security forces, asked Kapel, a native French speaker, to accompany him and the young Austrian Paul Kessler to Paris. Kessler was an active member of the 'Freies Österreich' group and could not speak a word of French.[509] Kapel joined the other two out of solidarity with Margulies.[510] Margulies hoped to see his wife and child again in Paris. Kapel could now hardly feel his leg; he had injured it jumping out of a first-floor window in Toulouse when the militia raided a meeting of Jewish Resistance activists. On their journey, they avoided major roads in the hope of staying away from the Feldgendarmerie, who were securing the Wehrmacht's retreat. Wherever they knocked on a door, they were admitted, given something to eat or offered a place to sleep. They were also provided with assistance in finding the way to Paris along the railway line. Even a Gendarme who checked them was satisfied with Kapel's papers and told them to 'clear off'. Kapel said this reconciled him to the French people. Finally, after several critical situations, they arrived in Paris. Maurice Margulies went from there to Yugoslavia to join Tito's partisans, joining the 2nd Austrian Battalion of the Yugoslav People's Army.[511]

Rose-Marie and Philippe Kohn pretended to be a loving couple as they crossed a bridge guarded by Germans, and arrived at St. Quentin, where they were hidden, as was Henry Pohoryles and some of his comrades, who had been hidden until the liberation in his school by the teacher Lucien Lebeau, who was also a member of the local Resistance.[512]

The Fate of Those Who Remained inside the Wagon

Paula Kaufmann and Alfred Fraenkel stated that after the escape was discovered, German policemen decided to shoot everyone as punishment. They were forced to get off the train and dig a pit. However, Brunner was angered by the policemen's autonomous actions and broke off the measure, sending the prisoners back to the wagon.[513]

During the journey, Armand Kohn threw a note with the address of his secretary through a gap in the floor of the freight wagon. It contained the following message:

> We are being deported and are without doubt being taken to Germany. We place our trust in God! Try to do something for us via the Red Cross. Try to meet the Paris City Councillor, Pierre Taittinger! May we see each other again soon! Think of us. Inform all friends and also the company I manage.[514]

After their arrival in Weimar on 25 August 1944, Armand Kohn was interned in Buchenwald concentration camp as a Jewish political prisoner.[515] On 16 September, he was transferred to the Witten-Annen subcamp, but soon returned to Buchenwald on 5 October 1944. There he was allocated to Block 9, the 'Kommandiertenblock', which housed prisoners who had to be directly available to the camp SS. The living conditions of the 'Kommandierten' were considerably better than those of the other prisoners with respect to food supplies and sanitary facilities, and they were not required to take part in the roll call. Armand Kohn's forced labour card includes the note by the Schutzhaftlagerführer that according to the Political Department, he was a privileged prisoner and could only be used for light work in the block.[516] Such preferential treatment was very unusual for a Jewish prisoner and suggests that Kohn was treated as an exchange hostage.

The grandmother Marie-Jeanne Kohn and Georges-André, the youngest son of the family, were deported to Auschwitz. The mother Suzanne Kohn and the eldest daughter Antoinette were sent to Bergen-Belsen. Georges-André was selected for the 'Sonderabteilung Heißmeyer' in Auschwitz. In April 1944, the SS doctor Kurt Heißmeyer began carrying out human experiments on prisoners in the Neuengamme concentration camp, using tuberculosis bacteria. After the experiments were completed, all victims were killed. Heißmeyer demanded twenty children from Auschwitz for a new series of experiments. On 27 November 1944, twenty children, including Georges-André Kohn, were taken from Auschwitz to Neuengamme. Shortly before Christmas 1944, all children were already severely ill as a result of the experiments. To hide the monstrous crime, shortly before the US army's arrival in April 1945, the children were murdered in a school in Bullenhuser Damm in Hamburg.[517]

The grandmother Marie-Jeanne Kohn died in Auschwitz, as did Suzanne and her daughter Antoinette in Bergen-Belsen, while the father returned from Buchenwald a few weeks after the liberation. Philippe Kohn only discovered the terrible fate of his little brother in Hamburg in 1979.[518]

Alfred Fraenkel, Max Windmüller, Paula Kaufmann, Ernst Hirsch and Kurt Reilinger from the Westerweel Group were interned in Buchenwald concentration camp on 25 August 1944. It is inexplicable that not a single witness account mentions the presence in the wagon of Max Windmüller, one of, if not *the* key figure in the Westerweel Group in France. From Buchenwald, Max Windmüller was initially transferred to the Flossenbürg concentration camp as an evacuation measure. He was shot dead in Cham during a death march from Flossenbürg to the Dachau concentration camp in April 1945.[519]

Alfred Fraenkel was initially transferred from the Buchenwald concentration camp to the Lippstadt subcamp and then to the Witten-Annen subcamp.[520] He survived the persecution.

Paula Kaufmann was sent to the Buchenwald concentration camp as a Dutch political prisoner and a 'Mischling 1. Grades',[521] from where she was sent to Auschwitz-Birkenau in September of 1944.[522] She was subsequently moved to Bergen-Belsen in late November.[523] On 10 February 1945 she was transferred to Raghun, a subcamp of Buchenwald that had only been established three days earlier.[524] Jewish women were required to work for the Heerbrandt factory there, a manufacturer supplying to Junkers heavy industry. A particularly large number of women forced to work there were either married to 'Aryans' or, like Paula Kaufmann, were 'Mischling 1. Grades'.[525] From there, she was transported to Theresienstadt, where she arrived on 20 April 1945 and was eventually liberated.[526]

Ernst Hirsch was also registered in the Buchenwald concentration camp on 25 August 1944.[527] His labour card was marked 'Austausch' ('Exchange').[528] It appears that, like Armand Kohn, he was regarded as a hostage. However, he died in April 1945 in the Bergen-Belsen concentration camp.[529]

After being interned in the Buchenwald concentration camp, Kurt Reilinger was transferred to the Mittelbau-Dora concentration camp on an unspecified date.[530] After the liberation, the Red Cross took him to Sweden to recover. From there, he returned to Holland. He died there in September 1945 in a car crash.[531]

Meta Lande (born in Vienna in 1924), who was engaged to Max Windmüller at the time and managed to avoid being arrested, recalls that the returning French people who had jumped from the last wagon assured her that the 'Dutch' had also jumped. When they did not return, Lande, who had received a pass from Jacques Lazarus, drove along the railway track by car. She was accompanied by Joseph Liennewiel, who also belonged to the Westerweel Group, as well as the AJ activist Henry Pohoryles, who had jumped from the train, and a French officer. The Frenchman talked to the inhabitants of the villages through which the train had passed, hoping for information.

The drive took a number of weeks and took them to Liège, without success. Meta Lande later heard from Paula Kaufmann that the French Resistance fighters had deliberately jumped without the 'Dutch' from the Westerweel Group.[532]

Retrospective Perception

In view of Meta Lande's account, the question arises why Henry Pohoryles, who had escaped from the wagon, should have participated in a search for the 'Dutch' over a period of weeks, if he knew that the search was in vain. Both Lazarus and Kapel state that thirty-six Jewish Resistance fighters from the AJ and the FTP had been in the wagon. Lazarus describes the members of the Westerweel Group as the 'Dutch group' of the AJ.[533] They had been the first that he had trained militarily in the Tarn region to establish an armed unit of the AJ, known as the M 7: they needed military skills before the winter journey via Spain to Palestine. There had been language difficulties. ('How could one talk to those young men that didn't speak a word of French?')[534] Perhaps this language problem was also responsible for misunderstandings when coordinating plans.[535] Immediately after being liberated, Lazarus described the events in a newspaper article. In the article, he abbreviated the names of the 'Dutch', since they were still in the hands of the Nazis. He named them the brave Dutch leaders, who had saved countless of their own kind by enabling them to flee via Belgium and France to the free countries.[536] In an article published in 1954, César Chamay also discusses the cooperation with the 'Dutch' and their leader Max Windmüller ('Cor'), but not in connection with the escape.[537] In a text published in 1995, Lazarus, like Henry Pohoryles in his witness account, mentions the 'Dutch' group, but not the fact that they were in the same wagon together.[538]

René Kapel at least asked himself why Max Windmüller and the others in his group – Paula Kaufmann, Ernst Hirsch, Kurt Reilinger and Alfred Fraenkel, whom he wrongly thought to come from the Netherlands – did not jump. Like all the others, they had been informed of the escape plan and had received a number and a blessing.[539] According to Kapel, the fact that none of the group used the chance to flee is an indication that they had come to a joint decision. In his autobiographical memoirs, he regrets that they, the French, had not known their intentions, because they would have done everything possible to convince the 'Dutch' group to jump. Kapel writes that the behaviour of Max Windmüller and his comrades might be explained by their deep exhaustion and tiredness, both physically and in terms of morale. This may be added to the – unjustified – sense of being foreign among comrades with a different range of experiences. Moreover, they had not known each other for long.

Chamay remains vague in his implications: with hindsight, there had been complaints, but in the wagon those who really wanted to sleep had slept, or at least pretended to. He did not know the motives of those who remained on the train. When he met Bloch by chance after being liberated, the industrial magnate had had the gall to complain that nobody had woken him when it was time to flee.[540]

Alfred Fraenkel provides another version. After the first nineteen prisoners had jumped, the train stopped because the tracks ahead had been damaged by an explosion. This is when the Germans discovered the absence of the nineteen prisoners.[541] However, this would mean that none of the Westerweel Group had drawn one of the first nineteen lots, which is unlikely, especially since other accounts state that Paula Kaufmann had drawn number ten and Max Windmüller number eleven.[542]

The inconsistencies and serious allegations that Paula Kaufmann made against those who jumped can no longer be clarified. The argument that it may have been language problems that hindered communication is not convincing: the FTP members also included the Austrian Maurice Margulies and Paul Kessler, who could speak German, but hardly any French. Ernest Appenzeller, son of an Austrian rabbi, also spoke German.[543] The members of the Westerweel Group who had German and Austrian origins could have communicated with them without any problems. So how could it have occurred that Paula Kaufmann describes all jumpers as French, which is just as untrue as the assumption of some AJ members that the members of the 'Dutch' group had been born in the Netherlands? The flight of a number of prisoners from the 'bourgeois' camp is also evidence against a secret escape by the Resistance fighters. Why would they have wanted to prevent the escape of members of the 'Dutch' group, but support the escape of the bourgeois prisoners? The historian Anat Gueta writes that the French Resistance members would have told everyone of their plans to escape. According to Gueta, the reports by the French survivors provide no explanation why none from the Westerweel Group jumped.[544]

In the memoirs of the AJ members Lazarus and Kapel, the 'groupe hollandaise' is mentioned in a very positive light. Furthermore, shortly after the liberation of France, Kurt Reilinger, Ernst Hirsch, Alfred Fraenkel, Max Windmüller, Léo Weil, Paula Kaufmann and Meta Lande were named by various AJ members as members of their organization in statements to the union of fighting Resistance groups.[545] This formed the basis for state remembrance of those who had fought for France's liberation.

Apart from Alfred Fraenkel, Paula Kaufmann and Kurt Reilinger, no-one from the group survived imprisonment in the concentration camps and there is no further evidence from that side. Thus, this partially incomplete reconstruction of the stories of persecution and escapes must suffice. The diverse variations and also the many discrepancies in the described details cannot be condensed to create a valid narrative that is free of uncertainties.

Notes

1. Esther Benbassa, *Geschichte der Juden in Frankreich*, Berlin/Vienna 2000, p. 130.
2. Ibid., p. 169.
3. Ibid., p. 187.
4. Ahlrich Meyer, '"Fremde Elemente". Die osteuropäisch-jüdische Immigration, die "Endlösung der Judenfrage" und die Anfänge der Widerstandsbewegung in Frankreich', in: *Arbeitsmigration und Flucht. Vertreibung und Arbeitskräfteregulierung im Zwischenkriegseuropa, Beiträge zur nationalsozialistischen Gesundheits- und Sozialpolitik*, Vol. 11, Berlin/Göttingen 1993, pp. 82–129, here p. 84.
5. Benbassa, *Geschichte der Juden*, pp. 187, 191; Ingrid Strobl, *Die Angst kam erst danach. Jüdische Frauen im Widerstand in Europa 1939–1945*, Frankfurt am Main 1998, p. 45.
6. Benbassa, *Geschichte der Juden*, p. 170.
7. Meyer, 'Fremde Elemente', p. 88; Stéphane Courtois, Denis Peschanski, and Adam Rayski, *L'Affiche Rouge. Immigranten und Juden in der französischen Résistance*, Berlin 1994, p. 15.
8. Courtois, Peschanski, and Rayski, *L'Affiche Rouge*, p. 13.
9. Meyer, 'Fremde Elemente', p. 88.
10. Lucien Lazare, 'Introduction: Les combattants de la résistance juive à vocation communitaire', in: Les Anciens de la Résistance juive en France, *Organisation Juive de Combat. Résistance/sauvtage, France 1940–1945*, 2006, pp. 19–36, here p. 23; Courtois, Peschanski, and Rayski, *L'Affiche Rouge*, p. 22.
11. For an extensive discussion of the history and significance of the MOI, see Courtois, Peschanski, and Rayski, *L'Affiche Rouge*.
12. Ibid., p. 33 ff.
13. Benbassa, *Geschichte der Juden*, p. 207.

14. Courtois, Peschanski, and Rayski, *L'Affiche Rouge*, p. 50.
15. Ibid., p. 56 f.
16. Volkhard Knigge and Detlef Hoffmann, 'Die südfranzösischen Lager', in: idem (Eds), *Das Gedächtnis der Dinge. KZ-Relikte und KZ-Denkmäler 1945–1995*, Frankfurt/New York 1998, pp. 208–22; Barbara Distel, 'Frankreich', in: Wolfgang Benz and Barbara Distel (Eds), *Der Ort des Terrors. Geschichte der nationalsozialistischen Konzentrationslager*, Vol. 9, Munich 2009, pp. 273–91, here p. 273 f.; see also the autobiographical study of the experience of the internee Lion Feuchtwanger, *Der Teufel in Frankreich*, Frankfurt am Main 1986.
17. Klaus-Michael Mallmann, 'Frankreichs fremde Patrioten. Deutsche in der Résistance', in: *Internationales Jahrbuch für Exilforschung* 15 (1997): Exil und Widerstand, pp. 33–65, here p. 40 f.
18. Stefan Martens (Ed.), *Frankreich und Belgien unter deutscher Besatzung 1940–1944. Die Bestände des Bundesarchiv-Militärarchivs Freiburg*, Stuttgart 2002 (revised by Sebastian Remus), p. XXIV; Gerhard Hirschfeld, 'Kollaboration in Frankreich – Einführung', in: Gerhard Hirschfeld and Patrick Marsh (Eds), *Kollaboration in Frankreich. Politik, Wirtschaft und Kultur während der nationalsozialistischen Besatzung 1940–1944*, Frankfurt am Main 1991, pp. 7–22, here p. 11 f.; Michael Wildt, *Generation der Unbedingten. Das Führungskorps des Reichssicherheitshauptamtes*, Hamburg 2003, p. 524 ff.
19. Bernd Kasten, 'Zwischen Pragmatismus und exzessiver Gewalt. Die Gestapo in Frankreich 1940–1944', in: Gerhard Paul and Klaus-Michael Mallmann (Eds), *Die Gestapo im Zweiten Weltkrieg. 'Heimatfront' und besetztes Europa*, Darmstadt 2000, pp. 362–82, here p. 362 f.; Wildt, *Generation der Unbedingten*, p. 514; Herbert, *Best*, p. 253.
20. Wildt, *Generation der Unbedingten*, p. 518.
21. Ibid., p. 520 f.; Meyer, *Täter im Verhör*, p. 37; Claudia Steur, *Theodor Dannecker. Ein Funktionär der 'Endlösung'*, Essen 1997, p. 45.
22. Meyer, *Täter im Verhör*, p. 21. For detailed information on the Vichy government's collaboration in identifying the Jewish population, removing their rights, expropriating and deporting them, see Michael R. Marrus and Robert O. Paxton, *Vichy France and the Jews*, Stanford 1995.
23. Mallmann, 'Frankreichs fremde Patrioten', p. 44; Herbert, *Best*, p. 251.
24. Herbert, *Best*, p. 310.
25. Ibid., p. 262 ff.
26. Henry Rousso, *Vichy. Frankreich unter deutscher Besatzung 1940–1944*, Munich 2009, p. 89.
27. Marrus and Paxton, *Vichy France and the Jews*, p. 242 f.; Serge Klarsfeld, *Vichy-Auschwitz. Die 'Endlösung der Judenfrage' in Frankreich*, Darmstadt 2007, p. 36; Steur, *Theodor Dannecker*, p. 51; Meyer, *Täter im Verhör*, p. 24.
28. Rousso, *Vichy*, p. 83; Mallmann, 'Frankreichs fremde Patrioten', p. 41; Klarsfeld, *Vichy-Auschwitz*, p. 32 f.; Herbert, *Best*, p. 262; Safrian, *Eichmann und seine Gehilfen*, p. 201.
29. Rousso, *Vichy*, p. 83; in detail: Anne Grynberg, *Les camps de la honte. Les internés juifs des camps français 1939-1944*, Paris 1999.
30. Rousso, *Vichy*, p. 83.
31. Herbert, *Best*, p. 306.
32. Ahlrich Meyer, *Die deutsche Besatzung in Frankreich 1940-1944. Widerstandsbekämpfung und Judenverfolgung*, Darmstadt 2000, p. 41; Klarsfeld, *Vichy-Auschwitz*, p. 385; Herbert, *Best*, p. 308.
33. Herbert, *Best*, p. 308.
34. Rousso, *Vichy*, p. 91 f.
35. Meyer, *Besatzung in Frankreich*, p. 21 f.; Herbert, *Best*, p. 308; Benbassa, *Geschichte der Juden*, p. 215; Safrian, *Eichmann und seine Gehilfen*, p. 204.
36. Benbassa, *Geschichte der Juden*, p. 216.
37. Rousso, *Vichy*, p. 90; Benbassa, *Geschichte der Juden*, p. 216.
38. Benbassa, *Geschichte der Juden*, p. 216.
39. Courtois, Peschanski, and Rayski, *L'Affiche Rouge*, p. 84.

40. Lucien Lazare, *La résistance juive en France*, Paris 1987, pp. 52 ff., 65.
41. In detail: Meyer, *Besatzung in Frankreich*, p. 54 ff.; see also Courtois, Peschanski, and Rayski, *L'Affiche Rouge*, p. 96.
42. Klarsfeld, *Vichy-Auschwitz*, p. 34 ff.; Herbert, *Best*, p. 309.
43. Herbert, *Best*, p. 310.
44. Ibid., p. 310 f.
45. Ibid., p. 311.
46. Ibid.
47. Ibid.
48. Cf. Klarsfeld, *Vichy-Auschwitz*, p. 31; Herbert, *Best*, p. 301 f.; Meyer, *Besatzung in Frankeich*, p. 22 ff.
49. Hilberg, *Quellen des Holocaust*, p. 229; Herbert, *Best*, p. 303; Meyer, *Besatzung in Frankreich*, p. 23.
50. Herbert, *Best*, p. 305.
51. Hilberg, *Quellen des Holocaust*, p. 229; Herbert, *Best*, p. 303 ff.
52. Herbert, *Best*, p. 314.
53. Martin Moll, *'Führer-Erlasse' 1939–1945*, Stuttgart 1997, p. 239 f.; Weinke, *Gesellschaft*, p. 103; Herbert, *Best*, p. 314.
54. Ruth Bettina Birn, *Die Höheren SS- und Polizeiführer. Himmlers Vertreter im Reich und in den besetzten Gebieten*, Düsseldorf 1986, p. 253.
55. Meyer, *Täter im Verhör*, p. 21; Wildt, *Generation der Unbedingten*, p. 652; Birn, *SS- und Polizeiführer*, p. 252; Marrus and Paxton, *Vichy France and the Jews*, p. 242.
56. Herbert, *Best*, p. 314; Birn, *SS- und Polizeiführer*, p. 252 f.
57. Klarsfeld, *Vichy-Auschwitz*, p. 53 f.
58. Oberg, Betr.: Kennzeichnung der Juden, 1 June 1942, BArch R 58, 6585; Lucy S. Dawidowicz, *Der Krieg gegen die Juden 1933–1945*, Wiesbaden 1979, p. 350 f.
59. Courtois, Peschanski, and Rayski, *L'Affiche Rouge*, p. 95 f.
60. Ibid., p. 109.
61. After the liberation, this did not stop the PCF from neglecting to mention the resistance by the FTP-MOI, which consisted mainly of immigrants, or from stressing that the Resistance was a national project by French Communists. See Ingrid Strobl, *'Sag nie, du gehst den letzten Weg'. Frauen im bewaffneten Widerstand gegen Faschismus und deutsche Besatzung*, Frankfurt am Main 1989, p. 136; Mallmann, 'Frankreichs fremde Patrioten', pp. 34 f., 43.
62. Arno Lustiger, *Zum Kampf auf Leben und Tod! Vom Widerstand der Juden in Europa 1933–1945*, Cologne 1994, p. 445; René S. Kapel, *Un rabbin dans la tourmente (1940–1944). Dans les campes d'internement et au sein de l'Organisation juive de combat*, Paris 1986, p. 125; Henry Pohoryles, Etats des services, CDJC, CCXVIII-58.
63. Lazare, *La résistance juive*, p. 78 ff. The following groups are reported to have been organized within the MJS: Jeunesse socialiste, PZ gauche, Misrahi, EIF and Hehaloutz. See Aron Lublin, 'L'organisation juive de combat (OJC)', in: *Le Monde Juif. Revue d'histoire de la Shoah* (1994) 152, p. 75; Anny Latour, *La résistance juive en France (1940–1944)*, Paris 1970, p. 84; Strobl, *Angst*, p. 84 f.; Pohoryles, Etats des services, CDJC, CCXVIII-58; Mompezat (Forces Francaises de l'interieur), 6 April 1945, CDJC, CMXX-6.
64. Cf. Lublin, 'L'organisation juive de combat (OJC)', p. 75; Latour, *La résistance juive*, p. 94; Benbassa, *Geschichte der Juden*, p. 222 f.; Kapel, *Un rabbin*, p. 205.
65. Knochen to Kosemann, Betr.: Aktionen gegen Judentum in Frankreich, 30 July 1942, CDJC, XXVb-105; Heinrichsohn, Besprechung zwischen Herrn Leguay und Kommandant Sauts mit SS-Unterscharführer Heinrichsohn, 27 August 1942, CDJC, XLIX-69; Röthke, Abschub der Juden aus dem unbesetzten Gebiet, 1 September 1942, CDJC, XXVb-147, cited in: Klarsfeld, *Endlösung*, p. 124; see also Meyer, *Besatzung in Frankreich*, p. 41.
66. Ahnert, Vermerk, Betr.: Evakuierung der Juden, 3 September 1942, CDJC, XXVI-60, cited in: Klarsfeld, *Endlösung*, p. 137.

67. Röthke to Knochen, Lischka, Hagen, Betr.: Plan für den Abtransport von Juden aus dem unbesetzten und besetzten Gebiet Frankreichs, 12 September 1942, CDJC, XXVI-63, cited in: Klarsfeld, *Endlösung*, p. 142; Röthke to Knochen, Lischka and Hagen, Betr.: Abschub von Juden aus dem unbesetzten Gebiet, 9 September 1942, CDJC, XXVb-156, cited in: Klarsfeld, *Endlösung*, p. 139.
68. Zeitschel, Aufzeichnung, 16 September 1942, cited in: Klarsfeld, *Endlösung*, p. 87.
69. Abetz to the Auswärtige Amt (Foreign Office), 2 July 1942, PA AA, R 99.417, No. 2231.
70. Patrik von zur Mühlen, *Fluchtweg Spanien – Portugal. Die deutsche Emigration und der Exodus aus Europa 1933–1945*, Bonn 1992, p. 41 f.
71. Röthke, Betr.: Abtransport von Juden aus dem Judenlager Drancy bei Paris nach Auschwitz, 21 January 1943, CDJC, XXc-195.
72. Knochen, 14 April 1944, cited in: *Europa unterm Hakenkreuz. Frankreich. Dokumentenedition. Dokumentenauswahl und Einleitung von Ludwig Nestler. Unter Mitarbeit von Friedel Schulz*, Berlin 1990, p. 308 ff.
73. Ibid.
74. Rousso, *Vichy*, p. 103.
75. Ibid., p. 102.
76. *Europa unterm Hakenkreuz. Frankreich*, p. 339.
77. For Drancy, see Janine Doerry, 'Das Lager Drancy und die Deportation der Juden aus Frankreich', in: Akim Jah et al. (Eds), *Nationalsozialistische Lager. Neue Beiträge zur NS-Verfolgungs- und Vernichtungspolitik und zur Gedenkstättenpädagogik*, Münster 2006, pp. 166–84; Jacques Durin, *Drancy 1941–1944*, Paris 1988, pp. 166–84.
78. Marrus and Paxton, *Vichy France and the Jews*, p. 253; Klarsfeld, *Vichy-Auschwitz*, p. 42; Rajsfus, *Drancy*, p. 81 ff.
79. Durin, *Drancy*, p. 29; Hans Catz, *The Eye of the Needle. A Story from World War II*, [self-published], Huizen 1999, p. 65.
80. Catz, *Eye of the Needle*, p. 65.
81. Anton Söllner, witness hearing, 19 September 1976, BArch B 162/4406.
82. Rajsfus, *Drancy*, p. 168 ff.
83. Author's interview with Louis Handschuh, Paris, 28 September 2008.
84. Klarsfeld, *Calendrier de la persécution*, pp. 59 f., 196; Safrian, *Eichmann und seine Gehilfen*, p. 268.
85. Georges Rueff, Interview Code 16236, VHA, USC Shoah Foundation Institute.
86. Durin, *Drancy*, p. 26; Marrus and Paxton, *Vichy France and the Jews*, p. 253.
87. Knochen to Eichmann, Abbeförderung von Juden aus Frankreich, 3 March 1943, CDJC, XXVc-235.
88. Klarsfeld, *Vichy-Auschwitz*, p. 273; Safrian, *Eichmann und seine Gehilfen*, p. 261 ff.
89. Author's interview with Louis Handschuh, Paris, 28 September 2008; see also Klarsfeld, *Vichy-Auschwitz*, p. 287; Safrian, *Eichmann und seine Gehilfen*, p. 264.
90. Distel, 'Frankreich', p. 285; Marrus and Paxton, *Vichy France and the Jews*, p. 253.
91. Eichmann to Knochen, 12 March 1942, cited in: Klarsfeld, *Vichy-Auschwitz*, p. 403 (original in CDJC, XXVb-10).
92. Günther to BdS Knochen, 16 May 1942, CDJC, XXVb-28.
93. For details, see: Meyer, *Täter im Verhör*, p. 238 ff.
94. Ibid., p. 242 f.
95. Dannecker, Richtlinien für die Evakuierung von Juden, 26 June 1942, printed in: Schoenberner, *Zeugen sagen aus*, p. 221; see also Georges Wellers, *De Drancy à Auschwitz*, Paris 1946, p. 112.
96. Rolf Weinstock, *Das wahre Gesicht Hitler-Deutschlands. Dachau-Auschwitz-Buchenwald. Häftling Nr. 59 000 erzählt von dem Schicksal der 10 000 Juden aus Baden, aus der Pfalz und aus dem Saargebiet in den Höllen von Dachau, Gurs-Drancy, Auschwitz, Jawischowitz, Buchenwald*, Singen 1948, p. 72; Catz, *Eye of the Needle*, p. 68.
97. Sylvain Kaufmann, *Le livre de la mémoire. Au-delà de l'enfer*, [Paris] 1992, p. 35.

98. Röthke, 29 July 1942, CDJC, XXVb-96, cited in: Klarsfeld, *Endlösung*, p. 98 ff.
99. Walter Bargatzky, *Hotel Majestic. Ein Deutscher im besetzten Frankreich*, Freiburg 1987, p. 127.
100. Ibid., p. 127 f.
101. Günther an Knochen, Betr.: Evakuierung von Juden aus Frankreich, 16 May 1942, CDJC, XXVb-28.
102. Brunner, 28 October 1943, CDJC, XLIX-30a.
103. Serge Klarsfeld, *Memorial to the Jews Deported from France 1942–1944. Documentation of the Deportation of the Victims of the Final Solution in France*, New York 1983, p. XXVII.
104. Weckmann, Bedarfsfahrplan Da 901, 30 April 1943, CDJC, XXVc-242; see also Meyer, *Täter im Verhör*, p. 232.
105. Meyer, *Täter im Verhör*, p. 232 f.
106. Catz, *Eye of the Needle*, p. 76 f.; Wellers, *Drancy*, p. 111; Yael Vered, *Là où il n'y a pas d'hommes tâche d'être un homme . . .* , Paris 2006, p. 309.
107. Anton Söllner, witness hearing, 19 September 1976, BArch B 162/4406; see also Catz, *Eye of the Needle*, p. 81; Gottlob Busch, witness hearing, 27 April 1972, BArch B162/4406.
108. Dannecker, 15 June 1942, cited in: Klarsfeld, *Vichy-Auschwitz*, p. 411 (original in the CDJC, RF-1219).
109. For example, Röthke to Niklas (Wehrmachtsverkehrsdirektion), Judentransport am Donnerstag, October 7, 1943 von Güterbahnhof Bobigny nach Auschwitz/O. S., 1 October 1943, CDJC, LXIX-29.
110. Röthke to Knochen and Lischka, Betr.: Abtransport von Juden aus dem besetzten und unbesetzten Gebiet Frankreichs, 28 July 1942, cited in: Klarsfeld, *Vichy-Auschwitz*, p. 446; see also Serge Klarsfeld, 'L'acheminement des Juifs de province vers Drancy et les déportations', in: *Une Entreprise publique dans la guerre: La SNCF 1939-1945. Actes du Ville Colloque de l'Association pour l'histoire des chemins de fer en France*, Paris 2001, p. 151 f.
111. Anton Söllner, witness hearing, 19 September 1976, BArch B 162/4405.
112. Correspondence between Brunner and Röthke, handwritten note, CDJC, XLIX-3.
113. Urban (1./SS-Pol. Rgt. 14), Bericht, 28 June 1943, CDJC, XLIX-8.
114. Röthke to Eichmann, 20 July 1942, CDJC, XXVb-86; Röthke, Betr.: Abtransport von Juden aus dem Judenlager Drancy bei Paris nach Auschwitz, 21 January 1943, CDJC, XXc-195.
115. Röthke, Betr.: Abtransport von Juden aus dem Judenlager Drancy bei Paris nach Auschwitz, 21 January 1943, CDJC, XXc-195.
116. Ibid.
117. Witness hearing, Friedrich Köhnlein, 11 November 1971, BArch B 162/4405.
118. Cf. Meyer, *Täter im Verhör*, p. 234 f.
119. Witness hearing, Gottlob Busch, 27 April 1972, BArch B 162/4406.
120. Patrick Coupechoux, *Mémoires de déportés. Histoires singulières de la déportation*, Paris 2003, p. 187; Catz, *Eye of the Needle*, p. 82; author's interview with Jacques Altmann, Paris, 19 June 2008; statement by Georges Wellers at the Eichmann trial, in: Schmorak, *Sieben sagen aus*, p. 85.
121. Joseph Wargon, in: Klarsfeld, *Calendrier de la persécution*, p. 978.
122. Nadine Heftler, Deportation of a fifteen-year-old French girl to Auschwitz, Wiener Library, Testaments of the Holocaust, 054-EA-0948.
123. Weinstock, *Gesicht Hitler-Deutschlands*, p. 75.
124. Ibid.
125. Author's interview with Jacques Altmann, Paris, 19 June 2008; see also Leo Bretholz and Michael Olesker, *Flucht in die Dunkelheit*, Vienna 2005, p. 173; Paul Chitelman, in: Klarsfeld, *Calendrier de la persécution*, p. 950; Joseph Wargon, in: ibid., p. 978.
126. Freispruch für Modest Alfred Leonhard Graf von Korff, Tatkomplex Schreibtischverbrechen, Tatort Chalons-sur-Marne, Gerichtsentscheidungen LG Bonn vom 17.11.1988, 24 N 3/83, BGH vom 30.11.1990, 2 StR 44/90, in: C. F. Rüter and D. W. de Mildt (Eds), *Justiz und NS-Verbrechen. Die deutschen Strafverfahren wegen nationalsozialistischer Tötungsverbrechen*, Vol. XLVII, Amsterdam 2011, p. 544 f.

127. Weinstock, *Gesicht Hitler-Deutschlands*, p. 76.
128. Jenny Spritzer, *Ich war Nr. 10291. Tatsachenbericht einer Schreiberin der politischen Abteilung aus dem Konzentrationslager Auschwitz*, Darmstadt 1980, p. 21.
129. Urban (1./SS-Pol. Regt. 14), Bericht, 28 June 1943, CDJC, XLIX-8.
130. Freispruch für Modest Alfred Leonhard Graf von Korff, in: Rüter and de Mildt, *Justiz und NS-Verbrechen*, p. 544 f.; testimony by Paul Chitelman, in: Klarsfeld, *Calendrier de la persécution*, p. 950.
131. Weinstock, *Gesicht Hitler-Deutschlands*, p. 75.
132. Spritzer, *Ich war Nr. 10291*, p. 21; Cohen, *The Abyss*, p. 78.
133. Testimony, Ida Fensterszab-Grinspan, in: Klarsfeld, *Calendrier de la persécution*, p. 958.
134. Joseph Wargon, in: ibid., p. 978.
135. Paul Chitelman, in: ibid., p. 950.
136. Nadine Heftler, Deportation of a fifteen-year-old French girl to Auschwitz, Wiener Library, Testaments of the Holocaust, 054-EA-0948.
137. Weinstock, *Gesicht Hitler-Deutschlands*, p. 76; Paul Chitelman, in: Klarsfeld, *Calendrier de la persécution*, p. 950.
138. Author's interview with Jacques Altmann, Paris, 19 June 2008. Between February and October 1944, he was forced to work at the ramp in Auschwitz and remove the bodies from the wagons.
139. Weinstock, *Gesicht Hitler-Deutschlands*, p. 76 f.
140. Lischka, 17 March 1942, in: Klarsfeld, *Endlösung*, p. 51 (original in CDJC, XXVb-15).
141. Dannecker, Richtlinien für die Evakuierung von Juden, 26 June 1942, cited in: Schoenberner, *Zeugen sagen aus*, p. 221.
142. Röthke, 18 July 1942, CDJC, XLIX-67, cited in: Klarsfeld, *Endlösung*, p. 93; Dannecker to RSHA IV B 4, the IKL and Auschwitz concentration camp command, Betr.: 2. Judentransport aus Frankreich, 5 June 1942, CDJC, XXVb-32; Delarue, Leutnant der Feldgendarmerie, Feldkommandantur 757 to the Kommandant of Greater Paris, Neuilly, 20 July 1942, ID 11179751#1, ITS Digitales Archiv.
143. Witness testimony, Friedrich Köhnlein, 11 November 1971, BArch B 162/4405.
144. Ahnert, Betr.: Bewachungsmannschaften für die Transportzüge der Juden, 10 August 1942, cited in: Klarsfeld, *Vichy-Auschwitz*, p. 454 (original in CDJC, XXVb-121).
145. Röthke, Betr.: Bewachungsmannschaften für die Transportzüge der Juden, 20 August 1942, cited in: Klarsfeld, *Vichy-Auschwitz*, p. 459 (original in CDJC, XXVb-134).
146. Meyer, *Täter im Verhör*, p. 236.
147. Witness statement by Gottlob Busch, 27 April 1972, BArch B 162/4406.
148. Meyer, *Täter im Verhör*, p. 237.
149. Röthke to RSHA, IKL, Auschwitz concentration camp, 2 September 1943, CDJC, XLIX-30a; see also Meyer, *Täter im Verhör*, p. 237.
150. Röthke to RSHA, IKL, Auschwitz concentration camp, 7 October 1943, 1.1.9.1, ID 111833487, ITS Digitales Archiv. The typewritten destination of 'up to the Reich frontier (Neuenburg)' was struck through in handwriting and replaced by 'Auschwitz'.
151. Röthke to Befehlshaber der Ordnungspolizei, Polizeirat Christoph, Betr.: Marschverpflegung für Begleitkommando der Ordnungspolizei, 6 October 1943, 1.2.7.18, ID 82198182, ITS Digitales Archiv; witness statement by Friedrich Köhnlein, 11 November 1971, BArch B 162/4405; testimony by Gustav Zuschneid, 7 December 1971, BArch B 162/4405; Günther (RSHA IV B a) to Röthke: Betr: Abbeförderung von Juden aus Frankreich, 24 October 1943, CDJC, XLIX-53.
152. Brunner to RSHA, IKL, Auschwitz concentration camp, 28 October 1943, 1.1.9.1, ID 11183574, ITS Digitales Archiv.
153. [unreadable] to RSHA, IKL, Auschwitz concentration camp, 7 December 1943, 1.1.9.1, ID 11183720, ITS Digitales Archiv.
154. Meyer, *Täter im Verhör*, p. 237 f.
155. Witness statement by Gottlob Busch, 27 April 1972, BArch B 162/4406.

156. Witness statement by Friedrich Köhnlein, 11 November 1971, BArch B 162/4405. The wagons were numbered and lists sorted by wagon. An example of the list for the 20th deportation train is printed as a facsimile in: Serge Klarsfeld, *Transport No. 20 du 17. 8. 1942, 530 enfants de moins de 16 ans*, Paris [c. 1980].
157. Witness statement by Gottlob Busch, 27 April 1972, BArch B 162/4406.
158. Gustav Zuschneid (born in 1896), a highly decorated World War I soldier, fought in 1919/29 in the Freicorps for the Grenzschutz Ost. From 1925 to 1933, he was a member of the Stahlhelm Bund der Frontsoldaten. In 1937 he again joined the SS, after having left it in 1932/33 for police duty. The convinced National Socialist took part in the campaigns in France and the East as a member of the Waffen-SS. He was then transferred back to the Ordnungspolizei and in 1943 became Bataillonskommandeur of II/SS Police Regiment 4, later of the 1st Police Guard Battalion, in France and Denmark. In June 1943, Zuschneid led the battalion as its commander in the 'fight against bandits in the district of Lublin'. Gustav Zuschneid, 27 March 1896, BArch B (formerly BDC), SSO Gustav Zuschneid.
159. Witness statement by Gustav Zuschneid, 7 December 1971, BArch B 162/4405.
160. Witness statement by Willi Nowak, 16 July 1971, BArch B 162/4408; witness statement by Gottlob Busch, 27 April 1972, BArch B 162/4406.
161. Zuschneid, Stellungnahme zu den Erfahrungsberichten über die Begleitung von Judentransporten am 9. 2., 11. 2. u. 13. 2. 1943, 15 February 1943, CDJC, XXVc-208.
162. Witness statement by Gottlob Busch, 27 April 1972, BArch B 162/4406.
163. Alfons Haberkorn, Schutzpolizei Meister in the Strasbourg police battalion, stated that he had heard colleagues say this. Witness statement, 13 June 1975, BArch B 162/4408.
164. Witness statement by Ernst Roth, 18 December 1974, BArch B 162/4408. Ernst Roth, Kompanieführer in the Strasbourg police battalion, stated that the then Ordonanzoffizier Ernst Trautz from Pforzheim had said this after reporting back from Auschwitz.
165. Witness statement by Gottlob Busch, 27 April 1972, BArch B 162/4406.
166. Witness statement by Otto Gehring, 11 June 1975, BArch B 162/4408.
167. Dannecker, Vermerk, 20 March 1942, in: Pätzold and Schwarz, *Auschwitz*, p. 123.
168. Günther, Betr.: Evakuierung von Juden aus Frankreich, 25 March 1942, CDJC, XXVb-20.
169. Dannecker, Vermerk, Betr.: Deportierung von Juden (27. 3. 42), 25 March 1942, CDJC, XXVb-22; Knochen to RSHA IV B 4, Betr.: Abtransport von 1000 Juden aus Compiègne bezw. Drancy, 20 March 1942, in: Klarsfeld, *Vichy-Auschwitz*, p. 406 (original in CDJC, XXVb-17).
170. Dannecker, Betr.: Deportierung von Juden, 25 March 1942, CDJC, XXVb-21.
171. Dannecker, Betr.: Bevorstehende Judentransporte, 26 March 1942, CDJC, XXVb-22.
172. Günther, Betr.: Evakuierung von Juden aus Frankreich, 25 March 1942, CDJC, XXVb-20.
173. Testimony by Georges Rueff, 16 June 1966, CDJC, CDLXXVI-25.
174. Georges Rueff, Interview Code 16236, VHA, USC Shoah Foundation Institute; testimony by Georges Rueff, 16 June 1966, CDJC, CDLXXVI-25.
175. Ibid.
176. Ibid.
177. Testimony by Georges Rueff, 16 June 1966, CDJC, CDLXXVI-25.
178. Georges Rueff, Interview Code 16236, VHA, USC Shoah Foundation Institute.
179. Ibid.; testimony by Georges Rueff, 16 June 1966, CDJC, CDLXXVI-25.
180. Statement by Georges Rueff, in: *Premier convoi*, documentary film by von Pierre Oscar Lévy, 1992; Georges Rueff, Interview Code 16236, VHA, USC Shoah Foundation Institute.
181. Georges Rueff, Interview Code 16236, VHA, USC Shoah Foundation Institute.
182. Interview with Rueff, in: *Premier convoi*, 1992.
183. Volker Mall and Harald Roth, *Jeder Mensch hat einen Namen. Gedenkbuch für die 600 jüdischen Häftlinge des KZ-Außenlagers Hailfingen/Tailfingen*, Berlin 2009, p. 150.
184. Bertha Goldwasser interviewed by David Boder, Paris, 4 August 1946, *Voices of the Holocaust*, http://voices.iit.edu/interviewee?doc=goldwasserB (accessed 31 October 2017).
185. Ibid.

186. Commission Shoah du Consistoire de Paris, *Les derniers témoins. Paroles de déportés. Recueillies par Jean-Pierre Allali, Adolphe Fuchs. Les copains d'abord*, 2005, p. 93.
187. Ibid., p. 95.
188. Ibid., p. 96.
189. Ibid., p. 97.
190. Ibid., p. 97 f.
191. Ibid., p. 97 ff.
192. Catz, *Eye of the Needle*, p. 18 ff.
193. Ibid., p. 39 f.
194. Ibid., p. 53.
195. Ibid., p. 58.
196. Ibid., p. 59 f.
197. Ibid., p. 68.
198. Ibid., p. 77.
199. Hans Catz writes their names Du Metz, but in deportation lists they are listed as De Metz. CDJC database, http://bdi.memorialdelashoah.org/internet/jsp/media/MmsMediaDetailPopup.jsp?mediaid=2350 (accessed 31 October 2017). See also Catz, *Eye of the Needle*, p. 81.
200. Catz, *Eye of the Needle*, p. 81.
201. Ibid.
202. Ibid., p. 83.
203. Ibid., p. 82.
204. Ibid., p. 83.
205. Ibid., p. 96 f.
206. Bretholz and Olesker, *Flucht in die Dunkelheit*, p. 52 ff.
207. Ibid., p. 139.
208. Ibid., p. 140 f.
209. Ibid., p. 149 ff.
210. Ibid., p. 154.
211. Ibid., p. 155.
212. Ibid., p. 157.
213. Röthke to Eichmann, Betr.: Abtransport von Juden aus dem Haftlager Drancy bei Paris nach dem Konzentrationslager Auschwitz O. S., 31 October 1942, CDJC, XXVc-192.
214. Ibid., p. 169 ff.
215. Leo Bretholz, Interview Code 8503, VHA, USC Shoah Foundation Institute.
216. Bretholz and Olesker, *Flucht in die Dunkelheit*, p. 172.
217. Ibid., p. 173.
218. Ibid., p. 176 f.
219. Ibid., p. 178 f.
220. Ibid., p. 181.
221. Abram Herskoviez, who had changed his name to Albert Hershkowitz in Belgium, did not survive Auschwitz. In Drancy, he was listed under his original name and the deportation list also uses that name. Written statement by Leo Bretholz to the author, dated 3 November 2008; see also Klarsfeld, *Memorial to the Jews*, p. 339.
222. Le Bretholz, Interview Code 8503, VHA, USC Shoah Foundation Institute.
223. An interview sequence from 1992, in which Leo Bretholz describes this escape, can be found at: United States Holocaust Memorial Museum, 'Personal Stories. Leo Bretholz', RG-50.042*0008, http://collections.ushmm.org/search/catalog/irn505562 (accessed 31 October 2017).
224. Leo Bretholz, Interview Code 8503, VHA, USC Shoah Foundation Institute.
225. Ibid.
226. For detailed information on this group, see: Marcel Gherson, *La Sixième*, CDJC, DLXI-29.
227. Written statement by Leo Bretholz to the author, dated 3 November 2008.

228. Klarsfeld, *Memorial to the Jews*, p. 336.
229. Metzer, 5 February 1943, CDJC, XXVc-203.
230. Witness statement by Willi Nowak, 16 July 1975, BArch B 162/4408; Nowak, testimony, 10 February 1943, CDJC, XXVc-208.
231. Nowak, testimony, 10 February 1943, CDJC, XXVc-208.
232. Written statement by Raoul Pageot to Serge Klarsfeld, 10 December 1985. The author thanks Serge Klarsfeld for providing this statement; Aus dem Freispruch für Modest Alfred Leonhard Graf von Korff, in: Rüter and de Mildt, *Justiz und NS-Verbrechen*, p. 551.
233. PB 323 was stationed in Tilsit (Sovetsk) in the summer of 1942, before being transferred to Paris. It was later renamed SS Police Regiment 4.
234. Zuschneid, Stellungnahme zu den Erfahrungen über die Begleitung von Judentransporten am 9. 2., 11. 2. u. 13. 2. 1943, 15 February 1943, CDJC, XXVc-208.
235. Nowak, testimony, 2 February 1943, CDJC, XXVc-208.
236. Serignan to Sauts, 5 March 1943, CDJC, XXVc-213.
237. Röthke, Flucht von Juden aus dem Judentransport am 13. 2. 1943, 3 March 1943, CDJC, XXVc-219.
238. Kassel, Erfahrungsbericht über Begleitung und Überwachung des Judentransportes am 11. 2. 1943 nach Neuburg/Mosel, 12 February 1943, CDJC, XXVc-208.
239. Ibid.
240. Ibid.
241. Ibid.
242. Ibid.
243. Röthke, Abschub von Juden französischer Staatsangehörigkeit aus dem Judenlager Drancy nach Auschwitz/O. S., 10 February 1943, CDJC, XXVc-204.
244. Klarsfeld, *Vichy-Auschwitz*, p. 506.
245. Röthke, Abschub von Juden französischer Staatsangehörigkeit aus dem Judenlager Drancy nach Auschwitz/O. S., 10 February 1943, CDJC, XXVc-204.
246. Ibid.; see also Klarsfeld, *Vichy-Auschwitz*, p. 506.
247. Röthke, Überwachung von Judentransporten, 12 February 1943, CDJC, XXVc-205.
248. Zuschneid, 12 February 1943, CDJC, XXVc-208.
249. Ibid.
250. Nowak, testimony, 14 February 1943, CDJC, XXVc-208.
251. Ibid.
252. Ibid.
253. Ibid.
254. Ibid.
255. Ibid.
256. Telegraph extract, Nancy, 15 February 1943, CDJC, XXVc-206.
257. Röthke, Flucht von Juden aus dem Judentransport am 13. 2. 1943, 10 March 1943, CDJC, XXVc-219.
258. Röthke, Judentransport am 13. Februar 1943, 22 February 1943, YVA O9-203 (original in CDJC, XXVc-236).
259. Zuschneid, Stellungnahme zu den Erfahrungen über die Begleitung von Judentransporten am 9. 2., 11. 2. u. 13. 2. 1943, 15 February 1943, CDJC, XXVc-208.
260. Ibid.
261. Ibid.
262. Ibid.
263. Niemann, Betr.: Judentransporte, 18 February 1943, CDJC, XXVc-208.
264. RSHA, IV B 4, Richtlinien zur technischen Durchführung der Evakuierung von Juden nach dem Osten (KL Auschwitz), 20 February 1943, cited in: Pätzold and Schwarz, *Auschwitz*, p. 140.
265. Serignan, Evasion de juifs au cours d'un transfèrement le 13 février 1943, 20 April 1943, CDJC, XXVc-238 (B).

266. Röthke, handwritten note on the document: Serignan, Evasion de juifs au cours d'un transfèrement le 13 février 1943, 20 April 1943, CDJC, XXVc-238 (B).
267. Röthke, 4 March 1943, CDJC, XXVc-211.
268. Röthke to RSHA IV 4 B a, Abschub von Juden aus dem Judenlager Drancy bei Paris nach Auschwitz und Cholm, 25 February 1943, BArch B 162/17057.
269. Röthke, 4 March 1943, CDJC, XXVc-211; Niemann (BdO) to HSSPF, Betr.: Judentransporte, 18 February 1943, CDJC, XXVc-208.
270. Autobiographical report by unknown author, 14 July 1978, CDJC, DCCXXXIV-3.
271. Küver to BdS, Betr.: Jakob Silber, geb. 13. 11. 1893 in Tarnow/Polen, wohnhaft in Lyon, Monte de la Grand 41, 8 March 1943, CDJC, XXVc-216.
272. Röthke, Den Juden Jakob Silber, geb. 13. 11. 1893 in Tarnow/Polen zuletzt wohnhaft: Lyon, Monte de la Grand 41, 11 March 1943, CDJC, XXVc-220.
273. Küver (BdS, Lothringen-Saarpfalz, Metz) to the BdS in Paris, Betr.: Judentransporte, 25 March 1943, CDJC, XXVc-231.
274. Klarsfeld, *Vichy-Auschwitz*, p. 524.
275. Röthke to RSHA, BdS Krakau, BdS Lublin, 6 March 1943, CDJC, XXVc-215; Zeug (Zentrale Stelle der Landesjustizverwaltungen), Ermittlungsverfahren 8 Js 1230/60 StA Wiesbaden gegen den Kriminalkommissar Walter Hess in Wiesbaden unter anderem wegen Mordes, 13 December 1961, BArch B 162/4429.
276. CDJC, database, C51_12, http://ressources.memorialdelashoah.org/zoom.php?code=50333&q=id:p_260022&marginMin=0&marginMax=0&curPage=0 (accessed 1 November 2017); CDJC, database, C51_36, http://ressources.memorialdelashoah.org/zoom.php?code=17639&q=id:p_232009&marginMin=0&marginMax=0&curPage=0 (accessed 7 February 2019).
277. Küver, Betr.: Jude Sal de Leeuwe, geb. am 4. 3. 1923, 17 March 1943, CDJC, XXVc-231.
278. Röthke, Betr.: Den Juden Sal de Leuwe, geb. am 4. 3. 1923 in Amsterdam, holländischer Staatsbürger, zuletzt wohnhaft in Aix/Frankreich, 22 March 1943, CDJC, XXVc-231.
279. Küver, Betr.: Jude Sal de Leeuwe, geb. am 4. 3. 1923, 17 March 1943, CDJC, XXVc-231.
280. Kurt Asser to Beate and Serge Klarsfeld, 8 July 1978. My thanks to Beate and Serge Klarsfeld for the information and for providing the letter.
281. Military Government of Germany, Fragebogen für Insassen der Konzentrationslager, Concentration Camp Inmates Questionnaire, 21 April 1945, 1.1.5.3, ID 5448872, ITS Digitales Archiv.
282. Deportation list, Kurt Asser, CDJC, database, C51_4, http://ressources.memorialdelashoah.org/zoom.php?code=68570&q=id:p_201432&marginMin=0&marginMax=0&curPage=0 (accessed 7 February 2019).
283. Kurt Asser to Beate and Serge Klarsfeld, 8 July 1978.
284. Military Government of Germany, Fragebogen für Insassen der Konzentrationslager, Concentration Camp Inmates Questionnaire, 21 April 1945, 1.1.5.3, ID 5448872, ITS Digitales Archiv.
285. For detailed information on the Brätz camp, see: Elisabeth Thalhofer, *Entgrenzung der Gewalt. Gestapo-Lager in der Endphase des Dritten Reiches*, Paderborn 2010, p. 213 ff.
286. Ibid., p. 215 f.
287. Martin Weinmann (Ed.), *Das nationalsozialistische Lagersystem*, Frankfurt am Main 1990, pp. 794, 269; see also Gabriele Lotfi, *KZ der Gestapo. Arbeitserziehungslager im Dritten Reich*, Frankfurt am Main 2003, p. 279.
288. Thalhofer, *Entgrenzung der Gewalt*, p. 214.
289. Häftlings-Personalkarte Kurt Asser, o. D., 1.1.5.3, ID 5448864, ITS Digitales Archiv.
290. Military Government of Germany, Fragebogen für Insassen der Konzentrationslager, Concentration Camp Inmates Questionnaire, 21 April 1945, 1.1.5.3, ID 5448872, ITS Digitales Archiv.
291. Niemann to the BdS, Betr.: Überwachung von Judentransporten, 9 March 1943, CDJC, XXVc-217.

292. Meyer, *Besatzung in Frankreich*, 'Die Razzien in Marseille im Januar 1943', p. 115 ff.
293. Röthke to Reichsbahninspektor Wolf, 18 March 1943, CDJC, XXVc-224; Röthke to Eichmann, 18 March 1943, CDJC, XXVc-224.
294. Eichmann to Röthke, 20 March 1943, CDJC, XXVc-224.
295. Lischka in Vertretung für Röthke und Metzger an den Befehlshaber der Ordnungspolizei im Bereich des Militärbefehlshabers in Frankreich, 20 March 1943, CDJC, XXVc-224.
296. Röthke, Betreff: Weigerung der französischen Gendarmerie, beim Abtransport von Juden französischer Staatsangehörigkeit mitzuwirken, 23 March 1943, CDJC, XXc-228.
297. Ibid.; emphasis in the original.
298. Hagen, Aktenvermerk, Betr.: Weigerung der französischen Polizei, beim Abtransport von Juden französischer Staatsangehörigkeit aus dem Lager Drancy nach Deutschland mitzuwirken, 27 March 1943, CDJC, XXVc-232.
299. Röthke, Betreff: Weigerung der französischen Gendarmerie, beim Abtransport von Juden französischer Staatsangehörigkeit mitzuwirken, 23 March 1943, CDJC, XXc-228.
300. Ibid.
301. Ibid.
302. Ibid.
303. Hermann Uhlemann joined the police force as a twenty-year-old in 1925. In 1937, he became a member of the National Socialist Party and joined the SS on 15 August 1941. In 1944, he was stationed in Litzmannstadt in Wach-Batl. VIII. The Reichsführer-SS, SS-Personalhauptamt, Dienstlaufbahn. o. D., BArch (formerly BDC), SSO, Hermann Uhlemann, 25 December 1905.
304. Uhlemann, 24 March 1943, CDJC, XXVb-75.
305. Ibid.
306. Ibid.
307. Ibid.
308. Ibid.
309. Ibid.
310. Ibid.
311. Ibid.
312. Witness statement by Franz-Ludwig Daigfuss, 9 November 1971, BArch B 162/4405.
313. Ibid.
314. Ibid.
315. Klarsfeld, *Vichy-Auschwitz*, p. 524.
316. Ibid., p. 526.
317. On 23 February 1943, all police regiments were renamed SS Police Regiments by order of RFSS Himmler in recognition of their brave and successful commitment. See Stefan Klemp, *Freispruch für das 'Mord-Bataillon'. Die NS-Ordnungspolizei und die Nachkriegsjustiz*, Münster 1998, p. 64.
318. Kassel, Erfahrungsbericht über die Begleitung und Überwachung des Judentransportes am 25. 3. 1943, nach Neuburg a/Mosel, 26 March 1943, CDJC, XXVI-75.
319. Klarsfeld, *Calendrier de la persécution*, p. 784.
320. Death certificates, Ville de Châlons-sur-Marne, by l'Officier de l'Etat Civil Délégué, official copy dated 8 December 1987. Thanks to Serge Klarsfeld for information on these death certificates.
321. Ville de Châlons-sur-Marne, cemetery record, Cimietière de l'Est, March 1943. Thanks to Serge Klarsfeld for providing this document.
322. Kaufmann, *Livre de la mémoire*, p. 55 ff. If not otherwise stated, Kaufmann's memoirs form the basis of this description of the escape.
323. Hugues Steiner, 'Le témoignage de Hugues Steiner', in: Henry Bulawko (Ed.), *Les Jeux de la mort et de l'espoir. Auschwitz/Jaworzno. Auschwitz – 50 ans après*, Paris 1993, p. 174 f.
324. A comparison of the personal data in the database of the Memorial de la Shoah shows that this must have been René Ardati (born in Ain Tolba in 1906).

325. Steiner, 'Le témoignage de Hugues Steiner', p. 176.
326. Ibid., p. 176 ff.
327. Oswald Poche lived under a false name in Dannenberg until his death. See Friedrich Hoffmann, *Die Verfolgung der nationalsozialistischen Gewaltverbrechen in Hessen*, Baden-Baden 2001, p. 129.
328. Poche to the BdS, 26 March 1943, CDJC, XXVc-234.
329. Klarsfeld, *Memorial to the Jews*, p. 424.
330. Hellenbroich, CDJC, XXVc-234 B.
331. Hans-Joachim Lang, *Die Namen der Nummern. Wie es gelang, die 86 Opfer eines NS-Verbrechens zu identifizieren*, Hamburg 2004, p. 51 f.
332. In 1947, a military court in Dachau convicted Heinz Hellenbroich of murdering Allied pilots in Hesse. He was sentenced to death and executed in 1948. See Hoffmann, *Die Verfolgung*, pp. 28, 149.
333. Kaufmann, *Livre de la mémoire*, pp. 61, 92.
334. Steiner, 'Le témoignage de Hugues Steiner', p. 176 ff.
335. Röthke to the Staatspolizeileitstelle Frankfurt/Main, Betr.: Judentransporte aus Frankreich nach dem Osten, 29 March 1943, CDJC, XXVc-234.
336. Hellenbroich an den BdS, Judentransporte nach dem Osten, 7 April 1943, CDJC, XXVc-234 D.
337. Staatspolizeistelle in Frankfurt a. M. to the BdS, Judentransport aus Frankreich nach dem Osten, 23 April 1943, CDJC, XXVc-239.
338. Lang, *Namen*, p. 55.
339. Ibid., pp. 147 ff., 288; Florian Schmalz, 'Die Gaskammer im Konzentrationslager Natzweiler. Experimentenanlage der Chemiewaffenforschung und Instrument des Massenmords für den Aufbau einer anatomischen Skelettsammlung', in: Günter Morsch and Bertrand Perz (Eds), *Neue Studien zu nationalsozialistischen Massentötungen durch Giftgas*, Berlin 2011, p. 310 ff.
340. Index card, Dachau concentration camp, Paul Guerin, 1.1.6.2, ID 10081610, ITS Digitales Archiv; Archive, Dachau Concentration Camp Memorial Site, database query, 6 November 2012.
341. Index card, Dachau concentration camp, Sylvain Kaufmann, 1.1.6.2, ID 10126955, ITS Digitales Archiv; Archive, Dachau Concentration Camp Memorial Site, database query, 6 November 2012.
342. The internment form at Auschwitz concentration camp with the name Hugo Israel Steiner is printed as a facsimile in: Klarsfeld, *Memorial to the Jews*, p. 425.
343. Steiner, 'Le témoignage de Hugues Steiner', p. 183.
344. Archiv der KZ-Gedenkstätte Mauthausen, Vienna, Häftlingszugangsbuch der politischen Abteilung, Y/36; Archiv der KZ-Gedenkstätte Mauthausen, Vienna, Zugangsliste, 29. 1. 1945, E/13/9/5; Häftlings-Personal-Karte Paul Fogel, o. D., 1.1.26.3, ID 1440787, ID 14407979, ITS Digitales Archiv.
345. Index card, Robert Fogel Gusen, 1.1.26.3, ID 1440797, ITS Digitales Archiv.
346. Death certificate, Robert Fogel, 2.3.3.3, ID 78095607, ITS Digitales Archiv.
347. Klarsfeld, *Calendrier de la persécution*, p. 783.
348. Zuschneid, Stellungnahme zu den Erfahrungsberichten über die Durchführung der Judentransporte am 23. und 25. 3. 1943, 27 March 1943, CDJC, XXVI-75.
349. Urban, Bericht, 28 June 1943, CDJC, XLIX-8.
350. Ibid.
351. Henri Moschkovitch, cited in: Rajsfus, *Drancy*, p. 320.
352. Author unknown, cited in: Klarsfeld, *Calendrier de la persécution*, p. 831.
353. Urban, Bericht, 28 June 1943, CDJC, XLIX-8.
354. Ibid.
355. Röthke to the RSHA, IKL and Auschwitz concentration camp, 20 November 1943, CDJC, XLIX-31a.

356. Köhnlein, 21 November 1943, CDJC, XXVI-78.
357. Köhnlein to Röthke, Bericht über Judentransport am 20. 11. 1943, 3 December 1943, CDJC, XXVc-249.
358. Testimony, André Ullmo, CDJC, DLXI-99.
359. Author's interview with Louis Handschuh, Paris, 28 September 2008.
360. Statement by Eugène Handschuh, in: *Mit dem Mut der Verzweifelten. Jüdischer Widerstand im Zweiten Weltkrieg*, documentary film by Rena and Thomas Giefer, 2006.
361. Ibid.
362. Author's interview with Louis Handschuh, Paris, 28 September 2008.
363. Ibid.; statements by Louis and Eugène Handschuh, in: *Le tunnel de Drancy*, documentary film by Claudine Drame, 1993; A. Drucker, Temoignage de Dr. A. Drucker, CDJC, CCXVI-66.
364. [Deportation list], CDJC, CMLXXV (33)-6.
365. Etat du Personnel, CDJC, CCCLXXVI-12.
366. Georg M. Hafner and Esther Schapira, *Die Akte Alois Brunner. Warum einer der größten Naziverbrecher noch immer auf freiem Fuß ist*, Frankfurt am Main 2000, p. 137. For 'Combat', see: Steffen Prauser, 'Frankreich: Résistance gegen Kollaboration und Besatzungsmacht 1940-1944', in: Gerd R. Ueberschär (Ed.), *Handbuch zum Widerstand gegen den Nationalsozialismus und Faschismus in Europa 1933/39 bis 1945*, Berlin/New York 2011, p. 100.
367. Statement by Serge Bouder, in: *Mit dem Mut der Verzweifelten*.
368. André Ullmo, in: Durin, *Drancy 1941-1944*, p. 76; statements by Serge Bouder and Eugène Handschuh, in: *Mit dem Mut der Verzweifelten*.
369. Statement by Roger Schandalow, in: *Drancy. Dernière étape avant l'abime*, documentary film by Cécile Clairval, 2002.
370. Statement by Roger Schandalow, in: *Le tunnel de Drancy*.
371. Statement by Serge Bouder, in: *Mit dem Mut der Verzweifelten*; Aussagen Louis und Eugène Handschuh, in: *Le tunnel de Drancy*.
372. André Ullmo and Louis Handschuh, cited in: Dubessay, Nadège, Le lourd passé. La Muette, CDJC, CMLXXV(3)-6; statements by Roger Schandalow, Serge Bouder, Louis and Eugène Handschuh, in: *Le tunnel de Drancy*.
373. Witness account, André Ullmo, CDJC, DLXI-99; Le tunnel de l'espoir, Drancy bulletin municipal, Nr. 6, 1993, CDJC, CMXI-10; statement by Roger Schandalow, in: *Le tunnel de Drancy*.
374. Equipe de Tunnel, 18 July 1945, CDJC, CDLLXXII-66; see also Durin, *Drancy*, p. 76; Janet Thorpe, *Nous n'irons pas à Pitchipoï. Le tunnel du camp de Drancy*, Paris 2004, p. 154.
375. Statement, Eugène Handschuh, in: *Le tunnel de Drancy*.
376. Statement, Roger Schandalow in: ibid.
377. Witness statement by Georges Wellers during the Eichmann trial, 9 May 1961, http://www.holocaustresearchproject.org/trials/wellers.html (accessed 31 October 2017).
378. Statement, Serge Bouder, in: *Le tunnel de Drancy*.
379. Hafner and Schapira, *Die Akte Alois Brunner*, p. 141.
380. Statement, Serge Bouder, in: *Le tunnel de Drancy*.
381. The tunnel was rediscovered in August 1980 during building work.
382. Nadège Dubessay, *Le lourd passé*, La Muette, CDJC, CMLXXV(3)-6.
383. Statement by Eugène Handschuh, in: *Le tunnel de Drancy*.
384. Hafner and Schapira, *Die Akte Alois Brunner*, p. 141.
385. Statement by Serge Bouder, in: *Le tunnel de Drancy*.
386. Statement by Serge Bouder, in: *L'évasion du convoi N° 62*, in the series 'Au Rendezvous de Souvenirs' by Mariana Grey, Jacques Muller and Monette le Boucher, c. 1965. Thanks to Robert Cajgfinger for providing me with a copy of the programme.
387. Statement by Eugène Handschuh, in: *Mit dem Mut der Verzweifelten*.
388. Author's interview with Louis Handschuh, Paris, 28 September 2008.
389. Thorpe, *Pitchipoï*, p. 165 ff.

390. Author's interview with Louis Handschuh, Paris, 28 September 2008; statement by Eugène Handschuh, in: *Le tunnel de Drancy*.
391. Statement by Oscar Handschuh, in: *L'évasion du convoi N° 62*; see also Michael Estorick, 'Louis Handschuh: French Resistance Operative, Who Survived One of the Most Daring Escapes of the Second World War', in: *The Independent*, 21 December 2009; Thorpe, *Pitchipoï*, p. 170.
392. Statement by Serge Bouder, in: *L'évasion du convoi N° 62*.
393. Statement by Roger Gerschel and Charles Mager, in: *L'évasion du convoi N° 62*; Jean-Christophe Erbstein, 'Le Juste retrouvé', *Est-Republicain*, 29 November 2008.
394. Written statement, Joseph Cajfinger to the author, 29 November 2009.
395. Lucien Lazare, *Dictionnaire des Justes de France (titres décernés de 1962 à 1999)*, Jerusalem/Paris 2003, p. 521 f.
396. This is unlikely if he was found near the place where Georges Gerschel jumped, since the latter had been the first to leap from wagon 6 together with his brother. Furthermore, Félix Goldschmidt stated that he was the nineteenth 'jumper'.
397. Statement by Charles Mager, in: *L'évasion du convoi N° 62*.
398. Rapports mensuels (1941–1944), 20 December 1943, Archives départementales de la Meuse, Versement de la Direction départementale des Renseignements généraux, 209 W 3; Rapport hebdomadaire du 27 novembre 1943 (période du 20 au 27 novembre), Archives départementales de la Meuse, Versement de la Direction départementale des Renseignements généraux, 209 W 2.
399. Vered, *D'hommes*, p. 157 ff.
400. Ibid., p. 314.
401. Ibid., p. 339.
402. Ibid., p. 344 f.
403. Ibid., p. 345.
404. Ibid.
405. Abraham Weichselbaum, Story of a Jewish Hero under Nazism, Wiener Library, Testaments of the Holocaust, London, 053-EA-0911, p. 11.
406. Wellers, *Drancy*, p. 222; Bargatzky, *Hotel Majestic*, p. 127 f.; Jorge Semprun, *Die große Reise*, Stuttgart 1981, p. 139.
407. Weichselbaum, Story of a Jewish Hero under Nazism, Wiener Library, Testaments of the Holocaust, London, 053-EA-0911, p. 11.
408. Liebehenschel, Betr.: Abbeförderung der Juden aus Frankreich, 25 November 1943, CDJC, XLIX-58.
409. Susan Zuccotti, *The Holocaust, the French, and the Jews*, New York 1993, p. 197.
410. Klarsfeld, *Vichy-Auschwitz*, p. 578.
411. Jizchak Katzenelson, *Oh mein Volk! Mein Volk ... Aufzeichnungen aus dem Internierungslager Vittel*, Berlin 1999.
412. Lustiger, *Zum Kampf auf Leben und Tod!*, p. 40; Sened Yonat, Foreword, in: Katzenelson, *Oh mein Volk!*, p. 15.
413. Nathan Eck, 'The Rescue of Jews with the Aid of Passports and Citizenship Papers of Latin American States', in: *Yad Vashem Studies on the European Jewish Catastrophe and Resistance* I (1957), pp. 12–152, here p. 128.
414. 'Biographische Notizen', in: Katzenelson, *Oh mein Volk!*, p. 273; Lustiger, *Zum Kampf auf Leben und Tod!*, p. 89.
415. Cf. Katzenelson, *Oh mein Volk!*, p. 82 f.
416. 'Biographische Notizen', in: ibid., p. 272.
417. Lustiger, *Zum Kampf auf Leben und Tod!*, pp. 40, 89.
418. Interview with Paula Kaufmann, 5 May 1998, YVA O.3 2.396 (original in Hebrew; thanks to Naomi Wiener for the translation); see also Élie Barnavi and Jean Frydman, *Tableaux d'une vie. Pour servir à l'histoire de notre temps*, Paris 2008, p. 73.
419. Klarsfeld, *Memorial to the Jews*, p. 595.

420. Interview with Paula Kaufmann, 5 May 1998, YVA O.3 2.396.
421. Author's interview with Jacques Lazarus, Paris, 19 September 2008.
422. For detailed information on Henry Pohoryles, see: Testimony, 1974, CDJC, DLIX-76; Marcel Gherson, *La Sixième*, CDJC, DLXI.
423. For detailed information on Jacques Lazarus, see: Testimony, 1973, CDJC, DLXI-56; Les Anciens de la Résistance juive en France, *Organisation Juive de Combat*, p. 88.
424. For detailed information on René Kapel, see: Kapel, *Un rabbin*, p. 20 ff.
425. Author's interview with Jacques Lazarus, Paris, 19 September 2008; testimony, Jacques Lazarus, 1974, CDJC, DLXI-56.
426. Author's interview with Jacques Lazarus, Paris, 19 September 2008.
427. Ibid.
428. For detailed information on Ernest Appenzeller, see: Les Anciens de la Résistance juive en France, *Organisation Juive de Combat*, p. 44; Sarah Kaminsky, *Adolfo Kaminsky. Ein Fälscherleben*, Munich 2011, p. 66 ff.
429. For detailed information on César Chamay, see: Testimony, 1973, CDJC, DLXI-13.
430. Kapel, *Un rabbin*, p. 138.
431. Author's interview with Jacques Lazarus, Paris, 19 September 2008.
432. Alfred Fraenkel, De arrestatie van het actief in Parijs, NIOD, 614 A, doc II.
433. Interview with Paula Kaufmann, 5 May 1998, YVA O.3 2.396; Alfred Fraenkel, 'Als afgevaardige van de ondergrondse uit Holland naar Italie', in: Adina Kochba (Ed.), *Het Verzet van de nederlandse Chaloetsbeweging en de Westerweelgroep tijdens de duitse Bezetting, Manuskript*, NIOD, 614 A, doc II, Ch. 7, p. 24; 'Overzicht van gebeurtenissen', in: Kochba, *Het Verzet van de nederlandse Chaloetsbeweging en de Westerweelgroep*.
434. The Hechaluz was founded in Russia in 1917 by J. Trumpeldor as a Zionist-Socialist pioneer organization. The German national association was founded five years later. Its aim was to prepare as many young Jews as possible for emigration to Palestine. Hechaluz is the Hebrew word for pioneer. For the Hechaluz movement in the occupied Netherlands, see Benjamin Yigael, *They Were Our Friends. A Memorial for the Members of the Hachsharot and the Hehalutz Underground in Holland Murdered in the Holocaust*, Tel Aviv 1990.
435. Index card, Joachim Simon, Buchenwald concentration camp, 1.1.5.3, ID 7117350#1, ITS Digitales Archiv.
436. Menachem Pinkhof, NIOD, 296 A, doc II; Vom Ringen des holländischen Hechaluz, 1945, NIOD, 614 A, doc II; see also Haim Avni, 'The Zionist Underground in Holland and France and the Escape to Spain', in: Yisrael Gutman and Efraim Zuroff, *Rescue Attempts during the Holocaust*, Jerusalem 1977, pp. 555–90, here p. 557; Adina Kochba, 'Joachim-Yachin Simon (Shushu)', in: Mirjam Pinkhof (Ed.), *De jeugdalijah van het Paviljoen Loosdrechtsche Rade 1939–1945*, Hilversum/Verloren 1998, p. 94 ff.
437. Dan Michman, 'Zionist Youth Movements in Holland and Belgium and Their Activities during the Shoah', in: Asher Cohen and Yehoyakim Cochavi (Eds), *Zionist Youth Movements during the Shoah*, New York et al. 1995, pp. 145–71, here p. 156.
438. Yehudi Lindeman, 'All or Nothing: The Rescue Mission of Joop Westerweel', in: David Scrase, Wolfgang Mieder, and Katherine Quimby Johnson, *Making a Difference. Rescue and Assistance during the Holocaust*, Burlington 2004, pp. 241–65, here p. 241; Nathan Mageen, *Zwischen Abend und Morgenrot. Eine Geschichte aus dem niederländischen Widerstand*, Düsseldorf 2005.
439. Paul Siegel, *In ungleichem Kampf – Von Köln nach Holland durch Westerbork über Frankreich und Spanien nach Israel 1924–1947. Christlich-jüdische Hilfsaktion der Westerweel-Gruppe*, Konstanz 2001, pp. 108, 143, 167 f.; interview with Menachem Pinkhof by Haim Avni, The Hebrew University, 8 July 1961, NIOD, 296 A, doc II; Avni, 'Zionist Underground in Holland and France', p. 557.
440. Hans Ehrlich, in: Kochba, *Het Verzet van de nederlandse Chaloetsbeweging en de Westerweelgroep*, Ch. 7, p. 29 f.; Hans E., in: Jakob and van der Voort, *Anne Frank war nicht allein*, p. 169 ff.; Vom Ringen des holländischen Hechaluz, NIOD, 614 A, doc II; Lazare, *La*

résistance juive, p. 188 f.; Jacques Lazarus, *Combattants de la liberté*, Paris 1995, p. 12; testimony, Henry Pohoryles, 1974, CDJC, DLIX-76.
441. Report by von Heinz Frankl, June 1956, Wiener Library, Testaments of the Holocaust, P.III.d. No. 230, 050-EA-0673; Henry Frank (formerly Heinz Frankl), Interview Code 1842, VHA, USC Shoah Foundation Institute; report by Walter Rosenberg, April 1956, Wiener Library, Testaments of the Holocaust, P.III.d. No. 229, 050-EA-0706.
442. Kochba, *Het Verzet van de nederlandse Chaloetsbeweging en de Westerweelgroep*, Ch. 7, p. 7.
443. Author's interview with witness Frida Wattenberg, Paris, 18 November 2012.
444. Lublin, 'L'organisation juive de combat (OJC)', p. 76; interview with Paula Kaufmann, 5 May 1998, YVA O.3 2.396; Joop (Ad) Linnewiel, 'Verzet en illegale acties', in: Kochba, *Het Verzet van de nederlandse Chaloetsbeweging en de Westerweelgroep*, Ch. 7, p. 32; Latour, *La résistance juive*, p. 104 ff.; Lazare, *La résistance juive*, p. 188; Les Anciens de la Résistance juive en France, *Organisation Juive de Combat*, p. 412.
445. Testimony, Jacques Lazarus, 1974, CDJC, DLXI-56.
446. Ibid.; see also Kapel, *Un rabbin*, p. 128.
447. Interview with Paula Kaufmann, 5 May 1998, YVA O.3 2.396; Paula Kaufmann, Arrestaties en Reddingspogingen, NIOD, 614 A, doc II; Hans Ehrlich, in: Kochba, *Het Verzet van de nederlandse Chaloetsbeweging en de Westerweelgroep*; see also Yigael, *They Were Our Friends*, p. 30.
448. Avni, 'Zionist Underground in Holland and France', p. 562 ff.; *Vom Ringen des holländischen Hechaluz*, 1945, NIOD, 614 A, doc II; Chanan Hans Flörsheim, Über die Pyrenäen in die Freiheit. Von Rotenburg an der Fulda über Leipzig nach Amsterdam und durch Frankreich und Spanien nach Israel 1923–1944, Konstanz 2008, p. 68 ff.
449. Author's interview with Shaul Sagiv (formerly Paul Siegel), Yakum Kibbutz near Tel Aviv, 3 October 2009; see also Presser, *Ashes in the Wind*, p. 283.
450. Avni, 'Zionist Underground in Holland and France', p. 586; Vom Ringen des holländischen Hechaluz, NIOD, 614 A, doc II.
451. Testimony, Jacques Lazarus, 1974, CDJC, DLXI-56; testimony, César Chamay, CDJC, DLXI-13; Kapel, *Un rabbin*, p. 140; testimony, Henry Pohoryles, CDJC, CCXVIII-58.
452. Testimony, César Chamay, 4 April 1973, CDJC, DLXI-13.
453. Author's interview with Jacques Lazarus, Paris, 19 September 2008; see also Jacques Lazarus, 'Dans le dernier wagon qui quitta Drancy', in: *La terre retrouvée I* (18 September 1944).
454. Jacques Lazarus, 'Dans le dernier wagon qui quitta Drancy', in: *La terre retrouvée II* (1 November 1944).
455. Kapel, *Un rabbin*, p. 154.
456. Ibid., pp. 156, 159; see also Lazarus, 'Dans le dernier wagon' (1 November 1944); Barnavi and Frydman, *Tableaux d'une vie*, p. 72.
457. Moritz Margulies was arrested in Vienna even before the 'Anschluss' expelled him from the country. He was active in various Jewish aid committees in Brussels and Toulouse and organized the routes to the International Brigades in Spain for volunteers. In 1940, he was consecutively interned in various camps. In 1943 he was transferred to the prison in Castres, from where he broke out together with thirty-seven other prisoners on 16 September 1943. Margulies joined the FTP-MOI in Paris and was arrested in August 1944. See Jonny Granzow, *Der Ausbruch aus dem Geheimgefängnis in Castres. Eine historische Reportage*, Berlin 2012, pp. 37, 135, 145 ff, 196; DÖW Akt 20 000/M 132, MA12 Opferfürsorge Akt Moritz Margulies.
458. Kapel, *Un rabbin*, p. 156.
459. René Kapel, J'étais l'aumonier des Camps du Sud-Ouest de la France (aout 1940 décembre 1942), o. D., CDJC, DCCCVII-1; Kapel, *Un rabbin*, p. 150 f.; DÖW Akt 20 000/M 132, MA12 Opferfürsorge Akt Moritz Margulies.
460. Kapel, *Un rabbin*, p. 156; Jacques Lazarus, 'L'enfant martyr du dernier wagonde deportation', in: *L'Arche*, January 2001, p. 79.
461. Jean-François Chaigneau, *Le dernier wagon*, Paris 1981, p. 41. Jean-François Chaigneau re-

counted the story of the last wagon in a documentary novel that is problematic in terms of its sources. During his research, he spoke to survivors. The book was recommended to me by two survivors who described it as conforming to the facts, which is why I have carefully integrated it into the reconstruction.

462. Kapel, *Un rabbin*, p. 163; Lazarus, 'L'enfant', p. 79.
463. Testimony, César Chamay, 4 April 1973, CDJC, DLXI-13.
464. Zuccotti, *The Holocaust*, p. 202.
465. Röthke, Überführung von internierten Juden in Altersheime, 30 July 1943, YVA, O.9 200 (original in CDJC, XXVc-248).
466. Klarsfeld, *Memorial to the Jews*, p. 595.
467. Les Aryens de l'Hopital Rothschild an Monsieur le Commandant Allemand du Camp de Drancy, 31 August 1943, CDJC, CMLXXXVI (13)-9.
468. Testimony, César Chamay, 4 April 1973, CDJC, DLXI-13.
469. Barnavi and Frydman, *Tableaux d'une vie*, p. 73 f.; interview with Paula Kaufmann, 5 May 1998, YVA O.3 2.396; interview with Philippe Kohn, raw material for the programme 'Brennt Paris?', Cassette No. 16, Prod. Nr. 437/00276, Archiv Redaktion Zeitgeschichte im ZDF, p. 8. Thanks to Sabrina Degenhardt for providing a transcript of the interview.
470. Lazarus, 'Dans le dernier wagon' (1 November 1944); Kapel, *Un rabbin*, p. 169; testimony, César Chamay, 4 April 1973, CDJC, DLXI-13.
471. Barnavi and Frydman, *Tableaux d'une vie*, p. 74; Chaigneau, *Le dernier wagon*, p. 55.
472. Author's conversation with Philippe Kohn, Paris, 26 June 2008; interview with Philippe Kohn, raw material for the programme 'Brennt Paris?', p. 8.
473. Anat Gueta, *Ha saba'hayhwdiy bSarpat qwrwteyha sel mahteret siywniyt lwhe met (The Jewish Army, the History of the Jewish Armed Underground in France)*, Israel 2001, p. 106 f. Thanks to Anat Gueta (Tel Aviv) for translating some passages of her study into English and the inspiring conversation about this escape; interview with Alfred Fraenkel, 1962, YVA O.3 10433 (original in Hebrew; thanks to Naomi Wiener and Catalina Körner for the translation).
474. Testimony, Jacques Lazarus, 1973, CDJC, DLXI-56; Kapel, *Un rabbin*, p. 165; testimony, César Chamay, 4 April 1973, CDJC, DLXI-13.
475. Interview with Alfred Fraenkel, 1962, YVA O.3 10433.
476. Testimony, César Chamay, 4 April 1973, CDJC, DLXI-13.
477. Honig and Salomon were Polish Jews who had emigrated to Antwerp and worked in the gemstone industry there. They fled from the Nazis to the unoccupied zone and were deported from Drancy to Auschwitz on the 29th transport (for the transport list, see CDJC, online database, http://bdi.memorialdelashoah.org/internet/jsp/core/MmsGlobalSearch.jsp#) (accessed 13 April 2013). In his account, Salomon writes that he was selected for labour in Cosel and spent eight months there in terrible living and working conditions until his escape. It was well known that those unable to work were sent to their death in Auschwitz. See Adam Rayski, 'Face à l'extermination et au secret', in: Courtois and Rayski, *Qui savait quoi?* p. 200 ff.
478. Chaigneau, *Le dernier wagon*, p. 117 f.
479. Barnavi and Frydman, *Tableaux d'une vie*, p. 75; author's conversation with Philippe Kohn, Paris, 26 June 2008; interview with Philippe Kohn, raw material for the programme 'Brennt Paris?', p. 11.
480. Testimony, César Chamay, 4 April 1973, CDJC, DLXI-13.
481. Ibid.; Kapel, *Un rabbin*, p. 168; testimony, Jacques Lazarus, 1973, CDJC, DLXI-56.
482. Testimony, César Chamay, 4 April 1973, CDJC, DLXI-13.
483. Testimony, Jacques Lazarus, 1973, CDJC, DLXI-56; Lazarus, 'L'enfant', p. 79; testimony, César Chamay, 4 April 1973, CDJC, DLXI-13.
484. Lazarus, 'L'enfant', p. 74 f.
485. Kapel, *Un rabbin*, p. 162 f.; David Knout, *Contribution à l'histoire de la Résistance juive en France, 1940–1944*, Paris 1947, p. 167.
486. Author's conversation with Philippe Kohn, Paris, 26 June 2008; interview with Philippe

Kohn, raw material for the programme 'Brennt Paris?', p. 12; Samuel Kapel, *Témoignage sur des choses vues et vécues en France durant l'occupation allemande (1940–1941)*, 31 July 1974, Jerusalem, CDJC, DLXI-45.
487. Chaigneau, *Le dernier wagon*, p. 125 f.
488. This may be true: see Eugen Kogon, *Der SS-Staat. Das System der deutschen Konzentrationslager*, Reinbek 1974, p. 338.
489. Barnavi and Frydman, *Tableaux d'une vie*, p. 77 f.
490. Testimony, César Chamay, 4 April 1973, CDJC, DLXI-13.
491. Lazarus, 'Dans le dernier wagon' (1 November 1944).
492. Barnavi and Frydman, *Tableaux d'une vie*, p. 78.
493. Testimony, César Chamay, 4 April 1973, CDJC, DLXI-13; Alfred Fraenkel, De arrestatie van het actief in Parijs, NIOD, 614 A, doc II.
494. Interview with Alfred Fraenkel, 1962, YVA O.3 10433.
495. Barnavi and Frydman, *Tableaux d'une vie*, p. 78.
496. Author's conversation with Philippe Kohn, Paris, 26 June 2008; interview with Philippe Kohn, raw material for the programme 'Brennt Paris?', p. 12.
497. Interview with Philippe Kohn, raw material for the programme 'Brennt Paris?', pp. 8, 13.
498. Author's conversation with Philippe Kohn, Paris, 26 June 2008.
499. Erinnerungsbericht Henry Pohoryles, 1974, CDJC, DLIX-76.
500. Samuel Kapel, *Témoignage sur des choses vues et vécues en France durant l'occupation allemande (1940–1941)*, 31 July 1974, CDJC, DLXI-45.
501. Testimony, Jacques Lazarus, 1973, CDJC, DLXI-56; Kapel, *Un rabbin*, p. 168; testimony, Henry Pohoryles, 1974, CDJC, DLIX-76; see also Barnavi and Frydman, *Tableaux d'une vie*, p. 78.
502. Lazarus also writes that no-one slept, but that it was two in the morning and the food had been distributed among everyone. Lazarus, 'Dans le dernier wagon' (1 November 1944).
503. Barnavi and Frydman, *Tableaux d'une vie*, p. 78.
504. Testimony, Jacques Lazarus, 1973, CDJC, DLXI-56.
505. Philippe Kohn, cited in: Guido Knopp, *Die Befreiung. Kriegsende im Westen*, Berlin 2004, p. 107.
506. Interview with Paula Kaufmann, 5 May 1998, YVA O.3 2.396. In the following testimony, she does not mention the journey: Paula Kaufmann, Arrestaties en Reddingspogingen, NIOD, 614 A, doc II.
507. Alfred Fraenkel, De arrestatie van het actief in Parijs, NIOD, 614 A, doc II.
508. Kapel, *Un rabbin*, p. 170.
509. Ibid., p. 171.
510. Ibid., p. 171 f.
511. Ibid., p. 150 f.; KPÖ confirmation, DÖW Akt 20 000/M 132, MA12 Opferfürsorge Akte Moritz Margulies; see also Granzow, *Der Ausbruch*, p. 196.
512. 'C'etait il y a vingt-huit ans! 19 patriotes s'échappaient d'un train de la mort près de Morcourt et participèrent, 10 jours plus tard, à la libération de notre ville', 26 August 1972, L'Aisne Nouvelle, CDJC, DLXI-11a; M. Lucien Lebeau, ancien instituteur à Morcourt raconte comment il a caché dans son école quelques-uns des évadés du 'train de la mort', 9 September 1972, L'Aisne Nouvelle, CDJC, DLXI-26a; see also testimony, Henry Pohoryles, 1974, CDJC, DLIX-76; Fondation pour la Mémoire de la Déportation, *Livre-mémorial des déportés de France arrêtés par mesure de répression et dans certains cas par mesure de persécution 1940–1945*, Vol. 3, Paris 2004, pp. 589, 592 f.; interview with Philippe Kohn, raw material for the programme 'Brennt Paris?', p. 13 f.
513. Interview with Paula Kaufmann, 5 May 1998, YVA O.3 2.396.
514. Armand Kohn, cited in: Günther Schwarberg, *Der SS-Arzt und die Kinder. Bericht über den Mord vom Bullenhuser Damm*, Göttingen 1989, p. 10.
515. Häftlings-Personal-Karte Armand Kohn, KL Weimar-Buchenwald, 1.1.5.3, ID 6305310, ITS Digitales Archiv.

516. Arbeitseinsatzkarteikarte Armand Kohn, 1.1.5.3, ID 6305312, ITS Digitales Archiv. Thanks to Sabine Stein, Archiv Stiftung Gedenkstätten Buchenwald und Mittelbau-Dora, for helpful support in interpreting notes on the document.
517. Interview with Philippe Kohn, raw material for the programme 'Brennt Paris?', p. 15; see also Schwarberg, *SS-Arzt*, p. 57 ff.; Fritz Bringmann, *Kindermord am Bullenhuserdamm. SS-Verbrechen in Hamburg 1945: Menschenversuche an Kindern*, Frankfurt am Main 1978.
518. Author's conversation with Philippe Kohn, Paris, 26 June 2008.
519. Häftlings-Personal-Karte Max Windmüller, KL Weimar-Buchenwald, 1.1.5.3, ID 7421603, ITS Digitales Archiv; 'Overzicht van gebeurtenissen', in: Kochba, *Het Verzet van de nederlandse Chaloetsbeweging en de Westerweelgroep*.
520. Häftlings-Personal-Karte Alfred Fraenkel, KL Weimar-Buchenwald, 1.1.5.3, ID 5880197, ITS Digitales Archiv; Alfred Fraenkel, Interview Code 17589, VHA, USC Shoah Foundation Institute.
521. Frauenkarteikarte Pauline Kaufmann, KZ Buchenwald, 1.1.5.4, ID 7610307, ITS Digitales Archiv.
522. Paula Kaufmann, Arrestaties en Reddingspogingen, NIOD, 614 A, doc II.
523. Interview with Paula Kaufmann, 5 May 1998, YVA O.3 2.396.
524. Karteikarte Arbeitseinsatz Pauline Kaufmann, 1.1.5.4, ID 14999/0002, ITS Digitales Archiv. Thanks to Sabine Stein, Archiv Stiftung Gedenkstätten Buchenwald und Mittelbau-Dora, for helpful support in interpreting the notes on the document; see also Irmgard Seidel, 'Jüdische Frauen in den Außenkommandos des KZ Buchenwald', in: Gisela Bock (Ed.), *Genozid und Geschlecht*, Frankfurt am Main/New York 2005, pp. 149–68, here p. 160.
525. Seidel, 'Jüdische Frauen', p. 160.
526. Interview with Paula Kaufmann, 5 May 1998, YVA O.3 2.396; Chawah Frenkel-Bihan, 'In Theresienstadt', in: Kochba, *Het Verzet van de nederlandse Chaloetsbeweging en de Westerweelgroep*, p. 257; written enquiry to the Theresienstadt/Terezin Memorial Site, 11 December 2011.
527. Häftlingspersonalkarte Ernst Hirsch, 1.1.5.3, ID 00091420/002; ITS Digitales Archiv.
528. Karteikarte Arbeitseinsatz Ernst Hirsch, KZ Buchenwald, 1.1.5.3, ID 00091420/003, ITS Digitales Archiv.
529. Karteikarte Krankenrevier Ernst Hirsch, KZ Buchenwald,1.1.5.3, ID 00091420/0011, ITS Digitales Archiv.
530. Karteikarte Krankenrevier Kurt Reilinger, KZ Mittelbau-Dora, 1.1.5.3, ID 00040310/0003, ITS Digitales Archiv; Postkontrollkarte Kurt Reilinger, KZ Mittelbau-Dora, 1.1.5.3, ID 00040310/0002, ITS Digitales Archiv.
531. Siegel, *In ungleichem Kampf*, p. 213.
532. Meta Lande, NIOD, 614 A, doc II.
533. Lazarus, 'L'enfant', p. 79; Kapel, *Un rabbin*, pp. 156, 159.
534. Author's interview with Jacques Lazarus, Paris, 19 September 2008.
535. Testimony, Jacques Lazarus, 1973, CDJC, DLXI-56.
536. Cf. Lazarus, 'Dans le dernier wagon' (18 September 1944).
537. César Chamay, 'Avec les survivants de l'OJC évadés du dernier train de déportation', in: *La terre retrouvée*, No. 2 (1954).
538. Lazarus, *Combattants de la liberté*; testimony, Henry Pohoryles, 1974, CDJC, DLIX-76.
539. Kapel, *Un rabbin*, p. 169 f.
540. Ibid., p. 79.
541. Interview with Alfred Fraenkel, 1962, YVA O.3 10433.
542. Chaigneau, *Le dernier wagon*, p. 175.
543. Kaminsky, *Adolfo Kaminsky*, p. 68.
544. Gueta, *The Jewish Army*, p. 106 f.
545. Lucien Rubel to Forces Francaises de l'interieur, Région 'Ile-de-France', 20 October 1944, CDJC, CDLXXVI-6; Organisation Juive de Combat, Proposition de Citation, 6 November 1944, CDJC, XI-31.

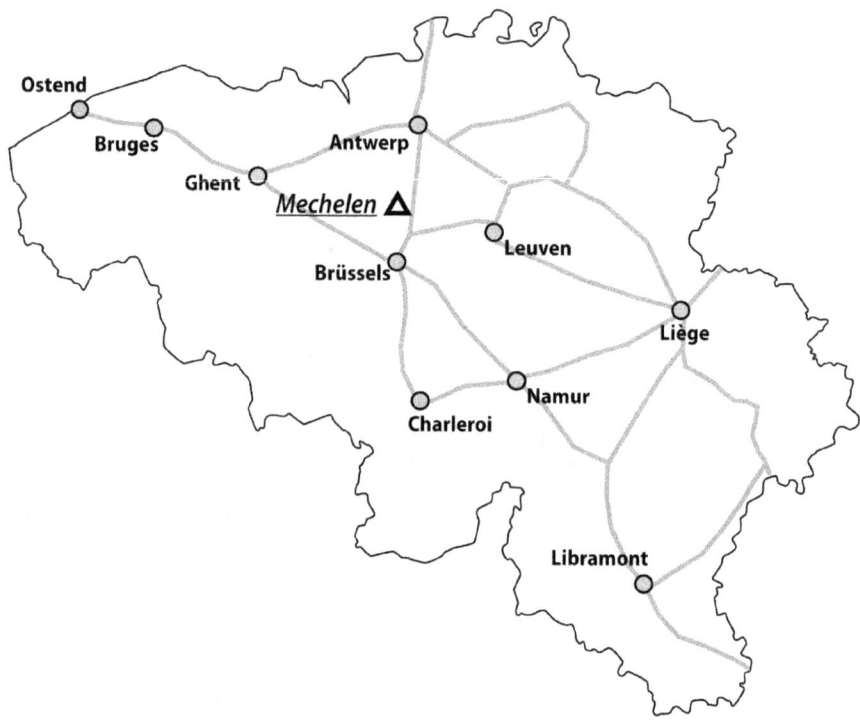

Railway Lines in Belgium

CHAPTER 3

Escapes by Jews from Deportation Trains in Belgium

The Initial Situation in Belgium
Before the Wehrmacht's Invasion

When Belgium became independent from the Netherlands in 1830, around one thousand Jews lived there. Due to the Antwerp seaport, Belgium became a transit country for many emigrating people in the following decades as they migrated overseas.

Between 1873 and 1935, almost three million people, including half a million Jews, left Europe from Antwerp's port to travel on the ships of the 'Red Star Line', which began operating in 1873, to migrate to the USA and Canada. Often, however, the emigration failed due to a lack of funds or entry papers, leaving many of those who wanted to emigrate overseas stranded in Belgium. From 1881 onwards, many of the Jews wanting to emigrate had fled from the pogroms in Eastern Europe. In 1880, only 4,284 Jews lived in Belgium, but by 1900 the number had increased to 17,250. By 1910, that figure had again almost doubled to 31,800.[1] In the 1920s, after the rebirth of the state of Poland and the associated increase in anti-Semitic persecutions, the number of Jewish migrants again increased significantly.

There were many organizations and parties in which the Eastern European Jews organized themselves. Most had a Socialist or Communist character, such as the Joodse arbeiders sportklub (JASK), Ainheit, Jeune Garde Socialiste Unifiée (JCSU), Rode Valken, Poale Zion, Bund and the Hashomer Hatzaïr,[2] to name just a few.

In the 1930s, Jewish refugees came to Belgium from Germany and Austria.[3] According to estimates, the figure was around ten thousand between January 1933 and February 1938. After the annexation of Austria in March and the pogrom of November 1938, a further thirty thousand Jews are reported to have fled to Belgium, of whom some, however, moved on to other countries or returned to their countries of origin when the situation there appearaed to have de-escalated.[4] In October 1938, the Belgian government established several camps for German Jewish refugees. One of its aims was to prevent anti-Semitic resentment from building among the Belgian population.[5]

At the time of the German invasion in 1940, around seventy-five thousand Jews lived in Belgium, which had a total population of eight million.[6] Only around 5 per cent of them had Belgian citizenship. Most of the Jews who had immigrated to Belgium originally came from Poland, the second largest group being from Germany.

As in the rest of Europe, Fascist movements gained strength in Belgium during the 1930s. In 1932, the anti-Semitic Vlaamsch Nationaal Verbond (VNV) formed in Flanders under the leadership of Staf de Clercq.[7] In Wallonia, Léon Degrelle founded the Fascist party Rex in 1935, which immediately won 12 per cent of the votes in the elections in 1936. During parliamentary elections in April 1939, only 2.4 per cent voted for the Rex party, while the VNV won 10.3 per cent of the votes.[8] The anti-Semitic group Volksverwering ('People's Defence'), which was founded in Antwerp, had existed since 1937 and would play a key role in the persecution of Jews in the following years.

Anti-Jewish Policy until the Start of Deportations in August 1942

On 10 May 1940, the German Wehrmacht invaded neutral Belgium. After eighteen days, the Belgian army capitulated on the orders of King Leopold III. Against the will of the government, which went into exile, Leopold III remained in the country and allowed himself to become a prisoner of war.[9] The invasion revived memories of the atrocities committed by German soldiers during their occupation in World War I and encouraged a strong anti-German attitude among much of the Belgian population.[10] As a result of the invasion, around ten thousand Jews fled from Belgium to France, but most returned after a short time as they could make little progress on the congested roads as a result of the outbreak of war. Furthermore, the Wehrmacht overtook them and was very willing to help the refugees to return.

The Belgian authorities arrested more than ten thousand German migrants without legal basis, including many Jews and political opponents of National Socialism, whom they suspected of being members of a 'fifth column'. Based on an agreement between the Belgian and French authorities, they were taken to the internment camps that already existed in southern France.[11]

The Germans established a Military Command under the Infantry General Alexander von Falkenhausen. The territory under his administration contained Belgium and also the two northern French Departments of Nord and Pas-de-Calais. The formerly German regions of Malmedy and Eupen, which had been ceded to Belgium under the terms of the Versailles Treaty, were annexed.

The Military Commander of Belgium and Northern France (Militärbefehlshaber von Belgien und Nordfrankreich, MBB), von Falkenhausen, and the Head of the Military Administration (Militärverwaltungschef), Eggert Reeder, who was responsible for civilian affairs, consolidated their power by preventing the establishment of a civilian administration and the deployment of a Higher SS and Police Officer (Höherer SS- und Polizeiführer, HSSPF) in Belgium. Above all, Reeder resolutely defended Himmler's attempts to expand the influence of the SS in occupied Belgium by deploying an HSSPF there.[12] Instead, the Commander of the Sicherheitspolizei and SD (BdS) stationed in Brussels reported to the MBB and the Head of the Military Administration.[13]

Initially, Max Thomas was appointed BdS in Brussels, before being replaced after only a few months by Constantin Canaris, who in turn made way for Ernst Ehlers in November 1941.[14] The position of a Judenreferent (offier for Jewish affairs) was created, who received official orders from Department IV B 4 of the RSHA. There were five consecutive Judenreferenten in Belgium: Viktor Humpert, Kurt Asche, Fritz Erdmann, Fritz Weidmann and Werner Borchardt.[15] The cooperation between the Military Commander of Belgium and Northern France and the BdS was characterized by few conflicts. The internment of political opponents and other declared enemies was the responsibility of the Military Commander of Belgium and Northern France.[16] He also issued the eighteen anti-Jewish laws and introduced the registration and deportation of Jews.[17]

After the occupation of Belgium, the German Embassy in Brussels was converted into a branch of the Foreign Office under Werner von Bargen. Compared to his colleagues Abetz in France and Bene in the Netherlands, von Bargen remained more in the role of an observer and reporter for his superior department in the Foreign Office.[18] Nevertheless, he supported the anti-Jewish policy of the MBB and the Sipo-SD, for instance proposing measures to identify and quantify Jews in Belgium. He cooperated in the search for ways of extending deportations to include Jews with Belgian citizenship and participated in the strategic planning of deportations.[19]

When the German occupiers arrived, the Jewish population in Belgium was confronted with anti-Jewish measures within a very short time: they were defined as a group in accordance with Nazi race ideology, segregated and expropriated. On 28 October 1940, the MBB ordered that all Jews aged fourteen and above had to be entered on a register at their place of residence.[20] Fifty-six thousand Jews complied with this demand.[21] Jews were also forbidden to work in specific professions. On 29 July 1941, Gerard Romsée (of the VNV), who had been named Belgian Minister of the Interior and of Public Health in April the same year, followed the demands of the occupiers and ordered that all Jews should have 'Jood-Juif' stamped on their ID papers.[22] From 29 August 1941, Jews were only permitted to live in the cities of Brussels, Antwerp, Liege and Charleroi. This measure was an attempt to socially isolate the Jewish population and concentrate them over a smaller area. On 25 November 1941, the MBB ordered the compulsory merger of all Jews in Belgium. This created the Association des Juifs en Belgique/Jodenvereeniging in België (AJB/JVB), which was occasionally described as the Judenrat.[23]

In the spring of 1942, all Jews and almost all companies owned by Jews were expropriated. The regional committees of the AJB/JVB had to list all Jewish families between March and May 1942, meaning that children were also recorded.[24] On 1 June 1942, a curfew from 20:00 to 07:00 was decreed. During those hours, all Jews were required to remain at the address entered in the Jewish register as their home. The identification, expropriation and isolation of Jews in Belgium was thereby completed.

On 15 June 1942, Reeder pointed out that the RSHA could begin the deportation of Jews in Belgium: 'With the above-stated measures, the *legislation on Jews* in Belgium can be regarded as *concluded*. The Jews now only have extremely limited livelihoods. The next step is their evacuation from Belgium'.[25]

The Forced Labour Camp of the Organisation Todt in Northern France

With the MBB's forced labour order for Jews on 6 March 1942, it was arranged that Jews would be 'deployed in a useful way for work that was important for the war' until their deportation.[26] On 13 June, 2,252 Jews were transferred to northern France as forced labourers for the OT.[27] The assignment orders were mainly for Jewish men from Antwerp, Liege and the surrounding region, since the police stations in these areas collaborated more than elsewhere.[28] In France, they were put into guarded groups and deployed to build the Atlantic Wall. They were accommodated in special youth camps.[29] Most of those forced into labour were sent to the Dannes-Camiers camp complex, while others were distributed in camps in the coastal region of Boulogne.[30] There were a total of twelve such OT camps in northern France. The OT had contracted various companies to build the Atlantic Wall, including H. Micka from the Saar, the Essen company Julius Berger, and the Euskirchen company Albert Jung. Guarded by their foremen, the Jewish forced labourers often had to work for fourteen hours a day in harsh conditions.[31] Both the accommodation and the food were very poor and there were reports of mistreatment leading to death and death by malnutrition.[32] A total of 196 Jewish forced labourers fled from these camps.[33]

On 15 September 1942, it was decided to deport the Jewish OT forced labourers to the East.[34] The Head of the Military Administration, Reeder, personally noted that they should be 'transported with their families'.[35]

The Persecution of Belgian Jews from 1943 Onwards

The Belgian Jews had originally been exempt from deportations, but there had long been signs that this would change. Unterstaatssekretär Luther, who had participated in the Wannsee Conference for the Foreign Office in Berlin, used the following anti-Semitic argument to state that from his perspective it was essential that Belgian Jews were also deported quickly:

> If today the remaining Jews in Belgium disobey the orders of the Military Commander, and even attempt by all means to veil their Jewish character and thereby hide away in corners that are difficult to cleanse, and if already initiatives by these Jews have been discovered to participate in active resistance against the occupying force, then forceful action should be taken to prevent the further spread of this source of danger.[36]

As early as 5 January 1943, von Bargen from the branch of the Foreign Office in Brussels informed the Foreign Office in Berlin that he had followed orders from Berlin and spoken to the MBB, the Head of the Military Administration and the Commander of the Sicherheitspolizei concerning the transportation of Belgian Jews. The result was that as soon as the deportations, which had been interrupted due to a lack of wagons, began again, Belgian Jews could forthwith be deported as well.[37] The hunt for Belgian Jews in Antwerp and Brussels began on the night of 3/4 September 1943 and was known as 'Aktion Iltis' ('Operation Polecat'). This 'major operation' also included the Devisenschutzkommando ('Currency Protection Squad'), which had already noted wealthy Jews in special lists.[38] The Devisenschutzkommando had the primary task of seeking money, gold and other valuables privately owned by Jews and making them useful for the German war economy.[39] It had far-reaching executive powers, including the power to arrest people. On 20 September 1943, Transport 22 B from the Mechelen transit camp was the first train to also deport a large number of Belgian Jews.

Collaboration

As the highest government officials, the remaining General Secretaries in Belgium were authorized to carry out the official duties of their superiors, who had gone into exile. In October 1940, the German occupiers tried to force the heads of department in the Belgian government to pass anti-Jewish laws in accordance with German law. They refused, however, referring to adherence to the Hague Conventions and existing Belgian law.[40] Thus, the occupying authority began to publish anti-Jewish regulations that did not have the status of law, but were nevertheless binding and were implemented by the Belgian administration. Although the Belgian administration was unwilling to pass anti-Jewish measures itself, it cooperated by enforcing these decrees. This passive collaboration ('collaboration passive') was regarded as legal.[41]

In addition to the state level, the Walloon Rexists and the Flemish VNV, which had around fifty thousand members in 1941, also collaborated. The VNV was the most important collaboration movement in Flanders, although there were tensions with the National Socialists because the VNV strived for an independent Flanders or a Flanders that was part of the Netherlands within a 'greater Netherlands' nation.[42] The German occupiers did not approve of this, as they regarded Flanders in the long term as an integral part of the 'Greater Germanic Reich'.[43]

In 1941, to counteract these separatist ambitions, the occupiers took over the German Flemish cultural association Kulturvereinigung Duitsch-Vlaamsche Arbeidsgemeenschap (DeVlag), which immediately campaigned for Flanders to join the German Reich.[44] Furthermore, two SS volunteer groups were established: the Wallonische Waffen-SS and the Allgemeine SS-Flandern. Members were canvassed with slogans of fighting together against Bolshevism. The Allgemeine SS-Flandern was founded in September 1940 and was actively involved with the persecution of Jews from the outset in Antwerp.[45] The membership of the Allgemeine SS-Flandern fluctuated between 1,800 and 3,200 volunteers.[46] In 1942, the Allgemeine SS-Flandern was renamed Germanische SS-Flandern. A year later, DeVlag was integrated into the Germanische SS-Flandern.[47]

As the historian Lieven Saerens has shown, the willingness to collaborate was especially high in Antwerp.[48] On 14 April 1941, a screening of the film *Der ewige Jude* in the city led to an anti-Semitic pogrom. The Jewish quarter was ransacked and plundered by two to four hundred members of the Volksverwering, the VNV militia known as the 'Schwarze

Brigade' and the Flemish SS, who were armed with clubs and iron bars. Two synagogues were set alight.[49]

After Alfred Thomas, the Head of Sipo-SD Department II in Brussels, failed to establish a 'General Commissariat for Jewish Affairs' ('Generalkommissariat für Judenfragen'), like its counterpart in France, a national anti-Jewish centre for Flanders and Wallonia was established together with the Volksverwering. Its full-time leader, Pierre Beeckmans, received his income from the German occupiers. The centre produced the 'Judenkartei' ('Register of Jews'), and used 'race classification studies' ('rassekundliche Untersuchungen') to decide on applications from people wanting to prove that they were not Jews. It ran its own search units that monitored the implication of and adherence to anti-Jewish measures.[50]

The Resistance Becomes Organized

The Belgian public initially accepted the occupiers' anti-Jewish measures without much protest. This changed in June 1942 with the introduction of the yellow star to denote Jews.[51] Not only did the general public resist this order, but the mayors of the nineteen Brussels districts also refused 'to participate in an order that so openly undermines the dignity of all people, whoever they may be'.[52] Until the introduction of the yellow star, anti-Jewish measures had been implemented without resistance by the City of Brussels. The historian Nico Wouters explains why this order was nevertheless resisted. In addition to the moral rejection of this stigmatizing measure, Wouters argues that there may have been legal provisos and a fear that issuing the yellow star would lead to an administrative overload since the Belgian municipalities were required to organize their sale themselves.[53] Furthermore, Wouters stresses that resistance to this law occurred at a time when the position of the German occupying force was no longer as powerful as in 1940, due to the progress of the war. The historian Maxime Steinberg points out that the mayors' solidarity with the Belgian Jews was based on the patriotic argument that 'a large number of Jews are Belgians'.[54] This in turn represents a lack of solidarity with Jews with other citizenships. The broad-based protests among large parts of the population against the requirement for Jews to identify themselves is regarded as the turning point in the mobilization of resistance in Belgium. Many underground journals appealed for solidarity with the persecuted Jews. The willingness to help within the non-Jewish population grew.

Before the German invasion, Jews and non-Jews had worked together in various left-wing groups. The left-wing parties and groups in Belgium had many Jewish members. Thus, many Belgian left-wing activists helped their Jewish comrades during the persecution, as can be seen below in the case of Claire Prowizur. The Communist Party of Belgium (PCB), which had been loyal to Moscow and was then paralysed by the Hitler-Stalin pact, began its active resistance to the German occupiers after the Reich's invasion of the Soviet Union.[55] In 1941, it initiated the foundation of the Front d'Indépendance/Onafhankelijkheidsfront.[56] This association of groups from different political persuasions became the Resistance organization with the largest membership, including the three major parties – the Catholic Christian Democrats, the Social Democrats and the Liberals – and the Communists. The total political spectrum of the Resistance organizations ranged from the right-wing conservative Belgian Legion (later the Armée Secrète/Geheim Leger) to the Communist resistance.[57] It is evident that there was greater Resistance activity in the francophone part of Belgium than in the Flemish part. This is shown by the far higher number of French-language underground journals, as well as the significantly diverging number of those who protected Jews from being captured by the Germans. They mainly came from the Walloon part of the country and the region surrounding Brussels.[58] By contrast, the number is particularly small in Antwerp and its environs.[59]

Yiddish-language underground newspapers were published by the social-democratic Bund and the left-wing workers' party Poale Zion,[60] whose publication *Unzer Wort* was produced a total of twenty-eight times between December 1941 and August 1944. As in France, the Main-d'œuvre immigrée (MOI) also existed in Belgium and was a type of 'Vorfeldorganisation' (party-affiliated organization) for foreign members of the Communist Party and was also organized into language groups in Belgium. Three groups were active in Brussels: one Yiddish, one Hungarian and one Russian-speaking unit. Most members of the MOI were Jewish, although they did not regard themselves as Jewish Resistance organizations but rather as a Communist group.[61] In the spring of 1942, the non-Jewish Political Secretary of the MOI, the Bulgarian-born Théodore Angheloff, formed the Mobile Corps of the Partisans from twenty-four members of these three groups.[62] Half of its members had fought in the Spanish Civil War. The group's operations included attacks on the Judenrat.

Conflicts between Resistance Groups and the Judenrat

According to its own assessment, the AJB/JVB, or the so-called Judenrat, pursued a policy of cooperation with the Germans in the hope of lessening the special hardship of Jews through skilful negotiation. The conflict with Resistance groups escalated, however, as they increasingly regarded the AJB/JVB as an establishment of Belgian-Jewish collaborators who were willing to deliver Jews without Belgian citizenship to the Germans in the hope of saving their own skins.[63] In an article in *Unzer Wort* on 10 May 1942, the second anniversary of the invasion of Belgium, the members of the Judenrat were rebuked as lackeys of the National Socialists, who in the hands of the Nazis had become hammers against the Jewish workers and masses.[64]

On 25 July 1942, four MOI members burst into the office of the AJB/JVB, which had only been established a few days earlier on Brussels' Boulevard du Midi. They set alight a register that the AJB/JVB had produced on the orders of the Judenreferent Kurt Asche, containing the names of all members of Jewish organizations. The attackers were unaware that it was a copy.[65] They justified the action with the argument that the AJB/JVB was aiding mass deportations to Poland by producing the register.[66]

The second armed attack by the MOI against the Judenrat was directed at Robert Holzinger, the functionary who sent out the deportation assignments. On 29 August 1942, three Jewish MOI partisans shot Holzinger dead on the streets of Brussels. In its September 1942 edition, the Communist underground newspaper *Le Drapeau Rouge* published its title story, 'Fight the Anti-Semitic Executioners and Attack Their Accomplices'.[67] The article stated that Holzinger, the Head of the Judenrat, did not hesitate to cooperate with the occupiers and hand over his fellow Jewish citizens. Now he had paid for his treachery. As a result, the Gestapo closed the now useless office. According to Maxime Steinberg and Laurence Schram, the assassination of Robert Holzinger put an end once and for all to the orderly procedure of the deportations that had begun three weeks earlier.[68]

Resistance after the Onset of Deportations in August 1942

On 4 August 1942, the first deportation train departed from Belgium in Mechelen. The Jews were told they were being sent to a labour assignment in the East. Initially, many Jews followed the orders to assemble for the labour assignment, but this changed within a few weeks. Raids and arrest operations were carried out, as a large number of people did not follow the orders to assemble and left their homes to avoid being captured. Many could rely on support from non-Jewish Belgians as they went into hiding, although they did not all have a positive attitude towards Jews.[69] For instance, 20 per cent of articles in the non-Jewish underground press contained disparaging remarks about Jews. The anti-Jewish measures were commented on very rarely by such sources, as were the deportations.[70] However, according to Saerens, many Belgians lay aside their anti-Jewish prejudice in the struggle against the common enemy, the German occupiers.[71]

Many Jews were active in the Resistance, in which the Comité de défense des Juifs (CDJ) played a leading role. It was founded in the summer of 1942 by members of the left-wing Zionist Poale Zion movement, who worked both with various political camps within the Jewish population and with non-Jewish Resistance groups, and organized themselves in the Front d'Indépendance.[72]

The CDJ provided adults with money, work, false papers, hideouts and clothing and attempted to smuggle them to Switzerland or England. Hiding places were organized for children and ID papers and Christening certificates were forged. Forty per cent of all Jews in Belgium at the time of the German invasion managed to survive in hiding, which is a high quota compared to the Netherlands.[73] The CDJ also published two newspapers, the French-language *Le Flambeau* and the Flemish *De Vrije Gedachte*.[74]

The Communist Resistance organization Travail allemand (TA) was founded by the underground structures of the exiled German, Austrian and Czech Communist parties, and existed in Belgium and France. It consisted of German-speaking Nazi opponents, including many Jewish refugees, with the aim of demoralizing the occupying forces in a variety of ways. For instance, young Austrian women risked their lives to come into contact with occupying soldiers to slip them the underground newspaper *Die Wahrheit* written by Hans Mayer (later: Jean Améry) and Marianne Bradt, and try to persuade them to desert.[75]

Jewish resistance in Belgium was relatively successful, mainly due to two extremely successful alliances: the CDJ, in which Jews from the entire social spectrum were organized, and the Front d'Indépendance, which united groups from different political camps under a single umbrella organization from 1941 onwards and was part of the CDJ. The high level of organization and the consolidated cooperation between politically heterogeneous camps made the Belgian Resistance relatively effective.

In July 1944, the last deportation train from Belgium departed for Auschwitz. The same month, the Military Administration was replaced by a Civilian Administration, as the Belgian territory was to be annexed by the German Reich as part of the 'Reichsgau Flandern' and the 'Reichsgau Wallonien'.[76] In September 1944, Allied troops liberated Belgium.

Deportations from Belgium

Summary of Deportations

The starting point for deportations from Belgium was the Mechelen transit camp. From there, a total of twenty-three trains transported 25,835 Jews to Auschwitz and a separate train transported 351 Roma, of whom fifteen survived Auschwitz.[77] Jews from the two northern French Departments under the jurisdiction of the MBB in Belgium were also deported to the East via Mechelen. In late December 1943, one transport took 132 women and men to the Ravensbrück and Buchenwald concentration camps.[78] In early 1944, forty-three Jewish prisoners were taken in two waves to Bergen-Belsen, presumably as prisoners in one of Himmler's putative exchanges of hostages with which Germans in enemy countries could be released. In fact, only very few such hostages were actually exchanged.

Sixty-three per cent of Jewish deportees were directly murdered in the gas chambers of Auschwitz. More than 95 per cent of all deportees did not survive.[79] Among the survivors, the group of Jews with Belgian nationality has a higher survival rate (two thirds) than the group of foreign or stateless Jews (around half). Overall, 45 per cent of all Jews in Belgium were deported.[80]

The Mechelen Transit Camp

The central transit camp for Jews was in the city of Mechelen (French: Malines), which is situated between Brussels and Antwerp, around 150 km by train from the border with the German Reich. The camp was established in the former Dossin barracks. On 15 July 1942, the Deputy Head of the Military Administration, Harry von Craushaar, instructed SS Sturmbannführer Philipp Schmitt, Camp Commander of the prison camp in Fort Breendonk,[81] operated by Sipo, to 'initiate the establishment of a transit camp in Mechelen for the Jewish labour assignments'.[82] On 9 March 1943, Philipp Schmitt was replaced as the Camp Commander by SS Sturmführer Gerhard Johannes Frank, a police Kriminalsekretär.[83] The Deputy Camp Commander was the extremely violent Max Boden, who had worked as a policeman in the BdS Judenabteilung since 1940 and was transferred to Mechelen in the summer of 1942.[84] The camp was under the jurisdiction of the BdS Judenreferat, which organized its operation and also guarded it from 1942 onwards. The responsible guards were provided by a separate BdS company, mainly consisting of Flemish SS men who were commanded by German SS officers.[85]

On 22 July 1942, the first labour orders were handed to the Judenrat, who were coerced into forwarding them with passive threats and false promises.[86] The labour orders included the items of provision that the Jews were required to take with them to the Mechelen camp, including: non-perishable food for fourteen days, a pair of working boots, one set of working clothes, an eating bowl, a drinking mug, a spoon, food and clothing cards and all ID papers.[87] On arrival at the camp, all Jews were registered by the reception office in different registers. Everyone received a cardboard sign that had to be worn visibly around the neck, on which was written their consecutive number, the number of the next transport and a letter denoting their status: an 'A' stood for 'Ausländer' ('foreigner'), a 'B' for Belgian, a 'Z' for 'Zigeuner' ('gipsy') and an 'E' for 'Entscheidungsfall' ('decision case') if the authorities had to check whether the person was a Jew according to National Socialist definition. Prisoners classified 'B' or 'E' were initially exempt from deportation.

Once a thousand numbers had been allocated, enough to fill a deportation train, the next new arrivals were given the next transport number and consecutive numbering began again from the beginning. All camp prisoners were recorded by name in a register. Once a transport was full, this register would be used to produce an alphabetical transport list.[88]

On entering the camp, which many survivors described as being very brutal and degrading, the prisoners were first stripped of their last valuables, papers and keys to their homes.[89] Their apartments were subsequently plundered by the 'Brüsseler Treuhandgesellschaft', which belonged to the Military Administration ('Möbelaktion').[90] The former camp internee Eva Fastag, who was forced to work in the reception office from the beginning, stated that scissors, knives, files and similar objects had to be handed over on arrival.[91] This practice was confirmed by Benita Hirschfeld, who later worked in parcel checking, where she was required to remove knives and other objects from parcels addressed to prisoners.[92] The parcels had already been checked, as the former Camp Commander Gerhard Johannes Frank stated: 'These parcels had to be handed to the Judenvereinigung in Brussels, which was required to check them for weapons and dangerous tools'.[93] This is relevant in connection with escapes from deportation trains, as a large number of prisoners attempted to acquire tools or knives before boarding the wagons to work on the walls, ceilings and floors.

When the Mechelen camp went into operation, the prisoners initially had to sleep on wooden floorboards covered with straw. Bunkbeds were built later.[94] Craftsmen, tailors and hairdressers worked in the camp[95] and workshops were set up where prisoners were forced to make boots, uniforms and other items for the Wehrmacht and the camp's SS guards.[96] The hygiene conditions and food supplies were very poor. In 1946, when the former Camp Commander Frank was in custody in Zwolle, he stated: 'when I arrived at the camp, I discovered that the internees were suffering inhumane torment'.[97] Frank described the long working day in the workshops from 7:00 to 21:00, insufficient and poor food, as well as cruel punishments. His predecessor Schmitt and Karl Meinshausen, who had become notorious through his violence, had forced prisoners who were not used in the workshops, including children, to exercise and march, often for hours, driving them to exhaustion. Sometimes prisoners were woken up at night and had to march in the yard of the former barracks for hours.[98] After the war, a large number of witnesses accused the Deputy Camp Commander Max Boden of serious crimes. He is reported to have enriched himself, sexually assaulted Jewish women during body searches and tortured prisoners.[99]

Deportation Procedure

The deportation of Jews from the Mechelen transit camp began on 4 August 1942. Initially, only prisoners who had been on Belgian territory when captured and did not have Belgian citizenship were deported. Around two thirds of all Jews transported from Belgium were deported in the following three months.[100] Between 4 August and 31 October 1942, fourteen deportation trains departed from Mechelen, transporting a total of 16,882 prisoners (in three cases – the 12th/13th, the 14th/15th and the 16th/17th transports – two transports were merged into one deportation train, so there were seventeen transports in a total of fourteen trains).[101]

The AJB/JVB called for cooperation: 'According to the assurance given to us by the authority, this is merely a labour assignment and not a deportation measure'.[102] However, only about 4,023 people heeded the at least twelve thousand labour assignment orders.[103] In 1968, Deputy Camp Commander Boden stated the following as a witness: 'It was the case that already after the second or third transport, the Jews no longer came voluntarily. At the time, they must have sensed what they were heading for. That is when the arrests of Jews really began'.[104] The announcement by the AJB/JVB led to a great loss of trust within the Jewish community: in Jewish Resistance circles, the 'Judenrat' was renamed the 'Judenverrat' ('Betrayal of the Jews').[105] The large-scale delivery of labour assignment orders and the imminent deportations led to 'considerable panic', as the MBB reported in its Activity Report No. 21.[106] Many attempted to flee to unoccupied France or acquire Belgian citizenship, which at the time still provided protection.

After the first wave of transports, hardly any Jews selected for labour assignments came to Mechelen freely. Only a month later, von Bargen, Head of the Brussels branch of the Foreign Office, reported to Berlin that doubt was spreading among Jews about the actual destination of the labour assignment. Since 'rumours of the butchering of Jews etc. caused them to ignore their labour assignment, the Jews were captured in raids and individual operations'.[107]

Between July and September 1942, partially with the help of the Belgian police, raids and other police arrest campaigns were carried out and captured Jews were sent to Mechelen.[108] According to Pim Griffioen and

Ron Zeller, the major raids in Antwerp and Brussels were ultimately counterproductive for the Germans since the measures meant that Jews did not wear their yellow stars, sought hiding places, acquired false papers and went underground.[109] Unlike in the Netherlands and France, the Germans were unable to systematically draw from local police forces for the first raids in Belgium in August 1942. They deployed police for night raids, but this remained unique and afterwards they were no longer involved.[110] In late September, Head of the Military Administration Reeder ordered the responsible units as follows: 'The Sicherheitspolizei office has received the order to carry out the operation in a way that attracts as little public attention as possible and does not make the population sympathize with the Jews'.[111]

More than half of all Jews deported from Belgium were arrested either individually or in small groups. This was a key difference from France and the Netherlands, where major arrest operations were the rule. One of the reasons for this was that the Belgian police had stopped participating in the arrest of Jews in the autumn of 1942.[112] The deportations lost momentum, 'because the required number of Jews could not be arrested', as the former Judenreferent Kurt Asche stated in 1966.[113] It took two and a half months for the next transport to depart, on 15 January 1943.

Once almost all foreign and stateless Jews had been deported, following pressure from Himmler, the deportation of Jews with Belgian citizenship was prepared for in the summer of 1943. In September 1943, the 'Aktion Iltis' ('Operation Polecat') suddenly began arresting and interning Belgian Jews.[114] Transport 22 B, which departed on 20 September 1943, contained the first Jews with Belgian citizenship. On 15 June 1944, the BdS reported that, forthwith, Jewish spouses of so-called 'mixed marriages' ('Mischehen') were 'for the greatest part layabouts and idlers . . . who must be assigned to the Ostministerium for labour'.[115]

It took three days and nights for a deportation train to travel the 1,200 km to Auschwitz.[116] Six transports (6, 7, 8, 9, 12, 13) stopped in Cosel, 100 km before Auschwitz, where some prisoners who were able to work were selected for forced labour in the camps of the Organisation Schmelt in Upper Silesia. One survivor describes the situation:

> Since most of these men did not want to be separated from their family . . . they hesitated to comply. The wagons were also suddenly raided by SS officers, who took all the men who seemed strong to them. . . . It is not difficult to guess that those separations were accompanied by heart-wrenching cries.[117]

A maximum of 1,334 men were affected by this compulsory recruitment, which meant for those affected that their extermination was postponed.[118]

The following five transports were merged from two administratively separate transports respectively: 12 and 13, 14 and 15, 16 and 17, 18 and 19, 22 A and 22 B. This means that the transports were separately administrated, but departed as one long train. The first and second transports departed from Mechelen station, where the Jews were taken by truck.[119] In mid August 1942, new railway tracks were laid that led directly to the transit camp. From the third transport, all deportation trains departed from there. To prevent escapes when boarding, the camp personnel formed special lines along which the prisoners walked from the camp to the wagons.[120] The train route went to Leuven, where the trains continued on the Brussels–Cologne line and eastwards through the German Reich.[121] One transport list was given to the Transportführer, while another remained in the camp and a third was sent to the BdS in Brussels.[122]

The Wagon Elder

As in France and the Netherlands, a wagon elder was named for each wagon. Former Camp Commander Frank stated in 1946:

> One 'warden' was allocated to each wagon, who also received a torch and an 'emergency flag'. In the connected train, I ordered that one medical wagon was set up and gave them a large metal box measuring 1 m x 40 x 60 cm – with medicine of all kinds. It included doctor's instruments and injection needles.[123]

Individual escape stories confirm the existence of a medical wagon, but they contained neither medical instruments nor medicine. Instead, the sick and dying were laid in the wagons without blankets or mattresses.

Wagons Used for Deportations

The first two trains that left from Mechelen station consisted of passenger wagons.[124] According to the Judenreferent in Belgien, Kurt Asche, this led to protests among the German population that the accommodation was too comfortable for the Jews, whereupon the Berlin Reichssicherheitshauptamt ordered the subsequent transportation of Jews in freight wagons.[125]

Other sources indicate that the large numbers of escapes from the 18th/19th transport led to the deployment of freight wagons, which were easier to guard. They had no windows through which deportees could escape.[126] The 20th deportation train and the transports after it consisted of freight wagons.[127] The hatches were nailed closed with wooden boards.

The wagons were painted with the following words in large letters: 'Nicht nahe treten. ANSTECKUNGSGEFAHR' ('Do not approach. RISK OF INFECTION').[128] The journey from the Mechelen camp to the German border normally lasted around five hours.[129] Passenger wagons for the guard teams were distributed between the freight wagons.[130]

The Situation in the Wagons

Before each deportation, the Judenrat organized food packages that the deportees took with them onto the trains.[131] A survivor of the 19th transport reports that everyone received 900 g of bread, 150 g of artificial honey, 25 g of butter and 50 g of sausage.[132] A survivor of Transport 22 B recalls that the food parcels provided by the AJB/JVB contained one loaf of bread, one ginger bread, one tin of sardines, one tin of meat, tissue paper and so on.[133] The Judenrat additionally provided provisions for two weeks, which the deportees were to receive at the destination. Simon Gutmann recalls that while the train stopped in Bremen station, women from the Red Cross refused to give them water because they were Jews.[134]

The provided supplies were loaded onto separate wagons along with the luggage. According to Frank, two wagons were generally required for this purpose. He had also received orders that Jews were not permitted to take their baggage with them onto the wagons.[135] According to a statement by a survivor, these wagons were decoupled from the respective deportation train immediately after crossing the German border.[136] The goods they contained were for the benefit of the German population.

The sick and dying people in the medical wagons were generally allocated to a doctor from among the deportees. One such 'Häftlingsarzt' in Transport 22 B stated that his wagon contained sixty people.[137] The hatches were secured using barbed wire, and apart from a bucket and two jugs, the wagons were empty. Transport 22 B stopped twice during its journey, at which times prisoners had access to a water supply.[138] One survivor reports that inside his wagon on the 24th deportation train, half the people were dead on arrival in Auschwitz because it was overcrowded, carrying eighty people.[139] In another wagon on the same transport, sixty-five people were crammed together with only two ventilation hatches. Straw was laid out on the floor. From time to time, the guards made sure that no-one had escaped.[140] One deportee who was taken on the penultimate deportation train to Auschwitz reports that they were literally beaten into the wagons with clubs and blows by the SS. The sixty people were crushed together and had to survive without water or food for three days and nights.[141]

In 1946, former Camp Commander Frank contradicted these survivors' reports with the following statement:

> I was responsible for giving the Jews 'marching provisions' for 3 days . . . and had to send interim supplies for 14 days according to the number of people. 48 people were loaded onto each train wagon. In each wagon I ordered straw to be laid out and provided 10 blankets, 2 toilet seats, 4 buckets, 2 water jugs and 1 broom. The Judenvereinigung gave each Jew a 'gift package' with plenty of food and consumables. . . . I believe I did everything to ease the Jews' journey.[142]

The Accompanying Guard Teams

From the outset, deportation trains were accompanied by Schutzpolizei guard units that travelled to Mechelen from western German cities.[143] They arrived at the transit camp one or two days before the departure of a transport.[144] They guarded the deportation train and were replaced by another Schutzpolizei unit, for instance in Aachen or Hamm, before the train continued eastwards.[145]

In 1966, Kurt Asche stated: 'From the Mechelen camp, the trains were guarded by units of the Schutzpolizei from the Cologne and Aachen region'.[146] Former member of the Department for Jewish Affairs, SS Hauptscharführer and Kriminaloberassistent Hans Rodenbüsch, stated that the guard teams for the deportation trains departing from Mechelen were provided by the Schutzpolizei from Cologne or Düsseldorf.[147] Each team consisted of one officer, the Transportführer, and fifteen men.[148] They were armed with machine guns and had orders to shoot.[149] Following the attack by Resistance fighters on the 20th deportation train from Mechelen to Auschwitz on 19 April 1943, members of the Judenreferat and the SS Guard Company ('Wachkompanie') in Brussels were deployed as reinforcements for the Schutzpolizei units and accompanied the train to the border.[150] The SS Wachkompanie initially consisted of German, Flemish and so-called 'Volksdeutsche' (i.e. 'ethnic Germans from abroad') and SS men from Hungary. Later, only the Zugführer and Gruppenführer were from the German Reich, while the units also included Walloons and 'Volksdeutsche' from Romania.[151] The guard team was subordinate to the BdS and was led by SS Obersturmführer Gerhard Lienke, who had been seconded by the Düsseldorf Staatpolizei.[152] It was responsible for the security of the Sipo building in Brussels. Its barracks were at the Sipo headquarters on Avenue Louise No. 453, where the SS men's tasks included guarding the Jews imprisoned in the cellars. They were also responsible for transporting them by truck to Mechelen.[153]

When the Wachkompanie was deployed for the deportation trains, their Zugführer Claudius Billerbeck and Ludwig Köpf were also the Transportführer and had the overall command of the guard teams. Different guard team sizes are indicated by different sources, consisting of between six and twenty men.[154] According to Ernst Böhlich, a former member of the Wachkompanie, the German SS men stationed in Belgium were certainly motivated to be deployed for guard duty on the deportation trains: 'The guard teams we provided for transportation trains were privileged with respect to exchanging German money into Francs. We all wanted that of course, because Belgian Francs were rare. It was not possible to pay with German money in Belgian shops'.[155] He stated that nobody in his guard team knew that the Jews were being transported to their deaths. Böhlich's statement is already implausible due to the fact that until he was posted in Belgium in September 1943, he had actively participated in the 'War of Annihilation' ('Vernichtungskrieg') in the Soviet Union. He had belonged to Einsatzgruppe B led by Arthur Nebe and then Einsatzkommando 8 under Dr Otto Bradfisch.[156] Another indication that at least some members of the Schutzpolizei knew the actual intention of the deportations is the statement by Erwin R., a Jew who originally came from Duisburg and was deported from Mechelen to Auschwitz. Immediately before the deportation, a Schutzpolizei officer warned him to try and save himself during the journey because it was impossible to come out of Auschwitz alive.[157]

Only two former members of the Schutzpolizei report escapes. One stated that he had heard of five or six 'fugitive prisoners' after the transport was completed, of whom two or three were recaptured shortly afterwards.[158] The former Transportführer Ludwig Köpf states that he had difficulties on his return because he was made responsible for the escape by two or three Jews who had fled from the wagons. Neither he nor other members of the guard unit had noticed.[159]

Belgium: Escapes and Attempted Escapes

In Belgium, the number of people who fled from deportation trains is relatively high compared to those in France and the Netherlands. The historian Laurence Schram has proven that 562 train fugitives undertook a total of 577 escapes (some fled from trains more than once).[160] Due to this large number, the following presents only selected examples of escape stories. Three events stand out: the escape of 229 former Jewish forced labourers for the Organisation Todt from the 16th transport on 31 October 1942, the flight of 215 deportees from the 20th transport on 19 April 1943 and the unique attack by Resistance fighters on the 20th transport, which also liberated a further seventeen people.

Walter Aron, Lipa Abraham Keller, Ludwig Keller – Escapes from the 12th/13th Transport on 10 October 1942

The 12th/13th transport that departed on 10 October 1942 was administrated separately, but in fact travelled as one train with a total of 1,684 prisoners. Of those, 356 men were selected for forced labour in Cosel, Upper Silesia, 116 were registered at Auschwitz concentration camp and the remaining 1,202 people were immediately killed in the gas chambers after arriving.[161] Ten deportees escaped from the train. Two prisoners on the 12th transport jumped from the wagon before reaching the German border. One of them was the 47-year-old Walter Aron (born in Waldhilbersheim/Germany in 1894). Aron was arrested in Belgium on the day of the German invasion and transferred as an enemy foreigner to the Gurs camp in the south of France. He escaped from Gurs on 26 December 1940 together with two other Germans.[162] The circumstances under which he was recaptured in Belgium and sent to Mechelen are unknown, as are details of his escape from the 12th transport. Walter Aron was able to avoid renewed Nazi arrest, survived and emigrated to the USA.[163]

The merchant Lipa Abraham Keller, born in Lemberg (Lvov) in 1885, and his son Ludwig Keller (born in Berlin in 1912) fled from the 13th transport. They had left their home in Berlin in December 1939 and initially went to Antwerp and then Brussels.[164] On 29 October 1940, both were interned as enemy foreigners in the camp in Gurs, from where they managed to escape on 7 March 1941.[165] The extant documents suggest that they managed to make their way to Belgium, where at least Ludwig Keller went underground. From 1941 to 1943, he was active in the Resistance; he transported anti-German books and flyers air-dropped by the Allies from Limbourg to Brussels and distributed them there.[166] On 8 October 1942, he was arrested in Brussels and transferred to Mechelen. Since Lipa Abraham Keller and Ludwig Keller were registered in Mechelen with consecutive numbers, it is likely that the father and son were arrested and taken to the camp together.[167] They were deported after two days' internment in the camp. Both managed to escape from the moving train in circumstances that are unknown. They were never recaptured by the Nazis.[168]

Ryla Wajnberg, Aron Schwarzbaum – Escapes from the 14th/15th Transport on 24 October 1942

The 14th/15th transport also departed from Mechelen as a single train with 1,474 internees on 24 October 1942. At least three deportees were able to escape before reaching the German border.

The hairdresser Ryla Wajnberg (born in Jamanow in 1893) managed to escape from the moving train. However, she was recaptured and transferred back to Mechelen on 30 October 1942. A day later, she was deported again on the 17th transport, after which all trace of her is lost.[169] The second escapee was Aron Schwarzbaum (born in Szezekony in 1899), who was a painter. He was arrested in Antwerp on 17 January 1941 and transferred to Breendonk a month later. He remained there in custody until his release on 26 October 1941.[170] Presumably in October 1942, he was arrested again and allocated to the 14th transport. Aron Schwarzbaum was able to escape from the train in the town of Visé, almost 30 km before reaching Aachen. A priest helped him to find a hideout in a café beside Visé station. In December 1943, he went underground in Brussels. He ultimately fled via France to Switzerland, where he was interned in camps in Geneva and Lausanne. He returned to Belgium after the end of the war.[171]

Otto Dawid – Attempted Escape from the 14th Transport on 24 October 1942

A third known escape from the 14th transport was prevented. It was undertaken by Otto Dawid (born in Vienna in 1915). Dawid had emigrated to Belgium in 1938.[172] On 29 October 1940, he was interned in the southern French camp in Gurs and transferred to the Les Milles camp on 8 April 1941, from where he fled.[173] On 14 October 1942, members of the Sipo arrested him and his wife, Anna, in Brussels. Among the policemen who arrested him was the Jewish informer 'gros Jacques', who had apparently betrayed him.[174] Otto and Anna Dawid were taken to Mechelen. He recalls the deportation as follows:

> I never heard the Germans reveal the fact that deportees to Auschwitz were condemned to die. During our internment in Mechelen, the Germans told us we would be deported to Germany for a labour assignment. During the transport to Germany, several prisoners, including myself, took the chance to flee while the train was standing in a Belgian station. The German prisoner called Leipziger and I were arrested by our guards, German Schutzpolizei officers, immediately after we left the wagon. They beat us and forced us to reboard the train. The journey continued without incident. Our guards did not fire a single shot.[175]

On 26 October 1942, Otto Dawid was registered in Auschwitz concentration camp.[176] Two days later, he was transferred to the Jawischowitz subcamp. From there he wrote two postcards to the Judenrat in Brussels; he seems to have answered an enquiry by the Judenrat, stating 'that the 14th transp. I belonged to arrived on Monday, Oct. 26, 1942/ 4 h aftern. at

Birkenau-Auschwitz railway station'.[177] In the second card, he requests information on the fate of his wife: 'I kindly request you inform me whether you have information on my wife Anna Dawid née Salzmann. . . . am healthy, work in a Coal mine'.[178] According to contradictory sources, Otto Dawid was either liberated on 29 January 1945 from Jawischowitz or at an unstated time from Buchenwald concentration camp.[179]

The Mass Escape of Jewish Forced Labourers from the 16th/17th Transport on 31 October/1 November 1942

In the autumn of 1942, the Sipo-SD in Belgium had difficulties arresting enough Jews to fill the deportation trains, as so many went into hiding to avoid being deported.[180] Like the previous transports, the 16th/17th deportation train departed as a single train. It contained a total of 1,937 prisoners, including 1,315 men who had been transferred by train to Mechelen from OT forced labour camps in northern France to fill the deportation trains to the East. At the station in Muizen, a suburb in the southeast of Mechelen, the wagons, which prisoners were not permitted to leave, were coupled with other wagons from the transit camp to form a deportation train to Auschwitz.[181] The first escape by a large group of prisoners occurred from this train: a total of 240 Jews escaped from the moving train, including 229 forced OT labourers.[182]

There were certainly a large number of reasons for the escapes by the forced labourers of the OT. The Sipo-SD had suggested to them and their dependants interned in Mechelen that families would be united to journey together to a labour assignment in the East. At least 160 women, daughters and sons in the transit camp had applied to join the transport in the hope of being reunited. However, the families were not reunited and instead deported in separate wagons without knowing of each others' whereabouts.[183] After the departure from Mechelen, they realized they had been deceived. The extent of the men's hopes of being reunited, and their disappointment when they were prevented from doing so, can be seen in the fact that all known escapes occurred after the train departed from Mechelen and none before. As Schram and Steinberg write, they were clearly more motivated to escape since they were not held back by the presence of members of their family.[184] Schram and Steinberg also propose that imprisonment for months in the OT camps had made the Jewish forced labourers more belligerent.[185] The fact that these men had first-hand experience of what it meant to be interned in a German camp and the forced labour there made them particularly resolved against renewed internship.

Of the 240 prisoners who jumped from the trains, 100 were recaptured and 94 were deported again.[186]

Israel Beck – Escapes from the 16th Transport on 31 October 1942 and from the 21st Transport on 31 July 1943

Israel Beck (born in Medyka/Poland in 1896) was among the fugitives from both of these transports. In June 1939, he had fled with his family from Berlin to Belgium.[187] His son Gabriel had been born in Berlin in 1936.[188] His wife Rosa Lessner, who was also from Poland, and the child Gabriel were deported on 8 September 1942.[189] Beck was forced into labour for the company Julius Berger in northern France from 26 June 1942. During this period, he was interned in the camp for Jews there known as 'Israel I'. After managing to escape from the 16th transport that departed on 31 October 1942, he was recaptured on 16 June 1943 and later taken to Mechelen. Six weeks later, on 31 July 1943, he was deported again on the 21st transport.[190] During the journey, he broke the door of the wagon open and jumped from the train. When the guards shot and wounded him, he pretended to be dead. His wounds were treated by a doctor under unknown circumstances.[191] He managed to avoid arrest and survived.[192]

Majlych Cykiert, Maurice Cykiert, Jakob Szolom, Wolf Wand – Escapes from the 16th Transport on 31 October/1 November 1942

Two of the forced labourers for OT who jumped from the train were Majlych Cykiert (born in Warki/occupied Poland in 1895) and his son Maurice Cykiert (born in Liège in 1926). Majlych Cykiert ran a hosiery store in Liège. In March 1942, he was expropriated on the orders of the German occupiers and his shop was deleted from the commercial register. He was charged 12 Francs for the store's deletion from the records.[193] On 3 August 1942, he was arrested together with his son Maurice and taken to the Dannes-Camiers camp in northern France.[194] His wife and second son remained behind. Only six days later, the father and son were deployed as forced labourers for the Organisation Todt on the Atlantic Wall building site operated by the company Albert Jung.[195] When they were transported to Auschwitz, Maurice Cykiert jumped from the moving train near Hasselt, while his son jumped 20 km further on in the region of Tongeren, about 30 km north of Liège.[196] On returning to Liège, Majlych Cykiert learnt that his wife and other son had been arrested. He never heard from them again.[197] Various people hid the father and son in different places in and around Liège until they were liberated. While the father only changed hideouts three times, Maurice was often forced to change his places of refuge and only just managed to avoid being arrested by German policemen.[198]

The Polish brothers Jakob Szolom (born in Kalisz in 1919) and Wolf Wand (born in Kalisz in 1923), who lived in Liège, had worked in the fur trade before their arrest. They too were forced to work for Albert Jung.[199] Both jumped from the 16th transport that departed on 31 October/1 November 1942. While Jakob Szolom managed to hide until the liberation, Wolf Wand was recaptured. On 4 April 1944, he was deported to Auschwitz and deployed in Monowitz (Auschwitz III). There, he apparently became so ill that he was transferred from the prisoners' centre for the sick in Monowitz to Birkenau on 22 January 1945.[200] During the evacuation from Auschwitz, he was transferred without any possessions to Buchenwald concentration camp.[201] The stockroom certificate that documents this is his last remaining sign of life.

Szulim Aronowicz – Escape from the 16th Transport on 1 November 1942

Szulim Aronowicz (born in Łódź in 1920) emigrated from Poland to Liège with his family as a ten-year-old.[202] From May 1941, he distributed the illegal pamphlets 'Le Coq Victorieux', 'Churchill Gazette' and 'La Libre Belgique'.[203] On 2 August 1942, he was arrested by the Feldgendarmerie in his apartment and was probably first taken to the local St. Léonard prison and then to the forced labour office at Place Saint Christophe in Liège.[204] He was arrested as a Jew, since the Gendarmes were apparently unaware that he handed out underground publications. His sister-in-law, who witnessed the arrest, secretly advised him to take the next opportunity to flee to avoid deportation to Germany.[205] The next day, he was transferred to the Dannes-Camiers camp near Boulogne-sur-Mer. The living conditions in the camp were terrible, with prisoners suffering torture and hunger on a daily basis.[206]

When Aronowicz was deported from Mechelen on 1 November 1942, he jumped from the moving train near Leuven on the same day. He was joined by an unnamed German.[207] He made his way to Brussels, where an acquaintance helped him to inform his fiancée and family of his successful escape.[208] The same day, another helper drove him to Liège, where he hid in private accommodation in Fléron thanks to support from the Resistance activist Jean Pirlot.[209] According to Pirlot's recollection, he was given asylum by a forester who lived in a kind of hut camp.[210] After three or four days, Aronowicz changed his hiding place and found shelter in Stoumont with a man named Schouns. On 15 November 1942, he was granted asylum in the seminary of Bastogne, where he remained until July 1943.[211]

After nine months, Aronowicz was betrayed and only just managed to flee back to Schouns. He again began to hand out underground publications, which he received from Pirlot. In the spring of 1944, he became active in the Durbuy Sector of the Resistance to the south of Liège. He requisitioned weapons and took over the dangerous transport of weapons and food. He fought in an armed unit and, for instance, managed to arrest an SS paratrooper.[212] A range of evidence points to his activity in the Resistance group Armée belge des Partisans between May and 14 October 1944.[213] On 25 July 1944, Szulim Aronowicz was apparently arrested and imprisoned firstly in Casteau to the south of Brussels, then in the Brussels district of Etterbeek and finally in the Siebenhirten subcamp of Mauthausen concentration camp.[214] His trace is lost there.

Ludwig Posener, Pinkus Fremder, Arja Kuper, David Herszaft, Jacheta Baum – Escapes from the 16th Transport on 31 October/1 November 1942

The German-born Ludwig Posener (born in Berlin in 1926) was only sixteen years old when he jumped from the 16th deportation train. Shortly after the November pogrom, the youth fled to Brussels with his remaining parent Kurt Friedrich (born in 1891). On 10 May 1940, his father was interned in Belgium due to his German roots. He was one of eight thousand German Jews who were deported to southern France as 'enemy foreigners' as a reaction to the invasion by the Wehrmacht. He was imprisoned in the camps in Gurs, St. Cyprien, Pithiviers and Rivesaltes, before being sent to Drancy at the age of fifty-one on 4 September 1942. Seven days later, on 11 September 1942, Kurt Friedrich Posener was deported on the 31st transport from France to Auschwitz.[215] He did not survive.

His son Ludwig Posener initially remained in Belgium in 1940. On 26 June 1942, he was ordered to the OT camps in northern France to carry out forced labour. When he was deported from there with others who shared the same fate, he jumped from the moving train between Mechelen and the German border. At first he was able to go underground, but was recaptured on 7 April 1943 and placed on the list for the 20th transport, which departed from Mechelen on 19 April 1943. Although a number of Jews fled from that transport and even from his wagon, he did not. In Auschwitz, Ludwig Posener was selected for labour and was soon moved to Auschwitz-Monowitz. Although his health deteriorated steadily and he spent long periods in the sickbay, he managed to survive until the liberation of Auschwitz by the Red Army on 27 January 1945.[216]

Pinkus Fremder (born in Warsaw in 1923), who jumped from the 16th transport on 31 October/1 November 1942, was also a former forced labourer for the OT. He had moved to Liège with his parents at the age of twelve. The City of Liège register of foreigners lists him as an apprentice in the leather processing industry.[217] He fled from the 16th transport train together with Arja Kuper and five other men who, like Fremder, had been used as forced labourers for the company Nick Garcon & Söhne, working on the Atlantic Wall fortifications.[218] Three of them were arrested after fleeing, including Kuper, who was again deported on 31 July 1943.[219] A document dated January 1944 shows that Kuper was a forced labourer in the 'Neu-Dachs' subcamp of Auschwitz in Jaworzno. The company founded by Albert Speer called Energieversorgung Oberschlesien (EVO) had established a mine camp there, in which almost 3,700 Jews were forced to work in 1944.[220]

After escaping from the moving train, Pinkus Fremder joined the Armée Secrete. He assumed the name of Jean-Paul Thonon and transported weapons, carried out acts of sabotage and fought in the armed Resistance.[221] In December 1943, there was an armed conflict near Liège with unspecified Germans. There is slightly conflicting information with respect to the day and location of the event. Pinkus Fremder must have been wounded by gunfire and arrested between 7 and 9 December 1943 in the village of Momalle near Liège. He was taken to the Seraing hospital on 9 December, where he is reported to have been shot dead.[222]

David Herszaft (born in Warsaw in 1921) managed to jump from the train. At the time of his forced labour order for the OT, the unemployed leather worker from the Brussels workers' district of Molenbeek was active underground as the contact between the Belgian Communist Party and the MOI. He was forced to work in northern France for the companies Dohrmann and Nick Garcon & Söhne. He fled from a wagon of the 16th deportation train. Other men who had previously worked for Dohrmann and Nick Garcon & Söhne also escaped from the wagons. One of them, Rudi Lachmann (born in Stargard in 1921), was shot dead by the Schutzpolizei while fleeing. After his escape, David Herszaft was helped by friends from the Communist Party in Molenbeek. The Resistance fighter Camille De Roeck took him to a hiding place where underground newspapers, twenty packages with explosives, hand grenades, rifle ammunition and pistol bullets were stored. The hideout was discovered under circumstances that are unclear. On 16 November 1942, Herszaft was taken to the prison in the Brussels district of Saint-Gilles. On 12 December 1942, he was executed together with Camille De Roeck by a firing squad in the woods of Hechtel in the Flemish city of Limbourg. The Sipo-SD publicly projected the image of Herszaft as a Jewish terrorist.[223]

Only two of the 240 deportees who fled from the train were women. One of them was Jacheta Baum (born in Czestochowa/occupied Poland in 1903), who probably jumped with her husband Szymon Imerglik (born in Wolbron/occupied Poland). Both were captured and taken together with their fourteen-year-old son Fiszel Imerglik to the Mechelen transit camp. On arrival, their son carried a youth hostel card, most probably with his photo, but issued in the name of Félix Baudon.[224] It was a widespread tactic to acquire not only an ID card with a false name, but also other cards, ideally with photos, such as library cards, fishing licences or youth hostel cards, since it made a more plausible impression if one had more than one form of ID when checked.[225]

The three members of the family were deported to Auschwitz with the 21st transport, after which all trace of them is lost.[226]

Monika and Hans Fritz and Margareta Magier – Escape from the 18th/19th Transport on 15 January 1943

Like the previous three transports, the 18th/19th transport departed from Mechelen as a single train. It had become increasingly difficult for the Sipo-SD to have a sufficient number of Jews in their custody; in this case, they needed two and a half months to fill the transport. This transport was the last composed of third-class passenger wagons. It departed with 1,625 prisoners, of whom a total of sixty-seven – fifty-five men and twelve women – fled from the moving train.[227]

The youngest person to jump from this train, or any other, was the four-year-old Monika Fritz (born in Brussels in 1938). Her parents, the mechanic Hans Fritz (born in Vienna in 1912) and Margareta Magier (born in Vienna in 1919) had fled from Austria. Hans Fritz had already been caught by the Gestapo in Koblenz in 1938,[228] but the couple managed to flee to Belgium, where their daughter Monika was born. In 1940, Hans Fritz was sent by the Belgian authorities to the southern French camp in St. Cyprien. After returning to Brussels, he hid together with his family. On 18 November 1942, he was discovered and arrested together with Margareta Magier's father Szlama Magier and eight other Jews. The three members of the family were initially taken to the prison in Saint-Gilles and then transferred to the Mechelen transit camp. When they were deported from there, the parents jumped with young Monika from the wagon.

Szlama Magier must also have jumped, though it is unknown whether he did so with the other three family members. Margareta Magier and Monika were not recaptured, but Hans Fritz and Szlama Magier were arrested again and deported on the 20th transport. Although Hans Fritz was locked inside a wagon that was especially reserved for fugitives from earlier transports, to which the guards paid greater attention, he managed to escape again between Tienen and Liège. The reunited family used false papers to flee to France, where they hid until the liberation. Szlama Magier survived Auschwitz and other camps, later returning to Belgium.[229]

Joseph Hakker – Escape from the 18th Transport on 15 January 1943

The oldest escapee from this train was the 56-year-old Joseph Hakker (born in Amsterdam in 1887). He worked as a baker in Antwerp. In late October 1942, he paid 45,000 Belgian Francs for illegal immigration into Switzerland, but his supposed helpers proved to be members of the Devisenschutzkommando and arrested him. Hakker spent two weeks in prison in Antwerp's Begijnenstraat before being transferred to Mechelen and deported on the 18th transport. He managed to wind down a window of his third-class passenger wagon and jump from the moving train near Boutersem, shortly after Leuven. He hid in the area of Liège and joined the Resistance. In July 1943, he wrote down his impressions of the transit camp in a text entitled 'De Geheimzinnige Kazerne Dossin' ('The Mysterious Dossin Barracks in Mechelen'), which was published in the underground pamphlet 'Coq Victorieux'. In September 1944, he published a collection with the same title, containing texts he had written for underground newspapers.[230]

Samuel Perl – Escapes from the 18th/19th Transport on 15 January 1943 and from the 20th Transport on 19 April 1943

In 1945, Hakker's accounts were corroborated by the diamond dealer Samuel Perl (born in Ruskova/Romania in 1920).[231] Perl's family was deported after a major raid in Antwerp on 15 August 1942. Perl himself initially fled to the unoccupied French zone. He smuggled Jews there from Belgium and provided them with false Dutch ID papers.[232] When the Wehrmacht occupied southern France, he returned to Antwerp and went underground.

On 4 December 1942, the Sicherheitspolizei arrested him as a Jew in a café in Antwerp's Gemeentestraat. He denied being a Jew and showed his papers. In 1945, Perl recounted: 'I had been able to acquire false ID papers to avoid being persecuted as a Jew by the Germans'.[233] After the Devisenschutzkommando had robbed him of two valuable diamonds, the Gestapo tortured him until he admitted to being a Jew. The same day, he was transferred to Mechelen and interned there for six weeks.[234] On 15 January 1943, he was deported on the 18th/19th transport. Samuel Perl describes his escape as follows: 'When the train was between Tirlemont and St. Trond, I and other Jews managed to jump from the train and flee'.[235] He made his way to Antwerp, where a married couple hid him in their apartment. He again received false ID papers. After eight days, Perl was arrested in the apartment together with the couple and another Jewish girl who had also been hiding there and taken to prison in Antwerp. He survived the interrogations and mistreatment without betraying the passport forger. On 28 January 1943, he was sent back to Mechelen. After arriving there, the Treuhand employee Dr Erich Krull tortured him by whipping him and burning him with a cigar.[236]

Perl was again deported on the next train, the 20th transport, and again escaped. The hatches of the freight trains in which Perl was transported were secured with barbed wire, but Resistance fighters had been able to hide saws and hammers in the wagon.[237] It had also been possible to smuggle a further saw into the wagon.[238] Samuel Perl describes his second escape as follows:

> Once we had passed St. Trond, I and a number of others again tried our luck in the darkness of night. . . . One young man had managed to steal a saw from the carpentry workshop, with which a piece of the wagon's rear wall was sawn open. We jumped through that opening and I ran towards Namur, where I remained hidden during the entire period of the German occupation.[239]

Members of the Schutzpolizei who were apparently posted in the brakeman's cab shot at the fugitives,[240] but Samuel Perl escaped and survived Nazi persecution.[241]

Fanny Abramowicz, Leopold Berger and Kurt Berger – Escape from the 18th/19th Transport on 15 January 1943

The family of Fanny Abramowicz (born in Bendzin/occupied Poland in 1892), Leopold Berger (born in Budapest in 1898) and their son Kurt Berger (born in Vienna in 1925) emigrated from Vienna to Brussels either in 1934 or 1938.[242] Kurt Berger was arrested in Brussels by the Gestapo on 16 December 1942 and taken to Mechelen. His parents were also captured and interned there. The three members of the family were deported on the 18th/19th transport.[243] They jumped from the train together.[244] After escaping, Kurt Berger, presumably together with his father, lived illegally in Brussels. It is unknown whether Fanny Abramowicz was with them. She managed to remain hidden until the liberation.[245] However, Kurt Berger was arrested again on 26 September 1943 and taken to Mechelen. His father Leopold Berger was also recaptured, though it is unknown whether he was arrested with his son. The father and son were guarded with special vigilance as they were deported to Auschwitz on the 24th transport on 4 April 1944.[246]

Only the continued suffering of Kurt Berger can be reconstructed for the time after that. Immediately after arriving in Auschwitz, he was transferred to the Laurahütte subcamp, which had been established in early April 1944, where he was forced to work for Rheinmetall-Borsig.[247] The arms manufacturer had previously moved its production site for anti-aircraft guns from Düsseldorf to Laurahütte.[248] From there, the evacuation took Kurt Berger on a journey lasting several days, which 134 fellow prisoners did not survive, to the Gusen II concentration camp.[249] He was registered there on 28 January 1945 as a new arrival with the professional description of mechanical assembly worker.[250] On 31 January, five hundred of the prisoners who had been evacuated from Laurahütte to Gusen II and found to be fit for work were transferred to the Neuengammer subcamp in Hannover-Mühlenberg.[251] There, the company Hanomag (Hannoversche Maschinenbau AG) produced the type of gun that was assembled in Laurahütte by Rheinmetall-Borsig.[252] The Hanover-Mühlenberg subcamp was evacuated on 6 April 1945. From there, Kurt Berger was forced onto an evacuation march to Bergen-Belsen, where he was ultimately liberated.[253] In late April, he was treated as an in-patient in a hospital in Hanover after contracting typhoid. On 8 May, he was transferred to the Hôpital des Anglais in Liège Lüttich. In June 1945, Kurt Berger returned to Belgium and was repatriated.[254]

Rudolf Schmitz – Escape from the 19th Transport on 15 January 1943

One of the most moving reports by a survivor of a train escape is the account by the baker Rudolf Schmitz (born in Kaiseresch in 1904). Before his flight to Belgium, he had lived in Cologne. After the liberation of Belgium, he wrote a report on his escape from the 19th deportation train, which was included in the trial documents of proceedings against Kurt Asche in Kiel in 1980:

> On 14 January, the Schutzpolizei from Cologne arrives to take over the transport. On the 15th, foreign SS officers appear to organize the loading. After hastily gulping down our soup, we are beaten out of our dormitory. And then we board the train by consecutive number according to the signs we are wearing around our neck. There is a shout 'Shut the windows! Shots will be fired without warning!' The doors are locked with keys. The wagon behind ours is for the police. We, that is some of the prisoners, had previously arranged to jump while the train is moving, at a hill beyond Leuven. Because we sense that nothing good awaits us. In our compartment, I am the first to open the window and look out. The police, around seventeen men, appear to be asleep. I try to convince my wife to climb through the window and jump. But she refuses because she is afraid. Meanwhile eleven people leave our compartment, including a man with a child in his arms. I take my wife and show her how easy it is. For the train is travelling slowly and stops from time to time. Probably the Belgian train driver is pretending that there is a technical problem. I do not want to jump before my wife has managed it. So the night passes at a slow pace. I think, consider our eight-year marriage, think that these devil-pos-

sessed SS men will part me from my wife, and think of my three children whom I have hidden in a monastery in Belgium. I want to see them again. I decide to jump alone. I first take the food from the baggage left behind by those who have escaped and put it in my wife's rucksack so that she has food until her arrival. Then I throw my rucksack out of the window and kneel on the window ledge ready to jump. When my wife realizes I am serious, she holds my leg and pleads: 'Don't leave me alone'. I answer that she should follow me. But she doesn't come. I jump.[255]

Unfortunately, Rudolf Schmitz jumped off the train at the guarded bridge Pont de Visé near Liège. A few minutes after leaping, he was arrested by two German military guards. He remained in custody in the Liège military prison until 9 February 1943 and was then transferred to Mechelen. On arrival in Mechelen, Schmitz encountered Karl Mainzhausen, the most senior luggage inspector, who was known to Schmitz. He mistreated Schmitz so badly that his right eardrum burst.[256]

For the following 20th transport, Schmitz was placed on a special list of people who were guarded with particular attention. Like Samuel Perl, who had also escaped from the 19th transport and been recaptured, Schmitz was given a special mark. Their numbers received a red horizontal band and their heads were also shaved to show that they were both fugitives from the 19th deportation train. Guarded in this way, Schmitz was deported to Auschwitz.[257] During the evacuation from Auschwitz, he was interned in Buchenwald concentration camp on 26 January 1945. His only possessions were the clothes he wore.[258] On 19 February 1945, he was allocated to an external labour unit.[259] It is unknown where Rudolf Schmitz experienced the liberation.

Meyer Tabakman – Escapes from the 19th Transport on 15 January 1943 and from the 20th Transport on 19 April 1943

Meyer Tabakman (born in Siedlce/occupied Poland on 3 September 1912) had emigrated from Poland in 1928 and had settled in the Brussels district of Saint-Gilles where he worked as a shoe leather cutter.[260] He was a member of the left-wing Zionist party Poale Zion and fought against the German occupiers as part of Alexander Livchitz's company in the Resistance.[261] In June 1942, Meyer Tabakman initiated a training camp for young Zionists preparing to emigrate to Palestine. Tabakman was arrested and interned in the Mechelen transit camp on 8 January 1943. He managed to escape from the deportation train that left seven days later by climbing out of the wagon window. In March 1943, the first edition of the underground newspaper *Le Flambeau*, which was published by the Front d'Indépendance, was being distributed in Belgium. In it, Tabakman describes his escape in an article entitled 'Je suis un evadé':

'I am an escapee.' That is not the title of a film with Paul Muni. No, it is an actual fact. The 19th transport train that was meant to take me to Poland, is travelling at 60 kilometres an hour. The doors are locked and every five minutes the route and the train are illuminated by floodlights. Deportation by the Nazis has become reality and it is synonymous with death. I decide to flee. There is the lowered window pane of the lower wagon door. And with one leap, I land on the cold earth. I remain lying stretched out there until dawn. I feel a terrible pain in my left arm. After escaping, I return with a broken arm. Am I an individual case? No, on every train, dozens of deportees resist death.[262]

Meyer Tabakman was recaptured on 10 April 1943 and sent on the next deportation train to Auschwitz.[263] He again managed to flee from the 20th transport with the help of a tool that his father, the Resistance fighter Szrul-Israël Tabakman, had arranged to be smuggled into the Dossin barracks from the outside.[264] When the train slowed down shortly after passing through Boutersem, Meyer Tabakman jumped.

On 1 December 1943, he was discovered again in the district of Forest while producing false papers and arrested. A day later, he was interned once more in Mechelen together with his wife Rosa Kibel. They were kept there until 15 January 1944 and finally deported on the 23rd transport. Due to his previous escapes, Meyer Tabakman was placed on a special list together with twenty-one other prisoners and loaded onto a separate wagon. The couple were selected for labour in Auschwitz. Rosa Kibel was initially deployed in Auschwitz, before being taken to Ravensbrück and from there to Neustadt in 1944, where she was liberated by American soldiers.[265] Her husband Meyer Tabakman was killed in January 1944 in Auschwitz, as were three of his siblings.[266]

The 20th Transport

The history of the 20th deportation train that left Mechelen on 19 April 1943 is unique not only in Belgium, but also throughout Europe. On the day of departure, three young men stopped the train, which was carrying 1,636 Jews to Auschwitz in forty wagons, in the open countryside during the night. The three men intended to free the prisoners.[267] It is the only train carrying Jewish deportees that was ever attacked by Resistance fighters. Seventeen people managed to escape as a result of the attack. However, many prisoners had already planned to flee from the train. Thus, ultimately, in addition to this spectacular liberation operation from the outside, another 215 deportees managed to escape from the train by their own efforts before reaching the German border. A total of 232 prisoners managed to escape.

The 20th deportation train was guarded by members of the Schutzpolizei from Cologne, who had arrived at the Mechelen camp on the evening before the departure.²⁶⁸ Third-class passenger wagons had been used until the 18th/19th deportation train. Their doors were locked, but the windows could be opened and many of those who had jumped had climbed through those windows. After this, freight wagons were used to make it more difficult for prisoners to flee. Unlike the passenger wagons, freight wagons had only one sliding door and two hatches that were secured with barbed wire and nailed boards. People intending to escape therefore increasingly required tools. Prisoners regularly managed to smuggle saws, files, pliers and other tools into the wagons, and many of them managed to break open the wooden walls from inside or clear the hatches.

The deportees of the 20th transport also had two other supporters: the Belgian train drivers Albert Simon and Dumon, who significantly reduced the train's speed on a number of occasions to allow people to escape.²⁶⁹ Members of the Comité de défense des Juifs (CDJ) had previously made sure of the railwaymen's support.²⁷⁰

The Attack on the 20th Transport

Meyer Tabakman's report on his escape from the 19th transport, which was published in *Le Flambeau* in March 1943, inspired the 38-year-old Ghert Jospa from Bessarabia to find a way to stop the trains and liberate the prisoners inside. Jospa himself had written in the same edition of *Le Flambeau*, stating that Nazi deportations were tantamount to a death sentence.²⁷¹ Together with his wife Yvonne, Ghert Jospa, who had been born in Romania, and Maurits Bolle ran the CDJ section 'Help for Partisans'. Jospa, Bolle and Roger Van Praag began planning an armed attack on the next deportation train.²⁷² However, when Jospa showed the plans to Jean Terfve, a Communist leader of the partisans, it was rejected for being too dangerous.²⁷³

Jean Terfve explained that to attack a train, at least twenty partisans with rifles and grenades were required to attack the German guards at the front and the rear of the train. Since the German guard team would immediately shoot, it would lead to a bloodbath. And this would be an unpredictable risk for the underground group, which was heavily depleted at the time. There was also a lack of transport for the escaping prisoners. If they began to seek shelter from the locals, it would endanger many other people who had gone into hiding to avoid their labour assignments.²⁷⁴

Partisan Groupe G also refused to help. They had only very limited means and hardly any men who could handle weapons. Groupe G carried out acts of sabotage, but was not accustomed to direct conflict or the handling of firearms, so they were not prepared to engage in an exchange of fire.²⁷⁵ Bolle, however, refused to give up his plan and responded that risk was a part of Resistance work. He pointed out that the deportation trains always travelled at night, which would provide protection for people attacking it. There was also the element of surprise since the Germans would certainly not expect an operation of this kind.

Georges Livchitz, also known as Youra, was also immediately fascinated by the idea of attacking the train.[276] He was a fellow student and friend of Bolle's daughter, and brother of the known Resistance fighter Alexander Livchitz. Eventually, Youra Livchitz managed to convince his non-Jewish former school friends to join him in his plan: Jean Franklemon, a 25-year-old Communist and former fighter in Spain, and the 22-year-old medical student Robert Maistriau, who had never before participated in a Resistance operation.[277] The CDJ provided the three men with 50,000 Belgian Francs, in 50-Franc notes, which were to be distributed among the prisoners who were freed from the wagons to fund their continued escape.[278] An old friend of Youra Livchitz, who was active in Groupe G, gave them a small-calibre revolver.[279]

The moon shone brightly that night as Youra Livchitz, Jean Franklemon and Robert Maistriau, equipped only with the pistol and a pair of pliers, stopped the 20th deportation train between Boortmeerbeek and Wespelaer, 13 km from Mechelen.[280] They had covered a storm lamp with red paper, which Maistriau placed on the track, making it look from a distance like an emergency signal.[281] The train driver did indeed brake. Maistriau ran to a wagon. He lost sight of his comrades as the initially surprised guards started shooting at them. Maistriau was in a good position behind the train, far from the guards posted at the front. He began opening the locked doors of the wagon, which was difficult because he held a lamp in one hand and worked with the pliers in the other. Once he had opened the door, he called out both in French and in a few words of German, since many of the prisoners could only speak German. His accent was enough for everyone to realize that he was not a German guard. Some escaped immediately from the train and others began to scream that nobody should flee, as it was very dangerous. Maistriau led two consecutive groups away from the train, giving each person a 50-Franc note so they would have a little money for their continued escape. He then returned to the train to open a second wagon. Due to the rifle shots fired towards him, he hesitated, and in that moment the train began to move again. The whole operation last between fifteen and twenty minutes.

The three attackers of the 20th transport initially escaped. Youra Livchitz was arrested on 14 May 1943, but was able to steal his guard's revolver, shoot him down and flee. Following his renewed arrest, he was taken to the police prison camp in Breendonk.[282] He was shot there on 26 June 1943 by the SD, who described him as the leader of a band of terrorists, for attacking a 'Judentransport'.[283] Jean Franklemon was also captured and survived in Sachsenhausen concentration camp until its liberation.[284] In 1968, he moved to the GDR, to Kleinmachnow, where he died in 1977.[285] In May 1944, Robert Maistriau was taken as a 'political Belgian' from the SD in Brussels to Buchenwald concentration camp.[286] He was transferred to the Mittelbau-Dora subcamp on 23 May 1944 and survived Nazi persecution.[287] In retrospect, Maistriau stated that the entire operation had been highly improvised and lacked any kind of logistical consideration. They had been only three men, with one revolver from Youra Livchitz and otherwise unarmed. As he commented, 'you probably had to be twenty-two years old to try something like that'.[288]

Hinda Vistinezki and Mendelis Judelis Goldsteinas – Escape from the 20th Transport on 19 April 1943

Among the prisoners in the wagon opened by Maistriau, which was fifteenth from the front of the train, were Hinda Vistinezki (born in Maryampoli/Lithuania in 1904) and Mendelis Judelis Goldsteinas (born in Maryampoli/Lithuania in 1901). The married couple had immigrated to Belgium from Lithuania in the 1920s and settled down in the district of Forest.[289] They were arrested and interned in the Dossin barracks on 19 February 1943. Mendelis Goldsteinas recalls their escape: when the deportation train stopped, it was initially unclear what was happening, but when the door opened, they began to flee from the train. He was one of the first to leap out. He called to his wife that she should also jump, but the others, mainly women, had begun to scream and the wagon elder wanted to stop people from escaping.[290] Hinda Vistinezki reports that the wagon elder tried to block her way through the open door. He and others wanted to prevent the escapes for fear of repercussions.[291] Once the couple had jumped off the wagon, they ran away, following the others. Shots were fired at them and they threw themselves to the ground. Then they continued to run. Goldsteinas stated that Robert Maistriau gave him a 50-Franc note and explained the way to Brussels. Once they had returned to Brussels, the couple went into hiding until the liberation of Belgium.[292]

Régine Krochmal – Escape from the 20th Transport on 19 April 1943

The trained nurse Régine Krochmal (born in The Hague in 1920) was at the very back of the train in the last wagon. Together with a doctor, it was her task to accompany the seriously ill and dying to Auschwitz. Régine Krochmal grew up in Brussels, the daughter of a German mother and a German-Polish father.[293] When her mother died after a long illness, Régine was forced to leave school at the age of twelve and manage the household for her father and brother. After the invasion of the Wehrmacht, she fled with her family to France, but since they were unable to continue, they turned back. Régine Krochmal managed to pass her nurse's exam shortly before Jews became ineligible for the profession. She became active in the Resistance group 'Travail allemand' – without any prior political education, as she stresses. This group included many organized veterans of the Spanish Civil War, most of whom had been active in Austria in the Communist or Socialist Party. At the Brussels registration office, she stole stamps, wrote many 'V' signs for victory against the Germans on house walls and tried to be charming to soldiers of the Wehrmacht to make them insecure and 'turn' them. The underground newspaper produced by her group was called *Die Wahrheit* ('The Truth'). One day, the Gestapo came into the apartment where the paper was produced. As had been arranged for such an event, while the others took the copying machine and the already produced newspapers to safety, Krochmal showed them ID papers that a colleague had stolen from the hospital. The deception failed and Régine Krochmal was taken to Gestapo headquarters on Avenue Louise. Two other prisoners in her cell, who had been badly tortured, advised her to throw herself out of the window, if possible, during her interrogation.

Régine Krochmal was taken to Mechelen, where she considered escaping. As a Polish citizen, she was forced to live in especially poor conditions and was exposed to violence. It was dangerous to reveal oneself as an active member of the Resistance, so it was often the case that Resistance members were unaware of each other in the transit camp. Régine Krochmal did not know the destination of the deportation trains, nor had she heard of successful escapes from previous trains, either previously or in the camp.

On 19 April 1943, she was called upon to board the 20th deportation train. The Jewish camp doctor, Dr Bach, allocated her to the wagon with the sick prisoners at the very end of the train. He secretly gave her a knife and told her to saw through the bars, because they would burn her where they were taking her. As usual, the Germans had threatened to shoot everyone in a wagon if one person attempted to escape from it.

Inside the wagon, Régine Krochmal was joined by a man of roughly the same age, and piles of people. Most of them were dead; a few still lived but were mortally sick. After the door closed, she looked around for a way to escape. The ventilation hatches were small and high up. She took out her knife and began sawing at the wooden bars. The young man asked her what she was doing and declared that if she fled, all those who remained behind would be shot. She replied that instead of being shot, they would all be burnt. He asked if she had gone mad and enquired about her profession. When she answered that she was a nurse, he replied that he was a doctor and that one cannot leave sick people alone and must instead help them. Régine Krochmal responded that they were at war and she was a member of the Resistance. She encouraged him to flee with her, but he replied: 'Never'.[294] There was a fight, in which she knocked him down. She was able to saw through the bars and pull herself up to the hatch. Although her train was travelling very quickly, she let herself drop shortly before Leuven. The moment she hit the ground, the train stopped. That was fortunate for her, since her cape would otherwise have been run over by the wheels. She heard shots and screams, but remained on the ground beside the track and filled her mouth with earth to stop her screaming if she were hit by a bullet.

When all was quiet, she stood up and walked to a signalman's hut opposite her. Armed with her knife and determined to defend herself to the utmost, she entered the hut. A young railwayman was sitting there. Krochmal told him that she had jumped from the wagon and if he intended to betray her, she would kill him. He placed his index finger on his lips as a sign that he would be silent and then quickly went to a side room that was filled with hay bales. The Germans arrived almost immediately with dogs and asked if there had been any incidents. The signalman said all was well and invited them in for a drink. The Germans stayed for a long time and their dogs fell asleep while Régine Krochmal hid in silence beneath the hay bales. The next morning, the signalman gave her something to eat and described the way to a tram stop, from where she could return to Brussels.

Régine Krochmal was helped by her Resistance group. Her hair was dyed blond and she was unable to leave the apartments where she hid for a month. Some time later, she began attempting to 'turn' young Wehrmacht soldiers again. When she went for a walk with a young soldier one day, she was recognized by another who knew about her 'ruse'. She was arrested and severely tortured. Until the liberation, she remained in custody in the Brussels Saint-Gilles prison, in Breendonk and in Mechelen. When asked whether she regarded her escape from the train as a form of resistance, she replied: 'One must do everything one can against an enemy that . . . makes war on life'.[295]

Louis J. Micheels – Attempted Escape from the 20th Transport on 19 April 1943

Régine Krochmal's account of the conditions in the wagons carrying sick and dying people is confirmed by Louis J. Micheels, who was born in the Netherlands in 1917 and was appointed Transport Doctor in a different wagon of the 20th transport. Together with his girlfriend Nora (surname unknown) and around twenty sick women and children, he was driven into a wagon with straw on the floor. The bars in front of the ventilation hatch had been nailed shut with boards from the outside. He and Nora tended the sick as well as they could. One woman was almost dead. They were unable to help anyone, however, as they had neither medical equipment nor medicines. He and Nora hugged each other and felt terribly alone. Micheels wrote about the situation in the wagon as follows: 'The others hardly seemed like human beings any more. We were surrounded by nameless death'.[296] He considered trying to escape. It might have been possible to remove the wooden boards over the hatch, but the guards were at the front, in the middle and at the end of the train, as well as on the roof. What if he got out, but his girlfriend did not? In his mind, he saw himself jump off the train, roll on the ground and be reborn as a free man.

Suddenly the train stopped abruptly. The wagon was illuminated, shots were heard. Louis J. Micheels said to Nora: 'This must be the attack by the partisans I was told about in Mechelen'.[297] The statement by Louis J. Micheels suggests that the plan to attack the 20th transport must already have been known to individuals in the Mechelen transit camp. Micheels looked through the hatch and saw people running towards a wooded area, some screaming in pain. He tried to break away the boards in front of the hatch to flee from the wagon as well, but he was not strong enough. The train set off again.[298]

Louis J. Micheels survived Auschwitz and other camps. He was liberated on a death march in Mittenwald, Bavaria.

Claire Prowizur and Philippe Szyper – Escape from the 20th Transport on 19 April 1943

A young married couple, Klara Prowizur (born in Altona in 1923), who changed her first name to Claire, and Frain-Wolf Szyper (born in Józefów/occupied Poland in 1916), who called himself Philippe, also managed to flee.[299] Claire Prowizur's father emigrated to Germany when he was just sixteen years old without family due to the strong anti-Semitism in Poland, and he married there. Klara was born and the family moved to Brussels where they soon experienced economic difficulties. Food became scarce; Claire's father lost his work permit, was repeatedly imprisoned and began to drink. Countless times, the police came to deport him back to Germany, but he returned each time. Claire Prowizur-Szyper wrote in 1978 that her father was a victim of a racist, unjust society. She therefore developed a growing sense of justice at the age of twelve, became active in the Socialist Faucons Rouges (Red Falcons) and was soon a member of the Jewish Socialist Bund. For her, the meetings were a place of refuge and she identified herself with the Socialist ideals presented there. Claire

Prowizur-Szyper reports on the miserable situation in which the German Jewish refugees found themselves, since they were not welcome in Belgium either as Jews or as Germans. A large number of people had attempted to emigrate overseas. Jews in Belgium had not known what to expect in the case of a German invasion. They were sympathetic to Jews who had been driven out of Germany, but for egoistic reasons they had wanted them to leave Belgian territory as soon as possible.

When the Wehrmacht invaded, the by now seventeen-year-old Claire Prowizur was a convinced Trotskyist, wrote slogans on walls at night, and distributed flyers in street postboxes, as well as the journal *La Lutte Ouvrière*. In the evenings she attended Marx courses at the Workers' University in Brussels. Together with Philippe Szyper and other young people, she built up a secret network of small, separately active cells that were only connected to each other via delegates. When the yellow star was introduced for Jews, members of the party decided not to wear it. As a Jew, Claire lost her employment; Philippe, who was a tailor, became self-employed. In January 1942 the couple married, despite family objections, without a religious ceremony. Claire Prowizur, who had attended a course in tailoring and sewing, then worked together with her husband. Their political activities took place in the evenings. Claire Prowizur proofread articles by mineworkers that were to be printed in an illegal magazine.

The pressure of persecution increased. Claire Prowizur's parents managed to hide with friends from the party. One problem of underground work was the lack of financial means and provisions. As Claire Prowizur describes, the problem was the lack of possibilities for Jews hiding underground to express themselves. They founded cells of non-Jewish members who cared for their Jewish comrades. Their cell consisted of Albert, Frédéric and Jacques. In October 1942, she learnt from an escaped eyewitness, a comrade from the French Trotskyist party, of the extermination of the Jews. Claire Prowizur-Szyper reports that she spoke to a number of fugitives from the 19th deportation train after their return to Brussels. This had been the first time that the occupiers had experienced open resistance. They, the escapees, dared to resist the enemy unarmed.

In Brussels, Claire became an eyewitness of her father's arrest. He had been betrayed by the Jewish Gestapo informer 'gros Jacques', who was also present at the arrest. In late January 1943, the Gestapo also arrested Claire Prowizur and Philippe Szyper. Anti-Nazi brochures had been found in their home. Szyper was taken to Gestapo headquarters on Avenue Louise, identified as a Jew and badly beaten. The two were taken to the Dossin barracks. After the humiliating reception procedure, during which the SS guards attempted to gain information on other members of her family, Claire met her father again. She reports that news of the defeat of the

German Wehrmacht near Stalingrad had reached the camp and that the mood among camp prisoners was therefore excited and tense.

Albert Clément, an acquaintance, was also interned and selected for work in the camp carpentry. He was required to build wooden bars with which to seal the ventilation hatches of the freight wagons. Clément collected saws with which the bars could be sawn off during the journey from the inside. One prisoner in each wagon was to receive a saw from Clément. He told those whom he trusted that everyone who intended to jump from the train would receive 50 Francs before their escape. In each future wagon group, there was someone whom Clément had organized to incite an escape from the wagon; their group included two Dutch men, a father and son, aged forty-five and twenty. Claire Prowizur, her father and Philippe Szyper were among those who intended to escape. Some refused, since they were responsible for the fate of their parents or children, who had also been allocated to the same wagon. Others were afraid or were unable to jump from the moving train due to their age or their physical or psychological condition.

Shortly before the departure of the 20th transport on 19 April 1943, the barracks were filled with hectic activity. Jews were brought from hospitals and care facilities to achieve the planned number of two thousand deportees. Claire Prowizur's father fell ill with a high fever. She reports that based on her registration number, she knew that she would be allocated to the third wagon, while her father would be in the first. Since her father was so sick, she did not want him to board a different wagon. She managed to find someone who was willing to switch with her father.

At 9:00, under heavy guard, they were forced to board the wagons in groups of one hundred people. The SS appointed the Dutch man with the saw as the wagon elder. At the same time, it informed him that he was responsible for the welfare of the one hundred people in the wagons and if anyone was missing on arrival, his fate would not be pleasant. Inside the wagon, it was apparently incredibly constricted and there was little air to breathe. The deportees tried to arrange themselves so that they could sit down. The Dutchman appointed as wagon elder and his son promised to jump first to serve as an example.

It was already night when the train departed. Those who had decided to escape discussed how they would do so. They had to flee on Belgian territory and under no circumstances in Germany. They calculated that they still had two hours before they reached the German border.[300] When someone tried to take the saw from the wagon elder's hand, he suddenly panicked: he screamed and gesticulated that nobody was to leave the wagon since he was responsible for a full count on arrival. Some people attempted to jump on top of him to end his madness, but he developed incredible strength and threatened anyone who approached him. Inside the wagon there was chaos and panic that is described as hellish. The son tried to approach his father, and precisely at that moment, a group of people threw themselves onto the wagon elder. With the son's help, they managed to overcome him and wrap him so tightly in blankets that they acted like a straitjacket.

The bars were sawn off. Suddenly the train stopped. They heard and saw that the Germans were shooting at fugitives and were pursuing them. Enormous floodlights were pointed at the field where the fugitives were fleeing. From the wagon, it had looked like a shadow play. After a while, the Germans returned with some fugitives; others had been shot dead. The train set off again.

Claire Prowizur-Szyper reports that the incident had no influence on their plans to escape, since they had been aware of the risks in advance. Her father, who was completely dehydrated and exhausted, had fallen into a coma during the journey. She knew that he could not flee with her, but she did not want to leave him alone. Her husband asked her urgently what the use was of such a sacrifice. She had to face the facts that her father was in a coma. Once they arrived in Auschwitz, they would be separated. Claire replied that he should put himself in her position. How could she let her father down? Philippe Szyper continued to try to convince her: if there was even a minimal chance of saving her father, he would not encourage her to jump, but that was not the case. After a long discussion, Claire Prowizur decided with a heavy heart to jump with her husband and leave her dying father behind in the wagon.

Philippe Szyper described to her exactly how she was to leap to minimize injuries. He said he would follow. As agreed, she climbed along the outside wall of the wagon until she was between two wagons. There she waited for a good moment to jump. She held her arms around her head and rolled over. Claire Prowizur-Szyper stated that had anyone asked her another time whether it was possible to leap from a train travelling at 80 km an hour, in full view of the enemy, she would have denied it.

When shots were fired, she was afraid that her husband had been hit. She ran in his direction, saw him, they embraced, cried and laughed. They looked dirty and dishevelled. In the tumult of events, they had left the money they had received for their escape behind in the wagon. They walked for some time and discovered the body of a fugitive who had been shot. In the next village, they found a church and told the priest: 'We are Jews and have jumped from the train. We have no money and ask for your help'.[301] The priest gave them 50 Francs. They were near Liège, to which they travelled by tram, as they had a relative who lived there. His wife received them and cared for them. From there, they sent a coded telegram to their cell in Brussels. Their fellow members collected the couple by car and took them back to Brussels. With the help of their cell, the couple managed to survive Nazi persecution.

Claire Prowizur-Szyper recounted how, twenty years later, a woman spoke to her on the streets of Tel Aviv. She said she had been looking for her for twenty years, as she had a message from her father. When her father regained consciousness and realized that the two had fled, he asked the woman, who had also been in the wagon, to seek her daughter wherever she was in the world and to tell her that he was happy that she jumped and that she should live in peace and could not have acted in a better way.

Simon Gronowski – Escape from the 20th Transport on 19 April 1943

One of the youngest fugitives from the train was Simon Gronowski (born in Brussels in 1931).[302] His father had emigrated to Belgium due to the severe anti-Semitism in Poland. There he married a Lithuanian-born woman and opened a leatherwork store. Ita and Simon were born seven years apart. The family spoke Yiddish and French. Little Simon was an enthusiastic scout. When the Wehrmacht invaded, the Gronowskis fled south like many others, but also like so many, soon returned to Belgium. Simon Gronowski describes his parents as apolitical, which is why his father was more helpless in the face of Jewish persecution by the German occupiers than, for instance, the Socialists and Communists, who had been able to defend themselves more effectively. The occupiers initially behaved in a polite and reserved way, but as the anti-Jewish measures mounted, so did the pressure of persecution.

Friends from Simon's scout club urged Simon's father to take the family into hiding. In September 1942, they were concealed in an apartment that was officially occupied by a woman who lived alone. Simon Gronowski tells how his father was careless due to his political naivety. The family remained together instead of splitting up into different hiding places, and they also left the house occasionally. When Simon's father had to go into hospital, their hideout was betrayed. On 17 March 1943, two German policemen came and took Simon, his mother and his sister to Gestapo headquarters on Avenue Louise. After one night, they were transferred to Mechelen. The induction procedure was terrible, violent and humiliating. Simon's sister was initially exempt from deportation since the sixteen-year-old had opted for Belgian citizenship.

In the camp, there were rumours that people had managed to escape from previous deportation trains. Simon believed that the only conceivable option was to leap to freedom. They had no idea of the actual plans of the National Socialists. In their dormitory, which accommodated one hundred people, there were three-storey bunkbeds. There were many children in Mechelen, with whom Simon simulated jumping from the train by leaping from the top bunk. The trams in Brussels were open at the time, allowing one to jump from them while they were still in motion. Simon had often done that, and states today: 'At the age of 11, I was a specialist, even when the tram was travelling at speed'.[303]

On the day of the deportation, the 'loading' of Jews onto the wagons began. The procedure lasted for hours and was very frightening. Simon's sister remained in Mechelen. Inside the wagon, it was dark as there were only two hatches. During the journey, the train suddenly stopped and they heard cries from the Germans and shots being fired. The train continued its journey. Simon slept in the arms of his mother while some men tried to open the wagon door. When they succeeded, his mother woke him, took his hand and led him to the open door. Two or three prisoners had jumped before him.[304] Simon waited his turn, then his mother helped him onto the running board. With his left hand he held onto a bar, while with his right hand he clung onto the floor of the wagon. His mother held him from above by his shoulders and clothes. She said to him in Yiddish: 'The train is moving too fast'.[305] Then it braked, Simon jumped and rolled down the railway escarpment. He immediately heard shots and the train stopped. Guards came in his direction, shouted and fired shots. Simon's first instinct was to run back to the wagon. He was afraid of the guards and wanted to be with his mother, who had been unable to jump due to the shots aimed at them by the Schutzpolizei. The way back to the wagon was now blocked by guards, so he ran away from the train, into the forest, and continued all through the night. He looked forward to seeing his father, his dog Bobby and his scout friends again. The next morning, he knocked at the door of a worker's house in the Flemish town of Borgloon. A woman opened the door. Afraid of collaborators, Simon said he was playing here in the town with other children, but had lost them and now wanted to return to his father in Brussels. The woman went with him to the Gendarmerie and handed him over to them. Simon was afraid that they would deliver him to the Gestapo, but instead, the Gendarme, Jean Aerts, took the young boy to his wife, who cared for him. But the story of the young French-speaking boy from Brussels who had 'lost his way' while playing with Flemish boys so far from home seemed implausible to the Gendarme. He went to the railway station and learnt of the escapes of the previous night. Jean Aerts drove home and told Simon: 'I know everything. . . . You escaped and don't need to be afraid. I'm a good Belgian and won't denounce you'. Simon Gronowski also recalls: 'I threw my arms around him and told him of my mother'.[306]

In the evening, for security reasons, Jean Aerts took Simon Gronowski by bicycle to a railway station that was further away, from where the boy travelled to Brussels without incident. There he boarded a tram and remained standing near the driver to be able to evade any ticket inspectors in time. He thought: 'I've managed to jump from the train, so I can also jump off a tram'.[307] As soon as he reached his scout friends, they took him to his father, who was living in hiding thanks to their help.

Simon Gronowski was separated from his father and hidden among two different families. He survived Nazi persecution. After the liberation of the Buchenwald and Dachau concentration camps, his father became aware of the Nazi atrocities and realized that his wife and daughter Ita, who had been deported on the 22nd transport from Mechelen, would never return. His father, who was sick and weak, died in July 1945 – as Simon Gronowski says, of despair. Later, Simon Gronowski learnt that three of the fugitives from his wagon had been shot dead while fleeing, including a young girl.[308]

Today, Simon Gronowski's story is known to many children in Belgium. It is told in a high-circulation picture book that is distributed and read at schools.[309]

Marie Neufeld and Günther Mendel – Escapes from the 20th Transport on 19 April 1943

Marie Neufeld (later married name Mendel) (born in Berlin in 1924) and Günther Mendel (born in Düsseldorf in 1919) jumped from different wagons of the 20th transport. In 1939, Marie Neufeld used the help of a smuggler, who was paid in jewellery, to flee across the German-Belgian border together with two friends at the age of only fifteen.[310] A Jewish aid committee arranged employment for her as a nanny in a Jewish family, where she also lived. She was very homesick. She also worked in a café in Brussels, where she engaged with German soldiers during the occupation. She pretended to them that she was from Luxembourg. Around 1941, a soldier from Berlin showed her war photos of mistreated and murdered Jews. Marie Neufeld recalls: 'All skeletons, like Auschwitz, heaps of bodies'.[311] The images later motivated her to flee. In 1942, she hid for two months with a Belgian couple, after which she was forced to return to her own apartments. A Jewish Gestapo informer denounced her in March 1943. She was arrested and taken to Gestapo headquarters, before being transferred to the Dossin barracks.

Marie Neufeld had been there a week when Günther Mendel was interned in the camp, arriving with a bruised face. They met and talked a great deal. Marie Neufeld shared her food package with him and Günther

Mendel told her how much his own and his family's lives had changed since the National Socialists had taken power. He had been forced to leave the Prinz-Georg-Gymnasium (secondary school) in Düsseldorf and began an apprenticeship as a machine operator. His father lost his job as a bank director because he was Jewish. During the November pogrom, men burst into his apartment, beat Günther's father and threw the furniture out of the window. It was a clear enough message that he had to flee any way he could.[312] Since his father ruled out the possibility of them all fleeing together, he accompanied Günther to the German-Belgian border and paid a smuggler to take the boy to his uncle in Brussels.

A month after his arrival, he was arrested in the apartment of his uncle by the Belgian police and placed in solitary confinement in the Brussels Saint-Gilles prison for six weeks. He was then taken to the camp in Huy Fortress near the German border. When war broke out, the internees were freed and the Jews among them fled from the approaching German soldiers. Günther Mendel made it to France, where the Germans overtook him. The German police initially took him to Aachen and deported him to Belgium from there. His parents wrote to him on 7 December 1941 from the Litzmannstadt (Łódź) ghetto. The postcard, requesting a sign of life, did indeed reach him in Brussels.[313] In 1942, when the Gestapo in Belgium began its hunt for Jews, Günther Mendel went underground with the help of false identity papers, for which he had paid.

In March 1943, the Jewish Gestapo informer 'gros Jacques' betrayed him. Günther Mendel was arrested and taken to the notorious Avenue Louise, where he was mistreated. His tormentors quickly discovered that his papers were false and wanted him to tell them where he had been living and whether other Jews were hidden there. He was then transferred to Mechelen. Since Günther Mendel had been living underground, he was treated especially badly by the camp administration and had to empty the latrines.

Marie Neufeld and Günther Mendel discussed the chance of fleeing from the train, since they had heard rumours of such escapes. Both were included on the list for the 20th transport. Günther, who was allocated to a different wagon, gave Marie 100 Francs before the departure and an address in Brussels where they could meet again.

In the case of Marie Neufeld, who had seen photos belonging to a German soldier that portrayed the murder of Jews, this knowledge motivated her to attempt an escape from the train.[314] She recalls that while on the train, she constantly saw in her mind's eye the piles of bodies that the soldier had shown her in the photographs.[315] She was locked into a wagon together with many elderly people. Only two younger people were also willing to flee. Marie Neufeld asked if she could jump first, since there was no-one else to lift her up to the hatch. As she jumped, she lost a shoe, but her 100 Francs were still hidden in her sock. She injured her head and was bleeding. On her way, she met another fugitive from the train and joined him. After some time, they came across an illuminated farmhouse. There, they exchanged the dripping wet 100-Franc note with the farmer for a pair of slip-on shoes and 50 Francs to pay for the return tickets.

In Brussels, Marie Neufeld followed her companion to the place where his family had been in hiding. Another man, who had also fled from the train and been injured by gunfire, also arrived there. The man explained that he had seen Günther Mendel jump from the train. Marie Neufeld was given a jacket because her coat was smeared with blood as a result of her fall. A doctor from the Jewish Committee came to treat the injured fugitive's bullet wound and Marie Neufeld's head injury. She went to her old apartment, where her caretaker was very pleased to see her. At eight in the evening, under cover of darkness, she went to the address that Günther Mendel had given her. His friends were very suspicious when she spoke of Günther's escape. They were afraid that she might by a spy, but when they saw her swollen knee they offered to let her wait there for Günther until 22:00. She would have to leave if he did not arrive by then. Günther came through the door punctually at 22:00.

Günther Mendel recounted that in his wagon, there was a discussion on how to return to the city after escaping, so he distributed his money among the others. Only a very small number of deportees decided to attempt to flee, however, because – in Günther Mendel's words – they lacked the courage to do so.[316] The hatch in the wagon had been boarded shut. A prisoner in the wagon had a screwdriver and managed to remove the screw from the boards within fifteen minutes of departing. Someone in the wagon gave them advice on how to jump:

> Don't put your head out and wait until we come to a bend, because the guards could shoot us from the cars where the Gestapo was. . . . So when I jumped out, I went out foot first and I got between the two cars, there is a platform, . . . I was holding myself on the platform and jumped off. Now you have to throw yourself backwards, because the train was maybe 30, 40 miles per hour, that's not too fast. Anyway, I still fell over, landed on my knees and hands, but that was OK. . . . and the train was gone. I was lucky I landed at an abandoned train station.[317]

Due to the curfew, Günther Mendel hid near Leuven in the open air beneath a tree around midnight. The next day, he returned to Brussels and met up with Marie Neufeld as hoped. They remained together and hid until the liberation in September 1944, together with a mutual friend, in the former apartment of Marie Neufeld. Her landlord shared food with them. Marie Neufeld and Günther Mendel married in August 1945.[318]

Izrael Sztejnberg – Escape from the 20th Transport on 19 April 1943

For years, Izrael Sztejnberg (born in Vilnius in 1890) had gathered experience in avoiding capture by the law. Due to a series of crimes, apparently pickpocketing, he had been convicted in Cracow, Memel (today's Klaipeda), Halle, Stuttgart, Vienna, Cattowice, Paris and, in 1937, Brussels. He was deported from Brussels to Austria and was again arrested in Vienna in 1938 and once more by the police in Brussels in 1939. From there he went to Italy, taking an unknown route, from where he was deported to Belgium.[319] Back in Belgium, he was again deported, but returned immediately. He was then arrested in Liège for theft.[320] Since it was impossible to deport him again due to the outbreak of war, he was sentenced to ten months' imprisonment.[321]

The Wehrmacht invaded Belgium while he was serving his sentence in the prisons in Forest and Saint-Gilles.[322] Izrael Sztejnberg was classified as an 'enemy foreigner' and taken to the Merksplas internment camp near Antwerp on 9 September 1940.[323] From there, the SD moved him to Breendonk on 4 October 1940, where he was mistreated and finally sent to Mechelen.[324] He jumped from the 20th transport in unknown circumstances. After his successful escape, he assumed the false name Alberto Ferrari and returned to Brussels. When he was again arrested, he stated that he had heard that the Belgians were not handing over any prisoners to the Germans and that he had therefore committed the crime. On 24 June and in November 1943, he was arrested for pickpocketing and sentenced to six months' imprisonment.[325]

Sztejnberg was subsequently interned in the camp in Rekem and then transferred to the Petit Château camp on 21 October 1945, where former Belgian members of the SS were imprisoned with him. In an appeal for a pardon, he stated that he had been forced to hear the other prisoners discuss the murderous crimes against the Jews and endure their anti-Semitism.[326] In 1946, he was freed from custody and repatriated to Vilnius. It seems that he did not find his family there and returned to Belgium.[327]

Willy Berler – Attempted Escape from the 20th Transport on 19 April 1943

Willy (Wilhelm) Berler (born in Czernowitz in 1918) was studying in Liège when the Wehrmacht invaded Belgium. Together with two friends, he initially fled south like so many other Jewish and non-Jewish Belgians. In late October 1940, when he realized that the idea of continuing via Marseille was unfeasible, he returned with a heavy heart to Liège. There, he tried to live as inconspicuously as possible and not identify himself as a Jew. But Willy Berler was denounced and arrested on 1 April 1942. After remaining in custody in Liège's citadel prison, he was transferred to Mechelen on 17 April 1943 and sent on a transport two days later. Willy Berler writes:

> In my wagon, there are two guys, ... They had already escaped from a train, . . . The two appear to be the only ones who know our destination and tell me. They are also the only ones who have a rough idea of what to expect in Auschwitz. Immediately after our departure, they decide to escape again. They use a penknife and quite quickly manage to break open the bars of the hatch. And then they wait for a good opportunity when the train stops somewhere in Flanders, to leap up. Then I suddenly hear shots being fired.[328]

These were the shots fired during the attack on the 20th transport. When the train set off again, they again focused on their escape plans:

> It is essential to jump while we are still in Belgium. The five or six of us decide on the order in which we should escape – I am last of all. I am excited as I watch the comrade whose turn is before mine as he disappears through the hatch and then I pull myself up. I see that the boy who jumped before me has not made it. It is a terrible sight. He was caught hanging on the wagon and his head has been squashed between two shock absorbers like a melon. It must have been the first time I had seen a dead person. I feel dizzy and I don't want to risk my life – and drop back down into the wagon. Cowering in the corner, I decide to continue on the great journey. After all, I thought, we were heading for a labour camp. I'm young and strong – it can't be all that bad. Had I only had the slightest inkling of what awaited me in the camp, I would have dared to jump despite fearing for my life. Later in the camp, I regretted my hesitation countless times.[329]

Wilhelm Berler survived for two years in Auschwitz. When the camp was evacuated in January 1945, he was taken to Gross-Rosen, from where he was transferred to Buchenwald on 10 February 1945 and finally liberated there by the US army.[330]

Sandor Weisz and Other Resistance Fighters – Escape from the 20th Transport on 19 April 1943

Some escapes were already planned in the camp. For instance, twelve members of the Jewish Resistance intended to flee and tried to manipulate the transport lists so they were together in the same wagon of the 20th transport and could flee together. The camp prisoner Eva Fastag helped them in her task of typing the transport lists while the new arrivals were registered in the Mechelen transit camp. These lists were also used as the loading documents for the individual wagons: she secretly replaced the existing transport list with a new one, so that the twelve prisoners would be allocated to the same wagon.[331] Five days before the departure, a number of those planning to escape broke into the workshops of the transit camp and took whatever tools they could find there.[332]

The 20th transport was scheduled to deport, among others, members of the CDJ, the Travail allemand, the MOI and members of the Mouvement National Belge (MNB). The prisoners included Sandor Weisz (born in Mandok/Hungary in 1911). Weisz had previously lived in Brussels-Schaerbeek and had been active as a Communist for the MOI. Earlier in 1936, he had fought in the International Brigades in the Spanish Civil War under the name of Istvan Molnar. There he had been, among other things, a Captain in the Hungarian Rakoczi Battalion, Deputy Commander of the XIIIth Brigade and finally Commander of the Polish Palafox Battalion. He returned to Belgium in 1939. He spent some time in Budapest and Paris, where he served as a volunteer in the Czech Legion of the French army. In April 1941, he returned to Brussels, where he led the Balkan Company of the Mobile Corps des Partisans together with Émile Lovenwirth.[333] One especially spectacular operation led by Sandor Weisz was the attack on the Marivaux cinema during a rally there by the DeVlag movement.

Although he possessed a false passport, Sandor Weisz was arrested as a Jew in unknown circumstances.[334] He was taken to Mechelen and allocated to the 20th transport. Together with the other Resistance group members, he jumped from the moving deportation train. After escaping, Weisz again became active in the Mobile Corps des Partisans, made up of Hungarian fighters. Sandor Weisz was shot dead on 4 July 1943 during a surprise German attack in the forest of Soignes to the south of Brussels.[335]

Summary of the 20th Transport

The 20th transport departed from Mechelen with 1,631 prisoners; 433 were above the age of fifty and 76 were over seventy years old; 237 deportees were children under fifteen.[336] Of the 232 people who escaped from the train, twenty-six were either shot dead while fleeing or died as a result of wounds sustained from jumping.[337] Thus, every tenth train fugitive was either killed directly while fleeing or died from their wounds.[338] Eighty-seven fugitives were recaptured after escaping and deported on a subsequent train. According to Menasche Maximilian Brunner, who was interned in Mechelen, fugitives who were recaptured were chained in the following transport.[339] The former Deputy Camp Commander Max Boden testified that a photo was produced of every prisoner who was shot while fleeing and posted in the camp. According to Boden, this was to determine their identity, but was undoubtedly also a method of deterrence.³⁴⁰ Four days after the escapes, the Belgian Resistance informed the BBC that numerous fugitives from the deportation train had been shot dead.³⁴¹ One hundred and nineteen escapees were not recaptured.³⁴²

The 21st Transport

Like the previous transport, the Sipo-SD had difficulties gathering sufficient numbers of Jews to fill another train. The transport list of the 21st transport was begun on 15 April 1943 and only completed on 27 July, four days before the departure.³⁴³ The transport deported 1,562 people from Mechelen. The proportion of 174 children was unusually low, while 321 people were over fifty years old.³⁴⁴ Fifty-seven prisoners had fled from a previous transport, forty-one of whom from the 20th transport.³⁴⁵ According to a survivor, the latter were deported in a separate wagon and immediately murdered after arriving in Auschwitz.³⁴⁶

In her microanalytical study, Insa Meinen investigates the countries of origin of the 1,562 prisoners on this deportation train and shows that its constitution corresponds to the different groups that lived in Belgium at the time. Thus, more than half of the deportees were born in Poland, followed by 430 people (a group around half the size) born either in Austria or Germany. Just under one hundred had been born in the Netherlands, thirty-five in Czechoslovakia and only twenty-three in Belgium.³⁴⁷

Meinen explains the fact that so many Jews from Germany leapt from deportation trains by a 'greater awareness of the dangers'³⁴⁸ among German Jews, who were therefore far more likely to be willing to risk their lives and attempt the dangerous jump. Another insightful conclusion by Meinen is that although an above-average number of Germans jumped from the train, they had lower than average access to false papers or hideouts before being sent to Mechelen, presumably because they lacked the contacts.³⁴⁹

The route of the 21st transport was changed in an attempt to prevent prisoners from escaping: instead of travelling towards Tirlemont, the train headed for Hasselt. Until they reached the border, the Schutzpolizei guard team was reinforced to include SS guard company units from the Sipo-SD and Judenreferat employees.³⁵⁰ The German Ordnungspolizei took over guard duties after leaving Belgium.³⁵¹

According to Schram, ten prisoners jumped from this transport. Four were shot dead by the guards.³⁵²

Chaj Bina and Josek Majer Benkiel – Death while Escaping from the 21st Transport on 31 July 1943

The circumstances of the death of the married couple Chaj Bina (born in Brzeziny/occupied Poland in 1910) and Josek Majer Benkiel (born in Brzeziny/occupied Poland in 1910) are described in a somewhat implausible account by their daughter. While Steinberg and Schram write that both were shot dead by guards as they jumped from the train, their daughter, who was born in Brussels in 1931, stated that she had heard the following from survivors in the wagon from which her parents escaped. A number of prisoners had broken a hole in the side wall through which to escape, but the Germans had discovered it. When no-one admitted that they had made the hole, the Germans threatened to kill all the prisoners. Thus, her father, Josek Majer Benkiel, admitted the deed, whereupon he was taken away by the guards. His wife, who did not want to remain behind alone, also admitted to the deed. Both were shot there and then.

This version of events is unlikely since it would have been the only case in which guards actually carried out their threat of punishing escapes or attempted escapes with immediate execution.[353]

The train arrived in Auschwitz on 2 August 1943. Before its arrival, new gas chambers and new crematoria with larger volumes had been completed. One thousand and eighty-seven deportees were immediately gassed to death on arrival; 468 were taken to Auschwitz camp and registered there. Only forty were alive by 8 May 1945.[354]

Alice (Annaliese) Bonheim and Salomon Kleinmann – Escapes from Transport 22 A on 20 September 1943

Deportation trains 22 A and 22 B on 20 September 1943 were the last of the double trains. Maurice Kubowitzki, who was currently interned in Mechelen, said that by this time, camp prisoners were discussing previous escapes, the intentions of their German guards to prevent further escapes and the duration of the journey up to the border with the German Reich – a period of five hours.[355] A total of 1,433 Jews were driven onto the train. Eight deportees, one woman and seven men, managed to escape before crossing the border.[356]

Transport 22 A comprised 639 Jews, including seventy-six children. The A stands for 'Ausländisch' or 'Foreign', that is, Jews who did not have Belgian citizenship. Seven deportees leapt from the train, including Alice Bonheim (born in Schwerin in 1911). Her 'foreigner's ID papers' were issued by the Brussels district of Saint-Gilles in October 1940. Bonheim was divorced and she had worked as a secretary.[357] On 3 August 1943, she was arrested as a Jew in Saint-Gilles. After being detained for two days at Gestapo headquarters, she was taken to Mechelen. She was forced to board the deportation train on 20 September 1943. After a two-day journey, by then already far within German territory, she threw herself out of the train, but was recaptured in Liegnitz, Upper Silesia and detained in a police prison. After ten days, she also managed to flee from there. She managed to make her way back to Belgium undiscovered and hid from October 1943 to the liberation on 15 September 1944 with friends in Liège.[358]

The Polish citizen Salomon Kleinmann (born in Krefeld in 1909) also jumped from the same train.[359] In 1938, he had been reported to the Gestapo in Krefeld by the Managing Director of the 'Hallischen Krankenkasse' ('Halle Health Insurance Fund'), Hans Rodd, for using the Hitler salute despite being a Jew.[360] During a Gestapo interrogation in Düsseldorf on 2 September 1938, Kleinmann denied the accusation, but the denouncer Rodd stood by his version of events. In late October 1938, Kleinmann's parents were expelled to Poland. It seems that during an operation to intern Jewish prisoners in the concentration camps in Buchenwald, Dachau and Sachsenhausen following the November pogrom, Kleinmann was arrested on 11 November 1938 and taken to the Dachau camp. A day later, he informed the Gestapo that he intended to emigrate to Mexico and had spoken to the Mexican Consulate in Essen two weeks earlier. His cousin Toni Herbst applied for his release from Dachau on 7 December 1938. Salomon Kleinmann was released ten days later.[361] Nothing is known of the period between his release and his renewed arrest and internment in the Mechelen camp, apart from the fact that he was caught with false papers.[362] Salomon Kleinmann escaped from Transport 22 A and was not captured again. After the liberation, he moved back to Krefeld.[363]

Michel Altschuler – Escape from Transport 22 B on 20 September 1943

Although Belgian Jews had initially been exempt from deportation, Transport 22 B on 20 September 1943 deported Jews with Belgian citizenship to Auschwitz for the first time. The letter 'B' stood for Belgian Jews.[364] The transport deported a total of 794 Jews. Only one of them, the metal worker Michel Altschuler (born in Brussels in 1925), escaped. Altschuler was active in an anti-German Resistance group and assigned to monitor Karin Hatker, who was an employee of an unspecified, apparently German propaganda department. She denounced him in September 1943, resulting in his arrest and internment in Mechelen on 25 September. After his escape, he was again denounced by Karin Hatker and arrested once more. His second internment in Mechelen is dated 25 October 1943. He was taken to Auschwitz on the 23rd deportation train.[365] According to a statement by his brother-in-law, the last message from him came from Monowitz.[366]

Charles Grabiner – Aborted Attempt to Escape from Transport 22 B on 20 September 1943

Maurice Kubowitzki reports on the following circumstances of Transport 22 B. At midday on 21 September, the second day after the train's departure, the train stopped in a large German city that had been heavily bombed and the wagons were opened. The prisoners were permitted to briefly stretch their legs and refill their water supplies. The medical service went from wagon to wagon. Later, when they were sitting in the wagon again, one of the prisoners, named Charles Grabiner, said that he had wanted to fill up his water supply and had looked for a water tap. He came across some stairs, which he descended without thinking. When he realized that he was unobserved, he slipped through the entrance of the station ruin and was suddenly completely alone on the station forecourt. He considered not returning but then thought of his wife Dora who would have had to continue the journey alone. He also had what he called a characteristic Jewish profile. Fate had decided that he should return to the wagon. When he told his wife what he had experienced, she asked him why on Earth he had returned.[367]

Schaja Cukier – Death while Attempting to Escape from the 23rd Transport on 15 January 1944

A special list existed for the 23rd transport on 15 January 1944, which was attached to the transport list. It presented all those who had previously been successful in escaping from deportation trains – in the case of Meyer Tabakman, even twice – and recaptured. They were to be guarded with special care. Meyer Tabakman, who had escaped from the 18th/19th and the 20th train, was finally deported to Auschwitz on this transport.

A total of 659 prisoners, including sixty-two children, were on board the train. Five of them tried to flee before the train reached the border.[368] It was not the first time that Schaja Cukier (born in Przytyk/occupied Poland in 1908) had attempted to escape; she had already fled from the 20th transport. When she was about to be recaptured again, she resisted, although she was injured. She was taken to a hospital in the Brussels district of Schaerbeek. From there she fled again, despite her injury. When Schaja Cukier was arrested for a third time, she was again transferred to the Mechelen transit camp and allocated to the 23rd transport. She was shot dead as she attempted to flee from this transport.[369]

Reina Blok – Escape from the 23rd Transport on 15 January 1944

Reina Blok (born in Groningen/the Netherlands in 1915) also jumped from the 23rd transport. She had come to Antwerp at the age of ten.[370] In

August 1942, when she received the labour assignment in Germany, she assumed a false identity and went underground.[371] With the help of her husband, she joined the Resistance group OF (Onafhankelijkheidsfront) and became active in it from July 1942 onwards, mainly distributing illegal texts in Antwerp and Brussels.[372] On 2 September 1943, she was detained in Brussels by two unknown Belgians, presumably Rexists. In addition to twenty-five copies of the underground pamphlet 'La Libre Belgique' she also had forged ID papers with her, but one of the two men seemed to know her true identity. She was taken to the Brussels prisons in Saint-Gilles and Forest. From there, she was transferred to the Sicherheitspolizei on Avenue Louise for interrogation.[373] As she reports, despite being beaten, she said nothing about the sources of the underground publication, but her persecutors did discover that she was Jewish.[374] Reina Blok was interned in Mechelen on 13 November 1943. Two months later, she was allocated to Transport 22. She leapt from the train, but injured herself,[375] was recaptured and deported to Auschwitz on the 24th transport under special surveillance on 4 April 1944.[376] On 2 December 1944, she was taken to Chemnitz to carry out forced labour for the Astra Werke AG.[377] As earlier in Auschwitz, she was forced to work there. After sabotaging machines, she was due to be transferred to Flossenbürg concentration in late April; on the way there, she again jumped out of the train.[378] After hiding for around a week in the open air among blueberry shrubs, she was liberated by Soviet soldiers on 10 May 1945, presumably in Kemtau near the German-Czech border.[379] Reina Blok initially received basic care in Prague and later in Pilsen. From there, she followed an American initiative, flying to Paris and then taking a train to Antwerp, where she arrived on 25 May 1945.[380]

Simon Apfeldorfer – Escape from the 23rd Transport on 15 January 1944

Simon Apfeldorfer (born in Mukacevo/Hungary in 1912) was another fugitive from the 23rd transport. Apfeldorfer was a citizen of Czechoslovakia and had migrated to Belgium in 1935. His 'foreigner's ID papers', which had been issued in April 1942 in Antwerp, where he resided, still exist with their red 'JOOD-JUIF' stamp. Another stamp on the document confirms that he was recorded in the register of Jews.[381] From 12 July 1942 to 3 October 1942, Apfeldorfer was forced to work for the German building company Max Früh GmbH & Co. KG, which still exists today. He was deployed in northern France for work on the Atlantic Wall defences.[382] For unknown reasons, he was taken to hospital in Calais, from where he fled and made his way back to Antwerp.[383] He was recaptured in the autumn of 1943 and interned in Mechelen in mid November. After escaping from the 23rd deportation train,[384] he was arrested once more. For his second deportation, on the 24th transport, he was included on a list that placed him under special surveillance.[385] Simon Apfeldorfer died in the spring of 1945 in Mauthausen concentration camp.[386]

Emil Weber – Escape from the 24th Transport on 4/5 April 1944

The 24th transport left the Mechelen transit camp on 4 April 1944 carrying 626 people, including fifty-four children. As for previous trains, the transport list was supplemented with a special list of names of those who had previously escaped from a train and were to be guarded more closely. Emil Weber (born in Hamburg in 1916) managed to escape from the freight wagon. It appears that the train had already reached German territory when he jumped. According to a file entry by the Aachen local court, Emil Weber was arrested again on 18 April 1944 – the arresting unit was the local Staatspolizei Judenreferat.[387] He was deported on the 25th transport to Auschwitz on 19 May 1944. Steinberg and Schram write that the train had stopped during its journey and around two hundred more Jews were driven onto it. It is unknown who these people were and where the train stopped.[388] It is quite possible that the stop was in Aachen and the train received more Jews there, including Emil Weber, who survived Nazi persecution.[389]

Notes

1. Jean-Philippe Schreiber, *L'immigration juive en Belgique du moyen âge à la première guerre mondiale*, Brussels 1996, p. 208.
2. De Kinderen van Gewapende joodse Partizanen van Belgïe (Ed.), *Gewapende Joodse Partizanen van Belgïe. Getuigenissen*, 1997, p. 5.
3. Hans-Dieter Arntz, *Judenverfolgung und Fluchthilfe im deutsch-belgischen Grenzgebiet: Kreisgebiet Schleiden, Euskirchen, Monschau, Aachen und Eupen/Malmedy*, Euskirchen 1990.
4. Lieven Saerens, 'Die Hilfe für Juden in Belgien', in: Wolfgang Benz and Juliane Wetzel (Eds), *Solidarität und Hilfe für Juden während der NS-Zeit. Slowakei, Bulgarien, Serbien, Kroatien mit Bosnien und Herzegowina, Belgien, Italien. Regionalstudien 4*, Berlin 2004, pp. 193–280, here p. 194; Insa Meinen and Ahlrich Meyer, *Verfolgt von Land zu Land. Jüdische Flüchtlinge in Westeuropa 1938–1944*, Paderborn 2013, p. 110 ff.
5. Insa Meinen and Ahlrich Meyer, 'Le XXIe convoi: études biographiques (Première partie)', in: *Les Cahiers de la Mémoire contemporaine, Bijdragen tot de eigentijdse Herinnering* 7 (2006–2007), p. 77.
6. Saerens, 'Hilfe für Juden in Belgien', p. 195.
7. Lieven Saerens, *Vreemdelingen in een wereldstad. Een geschiedenis van Antwerpen en zijn joods bevolking (1880–1944)*, Tielt 2000, p. 298.
8. Saerens, *Vreemdelingen*, p. 461.
9. Wolfgang Benz, 'Typologie der Herrschaftsformen in den Gebieten unter deutschem Einfluß', in: Wolfgang Benz, Johannes Houwink ten Cate, and Gerhard Otto (Eds), *Die*

Bürokratie der Okkupation. Strukturen der Herrschaft und Verwaltung im besetzten Europa, Berlin 1998, pp. 11–25, here p. 14.
10. Alan Kramer, '"Greueltaten". Zum Problem der deutschen Kriegsverbrechen in Belgien und Frankreich 1914', in: Gerhard Hirschfeld, Gerd Krumeich, and Irina Renz (Eds), *'Keiner fühlt sich hier mehr als Mensch . . .'. Erlebnis und Wirkung des Ersten Weltkriegs*, Essen 1993, pp. 85–114, here p. 104 ff.
11. Christian Eggers, *Unerwünschte Ausländer. Juden aus Deutschland und Mitteleuropa in französischen Internierungslagern 1940–1942*, Berlin 2002, p. 234 ff.
12. Nanno In't Veld, 'Höhere SS- und Polizeiführer und Volkstumspolitik: ein Vergleich zwischen Belgien und den Niederlanden', in: Benz, Houwink ten Cate, and Otto, *Die Bürokratie der Okkupation*, pp. 121–38.
13. Insa Meinen, 'Die Deportation der Juden aus Belgien und das Devisenschutzkommando', in: Johannes Hürter and Jürgen Zarusky (Eds), *Besatzung, Kollaboration, Holocaust. Neue Studien zur Verfolgung und Ermordung der europäischen Juden*, Munich 2008, pp. 45–79, here p. 46.
14. Maxime Steinberg, *La Persecution des Juifs en Belgique (1940–1945)*, Brussels 2004, p. 158; Maxime Steinberg and Laurence Schram, 'Mecheln-Auschwitz: The Destruction of the Jews and Gypsies from Belgium 1942–1944', in: Ward Adriaens et al., *Mecheln-Auschwitz 1942-1944. De vernietiging van de Joden en zigeuners van België. La destruction des Juifs et des Tsiganes de Belgique. The destruction of the Jews and Gypsies from Belgium*, Vol. 1, Brussels 2009, p. 186.
15. Meinen, *Shoah in Belgien*, p. 241.
16. Ibid., p. 19.
17. For a chronological list of anti-Jewish laws, see: Steinberg, *Persecution des Juifs en Belgique*, p. 307 ff.
18. Eckart Conze et al., *Das Amt und die Vergangenheit. Deutsche Diplomaten im Dritten Reich und in der Bundesrepublik*, Munich 2010, p. 242.
19. Von Bargen, 9 July 1942, PA AA, R 99.406, No. 5602; Dienststelle des Auswärtigen Amtes Brüssel an das Auswärtige Amt Berlin, Zahl der Juden in Belgien, 31 October 1940, PA AA, R 99.406, No. 5600; Unterstaatssekretär Luther, Auswärtiges Amt an die Vertretung des Auswärtigen Amts beim Militärbefehlshaber in Belgien und Nordfrankreich, Brussels, 4 December 1942, printed in: *Akten zur deutschen auswärtigen Politik 1918–1945. Aus dem Archiv des Auswärtigen Amts. Serie E: 1941–1945, Bd. IV, 1. Oktober bis 31. Dezember 1942*, Göttingen 1975, p. 450 f.
20. Verordnungsblatt des Militärbefehlshabers in Belgien und Nordfrankreich für die besetzten Gebiete Belgiens und Nordfrankreichs, 5 November 1940, PA AA, R 99.406, No. 5600.
21. The register of Jews has largely survived (with 45,000 entries) and is archived in the Musée Juif de Belgique, Brussels.
22. Steinberg, *Persecution des Juifs en Belgique*, p. 145.
23. Verordnungsblatt des Militärbefehlshabers in Belgien und Nordfrankreich für die besetzten Gebiete Belgiens und Nordfrankreichs, 2 December 1941, PA AA, R 99.406, No. 5601; Steinberg, *Persecution des Juifs en Belgique*, p. 203.
24. Saerens, 'Hilfe für Juden in Belgien', p. 210.
25. Reeder, Tätigkeitsbericht No. 20 der Militärverwaltung für die Zeit vom 15. März – 1. Juni 1942, 15 June 1942, Cegesoma, BA L 13.1/11.
26. Ibid.
27. Liste des Israélites domiciliés en Belgique en mai 1940, internés dans des camps de travail forcé du Nord de la France employés par des firmes effectuant des travaux pour l'Organisation Todt, 1.1.24.1, ITS Digitales Archiv.
28. Steinberg, *Les cent jours*, p. 145 ff.; Nico Wouters, 'La chasse aux Juifs, 1942–1944', in: Rudi van Doorslaer et al. (Eds), *La Belgique docile. Les autorités belges et la persécution des Juifs en Belgique durant la Seconde Guerre mondiale*, Brussels 2006, pp. 566, 598.
29. For example, Maxime Steinberg, *Un pays occupé et ses juifs. Belgique entre France et Pays-Bas*, Gerpinnes 1998, p. 22 ff.

30. Rapport Definitif No. 5, Camp de Calais, 17 August 1950, 2.3.5.1, ITS Digitales Archiv; Ministerie van Wederopbouw, Algemene Directie, Schade aan Personen, Iste Directie, Opzoekingen, Documentatie en Overlijden, Dienst 'Kampen', Alphabetische lijst van in de Eindverslagen behandelde kampen. Afgesloten op 31. 3. 1952, 2.3.6.1, ID 82377268, ITS Digitales Archiv; Steinberg, *Persecution des Juifs en Belgique*, p. 217.
31. Steinberg, *Persecution des Juifs en Belgique*, p. 219; idem, *Les cent jours*, p. 147 f.
32. Vereeniging van joodsche politieke gevangenen, Association des prisonnieres politiques Juifs to the Commissie der Oorlogsmisdadigers, 10 March 1947, Cegesoma, AA D 120-C-82.
33. Steinberg, *Les cent jours*, p. 147 f.
34. Klarsfeld and Steinberg, *Mémorial*, p. 28.
35. Militärbefehlshaber in Belgien und Nordfrankreich, Militärverwaltungschef Reeder, to the Feldkommandanturen und Oberfeldkommandanturen, Betr.: Evakuierung der Juden, 25 September 1942, cited in: Klarsfeld and Steinberg, *Endlösung*, p. 47.
36. Unterstaatssekretär Luther, Auswärtiges Amt an die Vertretung des Auswärtigen Amts beim Militärbefehlshaber in Belgien und Nordfrankreich, Brüssel, 4 December 1942, printed in: *Akten zur deutschen auswärtigen Politik 1918–1945. Aus dem Archiv des Auswärtigen Amts, Serie E: 1941–1945, Bd. IV*, p. 450 f.
37. Von Bargen, 5 January 1943, CDJC, DXX-1072, cited in: Klarsfeld and Steinberg, *Endlösung*, p. 60.
38. Erdmann, Einsatzplan, 1 September 1943, CDJC, CXCVI-18, cited in: Klarsfeld and Steinberg, *Endlösung*, p. 78 ff.
39. Meinen, *Shoah in Belgien*, p. 87 ff.
40. Ibid., p. 23 f.
41. Ibid., p. 25.
42. Saerens, 'Hilfe für Juden in Belgien', p. 214; In't Veld, 'Höhere SS- und Polizeiführer', p. 125.
43. Bruno de Wever, 'Benelux-Staaten: Integration und Opposition', in: Benz, Houwink ten Cate, and Otto, *Die Bürokratie der Okkupation*, pp. 69–115, here pp. 70, 73 f., 84; Berger an Reeder, 7 October 1941, in: *Europa unterm Hakenkreuz. Belgien, Luxemburg, Niederlande. Dokumentenedition. Dokumentenauswahl und Einleitung von Ludwig Nestler. Unter Mitarbeit von Heidi Böhme u. a.*, Berlin 1990, p. 165.
44. Saerens, 'Hilfe für Juden in Belgien', p. 242; Saerens, *Vreemdelingen*, p. 541; In't Veld, 'Höhere SS- und Polizeiführer', p. 128; CSSD Heydrich an alle Stapoleitstellen und andere nachgeordnete Dienststellen, 12 May 1942, in: *Europa unterm Hakenkreuz. Belgien, Luxemburg, Niederlande*, p. 179.
45. Witness statement, Samuel Perl, 29 January 1945, Collège des Procureurs, Conseil de Guerre Bruxelles, Cour Militaire Antwerpen, Berufungsverfahren Felix Lauterborn, Vol. III, No. 303/47; Der Militärbefehlshaber in Belgien und Nordfrankreich, Militärverwaltungschef: Tätigkeitsbericht No. 10 der Militärverwaltung für den Monat Oktober 1940, 2 November 1940, Cegesoma, BA L 13.1/11.
46. Saerens, 'Hilfe für Juden in Belgien', p. 214.
47. Meinen, *Shoah in Belgien*, p. 22.
48. Saerens, *Vreemdelingen*, p. 649 ff.
49. Saerens, 'Hilfe für Juden in Belgien', p. 219.
50. Ibid., p. 215; Meinen, *Shoah in Belgien*, p. 22 f.
51. De Wever, *Benelux-Staaten*, p. 99; Steinberg, *Persecution des Juifs en Belgique*, p. 48 ff.
52. Mayor of Brussels Jules Coelst to Oberfeldkommandeur Gentzke, 5 June 1942, cited in: Meinen, *Shoah in Belgien*, p. 28; see also Steinberg, *Persecution des Juifs en Belgique*, p. 49.
53. Wouters, 'La chasse aux Juifs', p. 549.
54. Steinberg, *Persecution des Juifs en Belgique*, p. 221.
55. Benoît Majerus, 'Belgien: Der Widerstand gegen die NS-Okkupation 1940–1945', in: Gerd R. Ueberschär (Ed.), *Handbuch zum Widerstand gegen den Nationalsozialismus und Faschis-*

mus in Europa 1933/39 bis 1945, Berlin/New York 2011, pp. 125–135, here p. 127; de Wever, *Benelux-Staaten*, p. 93.
56. Saerens, 'Hilfe für Juden in Belgien', pp. 227, 251; Majerus, 'Der Widerstand', p. 127.
57. Majerus, 'Der Widerstand', p. 128.
58. De Wever, *Benelux-Staaten*, p. 107.
59. Majerus, 'Der Widerstand', p. 127; Saerens, 'Hilfe für Juden in Belgien', p. 230 f.
60. Steinberg and Schram, 'Mecheln-Auschwitz', p. 205.
61. Ibid.
62. Steinberg, *Les cent jours*, p. 114; Maxime Steinberg, 'Le Bulgare Théodore Angheloff et ses partisans juifs de la MOI à Bruxelles (1942–1943)', in: Maxime Steinberg and José Gotovitch, *Otages de la terreur nazie. Le Bulgare Angheloff et son groupe de Partisans juifs Bruxelles, 1940–1943*, Brussels 2007, p. 57 ff.
63. Pierre Broder, *Des Juifs debout contre le nazisme*, Brussels 1994, p. 60; Ghert Jospa, *The Belgian Resistance and the Camps of Breendonck and Buchenwald*, April 1956, Wiener Library, Testaments of the Holocaust 052-EA-0861, P.III.g. No. 272.
64. Steinberg and Schram, 'Mecheln-Auschwitz', p. 205.
65. Ibid.
66. Ibid., p. 206; see also Steinberg, *Les cent jours*.
67. Printed as a facsimile in: Adriaens et al., *Mecheln-Auschwitz*, Vol. 1, p. 210; see also Steinberg, 'Le Bulgare Théodore Angheloff', p. 88 ff.
68. Steinberg and Schram, 'Mecheln-Auschwitz', p. 210.
69. Von Bargen to the Foreign Office, 24 September 1942, cited in: Klarsfeld and Steinberg, *Endlösung*, p. 45 f.
70. Schreiber, *L'immigration juive en Belgique*, p. 77.
71. Saerens, 'Hilfe für Juden in Belgien', pp. 226, 235.
72. Steinberg, *L'Étoile et le fusil*, Vol. I, p. 75 ff.; Saerens, 'Hilfe für Juden in Belgien', p. 251; Ghert Jospa, *The Belgian Resistance and the Camps of Breendonck and Buchenwald*, April 1956, Wiener Library, Testaments of the Holocaust, 052-EA-0861, P.III.g. No. 272.
73. Zeller and Griffioen, 'Judenverfolgung in den Niederlanden und in Belgien', p. 35; Comite de Defense des Juifs – C. D. J., *Groupement de résistance reconnu à la date du 1-3-1948. (Moniteur Belge), Affilie au 'Front de l'indépendance', Témoignages et documents recueillis entre 1947 et 1951 par René De Lathouwer. Liquidateur du C. D. J. au statut de la Résistance Civile*, p. 10 ff.
74. Ibid., p. 35; see also Steinberg, *L'Étoile et le fusil*, Vol. I, p. 83.
75. Jean Améry, *Jenseits von Schuld und Sühne. Bewältigungsversuche eines Überwältigten*, Stuttgart 1997, p. 85; Steinberg, 'Le Bulgare Théodore Angheloff', p. 59 f.; regarding Travail allemand, see Tanja von Fransecky, *Bis ans Maul der Bestie. Nelly Klein - Eine österreichische Jüdin im belgischen Widerstand*, Berlin 2019.
76. Moll, *'Führer-Erlasse'*, p. 338 f.; Benz, 'Typologie der Herrschaftsformen', p. 15.
77. Steinberg and Schram, 'Mecheln-Auschwitz', p. 242.
78. *Chronologie der Deportationen aus Belgien, Gedenkbuch – Opfer der Verfolgung der Juden unter der nationalsozialistischen Gewaltherrschaft in Deutschland 1933–1945*, http://www.bundesarchiv.de/gedenkbuch/chronicles.html?page=2 (accessed 13 December 2013).
79. The figures refer exclusively to the Jewish deportees and are drawn from the table 'The deportation from Mechelen to Auschwitz – general overview', in: Steinberg and Schram, 'Mecheln-Auschwitz', p. 235.
80. Steinberg, *Un pays occupé et ses juifs*, p. 27.
81. For Breendonk, see: Markus Meckl, 'Unter zweifacher Hoheit: Das Auffanglager Breendonk zwischen Militärverwaltung und SD', in: Wolfgang Benz and Barbara Distel (Eds), *Terror im Westen. Nationalsozialistische Lager in den Niederlanden, Belgien und Luxemburg 1940–1945*, Berlin 2004, pp. 25–38.
82. Craushaar, 15 June 1942, cited in: Joods Museum van deportatie en verzet, 'De Belgische tentoonstelling in Auschwitz', p. 75.

83. Steinberg and Schram, 'Mecheln-Auschwitz', p. 185.
84. Erdmann, 7 May 1942, printed in: Klarsfeld and Steinberg, *Endlösung*, p. 23 f.; statement, Max Hermann Boden, 19 February 1968, BArch B 162/4405; see also Schreiber, *Stille Rebellen*, p. 217 f.
85. Hearing statement, Walter Czunczeleit, 5 September 1966, BArch B 162/20350; hearing statement, Karl Heinrich Wilhelm Fielitz, 6 September 1966, BArch B 162/20350; see also Steinberg, *L'Étoile et le fusil*, Vol. II, p. 69; Saerens, 'Hilfe für Juden in Belgien', p. 216.
86. Saerens, 'Hilfe für Juden in Belgien', p. 212; Meinen, *Shoah in Belgien*, p. 42.
87. Ehlers, labour assignment, 8 August 1942, cited in: Klarsfeld and Steinberg, *Endlösung*, p. 39.
88. Interview with Eva Fastag, 9 June 2004, JMDV, Interviewsammlung Johannes Blum, No. 535; note on the hearing of Hans Rodenbüsch, 7 December 1964, Cegesoma, AA 377, Bd. VI, Bl. 1005.
89. For example, F. Gutmacher, 'Aus dem Lager Malines nach Auschwitz', in: Peter Longerich, *Die Ermordung der europäischen Juden*, Munich 1989, p. 267.
90. Statement, Max Hermann Boden, 19 February 1968, BArch B 162/4405.
91. Interview with Eva Fastag, 9 June 2004, JMDV, Interviewsammlung Johannes Blum, No. 535.
92. Interview with Benita Hirschfeld, 7 June 2005, JMDV, Interviewsammlung Johannes Blum, No. 631.
93. Statement, Gerhard Johannes Frank, 27 October 1946, NIOD, Mechelen, Kamp, 429 B, doc II.
94. Statement, Max Hermann Boden, 19 February 1968, BArch B 162/4405.
95. Ibid.
96. Interview with Eva Fastag, 9 June 2004, JMDV, Interviewsammlung Johannes Blum, No. 535.
97. Statement, Gerhard Johannes Frank, 27 October 1946, NIOD, Mechelen, Kamp, 429 B, doc II.
98. Marie Mendel, Interview Code 14125, VHA, USC Shoah Foundation Institute.
99. Witness statement, Icek Wolman, 11 June 1948, Collège des Procureurs, Conseil de Guerre Bruxelles, Sipo Brüssel, Vol. 10; see also Nico Wouters, 'Völkermord vor belgischen Militärtribunalen am Beispiel der gerichtlichen Ahndung von Verbrechen an Juden und Jüdinnen (1944–1951)', in: Heimo Halbrainer and Claudia Kuretsidis-Haider (Eds), *Kriegsverbrechen, NS-Gewaltverbrechen und die europäische Strafjustiz von Nürnberg bis Den Haag*, Graz 2007, pp. 171–91, here p. 188 f.
100. Witness statement, Icek Wolman, 11 June 1948, Collège des Procureurs, Conseil de Guerre Bruxelles, Sipo Brüssel, Vol. 10; see also Wouters, 'Völkermord vor belgischen Militärtribunalen', p. 188 f.
101. Ibid.; Wouters, 'La chasse aux Juifs', p. 577.
102. Cited in: Saerens, 'Hilfe für Juden in Belgien', p. 212 f.
103. Meinen, *Shoah in Belgien*, pp. 43, 84.
104. Statement, Max Hermann Boden, 19 February 1968, BArch B 162/4405.
105. Saerens, 'Hilfe für Juden in Belgien', p. 213.
106. Der Militärbefehlshaber in Belgien und Nordfrankreich, Militärverwaltungchef: Tätigkeitsbericht No. 21 der Militärverwaltung für die Zeit vom 1. Juni – 1. September 1942, 15 September 1942, Cegesoma, BA L 13.1/11; see also Steinberg, *Les cent jours*, p. 207 ff.
107. Von Bargen to the Foreign Office in Berlin, Betr.: Juden in Belgien, 11 November 1942, PA AA, R 100.862, No. 2215; von Bargen, cited in: hearing protocol Hans-Günther Heym, 2 April 1968, Cegesoma, AA 377, Bd. VII, p. 1244; and hearing protocol, Wilhelm von Hahn, 4 April 1968, Cegesoma, AA 377, Bd. VII, p. 1299.
108. Statement, Max Hermann Boden, 19 February 1968, BArch B 162/4405.
109. Zeller and Griffioen, 'Judenverfolgung in den Niederlanden und in Belgien', p. 52.

110. Schreiber, *L'immigration juive en Belgique*, p. 75.
111. Militärbefehlshaber in Belgien und Nordfrankreich to the Feldkommandanturen und Oberfeldkommandanturen, Betr.: Evakuierung der Juden, 25 September 1942, cited in: Klarsfeld and Steinberg, *Endlösung*, p. 48.
112. Steinberg, *Persecution des Juifs en Belgique*, p. 219; Meinen, *Shoah in Belgien*, pp. 84, 87.
113. Hearing statement, Kurt Asche, 8 September 1966, BArch B 162/20350.
114. Various documents regarding 'Aktion Iltis' can be found in Cegesoma, AA 556; Dr Artzt, Vermerk, 5 December 1961, Cegesoma, AA 377, Bd. I, p. 7 (original in BArch L); Erdmann, 'Einsatzplan Aktion "Iltis"', 1. 9. 1943', in: *Europa unterm Hakenkreuz. Belgien, Luxemburg, Niederlande*, p. 226 f.
115. BdS, Meldungen aus Belgien und Nordfrankreich, No. 12/44, Brussels, 15 June 1944, cited in: Klarsfeld and Steinberg, *Endlösung*, p. 87.
116. Steinberg and Schram, 'Mecheln-Auschwitz', p. 183.
117. Gutmacher, 'Lager Malines', p. 267.
118. Steinberg and Schram, 'Mecheln-Auschwitz', p. 240.
119. Hearing statement, Hans Rodenbüsch, 10 September 1966, BArch B 162/20350; statement, Max Hermann Boden, 19 February 1968, BArch B 162/4405.
120. Statement, Walter Kaiser, 7 October 1969, Cegesoma, AA 377, Bd. X, Bl. 1865.
121. Steinberg and Schram, 'Mecheln-Auschwitz', p. 183; statement, Max Hermann Boden, 19 February 1968, BArch B 162/4405.
122. Ibid.
123. Statement, Gerhard Johannes Frank, 27 October 1946, NIOD, Mechelen, Kamp, 429 B, doc II.
124. Hearing statement, Hans Rodenbüsch, 10 September 1966, BArch B 162/20350; statement, Max Hermann Boden, 19 February 1968, BArch B 162/4405.
125. Hearing statement, Kurt Asche, 8 September 1966, BArch B 162/20350; Zeugenaussage im Ermittlungsverfahren gegen ehemalige Angehörige der Dienststelle des Beauftragten des Chefs der Sicherheitspolizei und des SD für den Bereich des Militärbefehlshabers in Belgien und Nordfrankreich wegen Verdachts der Beihilfe zum Mord (NS-Gewaltverbrechen) Kurt Asche, 27 June 1967, Cegesoma, AA 377, Bd. V, Bl. 949 ff.
126. For example, Joseph Hakker, cited in: Maxime Steinberg and Laurence Schram, 'Transport XVIII', in: Ward Adriaens et al. (Eds), *Mecheln-Auschwitz. Gezichten van gedeporteerden: transporten 14–26. Visages des déportés: transports 14–26. Faces of the Deportees: Transports 14–26*, Vol. 3, Brussels 2009, p. 106.
127. Witness statement, Samuel Perl, 13 January 1945, Cegesoma, AA 377, Bd. XI, Bl. 2194 ff.
128. Statement, Menasche Maximilian Brunner, September 1959, Cegesoma, mic 122 (original in YVA O3/1404).
129. Witness statement, Herz Adler, 19 March 1948, Collège des Procureurs, Conseil de Guerre Bruxelles, Sipo Brüssel, Vol. 10.
130. Witness hearing, Leonard Koepf, 11 December 1968, BArch B 162/4405; witness hearing, Hans Lauer, 5 December 1968, BArch B 162/4405.
131. Witness statement, Theodore Herz, Cegesoma, Commission des Crimes de Guerre de Belgique, D 120; statement, Max Hermann Boden, 19 February 1968, BArch B 162/4405.
132. Joseph Hakker, *De Geheimzinnige Kazerne Dossin, Deportatiekamp der Joden, 1943*, Collège des Procureurs, Conseil de Guerre Bruxelles, Cour Militaire Antwerpen, Berufungsverfahren Felix Lauterborn, Vol. II.
133. Statement, Paul Halter, 26 April 1945, Cegesoma, Commission des Crimes de Guerre de Belgique, D 120.
134. Mall and Roth, *Jeder Mensch hat einen Namen*, p. 150.
135. Statement, Gerhard Johannes Frank, 27 October 1946, NIOD, Mechelen, Kamp, 429 B, doc II; Boden confirmed in 1969 that the luggage was loaded separately. Statement, Max Hermann Boden, 19 February 1968, BArch B 162/4405.

136. Statement, Menasche Maximilian Brunner, September 1959, Cegesoma, mic 122 (original in Yad Vashem).
137. Statement, Theodore Herz, Cegesoma, Commission des Crimes de Guerre de Belgique, D 120.
138. Statement, Paul Halter, 26 April 1945, Cegesoma, Commission des Crimes de Guerre de Belgique, D 120.
139. Meyer, *Wissen um Auschwitz*, p. 143.
140. Witness statement, Lily Cohen, Cegesoma, Commission des Crimes de Guerre de Belgique, D 120.
141. Witness statement, Adelin Hinkens, 17 July 1945, Cegesoma, Commission des Crimes de Guerre de Belgique, D 120.
142. Statement, Gerhard Johannes Frank, 27 October 1946, NIOD, Mechelen, Kamp, 429 B, doc II.
143. Note on the hearing of Hans Rodenbüsch, Vermerk, 7 December 1964, Cegesoma, AA 377, Bd. VI; [BdS, Judenreferat, fernschriftliche Meldung Abfahrt Deportationszug] an Eichmann und die IKL, 15 September 1942, YVA, O.29/9.
144. Statement, Eva Fastag, 7 April 1948, Collège des Procureurs, Conseil de Guerre Bruxelles, Sipo Brüssel, Vol. 10.
145. Statement, Ludwig Semmelbauer, 11 September 1968, BArch B 162/20347; witness hearing, Hans Lauer, 5 December 1968, BArch B 162/4405; statement, Hermann Max Rudolf Horlitz, 11 December 1967, Cegesoma, AA 377, Bd. V, Bl. 926 ff.; witness statement, Eva Fastag, 7 April 1948, Collège des Procureurs, Conseil de Guerre Bruxelles, Sipo Brüssel, Vol. 10; witness hearing, Leonard Koepf, 11 December 1968, BArch B 162/4405; statement, Menasche Maximilian Brunner, September 1959, Cegesoma, mic 122 (original in Yad Vashem).
146. Hearing statement, Kurt Asche, 8 September 1966, BArch B 162/20350.
147. Hearing statement, Hans Rodenbüsch, 10 September 1966, BArch B 162/20350. Hans Rodenbüsch (born on 27 August 1908) worked in the Federal Republic of Germany as a Kriminalinspektor at the Bundeskriminalamt.
148. Oberlandesgericht Schleswig, Beschluss, 8 March 1977, cited in: Klarsfeld and Steinberg, *Endlösung*, p. 128.
149. Statement, Menasche Maximilian Brunner, September 1959, Cegesoma, mic 122; Oberlandesgericht Schleswig, Beschluss, 8 March 1977, cited in: Klarsfeld and Steinberg, *Endlösung*, p. 128.
150. Witness hearing, Ernst Böhlich, 23 April 1968, Cegesoma, AA 377, Bd. VII, Bl. 1350 ff.; Mihr, Vors. Richter am OLG/Gribbohm, Richter am OLG/Welk, Richter am OLG, Beschluss, 1 March 1977, BArch B 162/19377; witness hearing, Robert Kamrath, 10 September 1968, BArch B 162/20374; Oberlandesgericht Schleswig, Beschluss, 8 March 1977, cited in: Klarsfeld and Steinberg, *Endlösung*, p. 128; statement, Max Hermann Boden, 19 February 1968, BArch B 162/4405; see also Meyer, *Wissen um Auschwitz*, p. 141.
151. Witness hearing, Leonard Koepf, 11 December 1968, BArch B 162/4405; witness statement, Walter Czunczeleit, 5 September 1966, BArch B 162/20350; statement, Ludwig Semmelbauer, 11 September 1968, BArch B 162/20347; see also statement, Walter Friedrich Hermann to the Kiel Public Prosecutor, 15 February 1968, Cegesoma, AA 377, Bd. VI, p. 1057 ff.; witness hearing, Ernst Böhlich, 23 April 1968, Cegesoma, AA 377, Bd. VII, Bl. 1350 ff.; witness hearing, Hans Lauer, 5 December 1968, BArch B 162/4405; witness hearing, Robert Kamrath, 10 September 1968, BArch B 162/20374.
152. Personalbedarf für das Einsatzkommando in Belgien u. Nordfrankreich auf Grundlage der Besprechung vom 1. August 1940 bei der Dienststelle Brüssel, Cegesoma, AA 588; Lienke, Diensteinteilung für die Zeit vom 22. 3. -28. 3. 43, 19 March 1943, Cegesoma, AA 588.
153. Witness hearing, Robert Kamrath, 10 September 1968, BArch B 162/20374.

154. Witness hearing, Hans Lauer, 5 December 1968, BArch B 162/4405; witness hearing, Ernst Böhlich, 23 April 1968, Cegesoma, AA 377, Bd. VII, Bl. 1350 ff.; statement, Ludwig Semmelbauer, 11 September 1968, BArch B 162/20347.
155. Witness statement, Ernst Böhlich, 23 April 1968, Cegesoma, AA 377, Bd. VII, Bl. 1350 ff.
156. Ibid.
157. Meyer, *Wissen um Auschwitz*, p. 143.
158. Witness hearing, Hans Lauer, 5 December 1968, BArch B 162/4405.
159. Witness hearing, Leonard Koepf, 11 December 1968, BArch B 162/4405.
160. Database Kazerne Dossin, Laurence Schram.
161. Klarsfeld and Steinberg, *Memorial*, p. 27.
162. Piany, Sous-Préfecture d'Oloron, Attestation, 30 June 1954, SVG, Dossier Walter Israel Aron; Dorlodot, Chef de la Mission en France, Mission belge en France an Braem, Direction du Service Recherches, Documentation et Décès, Ministere de la Santé publique et de la Famille, 24 March 1955, SVG, Dossier Walter Israel Aron.
163. Stockmans, Direction Générale, Dommages aux Personnes, Ministere de la Santé publique et de la Famille, 7 April 1953, SVG, Dossier Walter Israel Aron.
164. Ministere de la Santé publique et de la Famille, Renseignements extraits du registre des Juifs, SVG, Dossier Lipa Keller.
165. Sous-Préfet d'Oloron, Attestation, 24 April 1957, SVG, Dossier Lipa Keller; Chef de la Mission Belge, Mission Belge en France an Ministere de la Santé publique et de la Famille, 5 June 1957, SVG, Dossier Ludwig Keller.
166. Ludwig Keller, Inlichtingsformulier, January 1957, SVG, Dossier Ludwig Keller.
167. Questionnaire, 12 July 1951, SVG, Dossier Ludwig Keller.
168. Ministere de la Santé publique et de la Famille, Attestation, 7 February 1957, SVG, Dossier Lipa Keller; questionnaire, 12 July 1951, SVG, Dossier Ludwig Keller.
169. Steinberg and Schram, 'Mecheln-Auschwitz', p. 329.
170. Thanks to Dimitri Roden, Breendonk Memorial, for this written information dated 10 January 2010, and to Gert De Prins, SVG, written statement dated 24 February 2010.
171. Gert De Prins, SVG, written statement dated 24 February 2010.
172. Fiche de Renseignements, Ministere de l'Interieur, SVG, Dossier Otto Dawid.
173. Braem, Note a Mademoiselle de Dorlodot, Chef de la Mission Belge de Recherches à Arolsen, 1 October 1956, SVG, Dossier Otto Dawid.
174. The informer named 'Fat Jacques' was Icek Glogowski. He often accompanied members of the Judenabteilung on their hunt for people in hiding or Jews in Brussels who failed to identify themselves. The Germans had promised him that his collaboration would be rewarded with the return of his already deported wife and children. See Meinen, *Shoah in Belgien*, p. 161.
175. Witness statement, Otto Dawid, 6 May 1949, Conseil de Guerre Bruxelles, Sipo Brüssel, Vol. 10.
176. Häftlingskarteikarte, Konzentrationslager Auschwitz, SVG, Dossier Otto Dawid.
177. Otto Dawid an das jüdische Komitee, SVG, Dossier Otto Dawid.
178. Ibid.
179. Formulier voor Politieke Gevangenen, Nationale Confederatie en Rechthebbenden, [1947], SVG, Dossier Otto Dawid; Inlichtlingsblad, Formulaire de Renseignements, Ministerie van Wederopbouw, Ministere de la Reconstruction, [1957], SVG, Dossier Otto Dawid.
180. Steinberg and Schram, 'Mecheln-Auschwitz', p. 330.
181. Ibid.
182. Klarsfeld and Steinberg, *Mémorial*, p. 28.
183. Steinberg and Schram, 'Mecheln-Auschwitz', p. 330.
184. Ibid., pp. 29, 330; Steinberg, *Les cent jours*, p. 148.

185. Steinberg and Schram, 'Mecheln-Auschwitz', p. 330.
186. Ibid.
187. Request for Certificate of Incarceration, Allied High Commission for Germany, International Tracing Service, Headquarters, 9 June 1955, SVG, Dossier Israel Beck.
188. Renseignements Extraits du Registre des Juifs, Ministere de la Santé publique et de la Famille, Direction, Recherches, Documentation et Décès, SVG, Dossier Israel Beck.
189. Formulaire de Renseignement, Israel Beck, 17 October 1960, Ministere de la Santé publique et de la Famille, SVG, Dossier Israel Beck; see also Ward Adriaens et al., *Mecheln-Auschwitz 1942–1944*, Vol. 4, *Namenlijst van de gedeporteerden. Liste des noms des déportés. List of Names of the Deportees*, p. 235.
190. Vragenlijst, Israel Beck, 5 July 1951, SVG, Dossier Israel Beck; Comité international de la Croix-Rouge, Service International de Recherches, ITS Arolsen, Certificate of Incarceration, Certificat d'Incarcération, Inhaftierungsbescheinigung, 11 July 1956, SVG, Dossier Israel Beck.
191. Jorisch, Commission des Pensions de Réaration de Bruxelles, 14 June 1949, SVG, Dossier Israel Beck.
192. Étranger, Vreemdeling, Carte d'Identité, Identiteitskaart, Israel Beck, 6 November 1942, JMDV, Reliques Israel Beck.
193. Greffe du tribunal de commerce, Déclaration de décès, cessation, transport ou cession, 31 March 1942, Cegesoma, BA 50.506, ASLB La Mémoire de Dannes-Camier, Du permis de séjour à la déportation [document collection in the Appendix].
194. Statement, Maurice Cykiert, Rapport d'une Enquete faite le 5. 8. 1953 par Monsieur Dumonceau de Bergendahl, Objet: Majlich Cykiert, Maurice Cykiert, SVG, Dossier Majlych Cykiert.
195. Wage transfer by the company Albert Jung, Euskirchen, wage period from 20 September 1942 to 3 October 1942, Cegesoma, AA 1665; database extract, Aufstellung der jüdischen Zwangsarbeiter bei der Firma Albert Jung, Cegesoma, AA 1665; Braem, Attestation, Ministere de la Santé Publique et de la Famille, 8 June 1957, SVG, Dossier Majlych Cykiert.
196. Statement, Maurice Cykiert, Rapport d'une Enquete faite le 5. 8. 1953 par Monsieur Dumonceau de Bergendahl, Objet: Majlich Cykiert, Maurice Cykiert, SVG, Dossier Majlych Cykiert.
197. Witness statement, Majlych Cykiert, Pro-Justitia, Commissariat de Police, Ville de Liège, 1 March 1953, SVG, Dossier Majlych Cykiert.
198. Statement, Maurice Cykiert, Rapport d'une Enquete faite le 5. 8. 1953 par Monsieur Dumonceau de Bergendahl, Objet: Majlich Cykiert, Maurice Cykiert, SVG, Dossier Majlych Cykiert.
199. Wage transfer by the company Albert Jung, Euskirchen, wage period 20 September 1942 to 3 October 1942, Cegesoma, AA 1665; database extract, Aufstellung der jüdischen Zwangsarbeiter bei der Firma Albert Jung, Cegesoma, AA 1665.
200. HKB Monowitz, Überstellungsliste nach Birkenau, 1 May 1944, Cegesoma, AA 1665 (original in the Auschwitz State Museum).
201. Effektenkammerschein Wolf Wand, KZ Buchenwald, Cegesoma, AA 1665 (original in the ITS Arolsen); Ministre de la Reconstruction, Direction, Recherches, Documentation et Décès, Formulaire de Renseignements, 1950, Cegesoma, AA 1665; Veränderungsmeldung KZ Buchenwald, 22 January 1945, Cegesoma, AA 1665 (original in the Auschwitz State Museum).
202. Le Commissaire de Police, Ville de Liège, Certificat de bonnes conduite, vie et mœurs, 22 October 1946, SVG, Dossier Szulim Aronowicz.
203. Statement, Szulim Aronowicz, 26 April 1951, SVG, Dossier Szulim Aronowicz; statement, Jean Pirlot, 5 May 1951, SVG, Dossier Szulim Aronowicz.
204. Szulim Aronowicz, 9 March 1947, SVG, Dossier Szulim Aronowicz; Szulim Aronowicz, Formulaire pour Prisonniers Politiques et bénéficiaires, Confédération Nationale des Pri-

sonniers Politiques & Ayant Droit, September 1947, SVG, Dossier Szulim Aronowicz; statement, Szulim Aronowicz, 26 April 1951, SVG, Dossier Szulim Aronowicz.
205. Statement, Chawa Sendyk, 27 May 1951, SVG, Dossier Szulim Aronowicz.
206. Kaminski, 22 October 1946, SVG, Dossier Szulim Aronowicz.
207. Statement, Szulim Aronowicz, 3 August 1951, SVG, Dossier Szulim Aronowicz.
208. Ibid.
209. Statement, Szulim Aronowicz, 26 April 1951, SVG, Dossier Szulim Aronowicz.
210. Statement, Jean Pirlot, 5 May 1951, SVG, Dossier Szulim Aronowicz.
211. Statement, Szulim Aronowicz, 26 April 1951, SVG, Dossier Szulim Aronowicz.
212. Jean Henet, Armee belge des Partisans, 27 October 1946, SVG, Dossier Szulim Aronowicz; Arnoldy, 23 October 1946, SVG, Dossier Szulim Aronowicz.
213. De Ridder, Office de la Résistance, Ministere de la Defense, Attestation, 19 February 1948, SVG, Dossier Szulim Aronowicz.
214. A. Delmiche, Commissaire de l'Etat, Ministere de la Reconstruction, Statut des P. P. et A. D., 24 December 1951, SVG, Dossier Szulim Aronowicz.
215. Klarsfeld, *Mémorial*, p. 271.
216. Adriaens et al., *Mecheln-Auschwitz*, Vol. 3, p. 52.
217. Province de Liège – Administration Communale de Bressoux, Extrait des registres des Etrangers, 17 May 1956, SVG, Dossier Pinkus Fremder.
218. Database Kazerne Dossin, Laurence Schram.
219. Ibid.
220. Labour Camp E. V. O., [list], 18 January 1944, Cegesoma, AA 1665 (original in the Auschwitz State Museum); see also Andrea Rudorff, 'Neu-Dachs (Jaworzno)', in: Wolfgang Benz and Barbara Distel (Eds), *Der Ort des Terrors. Geschichte der nationalsozialistischen Konzentrationslager. Vol. 5: Hinzert, Auschwitz, Neuengamme*, Munich 2007, pp. 284–89; Franciszek Piper, 'Die Rolle des Lagers Auschwitz bei der Verwirklichung der nationalsozialistischen Ausrottungspolitik. Die doppelte Funktion von Auschwitz als Konzentrationslager und als Zentrum der Judenvernichtung', in: Ulrich Herbert, Karin Orth, and Christoph Dieckmann (Eds), *Die nationalsozialistischen Konzentrationslager. Entwicklung und Struktur*, Vol. I, Göttingen 1998, pp. 390–414, here p. 408.
221. Ministere des Travaux publics et de la Reconstruction, Commission d'Agréation pour Prisonniers Politiques et Ayants Droit, Decision, 18 March 1953, SVG, Dossier Pinkus Fremder; A. Delmiche, Le Commissaire de l'Etat, Statut des PP et AD. Ministere des Travaux publics et de la Reconstruction an Pirlet, Commissaire principal de l'Etat, 24 November 1952, SVG, Dossier Pinkus Fremder.
222. Ministere des Travaux publics et de la Reconstruction, Commission d'Agréation pour Prisonniers Politiques et Ayants Droit, Decision, 18 March 1953, SVG, Dossier Pinkus Fremder.
223. Steinberg and Schram, 'Mecheln-Auschwitz', p. 330; Steinberg, 'Le Bulgare Théodore Angheloff', p. 60 f.; Database Kazerne Dossin, Laurence Schram.
224. Youth hostel card, JMDV, Reliques Imerglik Szymon.
225. Gerhard Leo, *Frühzug nach Toulouse*, Berlin 1988, p. 17.
226. Paszport Rzeczpospolita Polska, JMDV, Reliques Jacheta Baum; Étranger, Vreemdeling, Carte d'Identité, Identiteitskaart, Jacheta Baum, 29 December 1942, JMDV, Reliques Jacheta Baum.
227. Steinberg and Schram, 'Mecheln-Auschwitz', p. 332.
228. Personenkartei Hans Fritz, Geheime Staatspolizei Koblenz, 1.2.3.3 Globale Findmittel, ID 12449239, ITS Digitales Archiv.
229. Meinen, *Shoah in Belgien*, p. 94 f.; Steinberg and Schram, 'Mecheln-Auschwitz', p. 332.
230. Steinberg and Schram, 'Transport XVIII', p. 106.
231. Witness statement, Samuel Perl, 13 January 1945, Prozessakten Verfahren gegen Kurt Asche, Cegesoma, AA 377, Bd. XI, Bl. 2194 ff.

232. Samuel Perl, 7 December 1998, Interview Code 49097, VHA, USC Shoah Foundation Institute.
233. Witness statement, Samuel Perl, 13 January 1945, Prozessakten Verfahren gegen Kurt Asche, Cegesoma, AA 377, Bd. XI, Bl. 2194 ff.
234. Samuel Perl, 7 December 1998, Interview Code 49097, VHA, USC Shoah Foundation Institute.
235. Witness statement, Samuel Perl, 13 January 1945, Prozessakten Verfahren gegen Kurt Asche, Cegesoma, AA 377, Bd. XI, Bl. 2194 ff.
236. Ibid.; Samuel Perl, 7 December 1998, Interview Code 49097, VHA, USC Shoah Foundation Institute.
237. Samuel Perl, 7 December 1998, Interview Code 49097, VHA, USC Shoah Foundation Institute.
238. Ibid.
239. Witness statement, Samuel Perl, 13 January 1945, Prozessakten Verfahren gegen Kurt Asche, Cegesoma, AA 377, Bd. XI, Bl. 2194 ff.
240. Samuel Perl, 7 December 1998, Interview Code 49097, VHA, USC Shoah Foundation Institute.
241. Ville de Bruxelles, Division Centrale de Police, Bureau des Etrangers et des Certificats an Monsieur le Directeur des Dommages de Guerre aux personnes, 25 February 1955, SVG, Dossier David Arari.
242. According to the 1934 'Judenregister'. The first entry in the register of foreigners dated 1938. Renseignements extraits du Registre des Juifs (Ordonnance allemande du 28 octobre 1940), SVG, Dossier David Arari; Ville de Bruxelles, Division Centrale de Police, 18 January 1955, SVG, Dossier David Arari.
243. Aufenthaltsbescheinigung Kurt Berger, Comité international de la Croix-Rouge, ITS Arolsen, 21 October 1959, SVG, Dossier Kurt Berger.
244. Database Kazerne Dossin, Laurence Schram.
245. Witness statement, Kurt Berger, 18 March 1955, SVG, Dossier David Arari; see also Adriaens et al., *Mecheln-Auschwitz*, Vol. 4, p. 13.
246. Attestation, Ministre de la Santé publique et de la Famille, 18 June 1958, SVG, Dossier Kurt Berger.
247. Ministerie van Wederopbouw, Ministere de la Reconstruction, Identiteit van de D. P.-Identité du D. P., Inlichtingsblad, Formulaire de Renseignement, [1952], SVG, Dossier Kurt Berger.
248. Andrea Rudorff, 'Laurahütte (Siemianowice Śląskie)', in: Benz and Distel, *Der Ort des Terrors*, Vol. 5, pp. 270–73, here p. 270.
249. Ibid., p. 273; Aufenthaltsbescheinigung Kurt Berger, Comité international de la Croix-Rouge, ITS Arolsen, 21 October 1959, SVG, Dossier Kurt Berger.
250. Zugangsliste Politische Abteilung, Archiv der KZ-Gedenkstätte Mauthausen, Y/36; Liste der Zugänge vom 28. Januar 1945 (Vom K. L. Auschwitz), [unreadable] Schutzhaftlager, 30 January 1945, Mauthausen (E/13/9/5).
251. Inhaftierungsbescheinigung, Allied High Commission for Germany, International Tracing Service, 18 January 1954, SVG, Dossier Kurt Berger; archive of the Mauthausen Concentration Camp Memorial Site, database.
252. Marc Buggeln, 'Hannover-Mühlenberg', in: Benz and Distel, *Der Ort des Terrors*, Vol. 5, pp. 440–43.
253. A. E. F. D. P. Registration Record, 6 June 1945, SVG, Dossier Kurt Berger.
254. Aufenthaltsbescheinigung Kurt Berger, Comité international de la Croix-Rouge, ITS Arolsen, 21 October 1959, SVG, Dossier Kurt Berger.
255. Rudolf Schmitz, cited in: Schreiber, *Stille Rebellen*, p. 189 f.
256. Ibid., p. 190.
257. Database Kazerne Dossin, Laurence Schram.

258. Effektenkammerschein Rudolf Schmitz KZ Buchenwald, 1.1.5.3 Globale Findmittel, ID 7047913, ITS Digitales Archiv.
259. Arbeitskarte Rudolf Schmitz, KZ Buchenwald, 1.1.5.3 Globale Findmittel, ID 7047915, ITS Digitales Archiv; Ausgabeschein Effekten Rudolf Schmitz, 1.1.5.3 Globale Findmittel, ID 7047917, ITS Digitales Archiv.
260. Maxime Steinberg and Laurence Schram, 'Transport XIX', in: Ward Adriaens et al., *Mecheln-Auschwitz. Gezichten van gedeporteerden: transporten 14–26. Visages des déportés: transports 14–26. Faces of the Deportees: Transports 14–26*, Vol. 3, Brussels 2009, p. 133.
261. Schreiber, *Stille Rebellen*, p. 198.
262. Meyer Tabakman, 'Je suis un evadé', *Le Flambeau*, March 1943, Cegesoma, BG microfiche 183. The French original is printed as a facsimile in: Joods Museum van deportatie en verzet, 'De Belgische tentoonstelling in Auschwitz', p. 133.
263. Steinberg and Schram, 'Transport XIX', p. 133.
264. Jean-Philippe Schreiber, *Dictionnaire biographique des Juifs de Belgique. Figures du judaïsme belge XIXe–XXe siècles*, Brussels 2002, p. 333.
265. Steinberg and Schram, 'Transport XIX', p. 133.
266. Schreiber, *Dictionnaire biographique*, p. 333.
267. Maxime Steinberg, 'L'exeption du vingtième transport', in: Steinberg and Schram, *Transport XX*, p. 15.
268. Meyer, *Wissen um Auschwitz*, p. 142.
269. Doorslaer et al., *La Belgique docile*, p. 1345 f.; Steinberg, 'L'exeption du vingtième transport', p. 23.
270. Comite de Defense des Juifs, *Témoignages et documents*, p. 38 f.
271. Steinberg, 'L'exeption du vingtième transport', p. 13.
272. Ibid.; Ghert Jospa, *The Belgian Resistance and the Camps of Breendonck and Buchenwald*, April 1956, Wiener Library, Testaments of the Holocaust, 052-EA-0861, P.III.g. No. 272.
273. Ghert Jospa, *The Belgian Resistance and the Camps of Breendonck and Buchenwald*, April 1956, Wiener Library, Testaments of the Holocaust, 052-EA-0861, P.III.g. No. 272.
274. Schreiber, *Stille Rebellen*, p. 201.
275. Ibid., p. 205.
276. Ibid., p. 202 f.
277. Ibid., pp. 224, 229; cf. Steinberg, 'L'exeption du vingtième transport', p. 14; Ghert Jospa is the only person to report that the other two were members of 'Groupe G'. Ghert Jospa, *The Belgian Resistance and the Camps of Breendonck and Buchenwald*, April 1956, Wiener Library, Testaments of the Holocaust, 052-EA-0861, P.III.g. No. 272.
278. Comite de Defense des Juifs – C. D. J., Temoignages et documents recueillis entre 1947 et 1951, JMDV, G 453; see also Steinberg and Schram, 'Mecheln-Auschwitz', p. 333.
279. Steinberg, 'L'exeption du vingtième transport', p. 14.
280. Steinberg and Schram, 'Mecheln-Auschwitz', p. 333; Steinberg and Schram, *Transport XX*, p. 151.
281. Steinberg, 'L'exeption du vingtième transport', p. 15.
282. Falkenhausen, Betr.: Erschießung von 6 Terroristen, 16 February 1944, Breendonk Memorial, NGFB XII; Vorschlagsliste des SD für die von Herrn Militärbefehlshaber aus Gründen von Sühnemaßnahmen angeordneten Erschießungen von Terroristen, JMDV, Mappe Convoi XX, Evadés + Sonderliste.
283. Bekendmakingen, Het Algemeen Nieuws, 19 February 1944, Breendonk Memorial, NGFB XII.
284. List of prisoners' numbers in the sick bay, 22 January 1945, Archiv Gedenkstätte und Museum Sachsenhausen, D 1 A/1231, Bl. 006 (original files in the Russian State Military Archive, Moscow 1367/1/231, Bl. 006).
285. Investigation report, BStU MfS AKK, 2076/75; see also Fritjof Meyer, 'Schnell! Schnell!', in: *Der Spiegel*, 5 February 2001.

286. Häftlings-Personal-Karte Robert Maistriau, KZ Buchenwald, 8 May 1944, 1.1.5.3, ID 6544966, ITS Digitales Archiv; Effekten-Verzeichnis Robert Maistriau, KZ Buchenwald, 1.1.5.3, ID 6544964, ITS Digitales Archiv.
287. Arbeitskarte Robert Maistriau KZ Buchenwald, 1.1.5.3, ID 6544965, ITS Digitales Archiv.
288. Robert Maistriaux, Cegesoma, AA 1593 M 251.
289. Étranger, Vreemdeling, Carte d'Identité, Identiteitskaart, 10 September 1942, Hinda Vistinezki, JMDV, Reliques Hinda Vistinezki; Étranger, Vreemdeling, Carte d'Identité, Identiteitskaart, Mendelis Goldsteinas, 28 November 1941, JMDV, Reliques Mendelis Goldsteinas.
290. Mendelis Goldsteinas, Cegesoma, AA 1593 M251.
291. Hinda Goldsteinas, Cegesoma, AA 1593 M251.
292. Mendelis Goldsteinas, Cegesoma, AA 1593 M251.
293. The following account is based on an interview by the author with Régine Krochmal in Brussels on 23 January 2009.
294. Ibid.
295. Ibid.
296. Micheels, *Doctor #117641*, p. 62.
297. Ibid., p. 63.
298. Ibid., p. 62 ff.
299. The following account is based on an interview by the author with Claire Prowizur-Szyper on 6 October 2009 in Tel Aviv, supplemented by her autobiographical report: *Conte à rebours: Une résistante juive sous l'occupation*, Brussels 1982.
300. Prowizur-Szyper, *Instantanés d'ici et d'ailleurs*, p. 89 f.
301. Author's interview with Claire Prowizur-Szyper in Tel Aviv on 7 October 2009.
302. Unless otherwise indicated, the following account is based on an interview by the author with Simon Gronowski in Brussels on 24 January 2009.
303. Ibid.
304. Statement, Simon Gronowski on the radio programme: 'Auschwitz Convoy Escape, Witness', BBC World Service, 18 April 2012.
305. Author's interview with Simon Gronowski in Brussels on 24 January 2009.
306. Ibid.
307. Ibid.
308. Statement, Simon Gronowski on the radio programme: 'Auschwitz Convoy Escape, Witness', BBC World Service, 18 April 2012.
309. Gronowski, *Le petit évadé*.
310. Unless otherwise indicated, the following account is based on: Marie Mendel, Interview Code 14125, VHA, USC Shoah Foundation Institute.
311. Ibid.
312. Unless otherwise indicated, the following account is based on: Günther Mendel, Interview Code 14173, VHA, USC Shoah Foundation Institute.
313. Postcard, December 1941, Archiv Mahn- und Gedenkstätte der Landeshauptstadt Düsseldorf; Marie Mendel, Interview Code 14125, VHA, USC Shoah Foundation Institute.
314. Marie Mendel, Interview Code 14125, VHA, USC Shoah Foundation Institute.
315. Unless otherwise indicated, the following account is based on: Marie Mendel, Interview Code 14125, VHA, USC Shoah Foundation Institute.
316. Unless otherwise indicated, the following account is based on: Günther Mendel, Interview Code 14173, VHA, USC Shoah Foundation Institute.
317. Ibid.
318. Marie Mendel, Interview Code 14125, VHA, USC Shoah Foundation Institute.
319. Ministerie van Justitie, Internationaal Boosdoener, 25 November 1954, Breendonk Memorial, Akte der Ausländerpolizei, 550; certificate, presumably 24 May 1939, JMDV, Reliques Israel Steinberg.

320. Division de Police, Ville de Bruxelles, 2 July 1939, BdS an das Ausländerlager Merksplas bei Antwerpen, 3 October 1940, Breendonk Memorial, Akte der Ausländerpolizei, 550.
321. Bob Moore, *Survivors. Jewish Self-Help and Rescue in Nazi-Occupied Western Europe*, Oxford/ New York 2010, p. 204.
322. BdS an das Ausländerlager Merksplas bei Antwerpen, 3 October 1940, Breendonk Memorial, Akte der Ausländerpolizei, 550.
323. Ibid.; Ministerie van Justitie, Weldadigheidswezen, Inlichtingen bij de intrede, Breendonk Memorial, Akte der Ausländerpolizei, 550.
324. Israel Szteinberg an den Justizminister, Breendonk Memorial, Akte der Ausländerpolizei, 550; BdS an das Ausländerlager Merksplas bei Antwerpen, 3 October 1940, Breendonk Memorial, Akte der Ausländerpolizei, 550; Ministrie van Justitie, Rijksveldadigheidskoloniën Merksplas, Inlichtingen bij het uitgaan, Breendonk Memorial, Akte der Ausländerpolizei, 550.
325. Police du Grand Bruxelles, Commissariat Central, Ville de Bruxelles, Rapport, 24 June 1943, Breendonk Memorial, Akte der Ausländerpolizei, 550.
326. Israel Szteinberg an den Justizminister, Breendonk Memorial, Akte der Ausländerpolizei, 550.
327. Moore, *Survivors*, p. 421 f.; Israel Szteinberg an den Justizminister, Breendonk Memorial, Akte der Ausländerpolizei, 550.
328. Willy Berler, *Durch die Hölle. Monowitz, Auschwitz, Groß-Rosen, Buchenwald*, Berlin 2003, p. 48.
329. Ibid., p. 50 f.
330. Nummernkarte Willy Berler KZ Buchenwald, 1.1.5.3, ID 5523855, ITS Digitales Archiv; Fragebogen für Insassen der Konzentrationslager, Concentration Camp Inmates Questionnaire, Military Government of Germany, 29 April 1945, 1.1.5.3, ID 5523858, ITS Digitales Archiv; see also Berler, *Durch die Hölle*, p. 152.
331. Steinberg, 'L'exeption du vingtième transport', p. 19; Schreiber, *Stille Rebellen*, p. 237 f.
332. Steinberg and Schram, 'Mecheln-Auschwitz', p. 333.
333. Schreiber, *Dictionnaire biographique*, p. 356; Steinberg, 'Le Bulgare Théodore Angheloff', pp. 69 f., 94, 109.
334. Étranger, Vreemdeling, Carte d'identité, Ideniteitskaart, 2 September 1942, JMDV, Reliques Sandor Weisz.
335. Schreiber, *Dictionnaire biographique*, p. 357; Steinberg, 'L'exeption du vingtième transport', p. 18.
336. Steinberg and Schram, 'Mecheln-Auschwitz', p. 333.
337. Steinberg, 'L'exeption du vingtième transport', p. 11; Vanacker, Sonderbericht über einen Unfall, 27 April 1943, Breendonk Memorial, NGFB XII.
338. Steinberg, 'L'exeption du vingtième transport', p. 11.
339. Statement, Menasche Maximilian Brunner, September 1959, Cegesoma, mic 122 (original in Yad Vashem, O.3. 1404).
340. Max Hermann Boden, Protocol, 19 February 1968, BArch B 162, 4405.
341. G. H./L. M. S. E. R. A, Section Politique, 24 April 1943, Cegesoma, D 120.
342. Steinberg, 'L'exeption du vingtième transport', p. 11; Laurence Schram, 'Les déportés du vingtième transport de Malines à Auschwitz', in: Steinberg and Schram, *Transport XX*, p. 35.
343. Steinberg and Schram, 'Mecheln-Auschwitz', p. 335.
344. Ibid., p. 334.
345. Ibid., p. 335; Meinen, *Shoah in Belgien*, p. 112.
346. Meyer, *Wissen um Auschwitz*, p. 126.
347. Meinen, *Shoah in Belgien*, p. 138 f.; Insa Meinen and Ahlrich Meyer, 'Le XXIe convoi: études biographiques (Deuxième partie)', in: *Les Cahiers de la Mémoire contemporaine, Bijdragen tot de eigentijdse Herinnering*, 2008, p. 64.

348. Meinen, *Shoah in Belgien*, p. 147.
349. Ibid.
350. Ibid., p. 160.
351. Steinberg and Schram, 'Mecheln-Auschwitz', p. 335.
352. Ibid.
353. Adriaens et al., *Mecheln-Auschwitz*, Vol. 4, p. 30; Meinen, *Shoah in Belgien*, p. 144; Rachel Arazi, Interview de Madame Rachel Arazi née Rachel Benkiel, 1 February 1968, Cegesoma, mic 122 (original in Yad Vashem).
354. Klarsfeld and Steinberg, *Mémorial*, p. 31.
355. Maurice Kubowitzki, 83 – 22 septembre 1943. Extraits de mes souvenirs, Cegesoma, mic 122 (original in Yad Vashem O.3. 1048).
356. Steinberg and Schram, 'Mecheln-Auschwitz', p. 336.
357. Étranger, Vreemdeling, Carte d'Identité, Identiteitskaart, Alice Bonheim, 18 October 1940, JMDV, Reliques Alice Bonheim.
358. Decision, Commission d'Agréation des Prisonniers Politiques et des Ayants droit, 6 November 1958, SVG, Dossier Alice Bonheim; Formulaire de demande, Status des Prisonniers Politiques et de leurs Ayant Droit, 25 October 1956, SVG, Dossier Alice Bonheim.
359. A. E. F. D. P. Registration Record, Salomon Kleinmann, 24 May 1945, SVG, Dossier Salomon Kleinmann.
360. Gestapo-Akte Salomon Kleinmann, LAV NRW R, RW 58, LAV 3.2012, No. 23939. Thanks to Dr Ingrid Schupetta from the NS Documentation Centre in Krefeld for information on this file.
361. Carte d'Identité, Ville de Bruxelles, JMDV, Reliques Salomon Kleinmann.
362. Ministere de la Sante publique et de la famille, Attestation, 25 June 1954, SVG, Dossier Salomon Kleinmann.
363. Ministere de la Sante publique et de la famille, Fichier 'Israélite', 16 July 1965, SVG, Dossier Salomon Kleinmann.
364. Steinberg, *Persecution des Juifs en Belgique*, p. 230.
365. F. Bosmans (Ministre de la sante publique et de la famille, Administration des Dommages aux Personnes. Direction, Recherches, Documentation et Décès), Attestation, 27 June 1961, SVG, Dossier Michel Altschuler; Comité international de la croix-rouge, Service international de recherches, Arolsen (Waldeck) Germany an Reg. Präs. Wiesbaden, Inhaftierungsbescheinigung, 2 March 1960, SVG, Dossier Michel Altschuler; Steinberg and Schram, 'Mecheln-Auschwitz', p. 336.
366. Alfred Cheval, Suchmeldung, SVG, Dossier Michel Altschuler.
367. Kubowitzki, Maurice, 83 – 22 septembre 1943. Extraits de mes souvenirs, Cegesoma, mic 122 (original in Yad Vashem O.3. 1048).
368. Ibid.; Database Kazerne Dossin, Laurence Schram.
369. Steinberg and Schram, 'Mecheln-Auschwitz', p. 338.
370. SD-Karteikarte Reina Blok, 13 November 1943, SVG, Dossier Reina Blok.
371. Vragenlijst, Tot erkenning als politieke gevangene, Consultatieve Commissie voor Politieke Gevangenen, 8 June 1949, SVG, Dossier Reina Blok.
372. Ibid.; Roels, Nationaal Secretairs O. F., Patriotische Milities van het Onafhankelijkheidsfront, Antwerpen, 22 March 1950, SVG, Dossier Reina Blok.
373. Vragenlijst, Tot erkenning als politieke gevangene, Consultatieve Commissie voor Politieke Gevangenen, 8 June 1949, SVG, Dossier Reina Blok.
374. Zeugenaussage Reina Blok, Proces Verbaal, 16 September 1949, SVG, Dossier Reina Blok; SD-Karteikarte Reina Blok, 13 November 1943, SVG, Dossier Reina Blok.
375. Attestation, Ministère de la Santé publique et de la Famille, Administration des Victimes de la Guerre, 8 October 1971, SVG, Dossier Reina Blok.
376. Ibid.

377. Royaume de Belgique, Œuvre Nationale des anciens Combattants, Déportés et Prisonniers Politiques de la Guerre 1914–1918, [questionnaire], 1 May 1946, SVG, Dossier Reina Blok; Ulrich Fritz, 'Chemnitz', in: Wolfgang Benz and Barbara Distel (Eds), *Das Konzentrationslager Flossenbürg und seine Außenlager*, Munich 2007, pp. 74–76.
378. Vragenlijst, Tot erkenning als politieke gevangene, Consultatieve Commissie voor Politieke Gevangenen, 8 June 1949, SVG, Dossier Reina Blok.
379. Ibid.; Royaume de Belgique, Œuvre Nationale des anciens Combattants, Déportés et Prisonniers Politiques de la Guerre 1914–1918, [questionnaire], 1 May 1946, SVG, Dossier Reina Blok; Interrogatoire pour Prisonniers politiques rentés, [unreadable] Belge au Repartement, SVG, Dossier Reina Blok.
380. Vragenlijst, Tot erkenning als politieke gevangene, Consultatieve Commissie voor Politieke Gevangenen, 8 June 1949, SVG, Dossier Reina Blok; A. E. F. D. P. Registration Record, 25 May 1945, SVG, Dossier Reina Blok.
381. Vreemdeling, Étranger Identiteitskaart, 29 April 1942, JMDV, Reliques Simon Apfeldorfer.
382. Ministere de la Santé Publique et de la Famille, Attestation, 16 January 1958, SVG, Dossier Simon Apfeldorfer.
383. Ville de Calais, Hospital, Attest, [unreadable, possibly 1 October] 1942, JMDV, Reliques Simon Apfeldorfer; Comité international de la croix-rouge, Service international de recherches an Bezirksamt für Wiedergutmachung, Inhaftierungsbescheinigung, 8 January 1959, SVG, Dossier Simon Apfeldorfer.
384. F. Bosmans (Ministre de la sante publique et de la famille, Administration des Dommages aux Personnes), Attestation, 3 July 1959, SVG, Dossier Simon Apfeldorfer.
385. Database Kazerne Dossin, Laurence Schram.
386. Comité international de la croix-rouge, Service international de recherches an Bezirksamt für Wiedergutmachung, Inhaftierungsbescheinigung, 8 January 1959, SVG, Dossier Simon Apfeldorfer.
387. Häftlingskarteikarte, Amtsgericht, Schöffengericht I, II, Staatsanwaltschaft, Strafkammer, Aachen, [18 April 1944], JMDV, Reliques Emil Weber.
388. Steinberg and Schram, 'Mecheln-Auschwitz', p. 343.
389. Adriaens et al., *Mecheln-Auschwitz*, Vol. 4, p. 410.

Railway Lines in the Netherlands

CHAPTER 4

Escapes by Jews from Deportation Trains in the Netherlands

The Initial Situation in The Netherlands
Before the Wehrmacht's invasion

Since 1796, the Jewish population of the Netherlands had enjoyed full civil rights and had undergone a process of assimilation and secularization.[1] Zionism, which was politically organized in the Zionistenbond and the Paalei Zion, was not widespread among Dutch Jews. Many were politically aligned towards Social Democracy.[2] There was no great interaction between the long-established Ashkenazic and the much smaller Sephardic communities.[3] The census in 1930 recorded 112,000 people belonging to the Jewish religion, out of a total population of around nine million.[4] Dutch Jews were poorer than average compared to the rest of the population.[5]

As in many other European countries, a Fascist party had formed in the Netherlands. The NSB (Nationaal Socialistische Beweging) was established in 1931 by Anton Adriaan Mussert. Its 1937 party manifesto shows a tendency towards racist anti-Semitism, declaring, among other things, that Dutch Jews, encouraged by German Jews, pursued the aim of using the powerful weapons of capitalism, Marxism and democracy to enslave the people of the Netherlands.[6] While the NSB managed to gain almost 8 per cent of the vote in the 1935 elections, this result was halved in the next election in 1939.

From 1933 onwards, Jews from Germany fled to the Netherlands. After the 'Anschluss' of Austria by the German Reich in March 1938, even more Jews decided to flee, seeking sanctuary in the Netherlands and elsewhere. Following the November pogrom in 1938, the number of refugees from Germany increased to four thousand. Many crossed the 'green border' without valid entry documents.[7] In May 1938, the Dutch government reacted to refugee movements from Germany and Austria by sealing off the Dutch-German border. From then on, only Jews who could prove that their deportation back to the Reich would risk their welfare and their life were permitted to enter.[8] Immediately after the November pogrom, a further two thousand Jewish refugees were officially permitted to enter the country. In December 1938, the Dutch government finally closed the border to Jewish immigrants and began interning male refugees in twenty-five different camps.[9] The measures were aimed at keeping them out of the employment market, preventing assimilation and maintaining pressure on them to emigrate to a different country.[10]

In reaction to the large number of refugees, Dutch Jews founded various aid committees from 1933 onwards. They later supported the internees, as they feared that anti-Semitism would also increase with the growing number of refugees from Germany; in coordination with the government, they attempted to support the refugees' emigration to other countries. Following the government decision on 13 February 1939 to establish a central refugee camp, the 'Centraal Vluchtelingenkamp Westerbork' near the village of Westerbork, Dutch Jewish organizations provided the funds for the camp to be built.[11] From then on, refugees illegally entering the country were interned there.

By far the largest Jewish community in the Netherlands lived in Amsterdam, with a size of eighty thousand people in 1940.[12] Over 90 per cent lived in fourteen of the total of fifty-six districts there, and specific streets were especially popular.[13] There were Jewish facilities such as schools and welfare organizations. Half of all Jews in the Netherlands worked in trade, for instance with used goods, while a third worked in the manufacturing industry, for instance in the diamond sector.[14]

From the Wehrmacht's Invasion to the Beginning of Deportations in July 1942

The Wehrmacht invaded the Netherlands on 10 May 1940. Five days later, the Dutch Commander in Chief General Winkelman and the Commander of the 18th Army, General Küchler, signed a ceasefire agreement.[15] The Dutch Queen Wilhelmina had gone into exile two days earlier together with her cabinet, but had instructed the remaining civil servants to continue their duties to ensure order in the country. The Dutch administration therefore remained in existence at the level of General Secretaries (which are comparable to State Secretaries in the German ministerial organization).[16] When the Dutch army capitulated, panic broke out among the Jewish population. A very large number of people attempted to reach England or Belgium by boat.[17] More than one hundred people committed suicide.[18] At the time, around 750 German Jewish refugees were interned in the Westerbork camp.[19]

After General Alexander von Falkenhausen was appointed Military Commander, Hitler ordered the formation of a civilian administration, an indication of his intention to integrate the occupied Netherlands into a 'Greater Germanic Reich' as a protectorate in the medium term, since National Socialist ideology regarded its population as 'Germanic'.[20] On 29 May 1940, von Falkenhausen handed over executive powers to the Austrian Arthur Seyß-Inquart, who had been appointed Reichskommissar by Hitler.[21] Since 1939, he had been actively involved in the development of an extremely bloody occupation regime as Deputy General Governor to Hans Frank in the German-occupied Generalgouvernement.[22] On the day he took office, Seyß-Inquart ordered the posting of bilingual announcements to 'the Dutch population of the occupied territories'. In them, he made it clear that the Dutch were regarded as 'racial' equals: 'I will, however, be ensuring that the Dutch population, with its close blood-relationship to the German population, does not disintegrate until less favourable living conditions than the given community of destiny and the destructive will of our enemies in these times requires'.[23]

Seyß-Inquart dismissed the parliament and the state council and placed the civil administration under the auspices of his four Generalkommissars Friedrich Wimmer (Administration and Law), Hans Fischböck (Finance and the Economy), Fritz Schmidt (NSDAP representative, appointed Generalkommissar zbV ['zur besonderen Verfügung', i.e. for special disposition]) and Hanns Albin Rauter (Generalkommissar for Security and Higher SS and Police Officer).[24] Apart from Fritz Schmidt, all were Austrian-born.

In addition to four hundred members of the Sicherheitspolizei, Rauter also commanded the three thousand Ordnungspolizei officers stationed in the Netherlands; he was also authorized to announce new regulations and control the entire Dutch police force (in 1944, twenty thousand police officers).[25] One of Rauter's aims for the occupation was, 'with the help of the SS, to educate the Dutch into "aware Germans" and "aware Germanic people" to prepare for the integration of the Netherlands into the "Greater Germanic Reich"'.[26] Otto Bene, the representative of the Foreign Office in the Netherlands who was of the same rank as the Generalkommissars, regarded the occupied country as 'Germanic territory . . . whose population must be led into the Germanic Reich in a spirit of comradeship'.[27] This conformed to Hitler's ideas of a German core region that was flanked to the west by protectorates. An annexation was not initially intended, also to protect the Dutch colonies.[28]

During the first months after the invasion, the German invaders were reserved, and in many areas there was even loyal cooperation between German occupying bodies and the Dutch General Secretaries, for instance in the introduction of identification requirements.[29] Unlike the Vichy government in France and the Belgian administration, the Dutch State Secretaries rarely expressed reservations with respect to anti-Jewish measures and some were even based on their initiative.[30] The lack of protection for Dutch Jews is one reason for the large number of Holocaust victims in the Netherlands. The political scientist Guus Meershoek writes, albeit without evidence, that the German side reacted to the refusal by the Vichy government to release French Jews for deportation with an immediate increase in the number of required deportees from the Netherlands from fifteen thousand to forty thousand, without any protest from the State Secretaries.[31]

The state of research on German bodies of Jewish persecution in the Netherlands does not present a uniform picture. There are discrepancies with respect to the chronology, tasks and relationships of subordination. If one follows the historians Geraldien von Frijtag Drabbe Künzel, Ron Zeller and Pim Griffioen in presuming that the Sonderreferat J and the Central Office for Jewish Emigration ('Zentralstelle für jüdische Auswanderung') were only established in September 1941, the question arises as to which administrative authority ordered the anti-Jewish measures until then.[32] According to von Frijtag Drabbe Künzel, the previous structure consisted of an unspecified team that was restructured into an administrative structure similar to the RSHA by BdS Wilhelm Harster[33] in the summer of 1941;[34] the historian Anna Hajkova names Seyß-Inquart as the originator of anti-Jewish measures.[35] However, the historian Johannes Houwink ten Cate states that the BdS restructured its authority along the lines of the RSHA administrative structure, including the establishment of a Judenreferat, in mid July 1940.[36] There is agreement that either in the summer of 1940 or in August/September 1941, the Sonderreferat Juden was founded in The Hague and was transformed in January 1942 into Referat IV B 4, with a staff of thirty-five led by SS-Sturmbannführer Wilhelm Zoepf.[37] His most important assistant, the clerk Gertrud Slottke, travelled regularly to the Westerbork camp to organize deportations from there, which came under the jurisdiction of the office of Referat IV B 4 in The Hague from mid 1942 onwards.[38]

In March 1941, Rauter followed orders from Reinhard Heydrich to establish a central office for Jewish emigration according to the examples in Vienna and Prague.[39] Mainly due to the problematic source material, there is no secured level of research with respect to the main motivation behind establishing the central office. Opinions differ regarding whether it was initially set up to organize the expropriation and emigration of Jews in the Netherlands, to systematically record them, or primarily to prepare for the deportations.[40] The Viennese lawyer Erich Rajakowitsch, who had previously proven useful in the persecution and deportation of Viennese Jews, was appointed Head of the Central Office for Jewish Emigration. He was succeeded in September/October 1941 by Ferdinand Hugo aus der Fünten.[41] Hajkova writes that the Central Office had become part of Referat IV B 4, which was established in the spring of 1942, but does not provide evidence.[42]

There is no valid state of research with respect to the history of the institutions of Judenreferat IV B 4 and the Central Office, or to the official relationship between the two authorities. However, it is possible to state that the core task of both bodies was to organize, record, expropriate and deport Jews. BdS Harster played an outstanding role in this respect. The anti-Semitic measures by the German occupiers were orientated towards the incremental model practised in Germany, beginning with the definition and classification of 'Jews' and continuing with the removal of their rights, expropriation, internment and finally their deportation and murder. In October 1940, Jews were dismissed from public office.[43]

On 10 January 1941, it was decreed that all Jews were required to be registered at their local registry offices. The 'Reichskommissar's order for the occupied Dutch territories on compulsory registration of all people of wholly or partially Jewish blood' ('Verordnung des Reichskommissars für die besetzten niederländischen Gebiete über die Meldepflicht von Personen, die ganz oder teilweise jüdischen Blutes sind') required everyone with at least one Jewish grandparent to be registered.[44] Thus, the responsible bodies defined Jews even more broadly than in the German Reich.[45] As Christoph Kreutzmüller indicates, another reason for the high number of deaths among Jews in the Netherlands is the modern standard of the population register. While the recording of Jews in the Netherlands was being prepared for in the summer of 1940, the German occupiers could use the population register introduced in the Netherlands in 1936, which was based on punch cards and also included information on the individuals' religious groups.[46] This thorough recording served as the basis for selecting and deporting those who were registered as Jews.[47] Furthermore, identification papers in the Netherlands were extremely difficult to forge, so it was almost impossible to avoid deportation by acquiring false documents.[48]

With a few exceptions, all Jews followed the order dated 10 January 1941 and were recorded in the register of Jews.[49] Due to the modernization of the central administration of registry offices, the central statistical office and the census carried out every ten years, records of the Jewish population were already very advanced at the time.[50] The number of those registered as 'full Jews' had increased significantly as a result of the refugees to 140,245. Around 22,500 of them did not have Dutch citizenship.[51] Of these foreigners, 14,500 came from Germany and 7,300 from other countries.[52] On 12 March 1941, the Germans began seizing Jewish property.[53] In early June 1941, Jews were banned from entering or visiting public places, including parks, hotels, restaurants, cinemas, sports facilities, beaches, swimming pools, libraries, museums and concerts.[54] From the second half of 1941 onwards, a 'J' for 'Jew' was stamped in their ID papers.[55] From 29 August 1941, Jewish children were no longer permitted to attend state schools.[56] It became easier to dismiss Jewish employees and measures such as a ban for Jews to work in specific professions led to a strong increase in unemployment among Jews.[57] Generalkommissar for Security and Higher SS and Police Officer Rauter immediately ordered that a large number of them were to be interned in labour camps.[58] A simultaneously implemented measure to concentrate the Jewish population forced Jews to move to Amsterdam.[59]

On 27 March 1942, BdS Harster announced that the principles of the Nuremberg Race Laws now applied in the Netherlands.[60] One month later, on 29 April 1942, he ordered the introduction of the yellow star for Jews within a period of three days.[61] Aus der Fünten instructed the Head of the Judenrat to administratively record Dutch Jews more quickly for the planned labour assignment, to allow their transportation in the near future.[62] In July 1942, the first Jews received orders to report to the Westerbork transit camp.

There was little protest by the Dutch population against the persecution of Jews. One exception was the February strike, which had a long history. In January 1941, the Jewish quarter in Amsterdam had experienced increasing conflicts between German and Dutch National Socialists and their Jewish and non-Jewish opponents.[63] In February 1941, the paramilitary wing of the NSB, the WA (Weer Afdeling, the paramilitary arm of the NSB), repeatedly made provocative marches into the Jewish quarter of Amsterdam. On 11 February, one member of the WA was killed. As a result, the quarter was sealed off. During the two-day operation, four hundred young Jews were arrested and taken to Mauthausen concentration camp. This wave of arrests caused workers in the Amsterdam public transport company and the waste removal services to announce a strike on 25 February 1941 in solidarity with the persecuted Jews. After seven hours, the whole of Amsterdam was on a general strike that was soon joined by other parts of the country.[64] The Germans brutally suppressed the strike and punished the demonstrators severely. In contrast to the myth of the resistance of the railwaymen, the Dutch railway company did not heed the strike call.

The occupiers' brutal force against those involved in the Amsterdam February strike led to widespread intimidation. Furthermore, within a few weeks, the relatives of the young men taken to Mauthausen concentration camp received death certificates. In the following period of more than two years, there was no further incident of organized resistance against the Germans in the Netherlands. This changed only in the spring of 1943, when Dutch men were recruited for forced labour in Germany. Many of them managed to avoid their labour deployment by going into hiding.[65] At the time, resistance structures were developing that also made it easier for the few remaining Jews to go into hiding.[66]

From a general perspective, there were individual resistance groups, but no overall organization. This can in part be explained by the bloody suppression of the February strike, the relatively good supplies received by the population and the appeal by the Dutch government in exile to adapt to the existing situation.[67] Furthermore, in some parts of the population there was a willingness to collaborate, which must partly be regarded as political approval. There were between twenty-five thousand and forty thousand Dutch Waffen-SS officers, which was the largest non-German volume compared to the population size.[68] The number of voluntary work applications by Dutch people was satisfactory from a German perspective.[69] The Fascist NSB led by Mussert collaborated with the German occupiers. Mussert had 'sworn loyalty to death to the Germanic Führer Adolf Hitler',[70] but was disappointed when he was not appointed to lead the Netherlands government. By contrast, the SS heavily criticized Mussert since he was not at all interested in the establishment of the 'Greater Germanic Reich' and was instead reported to be pursuing separatist aims.[71]

From the Beginning of Deportations in July 1942 to the Liberation

When the deportations began on 15 July 1942, the German and local police arrested Jews on a daily basis to fulfil the defined quotas.[72] The Commander of the Amsterdam police, the NSB supporter Sybren Tulp, regularly offered support from his police force to implement anti-Jewish measures. One effect of this was that in August 1942, eleven thousand Jews were arrested in a single month in Amsterdam. This would have been impossible without the help of the Dutch police.[73] To capture as many Jews as possible, a system of premiums was introduced that guaranteed the payment of 7.50 Guilders for each apprehended Jew. The bounty was offered to members of the Amsterdam police, employees of the Central Office for Jewish Emigration and 'Judenjäger' ('Jew hunters') of the so-called Kolonne Henneicke, most of whom were NSB members.[74]

A large number of professional groups followed the occupiers' orders. The appeal to railway workers by the Communist underground newspaper *De Waarheid* on 8 August 1942 was unsuccessful. The paper had called for them to refuse to work and given them the following warning: 'Railwaymen consider that your trains are loaded with slaves heading for the slaughtering block'.[75] In fact, the railwaymen ensured the transport of Jewish prisoners to Westerbork and from there to the German border. The Dutch military police, the Marechaussee, was used to guard transports inside the country.[76] There is evidence that individual military policemen blackmailed Jews during these journeys for valuables or forced Jewish women to commit sexual acts, promising to release them in return.[77] Other Dutch policemen guarded the Jewish prisoners they were allocated during the transports or in custody in a rather negligent way, thereby occasionally allowing people to escape.[78]

Within the Jewish population, compared to the Belgian and French population, there was a lack of effective political organization, which is why no specifically Jewish resistance developed.[79] One reason for this lies in the high level of assimilation and the legal parity of Dutch Jews that had been introduced generations earlier. Unlike the Jews who had fled to Belgium and France in the wake of persecution in Eastern Europe, Jews in the Netherlands had not been persecuted or experienced legal discrimination for generations. As a result, they had seen no reason to organize themselves in Jewish interest groups or self-defence associations. Thus, they lacked options for collective action. Nevertheless, there were rescue attempts. For instance, one employee of the Jewish Council managed very skilfully to smuggle Jews, including many children, out of the Hollandsche Schouwburg assembly camp in Amsterdam. Furthermore, a very large number of Jews had individually ignored orders to report to the Westerbork camp. One highly effective Resistance group was the Westerweel Group, which developed a wide range of strategies to rescue persecuted Jews. It consisted of mainly non-Jewish Dutch people and German and Austrian Jews who had already experienced National Socialist persecution.

Furthermore, there were several attempts to steal or destroy registration lists to make it impossible to identify registered Jews. For example, on 27 or 28 March 1943, when the deportations were already very advanced, a group of Jewish Resistance fighters committed an attack on a population register situated in Plantage Kerklaan near Amsterdam Zoo. The operation involved 'overcoming and gagging the guards and setting the building on fire, partially destroying the files'.[80] Another resistance group in Haarlem should also be noted, in which Hannie Schaft and Truus Menger were active. They provided Jewish friends with false ID papers, carried out sabotage operations and took part in armed resistance.[81]

Around twenty-five thousand Jews attempted to avoid deportation by going into hiding. Two thirds of them survived.[82] In Belgium, the same number of Jews also went into hiding,[83] but since far fewer Jews lived in Belgium compared to the Netherlands, the proportion of Jews hidden in Belgium compared to the overall Jewish population was much higher than in the Netherlands. The proportion of those who hid and survived is also higher in Belgium.[84]

Researchers have proposed a wide range of theses to explain the high number of Jews deported from the Netherlands. This study does not aim to make a conclusive assessment, but does add further aspects. Dutch society consisted strongly of vertical social 'columns', that is, relatively different political and religious groups that were strongly separated from each other. Furthermore, J. C. H. Blom and Dan Michman, among others, describe the 'typically Dutch' obedience to authority and law abidance.[85] According to Pim Griffioen and Ron Zeller, this obedience is expressed in the cooperative behaviour of the Joodse Raad, as well as the passive attitude displayed by the majority of Dutch Jews even in the face of persecution.[86] In Belgium and France, there was a much higher suspicion of the Germans among Jews and non-Jews alike.[87] Ahlrich Meyer argues that the high number of Dutch victims can be explained neither by the lack of awareness of the assimilated Jewish population in the Netherlands nor by the lack of rescue efforts, but instead by the following fact: a 'power block consisting of the civilian administration, SS and the Sicherheitspolizei represented a "maximalist line" with respect to the persecution of Jews, despite internal differences, that could not be established in France or Belgium'.[88]

The country's topography is often used as an argument for the high number of deaths. Due to the small size of the Netherlands, the lack of forests and the mainly flat countryside, there were very few opportunities to flee.[89] Griffioen and Zeller reject this argument, pointing out that with the introduction of forced labour in the Netherlands in the spring of 1943, a large number of people (namely those who ignored their labour assignments) were suddenly hidden away from the German authorities. In this way, between mid 1943 and the liberation, two to three hundred thousand Dutch people assigned to forced labour in the German Reich were hidden. Thus, the specific conditions of the Dutch topography can have had less influence than anti-Jewish sentiment in limiting the number of hidden Jews.[90]

The period of good collaboration between the Dutch administration and the German civil administration continued until the spring of 1943. Apart from the February strike and a number of other Resistance operations, the occupation went relatively smoothly from a German perspective until then. When in the autumn of 1942 it became compulsory to hand in radios and bicycles for use by the Wehrmacht, followed in the spring of 1943 by forced labour for young men in Germany, the cooperative stance became more confrontative.[91] The defeats of the German Wehrmacht near Stalingrad and in North Africa also indicated a turning point in the events of the war in favour of the Allies. Larger national disturbances occurred in late April 1943, when the Germans made demobilized Dutch officers retrospective prisoners of war. One hundred and sixteen reputed leaders of these uprisings were sentenced to death.[92] Generalkommissar for Security and Higher SS and Police Officer Rauter was forced to establish a 'Railwacht' consisting of police officers to prevent attacks on the railway system. Such attacks were committed to prevent the transportation of forced labourers to Germany and to sabotage the German military logistics.[93] In early 1943, the Dutch government in exile called upon employees in public service not to cooperate in the deportation of Jews and young Dutch men assigned for forced labour.[94] However, the appeal came far too late for the Jewish population in view of the very advanced stage of deportations, nor was it implemented: the deportations continued. On 20 July 1944, the envoy Otto Bene reported to the Foreign Office: 'The Jewish question can be described as solved for the Netherlands since a large majority of the Jews have been transported out of the country'.[95]

The last deportation train departed from the Westerbork camp on 4 September 1944. In mid September, Allied troops invaded the Netherlands, but the advance was resisted in Arnhem. Following the devastating winter of hunger in 1944/45, which resulted in twenty-two thousand deaths, the Netherlands was liberated on 5 May 1945.

Deportations from the Netherlands

Summary of Deportations

A total of 102 deportation trains transported 107,000 Jews and 245 Sinti and Roma from the Netherlands. The first fifty deportation trains ended in Auschwitz, the destination for a total of sixty-seven trains. Nineteen others went from Westerbork to Sobibór. Seven trains went to the Theresienstadt ghetto, which was described as an 'Altersghetto' ('ghetto for the elderly') for propaganda purposes.[96] In 1944, eight transports went to Bergen-Belsen, where prisoners were interned as 'Austauschjuden'. Most were Jews who might be used as hostages to be exchanged for Germans held in enemy states. In fact, only a fraction of such prisoners were exchanged and most were killed.[97]

One train carrying 869 patients and care personnel from the Jewish psychiatric hospital in Apeldoorn was sent directly from there to Auschwitz, while two trains departed to Auschwitz from the Vught concentration camp.[98] On 25 June 1943, Harster reported that of the 'full Jews originally registered in the Netherlands ... the 100,000th has now been removed from the national territory'.[99] This means that within eleven months, one hundred thousand Jews from the Netherlands were deported. Both the significantly high number of deportees and the incomparably short time in which most of the Jews were deported from the Netherlands is without precedent, not only in France and Belgium. The total number of Jews deported from the Netherlands is almost exactly 107,000.[100] Only 4,700 returned from the camps.

The Westerbork Assembly Camp

The Westerbork camp was established in 1939 by the Dutch government to intern Jewish refugees from the German Reich to the south of Assen in a sparsely populated area. After its enlargement in 1941, it came under the jurisdiction of BdS Harster on 1 July 1942 and was officially called 'Polizeiliches Durchgangslager Westerbork' ('Police Transit Camp Westerbork'). It was used as an assembly camp.[101] The Camp Commander was SS-Obersturmführer Albert Konrad Gemmeker. Harster described Westerbork's role as a '"store" for departing transports'[102] to Auschwitz and other camps.

The camp was newly fenced in with barbed wire and guarded by the Marechaussee, the Dutch military police.[103] To begin with, the lack of tight security made it possible for prisoners to escape from the camp.[104] Later, however, the camp administration threatened to immediately deport the family of anyone trying to flee, or their co-prisoners in the same hut.[105]

On arriving in the camp, new inmates were entered in the camp register. Prisoners had to appear for roll calls in the morning and work hard every day.[106] Some had enough to eat due to the food parcels sent to the camp, but others report permanent hunger.[107] The hygiene conditions were appalling. There are reports of water shortages, flooded toilets and a stench in the huts.[108] Westerbork inmate Etty Hillesum wrote as follows on the situation in the camp: 'The misery here is really indescribable. We are housed in large huts like rats in a sewer'.[109]

There were great differences between the first internees in the camp, who were German, and the Dutch Jews imprisoned there later, as many survivors recall.[110] The German Jews disliked the fact that the Dutch Jews had recommended and financed the establishment of the government camp to accommodate German Jewish refugees.[111] When the Dutch Jews were later also interned, the German prisoners had long organized daily life in the camp and assumed key prisoners' functions. These were associated with certain advantages, to which Dutch prisoners therefore had no access. Furthermore, German prisoners initially provided the internal camp Ordnungsdienst (OD) ('wardens'), which had sometimes been described as 'Jewish police' or, worse still, as the 'Jewish SS'. For instance, they read out the list of those selected for the next deportation train in each hut and took them to the train on the day of departure. There were markings in chalk on the trains denoting the number of people who had to be driven inside. OD members guarded the prisoners as they boarded and locked the wagon doors.[112]

In addition to the conflict between German and Dutch prisoners, the existence of social and cultural facilities was a special aspect of the camp. There was, for instance, a school, sports events were held and renowned artists and musicians performed to the prisoners at cultural events.[113] There were also craftsman's stores and workshops in the camp.[114] Since Westerbork was overcrowded for some time, a separately administrated subcamp, known as the Vught concentration camp (or the Herzogenbusch concentration camp), was temporarily run in the town of Vught in 1943 as an additional assembly camp.[115] Another assembly camp was set up in the former theatre of the Hollandsche Schouwburg in Amsterdam. From there, prisoners were generally taken to Westerbork. The conditions in the Hollandsche Schouwburg were described as abysmal.[116]

Deportation Procedure

Deportations began in the Netherlands six months after the systematic murder of all Jews in Europe had been decided upon at the Wannsee Conference in January 1942. First, from 15 July 1942, almost twenty-five thousand stateless and foreign Jews were deported within only four months on two special trains a week. The deportation of Dutch Jews was planned for the subsequent period.[117]

The Central Office for Jewish Emigration produced the orders to report to Westerbork. Those selected were ordered to appear at a specific station on a defined day and time, 'for possible participation in a labour assignment in Germany under police supervision', for the purpose of a medical examination in the Westerbork transit camp.[118] Attached were the obligatory travel permits for Jews and a ticket. The Jews receiving orders to report to Westerbork were given precise instructions on the everyday items and documents they had to bring with them and what was prohibited.[119]

On 5 July 1942, the Central Office sent the first four thousand orders to assemble by post. Most of those ordered to appear did not do so. The

Central Office reacted by sending orders by officers of the Amsterdam municipal police, though this did not help. Thus, on 14 July 1942, raids were carried out in the Jewish quarter and in a number of southern districts. Around 540 women and men were taken away. At the same time, a special edition of the last legal Jewish newspaper, the *Joodse Weekblad*, was released, announcing to those who had not appeared as ordered that if they did not report as instructed within a week, the seven hundred (in fact 540) arrested Jews were to be sent to German concentration camps as punishment. The article was signed by the two leaders of the Judenrat, Abraham Asscher and David Cohen. Furthermore, messengers of the Joodse Raad sent a serial letter to all Jews ordered to report to Westerbork, including an urgent appeal to consider the fates of the seven hundred arrested Jews when deciding on their actions.[120] As a result, a large number of people followed their orders to report to Westerbork.

On 15 July 1942, the first deportation train departed from Westerbork, while the second departed only a day later. Shortly afterwards, the organizers of the deportations were confronted with a new situation, which the representative of the Foreign Office in the Netherlands, Otto Bene, described as follows: 'The Jewish population has discovered [the measure's] purpose and knows what really lies ahead with the transports and labour assignments in the East'.[121] He reports that only four hundred out of a further two thousand selected Jews appeared, continuing: 'It is therefore difficult to fill both trains and it is as yet unclear how to fill the trains in the coming weeks'.[122] From September 1942 onwards, only around half of all Jews complied with their labour assignment orders.[123] Nevertheless, Generalkommissar for Security and Higher SS and Police Officer Rauter eagerly reported to his boss, Heinrich Himmler: 'I aim to receive three rather than two trains a week. . . . I hope that by Christmas, we will also be rid of these 30,000 Jews, so that a total of 50,000 Jews, or half, will have been removed from Holland'.[124] To capture them, more raids and individual arrests were carried out in apartments. According to Rauter, 'the Jewish population is to be outlawed on 15 October 1942'[125] and the male Jews interned in labour camps should be brought together with their families in transit camps on the pretence of uniting families.

To cover the short-term increase in capacity requirements, the additional camp section in Herzogenbusch concentration camp was to be completed as soon as possible. This order indeed led to an increase in the weekly number of deportees from 2,000 to 3,500, which, according to Bene, caused problems due to a lack of space in the camp and also the capacity of the trains.[126] Reichskommissar Seyß-Inquart ordered that the approximately sixty-one thousand remaining 'full Jews' in the Netherlands should be transported by 1 May 1943.[127] BdS Harster informed the responsible offices on 3 May 1943 that RFSS Himmler wishes 'that as many Jews are transported to the East this year as humanly possible'.[128] Thus, eight thousand Jews were to be deported in May, and fifteen thousand in June. Harster explained this high volume with the great need for labour through the new construction of a Buna factory in Auschwitz. The three-page notice announced and ordered several operations, such as raids in Amsterdam and the release by the Rüstungsinspektion of 'armaments Jews', who had previously been reserved for work in the weapons industry, for deportation. In the summer of 1943, most Jews in Amsterdam no longer followed the orders to report for labour assignment, probably also because of the increased hope that, following the North African invasion, there would also be an Allied invasion in Europe.

Until 12 December 1942, a transport departed from Westerbork almost every Tuesday and Friday. Until 1 November 1942, prisoners selected for deportation had to walk 5 km from Westerbork to the railway station in Hooghalen, guarded by the Marechaussee.[129] Tracks were subsequently laid to the camp.[130] The trains were driven by railwaymen from the Dutch railway company Nederlandse Spoorwegen, which also provided the wagons.[131] The trains travelled towards Groningen, crossed the border near Nieuweschans, passed Bremen, Magdeburg, Hoyerswerda and Kohlfurt and finally arrived at Auschwitz.[132] On a number of occasions, the train travelled via Zwolle to the south.[133] Between August and December 1942, six transports stopped in Cosel, Upper Silesia, and possibly also in Heydebrecht,[134] where a total of 3,540 men between the ages of fifteen and fifty were selected for forced labour in the numerous Jewish labour camps in the surrounding area.[135] Several former members of the Schutzpolizei who were among the guards stated that in Cosel, depending on how many prisoners were selected for work, the same number of prisoners who were no longer fit for labour or were sick were loaded onto the train 'so that the number of Jews in the train was correct'.[136]

The historian Gerhard Hirschfeld writes that despite its reservations, the Judenrat decided by majority decision to follow the German orders, in order to 'keep at least the important people here for as long as possible'.[137] It delivered the labour assignment orders from the Central Office and organized the administrative handling of those affected, including their declaration of assets.[138]

The head of the Central Office for Jewish Emigration, Ferdinand Hugo aus der Fünten, sometimes made minor concessions in the selection of people to be deported. In addition to specific professional groups (including diamond cutters and weapons industry workers), all members of the Joodse Raad were exempt from deportation.[139] Those exemptions, which were known as 'Sperren' ('blocks'), were an important instrument for keeping people quiet, since they implied the hope of being able to avoid deportation. Ultimately, none of them were effective.

Before Deportation in Westerbork

Before the departure of a transport, all prisoners in Westerbork who were not to be deported were required to remain in their blocks.[140] To handle the deportations, which took a long time every Tuesday, as smoothly as possible, Camp Commander Gemmeker ordered in early May 1943 that apart from activities required to uphold the camp's operations, all work was to be halted from Monday at midday to Tuesday morning.[141]

Most of the internees tried to remain in Westerbork as long as possible, because of their fear and insecurity regarding what awaited them at the end of the journey. A large number of prisoners attempted to be taken to the camp hospital and thereby qualify as unfit for travel.[142] On the day of the deportation, the list of those required to leave for the transport was read out in the huts early in the morning and the people on the list had half an hour to pack. There were scenes of despair.[143]

On 24 May 1943, the Camp Commander announced that the following rules applied for the transport due to depart the next day: 'I hereby order that the camp prisoners leaving on the transport are only permitted to take the following items with them onto the wagons determined for them: 1 bread bag with provisions, 1 canteen, 1 blanket, eating utensils, 1 set of cutlery (knife, fork, spoon)'.[144]

The remaining luggage was to be deposited in front of the hut. The foreman of the hut and the OD loaded the luggage in separate baggage wagons. A former guard team member confirms the accounts by many deportees that before the departure all wagon passengers were threatened that if they tried to escape they would be shot.[145]

The Wagon Elder

In the Netherlands too, one wagon elder was selected from among the prisoners in each wagon. He was responsible for 'securing the Jews' during stops at stations along the route and was occasionally permitted to gather water or food for the people in the wagon.[146] The dilemma in which the wagon elder was placed is described by Elie A. Cohen, who was deported from Westerbork to Auschwitz on 14 September 1943:

> One man was put in charge as the Wagonführer. All these Wagonführers had to report to the Obersturmführer some time before we left. Ours came back and said, 'Boys, I've been appointed Wagonführer, and I've been told that if as much as one

of you escapes, it'll cost me my life'. It was once more an appeal to our solidarity. Everyone thought: Ought you to escape when it can cost that man his life?[147]

The historian Jacques Presser interpreted the naming of a Transportführer, several wagon elders and a responsible doctor as a calming tactic and a deception strategy to conceal the actual purpose of the deportation.[148]

The Wagons Used

The first deportations from the Netherlands appear to have used freight wagons.[149] Information on the wagon types for later transports varies. Former Westerbork prisoners and Hans Ottenstein stated that between January and March 1943, passenger wagons were used, before switching back to freight wagons, with the exception of transports to Bergen-Belsen and Theresienstadt.[150] Other sources suggest that earlier transports already used passenger wagons, for instance the train on 30 November 1942. This is evident, for example, in the report that clearly states that the deportees were accommodated in compartments, that is, passenger wagons and – presumably to prevent escapes – that the windows were to be kept closed on Dutch territory: 'Until the border, compartment windows remain *closed*. On German territory, windows may be opened'.[151] A former member of the Schutzpolizei stated that some of the passenger wagons used did not have a toilet. One or two guards were posted in each wagon.[152]

The train departing from Westerbork on 30 March 1943 was the last transport to an extermination camp that consisted exclusively of passenger wagons.[153] In the spring/summer of 1943, a further transport destination was announced: Theresienstadt. It was quickly presumed that it was better to be deported to Theresienstadt than to Auschwitz, because 'Jews with former wartime or peacetime distinction' and 'Jews who had distinguished themselves in the removal of Jews from the Netherlands'[154] were sent to Theresienstadt. The transports to Theresienstadt used passenger wagons and were carefully compiled, while the transports to Auschwitz were put together in half a day and consisted of freight wagons.[155] According to the former prisoner Fred Schwarz, at an unspecified time later on, the trains consisted both of passenger wagons and freight wagons and it had been a matter of chance as to which wagon the prisoners were allocated.[156]

Camp Commander Gemmeker ordered that the wagons travelling to Auschwitz every week should be converted – presuming that the train would return with the same wagons. He instructed coopers to produce bottomless barrels with lids for the freight trains for use as toilets. Each wagon floor had a hole with the diameter of such a barrel cut into it and a barrel placed above it.¹⁵⁷ Twenty freight wagons were also equipped with wooden benches screwed to the floor and with iron railings attached to the ceiling, onto which straw mattresses were placed.¹⁵⁸ Signs with the text 'Westerbork-Auschwitz, Auschwitz-Westerbork, do not uncouple wagons, train must return closed to Westerbork' were fixed to the outside of the trains in Gemmeker's presence.¹⁵⁹ In practice, however, the plan clearly failed and only once did a train return with all the converted wagons.¹⁶⁰

When the train arrived the day before the departure, the following procedure began:

> Immediately after their arrival, the wagons were cleaned and disinfected thoroughly by a cleaning unit, while another group repaired the most serious damage to the wagons. Leaky roofs were repaired with roof felt. Hatches were opened, floors were sealed, nails hammered into walls. A third group dragged paper mattresses out of the wagons intended for the transportation of sick people, rolled water barrels to the train and set up barrels that replaced toilets on the journey.¹⁶¹

Judenreferent Zoepf was aware of the positive influence that the use of passenger wagons had. For instance, in a letter to Referat IV B 4 of the RSHA dated 15 April 1943, he requested permission to use passenger wagons for a transport from Amsterdam to Theresienstadt. In addition to technical advantages, Zoepf added another argument: 'Furthermore, the Reichskommissar especially values, in the Netherlands and for this train, a certain propaganda effect, since the train is a "change of residence" and is departing from Amsterdam rather than the camp'.¹⁶²

A train did indeed leave Amsterdam for Theresienstadt on 21 April 1943.¹⁶³

The Situation in the Wagons

Not much is known of the situation in the passenger wagons. They were apparently full, but not always overcrowded; one report states that attempts had been made to distract and calm down the prisoners with astronomical explanations of the sky or with everyday activities such as haircutting. There was a gloomy or oppressive silence.¹⁶⁴

By contrast, the freight wagons were completely overcrowded, carrying fifty-five to seventy-five people.¹⁶⁵ Deaths due to the conditions during the transport were taken into account by those responsible, as Gertrud Slottke, who was responsible for the processing by the Judenreferat, confirmed in 1967: 'I must therefore stress that the standard type of transportation (such as the overcrowding in the freight trains) combined with all ages and sick people should have made me think – as I said – that during the entire period a certain number would die'.¹⁶⁶

Jules Schelvis, who was deported from Westerbork to Sobibór on 1 June 1943, reports of terrible conditions during the journey. Prisoners stood with their luggage cramped together; the train stopped countless times along the way; the atmosphere was bleak and desperate; there were many arguments. Schelvis describes the atmosphere in the wagon shortly before arriving in Sobibór: 'We were so tired, we were no longer interested where we would end up. There was only one question: how do we get out of this stinking, overcrowded livestock wagon to get a breath of fresh air?'[167] Elie A. Cohen also reports that the atmosphere was bleak and prisoners were ashamed at having to relieve themselves in the barrel in front of others. They had attached a small curtain around the barrel to enable a little privacy.[168] At every stop, the guards attempted to take money and other valuables from the imprisoned Jews.[169]

On 6 April 1943, Levie Sluijzer was deported to Sobibór. He arranged with his brother Moses Sluijzer, who had remained in Westerbork, to hide a report on his journey at an agreed place on the underside of the wagon. After the train returned, Moses Sluijzer found the message from his brother. Levie Sluijzer described the terrible conditions in the wagon, how cramped it was, the freezing cold, the stench and the constant arguments. In the morning, members of the Ordnungspolizei went from wagon to wagon and asked whether there had been any deaths; in their wagon there had been two. The bodies were taken to the baggage wagon. Sluijzer states that this shows how the guards expected people to die in the wagons. He described their behaviour as very polite and friendly: 'It's bearable. At the many stations they give us water and bread with sausage and marmalade'.[170]

The water provisions apparently differed on each transport. Like Sluijzer, many other prisoners and former members of the guard units reported that water was provided on the journey.[171] However, Schelvis states: 'We were dying of thirst, . . .'.[172] No-one gave them water. Etty Hillesum noted back in Westerbork that prisoners could only take one bread bag onto the wagon and that they were locked up with seventy other people for three days and nights. She asked herself how many would arrive alive.[173] There are several reports on the deportation on 3 September 1944. Janny Brandes-Brilleslijper, for instance, states that the people crushed together in the wagon were forced to stand for the whole journey and that the conditions of the transport led to aggression among the prisoners:

> The longer the trip lasted, the more belligerent people became. . . . The kindest, gentlest people become aggressive when they've stood for a long time. And you get tired – so terribly tired that you just want to lean against something, or if possible,

even if only for a minute, to sit down on the straw. Then you sit on the straw and all that noise around you makes you aggressive . . . and then you, too, push and hit.¹⁷⁴

Georg H., another witness, recalls the same journey: 'We were taken in livestock wagons to Auschwitz. . . . The journey alone was indescribable. There are no words'.¹⁷⁵

The requirement to write letters and postcards to relatives can be regarded as a 'calming measure' and a deception tactic, both for the people on the train and for those left behind. The Ordnungspolizei gathered the post together.¹⁷⁶ Deportees also threw messages out of the wagon through cracks in the walls in the hope that they would be found and forwarded to the relevant addressees.

The Guard Teams

Due to a lack of sources, it has not to date been possible to prove consistently which police battalions were used to form the accompanying guards on deportation trains from the Netherlands.¹⁷⁷ During this study, it was possible to identify a number of Transportführer for the first time. This allows us to draw some conclusions on the battalions deployed. At least twice, these were members of PB 56, three times they were from PB 68 and several times from PB 105.¹⁷⁸

One Transportführer can be identified without doubt as the Oberleutnant der Schutzpolizei der Reserve Friedrich Degeler (born in Heidenheim in 1902), who was seconded from the police administration in Heidenheim.¹⁷⁹ In February 1943, he was appointed Kompanieführer with the rank of an Oberleutnant der Schutzpolizei in the newly founded I/Pol. 16 (previously PB 56)¹⁸⁰ under Bataillonsführer Major der Schutzpolizei Herbert Furck in its 2nd Company.¹⁸¹ He served in Tilbourg, the Netherlands.¹⁸² In at least two cases, on 31 August 1943 and 15 March 1944, he commanded the accompanying guards on transports from Westerbork to to Auschwitz and Bergen-Belsen.¹⁸³ After returning to Germany following a period as a Soviet prisoner of war, he was able to continue his life without any consequences and was regarded as a respectable civilian. From 1968 to 1972, he was a Christian Democrat member of the state parliament of Baden-Württemberg. Due to his local political engagement in his home community of Heidenheim, a square was even named after him: Friedrich-Degeler-Platz.

Another Transportführer was Alfred Käsewieter, Oberleutnant der Schutzpolizei der Reserve, who served as a Zugführer in the 7th Company of Battalion II, SS Police Regiment 3 (previously probably PB 68) from April 1942 to July 1944.¹⁸⁴ From 3 July 1944 to 15 August 1944, he was a Kompanieführer in the 6th Company of SS Police Regiment 3 in the Netherlands. During this period, his superior authority was situated in The Hague.[185] At least twice, on 7 September 1943 to Auschwitz and on 11 January 1944 to Bergen-Belsen, Käsewieter served as the Transportführer.[186] In March 1943, he was appointed Oberleutnant der Schutzpolizei der Reserve.[187] It was explained that his promotion was due to his 'inner soldier's attitude'.[188] Furthermore, Käsewieter is said to have led units independently on several occasions with a good level of success. Later assessments were also positive: 'His intelligent way of leading people should be stressed, with the right balance of care and firmness'.[189]

The size of the guard unit was recorded as between six or eight and twenty men.[190] They were posted in a passenger wagon at the centre of the train.[191] While PB 105 was stationed in the Netherlands, their tasks included guarding Jewish prisoners during deportations. A large number of guards report that they drove to the 'Jews' camp' the night before the deportation, stayed overnight there and then took over the train once the Jews had already been 'loaded' onto it.[192] Sometimes, when members of the Schutzpolizei in PB 105 had leave, they joined the deportation train for part of the journey and left it along the way to visit their parents or wives.[193]

The Transport Conditions from the Perspective of Former Members of the Schutzpolizei in Police Battalion 105

During investigation proceedings against Hans Helwes, the former Commander of Bremen PB 105, which began in 1964, on suspicion of violent National Socialist crimes, he and many of his former battalion members made statements. PB 105 was a reserve battalion that was established in 1939 and consisted of reserve policemen. Only the Kompanieführer, Zugführer and Gruppenführer came from active police duty.[194] PB 105 had been stationed in Arnhem since July 1942 and in The Hague from November 1942 to the autumn of 1944.[195]

The task of the guard unit was described by former member of the Schutzpolizei Walter Meyer as follows: 'The guard unit had the task of securing the terrain directly around the train if it stopped to prevent the Jews from attempting to escape'.[196] The chain of guards was established when the train made interim stops, as Georg Lüdeke, another former Schutzpolizei officer, stated, 'so that the Jews had no contact with people outside or dared to attempt an escape'.[197] Another guard, Ludwig Walter Coors, said: 'Basically, we had a "quiet time" on the transport and did little about the Jews even when the train stopped'.[198] Several of them could remember that they had been ordered to shoot in the case of an escape. For instance, the policeman Heinrich Falke said: 'We were told in advance that if more than one Jew tried to escape at the same time, warning shots and then targeted shots were to be fired. But we were never in a situation where we had to shoot'.[199] Another former Schutzpolizei officer, Wilhelm Holdhoff, stated that the Transportführer had ordered them 'to prevent the escape if necessary with firearms'.[200] They had been armed with carbines and pistols.[201]

Another policeman, Alfred Henke, reports that during the journey, his Transportführer had told him roughly the following:

> If one of them escapes from me on the way and we have to have to count 2,000 heads, that will take too much time. ... We had previously received orders to call out to people trying to escape and then – if they did not stand still – use our firearms.[202]

Only one of those questioned spoke of escapes, namely Helmut Rackwitz: 'I can say for sure that we were supposed to prevent the Jews from leaving the train. But some of them did do that and we did not stop them'.[203]

Several former Schutzpolizei officers confirmed that they stopped in Cosel, where there were desperate scenes of separation.[204] A former PB 105 guard, Alfred Henke, described the scene in detached terms: 'During that separation, I sometimes heard screaming, but I never saw or heard any mistreatment or shots'.[205] Another policeman, Johann Alberts, claimed: 'I am not aware of a single case where members of the battalion robbed or tormented Jews during the transport to Auschwitz'.[206] During the journey, the Jews had provided for themselves and drawn water from the pumps at the stations.[207] Only one guard, Heinrich Wiewerich, noticed that the wagons, in this case apparently passenger wagons, were 'overcrowded'.[208]

Once the Westerbork camp had been connected to the railway line in November 1942, the camp command organized the process of prisoners boarding the train. This had previously been handled by the guard teams. The prisoners were therefore already in the wagons when the guard units came to the train.[209]

The accompanying guard teams travelled the entire journey to Auschwitz without being relieved.[210] According to the general tone of the statements, once they had arrived and handed the train over to the SS, they had immediately returned home or spent the night in nearby SS accommodation. The task of guarding the deportation trains, which was known as the 'Judenkommando', was apparently popular among policemen of lower ranks. For instance, former Schutzpolizei member Julius Aschermann reports: 'It sometimes happened that the same people volunteered again. But they were sent back to the battalion with the words "You've already been on one"'.[211] One former colleague, Johann Alberts, explained why some people found the assignment so attractive:

It was far more the case that Major Helwes assembled the transport unit from a social perspective. For instance, if a member of the battalion had suffered material or personal loss as a result of air raids in Bremen, the respective member of the battalion was selected for the guard team. That way he was perhaps able to spend three days in Bremen.[212]

This brief, unofficial leave in Bremen on the return journey had been a great incentive. Alberts also stated that he never experienced his colleagues 'robbing or tormenting' Jewish prisoners.[213]

While the former Schutzpolizei officers describe and explain their actions as guards as always being decent, and that the transports were 'carried out correctly', they sometimes criticize in contrasting ways the 'harsh' treatment of the Jews on arriving in Auschwitz. According to Friedrich Behrens and Meinolph Derenthal, there had been 'unpleasant scenes'[214] and 'rough treatment';[215] Wilhelm Engels even speaks of 'raw violence – without human compassion'.[216]

The Netherlands: Escapes and Attempted Escapes

Juda Arnold Toff and Maurits Wolder – Escape on 11 January 1943

The first escape that became known in the Netherlands was undertaken in January 1943 by Maurits Wolder and Juda Arnold Toff.

Maurits Wolder (born in Amsterdam in 1925) had been ordered to report to Hollandsche Schouwburg for a labour assignment. As a result, he worked for the German war industry and had to produce waistcoats as a furrier for the Wehrmacht.[217] He escaped and assumed a false name.[218] On 17 December 1942, he was arrested by the Gestapo and taken to the prison in Amstelveenseweg.[219] There, as Maurits Wolder explained in an interview in 1996, he met the 28-year-old Juda Arnold Toff (born in Amsterdam in 1914), who had been imprisoned there on 22 December 1942 and shared a cell with him.[220] Toff spoke of his wife and baby[221] and declared: 'Come what may, I will flee'.[222] Wolder replied: 'Me too'.[223] The two were transferred to Westerbork on 9 January 1943.[224] They decided against fleeing from the train to Westerbork, since Toff was waiting for news of his wife and Wolder hoped to see his mother again in Westerbork.[225] Once they had arrived there, they were immediately sent to a punishment hut and sent directly on a transport train two days later, this time to Auschwitz.[226] Wolder recounts that they were lucky that they were in a passenger wagon and not cramped inside a freight car. The compartment doors were not even locked.[227] They were guarded by 'Greens' (the

Dutch expression for the Ordnungspolizei), who were posted in a separate wagon and armed with submachine guns.[228]

Maurits Wolder and Juda Arnold Toff decided to jump from the train.[229] Juda Arnold Toff informed the others in the wagon of their escape plans and offered to take messages to their families.[230] He took a number of letters, removed the yellow star from his clothing and jumped out of the moving train.[231] Maurits Wolder mustered all the courage he had and jumped shortly before Haren, presumably where the train made a sharp right turn at a slower speed.[232] The precise circumstances of how Toff and Wolder escaped from the wagon are unknown.

When the train stopped immediately after he had jumped, Wolder crawled under the train. The Schutzpolizei guard patrolled along the wagons, but did not see him.[233] He wore a hat to cover his clean-shaven head, which made him recognizable as a prisoner. A farmer waved to him and said: 'You've just escaped, no doubt from that train. Let's go home'.[234] He then took him to his house in Haren.[235] With the help of the farmer, Wolder managed to return to Amsterdam, where he rediscovered Toff in an unknown situation using a previously agreed, whistled 'signal melody'.[236] Maurits Wolder was subsequently hidden by a family in Zaandam, among others.[237] Juda Arnold Toff was captured and deported to Auschwitz. During its evacuation, he was taken to Mauthausen concentration camp on 25 January 1945.[238] From there, he was transferred to Ebensee, a subcamp of Mauthausen, where he died on 16 March 1945. The death certificate states general sepsis as the cause of death.[239]

Looking back, Wolder called Toff his hero for encouraging him to jump from the train to Auschwitz, where they would have been gassed and exterminated.[240]

Elsa Wijnperle and Her Son Nathan – Escape on 29 January 1943

On 5 May 1942, the six-person Wijnperle family from Amsterdam received orders to report to a specific bus stop within twenty-four hours, taking with them only a change of clothes. From there, they were taken to the abattoir that served as a collection point, which was already overcrowded. All Jews taken there were forced to undergo a medical examination. A German officer gave the father, Manus Wijnperle, the address of a different Jewish family that was to accommodate them in their apartment.[241] However, Manus Wijnperle sensed that this was a trap. Instead of going to the named address, the Wijnperle family hid with the grandmother. A week later, thanks to the tireless efforts of the father, they were able to move to the home of a business partner. During the time that followed, the family was forced to move from hideout to hideout, and was eventually forced to split up.[242]

The son, Nathan Wijnperle (born in Sittard in 1926), hid with his parents in an Amsterdam apartment. When he left it for the first time after a long period on 6 January 1943, in order to gather provisions, he was arrested by the notorious collaborator Abraham Puls and the police accompanying him. It seems that they had been watching the house for a long time. While Nathan and his mother Elsa (born in Sittard in 1901) were arrested, the father managed to escape unnoticed.[243]

Elsa and Nathan Wijnperle were held in custody overnight at the police station and interrogated the next morning at the SD headquarters on Euterpestraat.[244] Since 'going underground' was a crime, they both received a criminal record[245] and were taken to the prison in Amstelveenseweg, where they were separated.[246] After more than a week, Nathan Wijnperle was taken to the Jewish transit camp that had been established in the Herzogenbusch concentration camp in Vught due to capacity shortages. On 16 January 1943, the first transport arrived carrying 450 Jews from the Amsterdam Hollandsche Schouwburg assembly camp.[247] The chronological procedure described by Nathan Wijnperle makes it plausible that Elsa and Nathan Wijnperle were among those taken there, without knowing each other's whereabouts.

Every day, more trains arrived loaded with prisoners. Nathan constantly looked for his mother. The huts in Vught were so overcrowded that some prisoners had to sleep on the floor. Nathan Wijnperle was forced into hard labour outside the hut, but he recounts that he always preferred the work to spending time in the mouldy stench of the huts. Food supplies were very poor and mainly consisted of potato skins.[248]

On 28 January 1943, Nathan Wijnperle was driven to Vught railway station together with a large number of prisoners.[249] His despair grew with the fear of leaving his own country. In front of the train he saw a dishevelled group of women, among them his mother.[250] The joy at seeing her again was indescribable, but they kept still to avoid attracting attention. Elsa Wijnperle removed her headscarf and wrapped it around her son. They remained standing beside each other. As they boarded the train, SS guards tried to separate women and men, but Elsa and Nathan Wijnperle managed to get into the same compartment and sit beside each other by the door.

This transport was the first to take Jewish prisoners from Vught via Westerbork to Auschwitz. The surviving prisoners' records from Herzogenbusch concentration camp for Elsa and Nathan Wijnperle show that both of them travelled on this train.[251] In the archive of the Westerbork Memorial Centre, there is a note stating that apparently both were given luggage by the Joodse Raad on 29 January 1943 during one of the stops on the journey.[252]

It took hours for all the prisoners to board the train. When the Dutch conductor, accompanied by the SS, came to close the compartment door, Nathan pressed his knees gently against the door to prevent the latch from closing. The conductor turned the key, but the door remained open. Nathan Wijnperle believes the conductor deliberately helped him.[253]

When the deportation train departed, it was dark both outside and on the train. Suddenly the train stopped. Nathan saw through the window how guards jumped from the train and illuminated the train from below with torches and shone them into the compartments. Once the guards were convinced that all was well, they boarded the train again and it slowly set off. Nathan Wijnperle reports that at that moment, he thought: now or never. When the train was setting off and the locomotive produced a great deal of steam, he wanted to use the opportunity to flee from the train with his mother. He opened the compartment door, which was still unlocked, went outside and jumped. Elsa Wijnperle remained fearfully standing on the running board. The train accelerated. Nathan Wijnperle ran beside the train and sometimes lost sight of his mother due to the steam. Elsa Wijnperle stretched her hand out to him and he motioned to her that she should jump. She let herself drop beside the track.[254]

Nathan Wijnperle describes how they initially lay beside each other as if paralysed and looked at the train as it moved away. They then started running and, with the help of a passer-by, found the way to the nearby town of Dieren. There, Elsa Wijnperle rang the bell at the rectory.[255] When the Catholic priest opened the door, she said: 'My son and I have just escaped from the train to Auschwitz. We are Jews. We need help'.[256] The priest gave them the address of a Jew in Dieren, Mr Cats, who was married to a non-Jew.[257]

When they arrived there, Mrs Cats opened the door. A birthday party was taking place inside the house. Elsa Wijnperle started to explain their situation, but Mrs Cats quickly understood and asked them to enter. The people inside encircled the two fugitives and when they understood what had occurred, they brought them dry clothes and took them into the warm living room. While Elsa Wijnperle ate only a bread roll and drank a glass of milk, Nathan stated that he devoured enormous amounts of food. That night, they stayed in the apartment above Mrs Cats' art gallery. In the middle of the night, Nathan, who was sick from eating such large amounts of food after weeks of hunger, became so ill that they had to call a doctor.

In the meantime, the Dieren underground had received news of the escape. Some of its members contacted the Resistance fighter Twan Maintz, a friend from Elsa Wijnperle's youth, who had already helped her family several times.[258] Maintz brought a message to Manus Wijnperle in his hideout in Amsterdam, informing him that his wife and son were alive and he could take them to him. Wijnperle collapsed on hearing the news.[259]

Since Maintz feared a trap, he and Manus Wijnperle agreed that if Maintz had not returned with the other two by 21:00 the next day, Wijnperle should leave his hideout for the sake of his safety. Since Elsa and Nathan Wijnperle had had their false ID papers taken from them, the journey to Amsterdam was a great risk. To hide Nathan Wijnperle's shaved head, the doctor who had treated him the night before applied a bandage around it so it looked as though he had had an accident. Twan Maintz also gave them a copy of the NSB newspaper *Volk en Vaderland* as extra disguise. Elsa Wijnperle hid in the toilet for long periods of the journey. When they changed trains in Arnhem, the train to Amsterdam was delayed and it was after 21:00 by the time they arrived in Amsterdam. Manus Wijnperle had already given up hope, but was too shocked to flee. Thus, he was still in his hideout when his wife and son arrived.[260]

In the following period, all six family members were often forced to change their hiding places, but all of them survived Nazi persecution.[261]

Paul Siegel and Martin Uffenheimer – Escape on 1 February 1944

Paul Siegel (born in Cologne in 1924) grew up with his two sisters in a religious family in Cologne.[262] His parents ran a poultry store there. Paul's father, Salomon Siegel, travelled to Barneveld in Holland almost every week to the large poultry market. He had a business partner and friend there, Henk van der Iest. In 1928, Salomon Siegel bought two houses in the Netherlands, in Arnhem, which he rented out. When the National Socialists came to power on 30 January 1933, the father did not return from one of his Holland trips as a precaution. An acquaintance from the police had learnt that a complaint had been made about Salomon Siegel, claiming that he supported anti-German elements and owned an illegal weapon. The apartment was indeed searched, but nothing was found.

Anti-Semitism became more visible every day. Paul Siegel recalls the anti-Semitic propaganda by Joseph Goebbels and how the walls were smeared with 'Die Juden sind unser Unglück' ('The Jews are our misfortune') and 'Juda verrecke' ('Die Jew'). The boycott on 1 April 1933 made it clear to the parents that Hitler's rule would not be a brief episode. Salomon Siegel, who was already in the Netherlands, and the mother spoke to each other on the telephone. The business was to be liquidated and the mother and three children were to join him. However, the authorities demanded that the father personally approve the emigration of the two older children, or that the mother show his passport. Thus, only the mother and the youngest daughter, Ruth, were able to leave the country. The older sister Margot and Paul were initially looked after by Mrs Loeb, Margot's teacher. Ten days later, Henk van der Iest collected the children and secretly crossed the border with them.

After his Bar-Mizwa, Paul joined a Jewish youth club in the Netherlands, which had a Zionist orientation, but did not carry out any activities with the aim of emigrating to Palestine. After the German invasion of Poland, Paul, who had become a convinced Zionist, regarded it as a natural step to emigrate to Palestine. His father also feared that the expansion of the Nazis would not stop at the border with the Netherlands, but favoured Canada or the USA as a future residence. The opposing ideas about their emigration destination led to heated arguments. Paul decided to become a Palestine pioneer. The Palestine pioneers (Hechaluz) planned to emigrate and prepared themselves for the settlement of the country through appropriating agricultural and craftsman's skills (Hackshara). In July 1940, the Zionist organization Vereniging tot Vakopleiding van Palestina Pioniers ('Association for the Professional Training of Palestine Pioneers'), also known as the Deventer Vereniging ('Deventer Society') for short, arranged a job for him on a farm. In his free time, he met likeminded people from the Zionist youth movement. In early 1942, Paul and his sister Margot planned to flee to Switzerland, but the acquaintance who was paid in advance to help them escape deceived them and escaped alone to Switzerland with their money.

In July 1942, Paul Siegel received orders to report for labour duty. He prepared to avoid the forced labour by going into hiding. He went underground on 1 October 1942 and often changed hiding places from then on. On 19 November 1942, Paul managed to escape from a raid by the Dutch police on the farmhouse of the Visscher couple, where he had been hiding: the Brummen police inspector who took part in the raid told Paul Siegel he should flee and that he would not apprehend him. In view of the constant threat and the frequent changes of hiding places, however, Paul lacked the necessary optimism and strength to flee. He was arrested. At first he was held in custody at the Brummen police station, before being transferred to the Gestapo headquarters in Arnhem. On 28 November 1942, he was taken by train to Westerbork. Dutch policemen guarded the group of prisoners, declaring that they would shoot at anyone who tried to escape.

At the time, two trains travelled from Westerbork each week. Hut 64, where Paul Siegel was soon accommodated along with a comrade at his request, mainly contained members of various Zionist agricultural training organizations. Paul Siegel worked for an internal camp care service and had an armband marked with an 'F' for 'Fürsorgedienst' ('welfare service'). Among other tasks, he was required to carry the baggage for the old and weak, as well as women with children, to the deportation trains and give everyone in the wagons food parcels before the wagon doors were closed.

The Palestine pioneers of the Hechaluz movement were popular among other camp interns.[263] Even Camp Commander Gemmeker spared the group from deportation.[264] Gustel Moses, who also belonged to the Hechaluz movement, reports on the attempts by Hechaluz to prevent new arrivals at the camp from being registered:

> Immediately after arriving, they attempted to send them out for labour, even before they were registered, to allow them to flee. But that had to happen straight away the next morning. Once the people were registered and someone was missing from a group in the evening, the others were immediately sent to a concentration camp.[265]

When Paul Siegel was sent to the sick bay with angina and pneumonia, he suffered a shock. He later wrote: 'In the neighbouring beds, there were literally and visibly human skeletons'.[266] The thin, mistreated Jews had come from the Ellecom camp and the police transit camp in Amersfoort.[267] All kinds of rumours and alarming stories caused further unease. One deportee wrote a postcard from the destination, saying that all was well, including the work and provisions. But the postcard was signed 'Blinde Maupie' (Blind Moses), an expression that was well known among Amsterdam Jews to denote someone who winks and tells outrageous lies.

Paul Siegel wanted to avoid being deported at all costs. Together with his friend Hermann Italiaander (born in Amsterdam in 1923), he decided: 'We're not going to Poland!'[268] The oath became a morning greeting. It would not have been too hard for Paul Siegel to flee from Westerbork, but he had often seen the captors' retaliation measures: for every fugitive, ten inmates from the same hut were deported with the next transport.[269] Thus, he rejected some escape methods outright. Today, Paul Siegel regards the strong sense of cohesion and solidarity among the prisoners to be partly the result of the Socialist character of the Zionist youth movement.[270] His dilemma was organizing an escape that would have no consequences for anyone else. The will to flee was so strong that he deliberately did not have a romantic relationship with anyone, as it 'might hinder my escape when the time came'.[271]

In late September 1943, Ru Cohen, the former Chair of the Deventer group, was interned in Westerbork.[272] Cohen, whose brother was one of the Committee Members of the Joodse Raad, believed it was the duty of the Jewish youth to accompany the people on their difficult eastward journey and stand by their side in support.²⁷³ By contrast, Paul Siegel believed that the most important duty was to survive and fulfil the Zionist ideal.

He considered jumping out of the moving deportation train, but rejected the plan as it seemed too dangerous. He writes:

> Jumping out of the moving train that is guarded by accompanying SS personnel was not so easy. It only looks good in a movie. The time factor was also against us, since we would hardly have had enough time to leave the train on Dutch territory because Westerbork was situated close to the German border. The prospects of surviving in Germany were very slim; we could not assume that we would meet a German who would help us return to Holland.²⁷⁴

He considered how an escape could succeed without being noticed. 'The idea of jumping from the train kept coming back to me. I was certain that this was the only chance to escape without leaving traces and I conceived a wonderful plan: Why travel with the train at all? Why not escape from the train while it was still in the camp?'²⁷⁵ Thus, he devised a plan to escape without endangering himself or others. On transport days, no-one except those who were on duty on the platform was allowed to leave the huts. Through Alfred Fraenkel,²⁷⁶ who acted as a contact between the camp and the Resistance, Paul Siegel and Hermann Italiaander sent a request for false passes for external personnel who left the camp on a daily basis without police escort. The request was granted.

First, they stole a pass and smuggled it out of the camp to be used as a template for forgery. Shortly afterwards, a sufficient number of false passes were delivered. Paul Siegel and his friend Martin 'Uffi' Uffenheimer (born in Breisach in 1922) had themselves added to the list of deportees on the train leaving for Bergen-Belsen on 1 February 1944. Hermann Italiaander and Fritz Siesel, who also worked in the 'Fürsorgedienst' ('welfare service'), were informed and were to keep an eye on Paul Siegel and Martin Uffenheimer in addition to their usual tasks, helping them if necessary.

On the day of the deportation, both men's names were deleted from the internal list of prisoners as discharged when they left their hut. Paul Siegel boarded the deportation train that was standing in the camp. Under his jacket, he wore working clothes with an armband that identified him as a member of the Fürsorgedienst. Once on the train, which consisted of passenger wagons, he quickly took off his coat and before the guards boarded and locked the doors, he jumped back onto the platform. In doing so, he twisted his knee as he got stuck between the steps, causing him great pain. He knew this was a life and death situation, however, so he disappeared as quickly as he could between the huts and entered the hospital, where he was already awaited, and was hidden there.

In the evening, Paul Siegel met Martin Uffenheimer, who had used the same ploy, at an arranged hiding place in the attic of the horse stables near the camp gate. The next morning, both used their false passes to leave the camp. Outside the camp, they were received by comrades from the Westerweel Group and accommodated by a family in a nearby town.

These escape tactics were used by a dozen other comrades, including Hermann Italiaander, Lottie Wahrhaftig-Siesel (born in Berlin in 1926), Meta Lande (born in Karlsruhe in 1921), Kurt Walter (born in Bamberg in 1922) and about eight Hechaluz members whose names are unknown.[277] A further sixteen Hechaluz members used a similar trick to escape from deportations. On the way to the deportation train in Westerbork, they managed to slip between the huts and later use false passes to leave the camp.[278]

Paul Siegel went to Amsterdam and was taken by Joop Westerweel and Frans Gerritsen[279] to a family in The Hague two days later.[280] From there, Joop Westerweel and Jan Smit helped them cross the Belgian border.[281] Paul Siegel fled to France via Belgium, where he was reunited with Alfred Fraenkel, Susi Hermann, Paula Kaufmann and Meta Lande, among others. Westerweel accompanied the group of fugitives around Paul Siegel as far as the Pyrenees.[282] In March 1944, Paul Siegel reached Spain on foot, from where he took a boat to Palestine.

Soon after his arrival in November 1944, he met a survivor of the deportation train from which he and Martin Uffenheimer had fled. He reported that their absence had been noted during registration in Bergen-Belsen concentration camp after a comparison with the deportation list. Unlike the Auschwitz concentration and extermination camp, where there were no checks to see if the transports were complete, the arrivals at Bergen-Belsen were registered in the normal way. The administration at Bergen-Belsen camp did indeed report to Judenreferent Zoepf that Martin Uffenheimer and Paul Siegel had not arrived.[283] Once all the camp prisoners had been forced to stand in roll call for hours and were counted many times, the SS presumed in its report that Siegel and Uffenheimer had managed to jump from the moving train.

Paul Siegel changed his name to Shaul Sagiv. He has lived in the Yakum kibbutz near Tel Aviv since 1946.

Max Meijer Levy – Escape on an Unknown Date in 1943

Max Meijer Levy (later Max Gerard Mansveld Levy)[284] (born in Amsterdam in 1911) grew up in a secular family. Most of his friends were Jewish, which he says was due to Jewish segregation. As his report clearly states, he became a 'Jew' through the discriminating attributes of his non-Jewish environment. As a 'Jew', he was not permitted to join the canoe, hockey or rowing clubs.

Meijer Levy attended business school and in 1930 joined his father's company, which imported exotic fruits and almonds. He heard terrible stories from Jewish refugees from Germany and decided to emigrate. But this was impossible. The family was expropriated in 1941 and his parents and sisters went into hiding. One sister was denounced, deported and murdered. Max Meijer Levy was not a member of a Resistance group, but began to forge ID papers. He had learnt photography and when the German occupiers introduced identification certificates, he used his darkroom and studio to exchange photos in the papers and retouch stamps. Leon Horn, who was active in the Resistance, brought papers, and if someone had no photo, Meijer Levy produced one himself. He also forged papers for himself.

In late 1942, Meijer Levy was denounced and imprisoned in Havenstraat, where he lost all his possessions. From there, he was taken to the prison in Javastraat and two weeks later to Herzogenbusch concentration camp. He made contact with no-one. In an interview in 2003, he said he simply thought: 'I have to get out of here. How do I get out?'[285]

It is unclear when the Germans discovered that the ID forger was Max Meijer Levy. After two or three months' imprisonment in Vught, he was transferred to Westerbork. During the journey he tried to escape from the train, but he states that it was difficult to flee from the passenger wagon guarded by the Dutch military policemen of the Marechaussee. Nevertheless, at a moment when he was unnoticed, he wound down a window and was already hanging half out of the wagon when a Marechaussee prevented his escape.

When he arrived in Westerbork, he met his brother-in-law, Edgar Horn. Meijer Levy knew that trains were leaving regularly for 'labour assignments' in the East and prepared thoroughly for an escape attempt: 'Before I was on the train, I already knew I wanted to flee'.[286] He got himself a coat and hat to conceal his shaved head after escaping. He also inspected the wagon and noticed that the locks could be broken open. No more than a week after his arrival in Westerbork, he and Edgar Horn were selected for deportation. Meijer Levy states that he tried to convince Edgar Horn to flee with him and told him: 'Edgar, I'm jumping off the train. Come with me'.[287] But his brother-in-law did not dare to take the risk. Finally, they were driven into a freight wagon with fixed wooden benches. As soon as the train set off, Meijer Levy started working on the lock. The others in the wagon were frightened to death and appealed to him: 'Don't do that'.[288] The wagon door was not properly shut, making it easy for Meijer Levy: 'It was very simple for me to open the lock and slide the door back. Then I jumped out'.[289]

He was in a wooded area ahead of Beilen, only a few kilometres outside Westerbork. After jumping, he initially remained still to avoid being noticed by the guards in the rear section of the train: 'I thought, just stay lying down, then they will think the Jew is dead, we don't have to do anything'.[290] When the train had disappeared on its way to Sobibór, a passer-by with a horse and cart took Meijer Levy to the priest in Beilen, who lent him ten Guilders with which to buy a ticket. Until the train's departure, he hid in the station toilet, before boarding a train to Zwolle and taking a seat. Max Gerard Mansveld Levy recounts further: 'And who should sit beside me? The guards from Westerbork'.[291] He pulled his hat low over his face so they would not recognize him.

From Zwolle he took a bus to Bussum, where he was able to stay with an acquaintance. A few months later, he hid in the Biesbos forest area, which is now a national park. A lock-keeper took him in and allowed him to help him with his work. Max Gerard Mansveld Levy presumes that he did not know he was a Jew. From there, he went to Amsterdam and rented a small apartment. After the liberation, he and his father were given back the store they had owned and they managed it together from then on.

Escape of an Unnamed Young Girl in 1944

Betty Mannheim had been interned in Westerbork since 1942. One day in 1944, she helped the new arrivals after they got off the train. As she was giving the elderly women and children some milk, she noticed a young girl whom she had seen before in Westerbork. The interviewer who spoke to Betty Mannheim many years later described the situation as follows: 'In one of the arriving trains she recognized a young girl who had been in Westerbork before. And had fled from the moving deportation train on her way to the East'.[292] She was recaptured in Amsterdam. Betty Mannheim advised the girl to register under a different name, but the Head of the Jewish Ordnungsdienst, Kurt Schlesinger, then arrived and immediately reported her to Gemmeker. She was deported on the next train.[293]

Escape by Several Prisoners on the Last Train to Auschwitz on 4 September 1944

On 4 September 1944, the last deportation train left Westerbork for Auschwitz. By that time, more than one hundred thousand Jews had already been deported from the Netherlands. It was broad daylight when at least seven young Jews jumped from the train: Max Buys, Abraham 'Ab' Groenteman (born in Amsterdam in 1911), Herman Melkman, Jacques 'Sjaak' Posno (born in Amsterdam in 1913), Isidor Stoppelman, Ciska Telghuis and Sonja Wagenaar-van Dam. The escape can be reconstructed based on several reports by those involved and other survivors of the deportation train. There are, however, differing accounts of the escape's advance preparation and execution.

By the time she was arrested and interned in Westerbork, Sonja Wagenaar-van Dam, née Sera Jeannette van Dam[294] (born in Amsterdam in 1918), had an exhausting odyssey behind her, moving from one hideout to the next. She recalls how a friendship developed between her, a young woman named Ciska Telghuis and the young men Max Buys, Ab Groenteman, Sjaak Posno, Herman Melkman and Isidor Stoppelman. Together, they decided: 'If we're deported, we will saw a hole into the wagon'.[295] Since sick people and children were also being deported, they knew they were not being taken to a labour camp.[296]

One of the men worked in the camp sawmill. He managed to strap a small saw to his leg and smuggle it out of the mill. Wagenaar-van Dam recalls that a Jewish observer who noticed him said, 'Don't do it. You won't succeed and the consequences are terrible'.[297]

Before his arrest, Isidor Stoppelman (born in Amsterdam in 1917) had been active in a Communist Resistance group.[298] He had organized hiding places and food for people who had 'gone underground' and also distributed underground newspapers. An acquaintance denounced him and he was arrested, tortured and interned in Westerbork on 4 May 1944.[299] He was sent to the punishment hut there, had his head shaved and was equipped with an overall and wooden shoes. His parents and brother had already been deported, while his young daughter had managed to hide with friends. He apparently had connections to Herman Melkman and his wife even before his arrest; she later took Stoppelman's daughter from her hideaway to Friesland, as it was easier to provide for her there.[300]

Isidor Stoppelman was forced to work hard, initially in a forced labour group that laid telephone cables outside the camp. Later he had to unload coal from trucks and carry it to the boiler house. The punishment hut was separated from the rest of the camp by a fence. Max Buys (born in 1916 in Amsterdam)[301] was also in the punishment hut.[302] Max Buys had already jumped from the 19th deportation train from Mechelen on 15 January 1943 (he is the only known case of a deportee who attempted two separate escapes in two different countries). Later, he was arrested again in the Netherlands and interned in Westerbork on 6 April 1944.[303]

The third young man in the group was Herman Melkman (born in Amsterdam in 1914),[304] who had been badly mistreated in the Amersfoort police transit camp by the deputy Schutzhaftlagerleiter Josef Johann Kotälla, probably because he was suspected of being a Resistance fighter.[305] Herman Melkman arrived in Westerbork on 24 May 1944.[306]

Gerard Stoppelman recounts that he, Buys and Melkman began preparing for their escape in May 1944. They had smuggled a small saw and a drill into the punishment hut and gathered information on the condition of the wagons and the placement of the guard teams during the journey.[307] They realized that to flee, they would have to saw a hole in the rear wall of the wagon. The wood was not as thick there as the wagon floor and they would not be seen by the guards as they let themselves slip beneath the train between the wagons, while taking the movements of the train into account.[308] Gerard Stoppelman stresses that the three men conceived the plan; he only mentions Wagenaar-van Dam, Groenteman, Posno and Telghuis in his account of the situation in the wagon.[309]

Thus, the statement by Sonja Wagenaar-van Dam that the group of seven planned the escape together does not concur with Stoppelman's description, which states that he, Buys and Melkman had been confined to the punishment hut, where they were completely isolated from the other camp prisoners. However, Ab Groenteman[310] also states that he was involved with plans to escape.

Groenteman was arrested in January 1944 as a member of a Resistance group of medical students, in which he operated as a passport forger, and taken to Westerbork. According to his own statements, the plan to flee from the train became concrete as early as May 1944, after an attempted escape from the camp failed.[311] However, the Jewish Council index card recorded the date of his arrival in Westerbork as 20 July 1944.[312] It is impossible to ascertain whether the date on the index card is wrong or whether Groenteman was mistaken.

According to Groenteman, they researched for months in advance: the route, where the guards were stationed on the train, the conditions of the wagons, their coupling mechanism and the distance between the track bed and the wagon floor. In doing so, they realized that they could not jump to the sides due to the guards and they could not cut a hole in the floor because the boards were too thick. Since the Marechaussee officers were becoming friendlier as the Allied forces approached, it was possible to gain a range of information. A mechanic told them that the longest section of the route was between Meppel and Zwolle and that the train stopped at every station for the wagons to be checked.[313]

Ciska Telghuis, née Rine (born in Amsterdam in 1921),[314] had been brought to Westerbork in late July 1944. She intended to avoid arriving at Auschwitz at all costs, as she had heard of medical experiments being conducted on prisoners and she was afraid of sexual violence. Her family had already been deported. She recounts how she had organized a bread knife to use as a saw for her escape.[315] When the transport was assembled, it was essential for the small group to remain together so that they could flee as a group. Fifty to eighty people were crowded into the freight wagon.[316]

The former Westerbork prisoner Lies van de Kolk-Cohen, who was deported on the same train, reports that Groenteman, whom she knew before the war, had tried to convince her to join him in the same wagon – presumably in an attempt to enable her escape. When she asked why, he replied: 'You don't have to ask too many questions'.[317] She boarded the train in a different wagon. Due to a lack of space in the wagons, all prisoners were forced to stand. The SS appointed a German Jew as wagon elder in each wagon.[318]

Stoppelman describes their escape as follows. Immediately after the train's departure, they went to the rear wall of the freight wagon. Straight away and as discreetly as possible, he and Max Buys began to cut a hole in the wooden wall.[319] The others shielded them with their bodies.[320] Sonja Wagenaar-van Dam recalls that there were protests as soon as the sawing noise was heard: 'The men in our group had to protect us with their bodies. When we started, we explained our purpose. We had the right. We had the right to flee. Those who wanted to join us could do so'.[321]

Telghuis reports that the train stopped occasionally and that the Germans opened the doors. Each time, she and Stoppelman pretended to be lovers huddled up in front of the hole. In doing so, they inconspicuously held up boards that concealed the opening.[322] Eventually, light shone through the hole. Ciska Telghuis says she will never forget that moment: 'There was air, there was freedom'. When daylight shone through the hole and the other prisoners realized that some of them wanted to flee, panic broke out for fear of the threatened consequences. Groenteman recalls that they knocked down the wagon elder and things then became quieter.[323] Ten minutes later, the hole was large enough to climb through.[324]

They had counted the stops and presumed they had passed Meppel. If they jumped then, they knew there was a long stretch without any stops.[325] Max Buys was the first to crawl through the hole and leap, followed by Jacques Posno. Gerard Stoppelman reports that they dropped themselves on the track from the buffers. Ab Groenteman states that a girl named Ciska called: 'I want to go with you!' He states: 'I pushed her through the opening. When we were outside on the coupling, we made ourselves small and dropped onto the side of the track'.[326] Ciska Telghuis recalls that before climbing through the hole, she grappled with the coupling. She saw how two young men in front of her allowed themselves to drop under the train with a movement that resembled swimming. Someone urged her on: 'Jump. We have to be quicker. If the train stops, it's over'.[327] She felt the wind in her face. The train was travelling far too quickly. There were others behind her, waiting for their chance to escape. She had to act. She thought of mass graves, shots in the back of the neck and everything she had heard about Auschwitz. She describes the jump as follows:

> I let myself drop from the coupling and rolled onto my back. I only had one thought: head down, or it's off. The train rolled over me. I felt the drag. Then it was quiet. . . . I was free, reborn. I was lying between the tracks and knew I had to get away as quickly as possible. I wanted to use my hands to get up, but couldn't feel the ground. I looked at my hands: only the fourth and fifth fingers remained. The train had rolled over both my hands without me realizing. I rolled onto the grass beside the tracks. I felt powerless and asked myself why just my hands and not everything else at the same time.[328]

Sonja Wagenaar-van Dam was afraid she would not fit through the hole. She took off her jacket and threw it through the hole, then crawled threw it herself, sat on the buffer and looked down onto the sleepers as they rushed past. She was terribly afraid. Someone in the wagon called, 'Sonja, you have to go now'.[329] She dived under the train with a swimming movement. She cannot remember the jump, or the pain in her ankle, only the noise of the train rolling above her.[330]

Despite the high speed, all of them jumped from the train.[331] All seven escapees survived the jump. According to Groenteman, they had agreed to remain lying on the ground immediately after jumping and then seek a hiding place.[332] Events turned out differently, however. Telghuis was severely injured, as were Posno, who had also lost a hand, and Groenteman, who had fallen on his back.[333] A farmer with a horse and cart took the three to the Sofia Hospital in Zwolle, where they underwent emergency operations in secret.[334] Ciska Telghuis' hands had to be amputated. She reports that while she was still in hospital, she was denounced as a Jew and had to flee.[335] Groenteman was hidden in Zwolle after being discharged from hospital.

Stoppelman recounts that he, Buys and Melkman hid themselves in a potato cellar after escaping. When darkness fell, they knocked on the door of a nearby rectory in Zwolle, but were turned away.[336] Zwolle was full of SS men as news of the escape had spread quickly. They decided to walk along the railway track towards Friesland. There they met a railwayman who knew Hermann Melkman, possibly from the Resistance.

The railwayman immediately understood the situation and sent them to a nearby farmhouse in Nieuwleusen, where they hid in a pigsty. He provided them with food and organized new clothes for them with the help of the local Resistance. When the pigsty burnt down after an air raid a week later, they approached the farmer, a devout Christian. He arranged for the three fugitives to be hidden by a ship's mechanic in the engine room with the aim of taking them to Amsterdam. The boat was attacked by the British Air Force. They jumped into the water in panic, managed to swim to the shore and hid again on a farm. The next day, Resistance fighters collected them in Zwolle. Stoppelman also states that the other two remained in hiding with a hairdresser in Zwolle due to their Jewish appearance, while he became active again in the Resistance and organized hideout addresses. He received false papers and changed his first name to Gerard.[337] He kept the name after the liberation. Summarizing, he states: 'If we hadn't made that hole, we would not be alive today . . . As far as we were concerned, all 56 [prisoners in the wagon] should have jumped'.[338]

Justus Philip, who had been in the same wagon, survived Auschwitz and reported on his situation during the deportation. He was asked if he wanted to jump, but did not take their escape plan seriously and declined. In fact, he had been very depressed during the journey. It was very hot and muggy in the wagon; by the time they arrived in Gleiwitz, five men and three women were already unconscious.[339]

Sonja Wagenaar-van Dam reports that she never saw Ciska Telghuis again after the jump and did not have the courage to reunite with her,[340] and that her own survival was a 'bitter victory against the Germans'.[341] She lost her trust in people and became hardened as a result of the experience of persecution. For many years, she suffered from anxiety and nightmares, as well as feelings of guilt. She was still unable to speak of some of the things she had experienced.[342]

Notes

1. Dan Michman, 'Die jüdische Emigration und die niederländische Reaktion zwischen 1933 und 1940', in: Kathinka Dittrich and Hans Würzner (Eds), *Die Niederlande und das deutsche Exil 1933–1940*, Königstein 1982, pp. 93–108, here p. 82.
2. Gerhard Hirschfeld, 'Niederlande', in: Wolfgang Benz (Ed.), *Dimension des Völkermords. Die Zahl der jüdischen Opfer des Nationalsozialismus*, Munich 1991, pp. 137–66, here p. 138.
3. Ibid,; Moore, *Survivors*, p. 210.
4. Christoph Kreutzmüller, 'Die Erfassung der Juden im Reichskommissariat der besetzten niederländischen Gebiete', in: Hürter and Zarusky, *Besatzung, Kollaboration, Holocaust*, pp. 21–44, here p. 22.
5. Hirschfeld, 'Niederlande', p. 138; Moore, *Survivors*, p. 208.
6. Konrad Kwiet, '"Mussert Juden" und die "Lösung der Judenfrage" in den Niederlanden', in: Hermann Graml, Angelika Königseder, and Juliane Wetzel (Eds), *Vorurteil und Rassenhaß. Antisemitismus in den faschistischen Bewegungen Europas*, Berlin 2001, pp. 151–68, here p. 160.
7. Johannes Houwink ten Cate, 'Mangelnde Solidarität gegenüber Juden in den besetzten niederländischen Gebieten?', in: Wolfgang Benz and Juliane Wetzel (Eds), *Solidarität und Hilfe für Juden während der NS-Zeit, Dänemark, Niederlande, Spanien, Portugal, Ungarn, Albanien, Weißrußland. Regionalstudien 3*, Berlin 1999, pp. 87–133, here p. 88.

8. Bob Moore, *Refugees from Nazi Germany in the Netherlands 1933–1940*, Dordrecht 1986, p. 78 ff.
9. Ibid., p. 82 ff.; Anna Hajkova, 'Das Polizeiliche Durchgangslager Westerbork', in: Benz and Distel, *Terror im Westen*, pp. 217–48, here p. 217.
10. Nanda van der Zee, *'Um Schlimmeres zu verhindern.' Die Ermordung der niederländischen Juden: Kollaboration und Widerstand*, Munich/Vienna 1999, p. 32; Michman, 'Die jüdische Emigration', p. 83; Moore, *Refugees from Nazi Germany*, p. 88 ff.
11. Siegel, *In ungleichem Kampf*, p. 39.
12. Hirschfeld, 'Niederlande', p. 138.
13. Houwink ten Cate, 'Mangelnde Solidarität?', p. 87.
14. Dawidowicz, *Krieg gegen die Juden*, p. 356 f.
15. Benz, 'Typologie der Herrschaftsformen', p. 10.
16. Wolfgang Seibel and Jörg Raab, 'Verfolgungsnetzwerke. Zur Messung von Arbeitsteilung und Machtdifferenzierung in den Verfolgungsapparaten des Holocaust', in: *Kölner Zeitschrift für Soziologie und Sozialpsychologie* (2003) 2, pp. 197–230, here p. 202.
17. Spritzer, *Ich war Nr. 10291*, p. 10 ff.; Harry C. Schnur, 'Flucht aus Holland', in: Schoenberner, *Wir haben es gesehen*, p. 198 ff.; Micheels, *Doctor #117641*, p. 12 f.; Nathan Wijnperle, *Zou ik het willen overdoen? Het levensverhaal van een joodse overlevende*, Sittard 1996, p. 56 f.
18. Hirschfeld, 'Niederlande', p. 139.
19. Presser, *Ashes in the Wind*, p. 407.
20. Werner Röhr, 'System oder organisiertes Chaos? Fragen einer Typologie der deutschen Okkupationsregime im Zweiten Weltkrieg', in: Robert Bohn (Ed.), *Die deutsche Herrschaft in den 'germanischen' Ländern 1940–1945*, Stuttgart 1997, pp. 11–46, here p. 39; de Wever, 'Benelux-Staaten', p. 78 f.
21. Benz, 'Typologie der Herrschaftsformen', p. 13 f. For a detailed description of the structure of the Reichskommissariat in the Netherlands, see: Isabel Gallin, 'Machtstrukturen im Reichskommissariat Niederlande', in: Bohn, *Die deutsche Herrschaft*, p. 145 ff.
22. Introduction to *West- und Nordeuropa 1940–Juni 1942, Die Verfolgung und Ermordung der europäischen Juden durch das nationalsozialistische Deutschland 1933–1945*, Vol. 5, edited by Katja Happe, Michael Mayer and Maja Peers, Munich 2012, p. 30.
23. Reichskommissar Seyß-Inquart, announcement: 'Niederländer der besetzten Gebiete', 29 May 1940, printed as a facsimile in: Joods Historisch Museum Amsterdam, *Documents of the Persecution of the Dutch Jewry 1940–1945*, Amsterdam 1979, p. 37.
24. Dawidowicz, *Krieg gegen die Juden*, p. 356; Benz, 'Typologie der Herrschaftsformen', p. 11.
25. Christoph Spieker, 'Von der Germanisierung zur Repression: Funktion und Politik der deutschen Ordnungspolizei in den Niederlanden 1943', in: Norbert Fasse, Johannes Houwink ten Cate, and Horst Lademacher (Eds), *Nationalsozialistische Herrschaft und Besatzungszeit. Historische Erfahrung und Verarbeitung aus niederländischer und deutscher Sicht*, Münster 2000 (*Studien zur Geschichte und Kultur Nordwesteuropas*, Vol. 1), pp. 179–90, here p. 179. For biographical details on Hanns Albin Rauter, see: Birn, *Höheren SS- und Polizeiführer*, p. 408 ff.
26. Kwiet, 'Mussert Juden', p. 162; Bernd Wegner, *Hitlers politische Soldaten: Die Waffen-SS 1933–1945. Leitbild, Struktur und Funktion einer nationalsozialistischen Elite*, Paderborn 1999, p. 299.
27. Bene an das Auswärtige Amt, Betr.: Besuch des Reichskommissars beim Führer, 6. 10. 1942, printed in: *Akten zur deutschen auswärtigen Politik 1918–1945. Aus dem Archiv des Auswärtigen Amts, Serie E: 1941–1945, Bd. IV, 1. Oktober bis 31. Dezember 1942*, Göttingen 1975, p. 31 ff.
28. De Wever, 'Benelux-Staaten', p. 70.
29. Kreutzmüller, 'Die Erfassung der Juden', p. 24 f.; Peter Romijn, 'Kein Raum für Ambivalenzen. Der Chef der niederländischen inneren Verwaltung K. J. Frederiks', in: Gerhard

Hirschfeld and Tobias Jersak (Eds), *Karrieren im Nationalsozialismus. Funktionseliten zwischen Mitwirkung und Distanz*, Frankfurt am Main 2004, pp. 147–71.
30. Hirschfeld, 'Niederlande', p. 139.
31. Guus Meershoek, 'Machtentfaltung und Scheitern. Sicherheitspolizei und SD in den Niederlanden', in: Paul and Mallmann, *Die Gestapo im Zweiten Weltkrieg*, pp. 383–402, here p. 397.
32. Geraldien von Frijtag Drabbe Künzel, 'Das Gefängnislager Amersfoort', in: Benz and Distel, *Terror im Westen*, pp. 73–100, here p. 74; Zeller and Griffioen, 'Judenverfolgung in den Niederlanden und in Belgien', Part 1, pp. 44, 46.
33. For biographical information on Harster, see: Meershoek, 'Machtentfaltung und Scheitern', p. 385 f.
34. Von Frijtag Drabbe Künzel, 'Das Gefängnislager Amersfoort', p. 74.
35. Anna Hajkova, 'The Making of a Zentralstelle: Die Eichmann-Männer in Amsterdam', in: *Theresienstädter Studien und Dokumente 10* (2003), pp. 353–81, here p. 357.
36. Johannes Houwink ten Cate, 'Der Befehlshaber der Sipo und des SD in den besetzten niederländischen Gebieten und die Deportation der Juden 1942–1943', in: Benz, Houwink ten Cate, and Otto, *Die Bürokratie der Okkupation*, pp. 197–223, here p. 199.
37. Ibid.; Hajkova, 'The Making of a Zentralstelle', p. 365.
38. Elisabeth Kohlhaas, 'Gertrud Slottke. Angestellte im niederländischen Judenreferat der Sicherheitspolizei', in: Mallmann and Paul, *Karrieren der Gewalt*, pp. 207–18, here p. 211.
39. Anschriftenverzeichnis der Dienststellen des Befehlshabers der Sicherheitspolizei und des SD für die besetzten niederländischen Gebiete, Stand: 1. 4. 1941, NIOD, 270 g, 3.3.; Hajkova, 'The Making of a Zentralstelle', p. 355.
40. Houwink ten Cate, 'Der Befehlshaber der Sipo und des SD', p. 206 ff.; Meershoek, 'Machtentfaltung und Scheitern', p. 396; Hajkova, 'The Making of a Zentralstelle', p. 355 f.; Hirschfeld, 'Niederlande', p. 144 f.
41. Houwink ten Cate, 'Der Befehlshaber der Sipo und des SD', p. 207.
42. Hajkova, 'The Making of a Zentralstelle', p. 355.
43. Benz, 'Typologie der Herrschaftsformen', p. 17.
44. Ibid.; Dawidowicz, *Krieg gegen die Juden*, p. 357; Kreutzmüller, 'Die Erfassung der Juden', p. 29 f.
45. Steinberg, *Un pays occupé et ses juifs*, p. 18; Hirschfeld, 'Niederlande', p. 137 f.
46. Kreutzmüller, 'Die Erfassung der Juden', p. 22 f.
47. Ibid., p. 43.
48. Ibid.
49. Marnix Croes, 'Gentiles and the Survival Chances of Jews in the Netherlands 1940–1945. A Closer Look', in: Beate Kosmala and Feliks Tych (Eds), *Facing the Nazi Genocide: Non-Jews and Jews in Europe*, Berlin 2004, pp. 41–72, here p. 49.
50. Kreutzmüller, 'Die Erfassung der Juden', p. 22.
51. Hirschfeld, 'Niederlande', p. 137.
52. Hirschfeld, 'Verfolgung und Vernichtung', p. 102.
53. Dawidowicz, *Krieg gegen die Juden*, p. 357; Hirschfeld, 'Niederlande', p. 145.
54. Hirschfeld, 'Verfolgung und Vernichtung', p. 104; Strobl, *Die Angst*, p. 178.
55. Marrus and Paxton, *The Nazis and the Jews*, p. 701.
56. Ibid.
57. Sytske de Jong, 'Die jüdischen Arbeitslager in den Niederlanden', in: Benz and Distel, *Terror im Westen*, pp. 131–48, here p. 132.
58. For underlying information, see: ibid., p. 131 ff.
59. Zeller and Griffioen, 'Judenverfolgung in den Niederlanden und in Belgien', Part 1, p. 47.
60. Harster an alle Außenstellen des BdS, an alle Gruppen und Referate im Hause, an die Zentralstelle für jüdische Auswanderung, Betr.: Behandlung des Judentums in den Niederlanden nach den Nürnberger Rassengesetzen, 1 April 1942, NIOD, 270 g, 2.2.

61. Harster an Wimmer, Generalkommissar für Justiz und Verwaltung, Betr.: Einführung des Judensterns, 29 April 1942, printed as a facsimile in: Joods Historisch Museum Amsterdam, *Documents of the Persecution*, p. 54 f.
62. Hirschfeld, 'Verfolgung und Vernichtung', p. 108.
63. Hirschfeld, 'Niederlande', p. 141.
64. Joods Historisch Museum Amsterdam, *Documents of the Persecution*, p. 59; Meershoek, 'Machtentfaltung und Scheitern', p. 388 f.
65. Ron Zeller and Pim Griffioen, 'Judenverfolgung in den Niederlanden und in Belgien während des Zweiten Weltkriegs: eine vergleichende Analyse', Part 2, in: *1999. Zeitschrift für Sozialgeschichte des 20. und 21. Jahrhunderts 3* (1997) 1, pp. 29–48, here p. 34 f.
66. Ibid., p. 43.
67. Ibid., p. 31.
68. Gerhard Hirschfeld, 'Kollaboration in Hitlers Europa als ein historisches Tabu: Vichy-Frankreich und die Niederlande', in: Nicole Colin, Matthias N. Lorenz, and Joachim Umlauf (Eds), *Täter und Tabu. Grenzen der Toleranz in deutschen und niederländischen Geschichtsdebatten*, Essen 2011, pp. 49–59, here p. 56; Kwiet, 'Mussert Juden', p. 163.
69. Houwink ten Cate, 'Der Befehlshaber der Sipo und des SD', p. 197.
70. Luther to the Reich Foreign Minister, 3 January 1942, printed in: *Akten zur deutschen auswärtigen Politik 1918–1945. Aus dem Archiv des Auswärtigen Amts, Serie E: 1941–1945, Bd. I, 12. Dezember 1941 bis 28. Februar 1942*, Göttingen 1969, p. 156.
71. Birn, *Höheren SS- und Polizeiführer*, p. 208.
72. Friedländer, *Jahre der Vernichtung*, p. 12.
73. Meershoek, 'Machtentfaltung und Scheitern', p. 398.
74. Ad van Liempt, *Kopfgeld. Bezahlte Denunziation von Juden in den besetzten Niederlanden*, Munich 2005, p. 9.
75. *De Waarheid*, No. 51, 8 August 1942.
76. Croes, 'Gentiles and the Survival Chances', p. 56.
77. Gemmeker to Deppner, Betr.: Vorläufige Festnahme eines niederl. Polizeibeamten vom Judentransport am August 6/7, 1943, 8 August 1943, NIOD, 250 i, 204; see also Egbert J. van der Veen, 'Yaagje naar de vrijheid. De sprong naar het leven van Sonja Wagenaar-van Dam', in: *Westerbork Cahiers 6* (1998), p. 66; Siegel, *In ungleichem Kampf*, p. 94.
78. Lankenau (BdO), Betr.: Massnahmen zur Sicherung von Gefangenen, 17 March 1943, BArch R 70, 3; Lager Westerbork: Spesenabrechnungen, NIOD, 250 i, 328.
79. Strobl, *Die Angst*, p. 187.
80. Arlt (BdS for the occupied Dutch territories), Betr.: Bewachung der Melderegister, 9 April 1943, BArch R 70, 42.
81. Conversation with Truus Menger, 29 October 2006 in Haarlem; for details on the activities of the above-mentioned Resistance groups, see: Tanja von Fransecky, *Sie wollten mich umbringen, dazu mussten sie mich erst haben. Hilfe für verfolgte Juden in den deutsch besetzten Niederlanden*, Berlin 2016.
82. Kwiet, 'Mussert Juden', p. 164.
83. Zeller and Griffioen, 'Judenverfolgung in den Niederlanden und in Belgien', Part 2, p. 35.
84. Ibid.
85. Moore, *Survivors*, p. 208; de Wever, 'Benelux-Staaten', p. 71; Blom, *Persecution*, p. 344 f.; Michman, 'Zionist Youth Movements', p. 155.
86. Zeller and Griffioen, 'Judenverfolgung in den Niederlanden und in Belgien', Part 1, p. 40 f.
87. Cf. Bob Moore, 'The Rescue of Jews from Nazi Persecution: A Western European Perspective', in: *Journal of Genocide Research* (June 2003) 2, pp. 293–308, here p. 296.
88. Meyer, *Wissen um Auschwitz*, p. 54 f.
89. Blom, *Persecution*, p. 341.
90. Zeller and Griffioen, 'Judenverfolgung in den Niederlanden und in Belgien', Part 1, p. 40.

91. Kreutzmüller, 'Die Erfassung der Juden', p. 24; Houwink ten Cate, 'Der Befehlshaber der Sipo und des SD', p. 197. For detailed information on the cooperation between the German supervisory administration and the Dutch administration, see: Peter Romijn, 'Die Nazifizierung der lokalen Verwaltung in den besetzten Niederlanden als Instrument bürokratischer Kontrolle', in: Benz, Houwink ten Cate, and Otto, *Die Bürokratie der Okkupation*, pp. 93–121; Bob Moore, 'Niederlande: Anpassung – Opposition – Widerstand', in: Ueberschär, *Handbuch zum Widerstand*, pp. 111–23, here p. 112 f.; Meershoek, 'Machtentfaltung und Scheitern', p. 383.
92. Meershoek, 'Machtentfaltung und Scheitern', p. 383 f.
93. Birn, *Höheren SS- und Polizeiführer*, p. 212; Moore, 'Niederlande: Anpassung – Opposition – Widerstand', p. 115.
94. Meershoek, 'Machtentfaltung und Scheitern', p. 398.
95. Bene to the Foreign Office, Betr.: Juden in den Niederlanden, 20 July 1944, PA AA, R 99.429, No. 5657.
96. Hirschfeld, 'Niederlande', p. 158.
97. Eberhard Kolb, Bergen-Belsen. *Vom 'Aufenthaltslager' zum Konzentrationslager 1943 bis 1945*, Göttingen 1996, p. 29; Hirschfeld, 'Niederlande', p. 158 f.
98. Hirschfeld, 'Niederlande', pp. 150 f., 162 f.
99. Harster to Seys-Inquart, 25 June 1943, in: *Europa unterm Hakenkreuz. Belgien, Luxemburg, Niederlande*, p. 216.
100. Hirschfeld, 'Verfolgung und Vernichtung', p. 114 f.
101. Presser, *Ashes in the Wind*, p. 407 f.
102. Statement, Wilhelm Harster, 14 September 1966, BArch B 162/5610.
103. Der BdS für die bes. niederländ. Gebiete, Zentralstelle für jüdische Auswanderung, Einsatzbefehl für Amsterdam, 1 October 1942, BArch B 162/4106; Lankenau (Der BdO), Betr.: Massnahmen zur Sicherung von Gefangenen, 17 March 1943, BArch R 70, 3; Lager Westerbork, Spesenabrechnungen, NIOD, 250 i, 328.
104. Mirjam Bolle, *'Ich weiß, dieser Brief wird Dich nie erreichen'. Tagebuchbriefe aus Amsterdam, Westerbork und Bergen-Belsen*, Frankfurt 2006, p. 71.
105. Abuys and Mulder, 'Een gat in het prikkeldraad', pp. 20 f., 26, 29 f.
106. Schwarz, *Züge auf falschem Gleis*, p. 104. For information on everyday life at the camp, see: Hajkova, 'Das Polizeiliche Durchgangslager Westerbork', p. 233 ff.
107. Philip Mechanicus, *Im Depot. Tagebuch aus Westerbork*, Berlin 1993, p. 127; Cohen, *Abyss*, p. 71; Coen Rood, *'Wenn ich es nicht erzählen kann, muß ich weinen'. Als Zwangsarbeiter in der Rüstungsindustrie*, Frankfurt am Main 2002, p. 22.
108. Rood, *Wenn ich es nicht erzählen kann*, p. 22.
109. Etty Hillesum, *Das denkende Herz. Die Tagebücher von Etty Hillesum 1941–1943*, Reinbek 1988, p. 208.
110. Siegel, *In ungleichem Kampf*, p. 111; Bolle, *Ich weiß, dieser Brief*, p. 71; Mechanicus, *Im Depot*, p. 31 ff.
111. Siegel, *In ungleichem Kampf*, p. 39.
112. Hans Margulies, in: Lindwer, *Kamp van hoop en wanhoop*, p. 138; *Aufschub*, film by Harun Farocki, 2007.
113. Abuys and Mulder, 'Een gat in het prikkeldraad', p. 15; Barbara Felsmann and Karl Prümm, *Kurt Gerron – Gefeiert und gejagt 1897–1944. Das Schicksal eines deutschen Unterhaltungskünstlers. Berlin, Amsterdam, Theresienstadt, Auschwitz*, Berlin 1992; Siegel, *In ungleichem Kampf*, p. 121 f.
114. Israel Taubes, *The Persecution of Jews in Holland. 1940–1944, Westerbork and Bergen-Belsen, Juni 1945*, Wiener Library, Testaments of the Holocaust, Jewish Survivors Report. Documents of Nazi Guilt, Document Reference: 068-WL-1632, p. 19 f.
115. For an extensive description, see: Hans de Vries, 'Das Konzentrationslager Herzogenbusch bei Vught: "streng und gerecht"?', in: Benz and Distel, *Terror im Westen*, pp. 197–216.

116. Prof. Dr D. Cohen, Joodsche Raad vor Amsterdam an die Zentralstelle für jüdische Auswanderung, 20 July 1942, NIOD, 77/1452; for an extensive description, see: Katja B. Zaich, 'Das Sammellager Hollandsche Schouwburg in Amsterdam', in: Benz and Distel, *Terror im Westen*, pp. 181–96.
117. Bene to the Foreign Office, Inhalt: ausländische Juden, 3 July 1942, PA AA, R 100.869, No. 2231.
118. Cited in: Hirschfeld, 'Verfolgung und Vernichtung', p. 108.
119. Central Office for Jewish Emigration, Oproeping! Printed as a facsimile in: Joods Historisch Museum Amsterdam, *Documents of the Persecution*, p. 85; see also the list 'Uitrusting voor Werkverruiming in Duitsland', NIOD, 250 i, 329.
120. Hirschfeld, 'Verfolgung und Vernichtung', p. 108 f.
121. Bene to the Foreign Office, Betr.: Abtransport der Juden, 13 August 1942, printed in: *Akten zur deutschen auswärtigen Politik 1918–1945. Aus dem Archiv des Auswärtigen Amts, Serie E: 1941–1945, Bd. III, 16. Juni bis 30. September 1942*, Göttingen 1974, p. 315 f.; Bene to the Foreign Office, Abtransport ausländischer Juden, 17 July 1942, PA AA, R 100.869, No. 2231.
122. Bene to the Foreign Office, Betr.: Abtransport der Juden, 13 August 1942, printed in: *Akten zur deutschen auswärtigen Politik 1918–1945, Bd. III*, p. 315 f.
123. Marnix Croes, 'The Holocaust in the Netherlands and the Rate of Jewish Survival', in: *Holocaust and Genocide Studies* (2006) 3, pp. 474–99, here p. 487.
124. Rauter to Himmler, Betr.: Judenabschiebung, 24 September 1942, printed as a facsimile in: Joods Historisch Museum Amsterdam, *Documents of the Persecution*, p. 90 ff.
125. Ibid.
126. Ibid.
127. Bene to the Foreign Office, Abtransport der Juden, 16 November 1942, printed in: *Akten zur deutschen auswärtigen Politik 1918–1945, Bd. IV*, p. 328 f.
128. Harster to the Zentralstelle für jüdische Auswanderung, das Lager Westerbork, das KL Hertogenbosch und sämtliche Außenstellen, Betr.: Endlösung der Judenfrage in den Niederlanden, 5 May 1943, printed as a facsimile in: Joods Historisch Museum Amsterdam, *Documents of the Persecution*, p. 95 ff.
129. Anna Hajkova, 'Das Polizeiliche Durchgangslager Westerbork', p. 220 f.; Presser, *Ashes in the Wind*, p. 457.
130. Presser, *Ashes in the Wind*, p. 457.
131. Ibid., p. 456.
132. Handwritten note on the deportation, 30 November 1942, Herinneringscentrum Kamp Westerbork; G. (written by a nurse), handwritten note on the deportation; N.V. Nederlandsche Spoorwegen, Baanvakken/Strecken, 29 October 1942, NIOD, 250 i, 186.
133. 'Vermetele ontsnapping uit Westerbork. Moedige joodse groep ontvluchtte de dodentrein naar Auschwitz', in: *De Waarheid*, 4 May 1966.
134. Witness statement, Theodor Krämer, 11 December 1967, BArch B 162/4103.
135. Bert Jan Flim, 'Opportunities for Dutch Jews to Hide from the Nazis, 1942–1945', in: Chaya Brasz and Yosef Kaplan (Eds), *Dutch Jews as Perceived by Themselves and by Others. Proceedings of the Eighth International Symposium on the History of the Jews in the Netherlands*, Leiden/Boston/Cologne 2001, pp. 289–305, here p. 295; Hirschfeld, 'Verfolgung und Vernichtung', p. 111.
136. Witness statement, Willi Teege, 8 December 1967, BArch B 162/4103; see also witness statement, Friedrich Goßrau, 4 September 1967, BArch B 162/4102.
137. Hirschfeld, 'Niederlande', p. 151.
138. Ibid.
139. Hirschfeld, 'Verfolgung und Vernichtung', p. 108; Houwink ten Cate, 'Mangelnde Solidarität?', p. 109 ff.; Hans Ottenstein, Lager Westerbork. Een persoonlijk verslag, 1946, NIOD, 250 i, 510, p. 16 ff.; Israel Taubes, *The Persecution of Jews in Holland 1940-1944*.

Westerbork and Bergen-Belsen, June 1945, Wiener Library, Testaments of the Holocaust, Jewish Survivors Report. Documents of Nazi Guilt, Document Reference: 068-WL-1632, p. 22.
140. For example, testimony, Herbert N. Kruskal, Two years behind barbed wire, July 1944, Wiener Library, Testaments of the Holocaust, London, Document Reference: 058-EA-1252, p. 28.
141. Lagerkommandant SS-Obersturmführer Gemmeker, Lagerbefehl Nr. 49, 3 May 1943, http://www.jhm.nl/collectie/documenten/00000597 (accessed 13 December 2013); Lagerkommandant SS-Obersturmführer Gemmeker im Auftrag von Harster, Lagerbefehl Nr. 8, 17 February 1943, http://www.jhm.nl/collectie/documenten/00000565 (accessed 13 December 2013).
142. Gemmeker to Zoepf, Abtransport von kranken Juden, 4 February 1944, NIOD, 250 i, 335.
143. Dr Curt Friedmann, Dutch workers strike in support of the Jews, Wiener Library, Testaments of the Holocaust, London, Document Reference: 055-EA-1056; Israel Taubes, *The Persecution of Jews in Holland 1940–1944. Westerbork and Bergen-Belsen*, June 1945, Wiener Library, Testaments of the Holocaust, Jewish Survivors Report. Documents of Nazi Guilt, Document Reference: 068-WL-1632, p. 23; see also Siegel, *In ungleichem Kampf*, pp. 97, 100.
144. Lagerkommandant SS-Obersturmführer Gemmeker, Lagerbefehl Nr. 35, 24 May 1943, http://www.jhm.nl/collectie/documenten/00000982 (accessed 13 December 2013).
145. Witness statement, Ernst Rautenhaus, 12 December 1967, BArch B 162/4103.
146. Witness statement, Ernst Heins, 18 September 1967, BArch B 162/4102; Hans Ottenstein, Lager Westerbork. Een persoonlijk verslag, 1946, NIOD, 250 i, 510, p. 82a.
147. Cohen, *Abyss*, p. 76 ff.
148. Presser, *Ashes in the Wind*, p. 458.
149. Hans Ottenstein, Lager Westerbork. Een persoonlijk verslag, 1946, NIOD, 250 i, 510, p. 82.
150. Ibid.; Wijnperle, *Zou ik het willen overdoen?*, p. 64; Sobiborinterviews NL, http://www.sobiborinterviews.nl/en/nederlandse-overlevenden/cato-polak (accessed 13 December 2013); for a contradictory account: witness statement, Jonas Pront, 27 October 1949, BArch B 162/29680.
151. Account by a deportee on the transport from Westerbork to Auschwitz on 30 November 1942, in: Bob Cahen, *Brieven uit de trein Westerbork-Auschwitz (enkele reis)*, Haarlem 1996, p. 11 ff. (emphasis in the original text); see also Schwarz, *Züge*, p. 149.
152. Witness statement, Karl Jacke, 14 November 1967, BArch B 162/4103.
153. Jules Schelvis, *Vernichtungslager Sobibór*, Hamburg/Münster 2003, p. 54; Hillesum, 'Die Nacht vor dem Transport', p. 227; Mrs Elfriede Snyders, 1957, Testaments to the Holocaust, from the Wiener Library, Testaments of the Holocaust, London, 054-EA-0970, p. 8.
154. Zoepf, Juden mit früheren Kriegs- oder Friedensverdiensten für Deutschland, 7 March 1943, NIOD, 77/1292; see also Slottke, Theresienstadt, 25 January 1943, NIOD, 77/1290.
155. Schwarz, *Züge*, pp. 164, 175.
156. Ibid., p. 151; *Aufschub*, film by Harun Farocki, 2007.
157. Schwarz, *Züge*, p. 153 f.
158. Ibid., p. 154; Presser, *Ashes in the Wind*, p. 458.
159. Schwarz, *Züge*, p. 154.
160. Ibid., p. 155; witness statement, Ludwig Walter Coors, 11 May 1967, BArch B 162/4101; Hans Margulies, in: Lindwer, *Kamp van hoop en wanhoop*, p. 137; Arno Levi, in: Adina Kochba (Ed.), *Het Verzet van de nederlandse Chaloetsbeweging en de Westerweelgroep tijdens de duitse Bezetting*, manuscript, no date, NIOD, 614 A, doc II, p. 237.

161. Jacob Harari, *Die Ausrottung der Juden im besetzten Holland. Ein Tatsachenbericht*, Tel Aviv 1944, Cegesoma, mic 122, p. 87; Dr Curt Friedmann, Dutch workers strike in support of the Jews, no date, Wiener Library, Testaments of the Holocaust, Document Reference: 055-EA-1056.
162. Zoepf to RSHA, IV B 4, Betr.: Zug aus den Niederlanden nach Theresienstadt, 15 April 1943, BArch B 162/4106.
163. Hirschfeld, 'Niederlande', p. 163.
164. Rood, *Wenn ich es nicht erzählen kann*, p. 31 ff.
165. Schelvis, *Vernichtungslager Sobibór*, p. 59.
166. Hearing, Gertrud Slottke, 27 January 1967, NIOD, 270 g, 1.2.
167. Schelvis, *Vernichtungslager Sobibór*, p. 65.
168. Cohen, *Abyss*, p. 76 ff.
169. Ibid., p. 78.
170. Levie Sluijzer, cited in: Schelvis, *Vernichtungslager Sobibór*, p. 63 f.
171. For example: witness statement, Karl Jacke, 14 November 1967, BArch B 162/4103; witness statement, Heinrich Hofmann, 16 November 1967, BArch B 162/4103.
172. Schelvis, *Vernichtungslager Sobibór*, p. 65.
173. Hillesum, *Das denkende Herz*, p. 208 f.
174. Janny Brandes- Brilleslijper, cited in: Dick van Galen Last and Rolf Wolfswinkel, *Anne Frank and After. Dutch Holocaust Literature in Historical Perspective*, Amsterdam 1996, p. 115.
175. Georg H., 'Der Traum von Israel', in: Volker Jakob and Anne van der Voort, *Anne Frank war nicht allein*, Berlin/Bonn 1988, p. 39.
176. Report by a deportee on the transport on 30 November 1942, in Cahen, *Brieven uit de trein*, p. 11 ff.
177. Regarding Orpo in the Netherlands, see: Browning, *Ganz normale Männer*, p. 26; for the significance of the Ordnungspolizei in the Netherlands, see among others: Houwink ten Cate and Kenkmann, *Deutsche und holländische Polizei*, p. 67 ff.
178. Lager Westerbork, [Quittungen Übernahme von Lebensmitteln durch den Transportführer], 7 September 1943, 11 January 1944, NIOD, 250 i, 330; Jupp Henneboel, 'Ich konnte nicht anders', in: Christoph Spieker (Ed.), *Freund oder Vijand? Eine groene politieman in het Nederlandse verzet. Ein 'Grüner Polizist' im niederländischen Widerstand*, Münster 2004, pp. 147–232, here p. 169 ff.
179. The Reich Minister of the Interior, memorandum, 30 October 1942, BArch R 19/482.
180. Klemp, *'Nicht ermittelt'*, p. 423.
181. BdO. im Wehrkreis I, [Neuaufstellung des I/Pol. 16], 6 February 1943, BArch R 19/108.
182. Der HSSPF beim Oberpräsidenten von Ostpreußen im Wehrkreis I, Betr.: Verwaltungsbeamte und Abwicklung beim I. und II/Pol.16, BArch R 19/108.
183. Lager Westerbork, [Quittungen Übernahme von Lebensmitteln durch den Transportführer], 31 August 1943, 15 March 1944, NIOD, 250 i, 330.
184. Klemp, *'Nicht ermittelt'*, p. 448.
185. Koch (II./SS-Pol. 3), Beurteilungsnotiz (vorgelegt aus Anlaß Aufhebung der Abordnung zum II./SS-Pol. 3), 20 August 1944, BArch R 19, 19.
186. Lager Westerbork, [Quittungen Übernahme von Lebensmitteln durch den Transportführer], 7 September 1943, 11 January 1944, NIOD, 250 i, 330.
187. Kärgel, Major d.SchP. u. Btl.-Kdr., Beurteilung des Leutnants d. SchP. d. R. Alfred Käsewieter zur Beförderung zum Oberleutnant d. Sch. P. d. R., 23 March 1943, BArch R 19, 19.
188. Ibid.
189. Koch (II./SS-Pol. 3), Beurteilungsnotiz (vorgelegt aus Anlaß Aufhebung der Abordnung zum II./SS-Pol. 3), 20 August 1944, BArch R 19/19.
190. Witness hearing, Hans Lauer, 5 December 1968, BArch B 162/4405; witness hearing,

Ernst Böhlich, 23 April 1968, Cegesoma, AA 377, Bd. VII, Bl. 1350 ff.; statement, Ludwig Semmelbauer, 11 September 1968, BArch B 162/20347.
191. Witness hearing, Hans Lauer, 5 December 1968, BArch B 162/4405.
192. Statement, Hans Ebert, 11 July 1967, BArch B 162/4102; statement, Johann Eickworth, 11July 1967, BArch B 162/4101; statement, Friedrich Goßrau, 4 September 1967, BArch B 162/4102; statement, Alfred Henke, 19 September 1967, BArch B 162/4102.
193. For example: witness statement, Gustav Lassowski, 28 December 1967, BArch B 162/4103.
194. Landeskriminalamt SK, Schlußbericht. Ermittlungsverfahren der Staatsanwaltschaft Bremen gegen den ehemaligen Kommandeur des Polizei-Bataillons 105, Major Hans Helwes, 8 February 1968, BArch B 162/4104. For a detailed history of this battalion, see: Schneider, *Auswärts eingesetzt*.
195. Klemp, 'Einsatz im Westen', pp. 32, 34; Schneider, *Auswärts eingesetzt*, p. 289.
196. Witness statement, Walter Meyer, 9 September 1967, BArch B 162/4102.
197. Witness statement, Georg Lüdeke, 2 October 1967, BArch B 162/4102.
198. Witness statement, Ludwig Walter Coors, 11 May 1967, BArch B 162/4101.
199. Witness statement, Heinrich Falke, 7 August 1967, BArch B 162/4102.
200. Witness statement, Wilhelm Holdhoff, 21 September 1967, BArch B 162/4102. See also, for example: witness statement, Ferdinand Geerken, 12 December 1967, BArch B 162/4103.
201. Witness statement, Claus Lange, 19 December 1967, BArch B 162/4103.
202. Witness statement, Alfred Henke, 19 September 1967, BArch B 162/4102.
203. Witness statement, Helmut Rackwitz, 26 October 1967, BArch B 162/4103.
204. For example: witness statement, Claus Lange, 19 December 1967, BArch B 162/4103.
205. Witness statement, Alfred Henke, 19 September 1967, BArch B 162/4102.
206. Witness statement, Johann Alberts, 4 July 1966, BArch B 162/4100.
207. Witness statement, Ludwig Walter Coors, 11 May 1967, BArch B 162/4101.
208. Witness statement, Heinrich Wiewerich, 6 November 1967, BArch B 162/4103.
209. Witness statement, Ludwig Walter Coors, 11 May 1967, BArch B 162/4101.
210. A. J. van der Leeuw (NIOD) an den Ersten Staatsanwalt Huber, 25 August 1966, NIOD, 270 g, 2.1.
211. Witness statement, Julius Aschermann, 8 July 1966, BArch L 162/4100.
212. Witness statement, Johann Alberts, 4 July 1966, BArch B 162/4100; see also witness statement, Herbert Arnold, 7 July 1966, BArch B 162/4100.
213. Witness statement, Johann Alberts, 4 July 1966, BArch B 162/4100.
214. Witness statement, Friedrich Behrens, 31 August 1966, BArch B 162/4100.
215. Witness statement, Meinolph Derenthal, 10 July 1967, BArch B 162/4102.
216. Witness statement, Wilhelm Engels, 10 July 1967, BArch B 162/4102.
217. Maurits Wolder, Interview Code 8590, VHA, USC Shoah Foundation Institute.
218. Ibid.
219. Ibid.
220. Emanuel Tov, statement in his personal diary, 1995. Thanks to Juda Arnold Toff's son, Emanuel Tov, for the extracts shown to me.
221. Maurits Wolder, Interview Code 8590, VHA, USC Shoah Foundation Institute.
222. Wolder, cited in: W. S. 't Hart-Velt, *Ik zou in mijn tranen willen wegzwemmen. Ontvluchtingen van Kamp Westerbork 1940–1945*, unpublished dissertation, 2003, p. 52.
223. Ibid.
224. Ibid., p. 51; written and verbal statement by Max Flietstra, Maurits Wolder's son, 27 January 2011, 8 March 2011.
225. Maurits Wolder, Interview Code 8590, VHA, USC Shoah Foundation Institute.
226. Ibid.

227. Ibid. There is evidence that freight wagons were also used on this transport; witness statement, Jonas Pront, 27 October 1949, BArch B 162/29680.
228. Maurits Wolder, Interview Code 8590, VHA, USC Shoah Foundation Institute.
229. Ibid.
230. Ibid.
231. Ibid.
232. Ibid.
233. Ibid.
234. Wolder, cited in: 't Hart-Velt, *Tranen*, p. 52.
235. Maurits Wolder, Interview Code 8590, VHA, USC Shoah Foundation Institute.
236. Ibid.
237. See 't Hart-Velt, *Tranen*, p. 52.
238. Liste der Zugänge vom 25. Januar 1945, Häftlinge vom K. L. Auschwitz, 26 January 1945, KZ-Gedenkstätte Mauthausen, Register (Y/50). Zugangsliste Politische Abteilung, KZ Gedenkstätte Mauthausen, Register der Politischen Abteilung (Y/36).
239. Sterbebuch KZ Mauthausen, KZ Gedenkstätte Mauthausen (Y/46).
240. Letter from Maurits Wolder to Emanuel Tov, 23 August 1996, privately owned by Emanuel Tov.
241. Mandy R. Evans, *Lest We Forget*, Berrien Springs/Michigan 1991, p. 43 ff.; Wijnperle, *Zou ik het willen overdoen?*, p. 60.
242. Evans, *Lest We Forget*, p. 47 ff.; Wijnperle, *Zou ik het willen overdoen?*, p. 61.
243. Evans, *Lest We Forget*, p. 72 ff.; Wijnperle, *Zou ik het willen overdoen?*, p. 62.
244. Evans, *Lest We Forget*, p. 81; Wijnperle, *Zou ik het willen overdoen?*, p. 63.
245. Wijnperle, *Zou ik het willen overdoen?*, p. 63.
246. Evans, *Lest We Forget*, p. 84.
247. De Vries, *Herzogenbusch (Vught)*, p. 140. Thanks to Hans de Vries (NIOD) for this information.
248. Wijnperle, *Zou ik het willen overdoen?*, p. 63.
249. Prisoner's index card, Nathan Herman Wijnperle, Herzogenbusch concentration camp, no date, 1.1.12.2, ID 423934#1, ITS Digitales Archiv.
250. Wijnperle, *Zou ik het willen overdoen?*, p. 64; Evans, *Lest We Forget*, p. 128.
251. Prisoner's index card, Elsa Wijnperle-Silberberg, Herzogenbusch concentration camp, no date, 1.1.12.2, ID 423931#1, ITS Digitales Archiv; prisoner's index card, Nathan Herman Wijnperle, Herzogenbusch concentration camp, no date, 1.1.12.2, ID 423934#1, ITS Digitales Archiv. Thanks to Hans de Vries for informing me of these documents.
252. Written statement by Guido Abuys, Herinneringscentrum Kamp Westerbork, 15 May 2012.
253. Wijnperle, *Zou ik het willen overdoen?*, p. 64.
254. Ibid., p. 64 f.
255. Ibid., p. 65.
256. Evans, *Lest We Forget*, p. 132; Wijnperle, *Zou ik het willen overdoen?*, p. 65.
257. Evans, *Lest We Forget*, p. 132.
258. Wijnperle, *Zou ik het willen overdoen?*, p. 65.
259. Evans, *Lest We Forget*, p. 133.
260. Wijnperle, *Zou ik het willen overdoen?*, p. 66.
261. Kring van Nederlandsche Joden in Engeland, Tiende Lijst, Teruggevonden in Zuid Limburg, 27 November 1944, Liste von zurückgekehrten Juden nach Süd-Limburg, 10. Liste, 3.1.1.3, ID 78773036#1, ITS Digitales Archiv.
262. Unless otherwise indicated, the following account is based on an interview by the author with Shaul Sagiv (formerly Paul Siegel) on 3 October 2009 in the Yakum kibbutz near Tel Aviv.

263. The Hechaluz movement was founded by J. Trumpeldor in Russia in 1917 as a Zionist pioneer organization. For details on the Hechaluz movement in the occupied Netherlands, see: Yigael, *They Were Our Friends*.
264. Hajkova, 'Das Polizeiliche Durchgangslager Westerbork', p. 230.
265. Conversations with Gustel Moses, in: Marianne Claudi and Reinhard Claudi, *Die wir verloren haben. Lebensgeschichten Emder Juden*, Aurich 1991, p. 27.
266. Siegel, *In ungleichem Kampf*, pp. 34 f., 106.
267. De Jong, 'Die jüdischen Arbeitslager', p. 142; von Frijtag Drabbe Künzel, 'Das Gefängnislager Amersfoort', esp. p. 90 ff.; Mechanicus, *Im Depot*, pp. 21, 25; Presser, *Ashes in the Wind*, p. 230.
268. Author's interview with Shaul Sagiv (formerly Paul Siegel) on 3 October 2009 in the Yakum kibbutz.
269. Louis de Wijze, in: Lindwer, *Kamp van hoop en wanhoop*, p. 160.
270. Author's interview with Shaul Sagiv (formerly Paul Siegel) on 3 October 2009 in the Yakum kibbutz.
271. Siegel, *In ungleichem Kampf*, p. 127.
272. For details on Ru Cohen, see: Lore Siesskind-Zimmels, 'Het Beth-Chaloets te Amsterdam', in: Adina Kochba (Ed.), *Het Verzet van de nederlandse Chaloetsbeweging en de Westerweelgroep tijdens de duitse Bezetting Palestina-Pioniers*, manuscript, NIOD, 614 A, doc II, p. 81.
273. Lore Siesskind-Zimmels wrote that Joop Westerweel told her Ru regarded it as his duty to take the same path as the overwhelming mass of Jews. Lore Siesskind-Zimmels, 'Het Beth-Chaloets te Amsterdam', in: Adina Kochba (Ed.), *Het Verzet van de nederlandse Chaloetsbeweging en de Westerweelgroep tijdens de duitse Bezetting Palestina-Pioniers*, manuscript, NIOD, 614 A, doc II, p. 81.
274. Siegel, *In ungleichem Kampf*, p. 127.
275. Ibid., p. 142.
276. Alfred Fraenkel was a member of the Westerweel Group who did not jump from the 79th deportation train in France. See Chapter 2 in this volume, on escapes from deportation trains leaving France.
277. Author's interview with Shaul Sagiv (formerly Paul Siegel) on 3 October 2009 in the Yakum kibbutz; Lottie Wahrhaftig-Siesel, *Van schuilplaats naar schuilplaats*, NIOD, 614 A, doc II, p. 193; *Naar de Vrijheid*, NIOD, 614 A, doc II.
278. *Vom Ringen des holländischen Hechaluz*, NIOD, 614 A, doc II; *Naar de Vrijheid*, NIOD, 614 A, doc II.
279. For details about Frans Gerritsen, who was already a peace activist in the JVA (Jongere Vredes Actie), among others, even before the Wehrmacht's invasion, see: *Vragenlijst*, NIOD, 296 A, doc II; see also Siegel, *In ungleichem Kampf*, fn 94, p. 138 f.
280. Paul Siegel, 'De laatste ontmoeting', in: Adina Kochba (Ed.), *Het Verzet van de nederlandse Chaloetsbeweging en de Westerweelgroep tijdens de duitse Bezetting Palestina-Pioniers*, manuscript, NIOD, 614 A, doc II, p. 158.
281. Ibid.
282. Ibid.
283. Seidl (SS camp Bergen-Belsen) to Zoepf, Betr.: Transport aus Westerbork am 2. 2. 1944, 7 February 1944, NIOD, 77/1299.
284. In 1958, Meijer changed his surname to Mansveld Levy, having already changed his first name to Max Gerard in 1946.
285. Interview with Max Gerard Mansveld Levy on 25 February 2003 by Guido Abuys, Herinneringscentrum Kamp Westerbork. Thanks to Nadine Schröder for the translation.
286. Ibid.
287. Ibid.
288. Ibid.

289. Ibid.
290. Ibid.
291. Ibid.
292. Betty Mannheim, From Westerbork to Theresienstadt, November 1957, Wiener Library, Testaments of the Holocaust, P.III.h. No. 834 (Westerbork), 058-EA-1283.
293. Ibid.
294. Index card, Jewish Council, Sonja Wagenaar-van Dam, Herinneringscentrum Kamp Westerbork.
295. Author's interview with Sonja Wagenaar-van Dam in Groningen on 18 May 2008.
296. Ibid.
297. Wagenaar-van Dam, cited in: van der Veen, 'Yaagje naar de vrijheid', p. 66.
298. Legitimatie, Identity Card Gerard Stoppelman, 15 April 1945, Herinneringscentrum Kamp Westerbork.
299. Index card, Isidor Stoppelman, database, Herinneringscentrum Kamp Westerbork [Isidor was Stoppelman's original first name].
300. Interview with G. Stoppelman by E. Doosje, 19 March 1998, Herinneringscentrum Kamp Westerbork. Thanks to Kristof Meerts for translating the interview.
301. Index card, Jewish Council, Max Frits Buys, Herinneringscentrum Kamp Westerbork.
302. Ibid.
303. Ibid.; see also Adriaens et al., *Mecheln-Auschwitz*, Vol. 4, p. 58.
304. Index card, Jewish Council, Herman Melkman, 1.2.4.2, ID 12773595#1, ITS Digitales Archiv.
305. Interview with G. Stoppelman by E. Doosje, 19 March 1998, Herinneringscentrum Kamp Westerbork.
306. Index card, Jewish Council, Herman Melkman, 1.2.4.2, ID 12773595#2, ITS Digitales Archiv.
307. This is confirmed by Ab Groenteman, 'Vermetele ontsnapping uit Westerbork. Moedige joodse groep ontvluchtte de dodentrein naar Auschwitz', in: *De Waarheid*, 4 May 1966.
308. Interview with G. Stoppelman by E. Doosje, 19 March 1998, Herinneringscentrum Kamp Westerbork.
309. Ibid.
310. Index card, Jewish Council, Ab Groenteman, Herinneringscentrum Kamp Westerbork.
311. 'Vermetele ontsnapping uit Westerbork. Moedige joodse groep ontvluchtte de dodentrein naar Auschwitz', in: *De Waarheid*, 4 May 1966.
312. Index card, Jewish Council, Ab Groenteman, Herinneringscentrum Kamp Westerbork.
313. 'Vermetele ontsnapping uit Westerbork. Moedige joodse groep ontvluchtte de dodentrein naar Auschwitz', in: *De Waarheid*, 4 May 1966.
314. Index card, Jewish Council, Rachel Telghuis, Herinneringscentrum Kamp Westerbork.
315. J. P. M. van Elswijk, 'Om te ontsnappen aan Auschwitz restte Ciska Telghuis slechts één kans. Sprong op leven en dood', in: *De Telegraaf*, 30 August 1969.
316. Interview with G. Stoppelman by E. Doosje, 19 March 1998, Herinneringscentrum Kamp Westerbork; 'Vermetele ontsnapping uit Westerbork. Moedige joodse groep ontvluchtte de dodentrein naar Auschwitz', in: *De Waarheid*, 4 May 1966.
317. Interview with Lies van de Kolk-Cohen by Guido Abuys, 2 November 1999, Herinneringscentrum Kamp Westerbork.
318. 'Vermetele ontsnapping uit Westerbork. Moedige joodse groep ontvluchtte de dodentrein naar Auschwitz', in: *De Waarheid*, 4 May 1966.
319. Interview with G. Stoppelman by E. Doosje, 19 March 1998, Herinneringscentrum Kamp Westerbork; van der Veen, 'Yaagje naar de vrijheid', p. 67.
320. Interview with G. Stoppelman by E. Doosje, 19 March 1998, Herinneringscentrum Kamp Westerbork.
321. Van der Veen, 'Yaagje naar de vrijheid', p. 67.

322. Van Elswijk, 'Om te ontsnappen aan Auschwitz', in: *De Telegraaf*, 30 August 1969.
323. 'Vermetele ontsnapping uit Westerbork. Moedige joodse groep ontvluchtte de dodentrein naar Auschwitz', in: *De Waarheid*, 4 May 1966.
324. Ibid.
325. Ibid.
326. Ab Groenteman, cited in: 'Vermetele ontsnapping uit Westerbork. Moedige joodse groep ontvluchtte de dodentrein naar Auschwitz', in: *De Waarheid*, 4 May 1966.
327. Ciska Telguis, cited in: Van Elswijk, 'Om te ontsnappen aan Auschwitz', in: *De Telegraf*, 30 August 1969.
328. Ibid.
329. Author's interview with Sonja Wagenaar-van Dam in Groningen on 18 May 2008.
330. Ibid.
331. The escape has been confirmed several times: Betje Rachel Boektje and Sera Sophia Boektje, statement, 5 September 1947, NIOD, 250 i, 1106; Index card, Jewish Council, Ab Groenteman, Herinneringscentrum Kamp Westerbork; index card Abraham Groenteman, 1.2.4.2, ID 12731793, ITS Digitales Archiv. However, this is clearly the index card of Abraham Groenteman, born 22 June 1877 and the remark 'Springer' undoubtedly refers to Abraham Groenteman, born in 1922, meaning the index card recorded the wrong Groenteman.
332. 'Vermetele ontsnapping uit Westerbork. Moedige joodse groep ontvluchtte de dodentrein naar Auschwitz', in: *De Waarheid*, 4 May 1966.
333. Ibid.; interview with G. Stoppelman by E. Doosje, 19 March 1998, Herinneringscentrum Kamp Westerbork.
334. Van der Veen, 'Yaagje naar de vrijheid', p. 69; interview with G. Stoppelman by E. Doosje, 19 March 1998, Herinneringscentrum Kamp Westerbork.
335. Van Elswijk, 'Om te ontsnappen aan Auschwitz', in: *De Telegraaf*, 30 August 1969.
336. Interview with G. Stoppelman by E. Doosje, 19 March 1998, Herinneringscentrum Kamp Westerbork.
337. Ibid.
338. Ibid.
339. Statement, Justus Philip, 1947, NIOD, 250 i, 1106. Thanks to Kristof Meerts for translating this document.
340. Author's interview with Sonja Wagenaar-van Dam in Groningen on 18 May 2008.
341. Sonja Wagenaar-van Dam, cited in: van der Veen, 'Yaagje naar de vrijheid', p. 70.
342. Author's interview with Sonja Wagenaar-van Dam in Groningen on 18 May 2008.

CHAPTER 5

Summary

Two connected questions were key research factors for this study and will now be addressed in a summary. The first complex set of questions refers to overriding structural factors regardless of the situation, which enabled or hindered escapes. The second field refers to the situational factors that were decisive in the wagons for prisoners deciding to flee or to prevent others from fleeing.

Empirical data derived from this study refer to the number of escapes by Jewish deportees on transports to the extermination centres. I was able to document 158 escapes from France, 575 from Belgium and 31 from the Netherlands.[1] To explain these starkly contrasting figures, the following structural and relevant incidental factors are named and classified within the respective national contexts.

Structural Factors

Structural factors that aided escapes from deportation trains can essentially be shown on the individual micro-level and on the organizational meso-level (conditions/processes).

One structural factor on the social macro-level that was important for decisions on the micro-level was the residence status and therefore the connected social situation of the Jewish population in the three countries in which Jews form only a very small minority.

The Persecution Experience of Jewish Refugees

In the Netherlands, around 84 per cent (118,500) of all Jews living there were Dutch citizens. A very large proportion of the foreign or stateless Jews there – 16 per cent of the Jewish population at the time (21,750) –

had recently fled from the National Socialists in the Third Reich and the annexed Austria. Belgium contrasts greatly with the Netherlands in the fact that only around 5 per cent of the 55,600 Jews living there actually had Belgian citizenship. The remaining 95 per cent had immigrated recently, often from Eastern European countries.[2] As a result of this migration, a large group of Eastern European Jews had settled in France. When the Wehrmacht invaded France, there were three hundred thousand Jews living in the country, roughly half of whom were French citizens.[3]

In addition to economic factors, it was above all anti-Semitic discrimination and pogroms in their countries of origin that led to migration from Eastern Europe.

From 1933 onwards, and increasingly so after 1938, Jews also fled from the German Reich and Austria to the three Western European countries studied in this volume. Often, they had been forced to cross the border illegally several times. This group and the refugees from Eastern Europe still remembered the deadly or extremely dangerous anti-Semitism in their home countries, which was not the case with assimilated Jews in the Netherlands, for instance. The refugees had already experienced a situation that caused them to flee to safety from the country in which they lived. This appears to have made it easier for them to decide to flee once again; a strikingly large number of train fugitives in Belgium and France were not born in those countries and instead came from Eastern European countries, the German Reich or Austria.

A large number of escape stories show that many of the escapees had already fled not only from their homelands but also from French internment camps, Organisation Todt labour camps, prisons and transports from one prison to the next, before they jumped from the deportation train.[4]

The Level of Organization among Jewish Migrants

As the reconstruction of escapes in France and Belgium shows, many Jewish migrants in those countries were organized in Socialist, Social Democratic, Communist or Zionist groups.[5] Many of them joined Resistance networks that had emerged from the left-wing and self-organized migrant Jewish communities. Thus, when the German occupiers began to introduce anti-Jewish laws, they were far more able to act than Jews who had no comparable organizational embedding. For instance, Bob Moore recognizes a comparatively early and powerful Jewish self-help organization that opposed the National Socialist occupying policy in Belgium and France, unlike the Netherlands. In Belgium and France, many Jews were united in organizations that can be regarded as precursors of the Resistance; in fact, in Belgium there was even an umbrella organization for various Jewish groups, the Comité de défense des Juifs (CDJ), which closely connected different Jewish groups via the Front de l'Indépendance/Onafhankelijkheidsfront with the non-Jewish Resistance. Their willingness to defend themselves against the German occupiers together, thereby overcoming their political differences, allowed the Jews organized within the CDJ to create a (partially militant) opposition to the Judenrat.[6]

Justified Hope of Support after Leaping from a Train

To act effectively, networks must be able to take decisions, have access to resources and have a highly developed infrastructure.[7] It was easier for people to decide to jump from a moving train if they knew they could expect help from an underground organization after fleeing, for instance through forged documents, money or hideouts.[8] For example, the Handschuh brothers knew that the MOI had false papers ready for them in Paris and they only had to reach the city to be relatively safe.

Knowledge of the Mass Extermination of European Jews

Another factor that could influence the decision to flee was knowledge of the actual purpose of the deportations and the distribution of reports on the mass murder of Jews in German-occupied Eastern Europe. In the second half of 1942, there was an increasing amount of information on the genocide 'in the East', which was spread by underground newspapers, political networks and also radio broadcasters.

Leo Bretholz, for example, secretly listened to the BBC, so he heard early reports of the atrocities and murders committed by the Germans against Jews in Eastern Europe. He and Manfred Silberwasser, a neighbourhood friend from his boyhood in Vienna, decided in Drancy to jump from the train if they were selected for deportation, regarding it as their last chance to escape death.[9] Similarly, Marie Neufeld had seen photos belonging to a Berlin soldier that showed how Jews were murdered, which motivated her to flee from the train.[10]

It is unknown how widespread the knowledge of the extermination was with respect to Nazi 'euthanasia'. We know from Louis Micheels and Régine Krochmal that they had at least heard of the murder of sick patients, people who were unable to work and social outsiders in Germany, and knew that the National Socialists had begun with a programme of murder against a defined population group.[11]

Knowledge of Successful Escapes from Deportation Trains

In 1942, there were frequent reports of successful escapes from deportation trains. Underground newspapers from France and Belgium have survived that report on deportees managing to jump from the moving trains, combined with a call for others to do the same. One former inmate at Drancy, who called himself Ernest, came from Nice and was interned in the assembly camp from 15 October 1943 until his escape from the camp on 2 January 1944. He wrote a report immediately after escaping, which was aimed at the Resistance community. It includes detailed advice on ways to escape from the assembly camp, as well as reporting that it was possible to leap from the deportation trains. In fact, he stated that between ten and thirty people fled from every train during its journey.[12] Meyer Tabakman's report 'Je suis un evadé' ('I Am an Escapee') has been shown to have encouraged people to escape and inspired Resistance fighters to attack the 20th deportation train on 19 April 1943.[13] Indeed, escapes after the autumn/winter of 1942/43 increased so sharply in Belgium and France that some prisoners were locked into the wagons without any clothing, without shoes – even in winter – or with special markings, and with guards in the wagons to prevent further escapes.[14]

It is difficult to quantify the importance of knowledge of the genocide with respect to escapes in France and Belgium, since it is not known how widespread the underground newspapers were. The increased number of escapes also coincides, among other events, with the defeat of the 6th Army near Stalingrad, destroying the illusion of the invincible German occupiers and kindling hope that the war would soon end. Thus, the fact that people were more motivated to resist certainly played a part in the increased number of escapes.

The Geographical Location of the Assembly Camps

One factor on a structural-organizational level (the meso-level) that aided or hindered escapes was the assembly camp's distance from the German border, which varied greatly. Since the German population was regarded as hostile and Jewish people could not expect any support from them, escapes on German territory were generally regarded as hopeless.

The small number of escapes from trains in the Netherlands can without doubt be explained by the fact that Westerbork was only 30 km from the German border as the crow flies. Since the deportation trains had to take a detour northwards or southwards due to the railway route, the journey to the border actually covered 80 km.[15] The train, with a maximum speed of between 45 and 60 km/h, probably needed less than three hours to reach the border, a very short period for extensive escape preparations such as sawing at wagon walls.[16] Mechelen, the central transit camp in Belgium, was approximately 150 km from the German Reich. From Drancy, the central assembly camp in France, the distance was more than 300 km, so every train required around twelve hours to travel to the border.[17] These long periods within France and Belgium increased the chance of escapes.

The Quality and Type of Wagons Used

The different wagon types, namely passenger or freight cars, as well as their condition, were also relevant factors affecting the chance of escape.

As presented in the chapters on the individual countries, the type of wagons used for the deportations varied. It was easier to flee through the windows and doors of passenger wagons than through the barred hatches of a freight wagon or by breaking open or sawing a hole into the wagon wall, which also required smuggled tools.

It is likely that the more unbearable the situation in the wagon was, the more people were willing to escape. The type of wagon used plays a key role in this respect. The situation in the passenger wagons was generally described as less unbearable than in the freight wagons. This appears to have led to a situation in which people transported in passenger wagons were more inclined to believe the myth of the 'labour assignment in the East' than those who could already judge how little their lives were worth in view of the transport conditions.[18] The BdS Judenreferent in the Netherlands, Wilhelm Zoepf, was well aware of the 'propaganda effect'[19] of using passenger wagons. Between fifty and one hundred people were crammed into the freight wagons without respite for three days and nights.[20] When the wagon held around fifty people, there seems to have been space for people to move a little. However, many descriptions state that it was standard practice to fill the trains with more prisoners.[21]

To conclude, it follows that the more frequent use of passenger wagons in the Netherlands, which was comparatively a more humane form of transport, encouraged the deportees to presume that they were travelling to a labour camp. By contrast, the use of increasingly dilapidated, overcrowded freight trains in Belgium and France motivated people to escape from the trains.

Inside the Wagons: Incidental Factors

What Happened inside a Wagon When People Expressed Their Intention to Escape?

Generally, other wagon inmates reacted when they became aware of people's intentions to flee. Only few people speak of indifference or apathy. The reactions ranged from fierce discussion and arguments to moral pressure and physical violence: the prisoners inside the wagons often interpreted the situation in which they found themselves in very different ways. The threat of collective punishment if one person fled was the greatest factor in conflict and even violence when it became known that people were trying to escape. As described by many witnesses, including Sonja Wagenaar-van Dam and Sylvain Kaufmann, panic was often the result.[22] This aspect is described in almost every escape story. Another key factor in these conflicts was the role played by the wagon elder, who was responsible for peace and order during the journey and the 'loading' procedure.[23]

Just as there were many different kinds of motivation behind fleeing or not fleeing, so the deportees also developed various strategies to prevent escapes, to enable their own escape or to help others flee from the train.

Moral Pressure

Moral pressure was a reason to decide against fleeing. Some reports describe how the wagon elder and other prisoners in the wagons appealed to the moral responsibility towards their fellow prisoners. For instance, Addy Fuchs and his comrades decided not to flee after an older Jew impressed upon them that they would be responsible for the deaths of babies, pregnant women and old people in the wagon.[24] The Germans made the wagon elders responsible for events in the wagons, as described, for instance, by Elie A. Cohen. The appointed wagon elder told his fellow prisoners that he would pay with his life for anyone fleeing and thereby appealed to their solidarity. Elie A. Cohen subsequently asked himself whether he really could escape if the price was this man's life.[25] Elie A. Cohen exemplifies the moral dilemma in which people intending to flee found themselves: can one flee if other people may lose their lives as a result?

Alarming the Guards

One of the strategies to prevent an escape was to call the guards. For instance, when Georges Rueff grabbed the door handle in his passenger wagon, other deportees began to scream to draw the guards' attention to the attempted escape and thereby avoid collective punishment.[26] In another case, on the 53rd deportation train from France, a young man ordered the group around Sylvain Kaufmann to stop sawing at the wagon and threatened to inform the guards. He was tied, gagged and hidden beneath the baggage before he could raise the alarm.[27] This strategy is also described in reports from the 20th deportation train that left Mechelen on 19 April 1943.

The Use of Physical Violence

There are several reports of attempts by fellow prisoners to prevent an escape by force.[28] For example, Maurice Rondor began sawing at the metal bars in front of the hatch on a deportation train in March 1944. The other prisoners began to panic when they realized he intended to escape, due to the previously made threat that they would be executed. They threw themselves on him and pinned him to a corner of the wagon. He was unable to free himself from that situation.[29] Inversely, it was also possible to use violence to assert one's intention to flee. Régine Krochmal knocked down another prisoner, a doctor who wanted to prevent her escape, and then indeed fled. Often, the wagon elder was attacked if he attempted to prevent escape efforts.[30] Joseph Silber, who was deported on the 20th transport from Mechelen, knocked the wagon elder to the ground when he tried to prevent him from fleeing.[31]

Group Action

One way of counteracting the resistance from other prisoners in the wagon was to act as a group. Some reports indicate that if members of an already existent (Resistance) group attempted to flee collectively, the other deportees did not dare to oppose them. Serge Bouder recalls that the other prisoners in his wagon almost went insane out of fear of the consequences when he and the other escapees began working on the walls. The others wanted to prevent the escape, but were unable to hold back a strong group of fourteen people.[32] The group from the last deportation train from Westerbork is an example of how a committed group was able to overcome the panicked reactions of other prisoners.[33]

Acting Together with Other Family Members

In several cases, deportees would only flee with their loved ones and tried to encourage them to join them in escaping – sometimes successfully, sometimes not. Of the twelve tunnel diggers who leapt from the 62nd deportation train on 20 November 1943, five were related: Oscar Handschuh and his two sons, and the brothers Roger and Georges Gerschel. An especially large number of pairs of brothers, including the Catz brothers, fled together. Some people still escaped despite failing to convince others to join them. For instance, Rudolf Schmitz was in a wagon with his wife, while his three children were hidden in a monastery in Belgium. After a long, unsuccessful attempt to convince his wife to jump, he eventually escaped without her from the 19th transport departing from

Mechelen on 15 January 1943. He did not wish to leave his children behind alone.[34]

In some cases, deportees did not jump because their relatives were unable or unwilling to join them, being in a different wagon, physically weak or having decided against fleeing for other reasons.[35] Jaak Spitz, who was in a wagon on the 18th transport from Mechelen, was encouraged to escape by a man sitting opposite him, who said: 'Jump. I can't because my wife is in the other wagon, but you're alone'.[36] Claire Prowizur-Szyper did not initially wish to leave her terminally ill father behind in the wagon. Only her husband's imploring words managed to change her mind after a long period of hesitation.[37]

So there were not only behavioural patterns and forms of action that prevented escapes, but also ways of arguing and strategies to enable an escape and encourage people in their plans to flee.

Political Arguments

The nurse Régine Krochmal, who was active in the Resistance in Brussels, argued in the wagon that they were at war and action against the Germans was necessary, rather than remaining on the train and being killed. In an interview, she also explained that there was no medicine, water or food to care for the sick and dying people in the wagon, so she had no means of helping them.[38] The survivor Joseph Silber called the escapes from the transport trains a 'Jewish revolt against deportation'.[39] In his report 'I Am an Escapee', Meyer Tabakman declared that attempting to escape meant resisting death. Thus, escapes from deportation trains are clearly described as acts of Jewish resistance.

Gender-Specific Socialization

The escape events I have studied in France, Belgium and the Netherlands show that many more men than women jumped from deportation trains; only 14 per cent of all escape attempts in the underlying sample for this study were carried out by women. One significant factor in deciding in favour or against jumping was whether dependants, loved ones or people needing support were also in the wagon, whom they did not wish to leave behind. So why did so many more men than women jump?[40] Presumably for two main reasons. Due to their social roles, women were more likely than men to assume caring responsibilities and did not wish to let down those they cared for.[41] It is also possible that women and men had different confidence levels with respect to their physical ability to survive the jump from a moving train without severe injury.

The Moral Dilemma

Almost all deportees intending to flee from deportation trains were confronted by a moral dilemma. Paul Siegel, who was selected for deportation on 1 February 1944, describes this phenomenon in detail. He and his friends abandoned their plans to jump out of the moving train because they did not know of a way to do it without others suffering as a consequence. In the end, they devised the plan of stealing away during the 'loading' process. It was the only escape they could conceive that was in harmony with their feelings of responsibility towards their fellow inmates.[42]

A moral dilemma is created if a person wishes to adhere to two values that cannot be achieved simultaneously on the same level of action, as they are mutually incompatible.[43] Whatever decision one makes, it must be assumed that it may have negative effects on others. In the case of Jews attempting to flee from deportation trains, leaving people behind who required help often led to inner and outer conflict. Furthermore, those who jumped could not be certain whether those who stayed behind would pay with their lives or not. Each person simply had to make a decision for themselves. The wagon prisoners were in a predicament that they had not chosen themselves, but in which they had to make individual choices with respect to escaping.

A moral dilemma cannot be solved rationally; there is no generally applicable hierarchy of values that can be derived to decide which is the most morally sound decision in a given situation.[44] Many surviving escapees from deportation trains, and also people who prevented escapes, had to live with the decisions they made in the framework of these competing values.

Notes

1. The figures for France and the Netherlands are a significant result of my research work, while the figure for Belgium is based on underlying research by Laurence Schram.
2. Moore, *Survivors*, p. 3; Steinberg, *Un pays occupé et ses juifs*, p. 27.
3. Marrus and Paxton, *The Nazis and the Jews*, p. 706 f.
4. For instance, Walter Aron (born in Waldhilbersheim) fled several times, see Piany, Sous-Préfecture d'Oloron, Attestation, 30 June 1954, SVG, Dossier Walter Israel Aron; and Moritz 'Maurice' Margulies, see Granzow, *Der Ausbruch*, p. 135; and Leo Bretholz, as presented in Chapter 2 on France.
5. Lazare, 'Introduction', p. 23; Courtois, Peschanski, and Rayski, *L'Affiche Rouge*, p. 22; Mallmann, 'Frankreichs fremde Patrioten', p. 40 f.
6. Moore, 'The Rescue of Jews', p. 296 ff.
7. Michael L. Gross, 'Jewish Rescue in Holland and France during the Second World War: Moral Cognition and Collective Action', in: *Social Forces* (1994) 2, pp. 463–96, here p. 489.

8. Author's interview with Louis Handschuh on 28 September 2008 in Paris; statement by Eugène Handschuh, *Le tunnel de Drancy*, documentary film by Claudine Drame, 1993.
9. Bretholz and Olesker, *Flucht in die Dunkelheit*, p. 137 ff.
10. Marie Mendel, Interview Code 14125, VHA, USC Shoah Foundation Institute.
11. Micheels, *Doctor #117641*, p. 27; interview with Régine Krochmal, Brussels, 23 January 2009.
12. Ernest, CDJC, CMXXI-28.
13. Meyer Tabakman, 'Je suis un evadé', *Le Flambeau*, March 1943, Cegesoma, BG microfiche 183.
14. Köhnlein to Röthke, Bericht über Judentransport am 20. 11. 1943, 3 December 1943, CDJC, XXVc-249. See also Meyer, *Täter im Verhör*, p. 262 f.; Bargatzky, *Hotel Majestic*, p. 127 f.; Meyer, *Wissen um Auschwitz*, p. 124.
15. Van der Zee, '*Um Schlimmeres zu verhindern*', p. 37; 'Enkele Medelingen betreffende transporttreinen vanuit Westerbork naar Duitsland', p. 8, Herinneringscentrum Kamp Westerbork.
16. N. V. Nederlandsche Spoorwegen, [timetable], 29 October 1942, NIOD, 250 i, 186.
17. Weckmann (Hauptverkehrsdirektion Paris), Betr.: Bedarfsfahrplan Da 901, 30 April 1943, CDJC, XXVc-242.
18. Abraham Margulies, [witness statement], 15 May 1962, LAV NRW W, Staatsarchiv Münster, Staatsanwaltschaft Dortmund Zentralstelle für NS-Verbrechen, No. 4476.
19. Zoepf (BdS Den Haag IV B 4) to RSHA, IV B 4, Betr.: Zug aus den Niederlanden nach Theresienstadt, 15 April 1943, BArch B 162/4106.
20. Weinstock, *Gesicht Hitler-Deutschlands*, p. 75.
21. Ida Fensterszab-Grinspan, cited in: Klarsfeld, *Calendrier de la persécution*, p. 958.
22. Author's interview with Sonja Wagenaar-van Dam in Groningen on 18 May 2008; Kaufmann, *Livre de la mémoire*, p. 58.
23. Adler, *Theresienstadt*, p. 70 f.; Hauptw. d. Sch. Salat, Betr.: Gestellung von Transportkommandos, 24 October 1941, 1.1.0.4 Vernichtungspolitik (Bürokratie), ID 82292612, ITS Digitales Archiv.
24. Commission Shoah du Consistoire de Paris, *Les derniers témoins*, p. 97 f.
25. Cohen, *Abyss*, p. 76 ff.
26. Testimony, Georges Rueff, 16 June 1966, CDJC, CDLXXVI-25; see also testimony, César Chamay, 4 April 1973, CDJC, DLXI-13.
27. Kaufmann, *Livre de la mémoire*, p. 58.
28. For example the account by Fiszel Abram Lipszyc of the 20th deportation train, in: Adriaens et al., *Mecheln-Auschwitz*, Vol. 3, p. 152.
29. Maurice Rondor, cited in: Rajsfus, *Drancy*, p. 320.
30. Urban (1./SS-Pol.-Rgt.14), report, 28 June 1943, CDJC, XLIX-8.
31. Joseph Silber (Fédération nationale des anciens combattants et résistants juifs de Belgique (FNACRAJB) to Czertok (CDJC), Remarques sur la note sur l'historique et les activités du CDJ, 18 May 1964, CDJC, CDLXI-20.
32. Serge Bouder, in: *L'évasion du convoi N° 62*, in the series 'Au Rendez-vous de Souvenirs' by Mariana Grey, Jacques Muller, and Monette le Boucher, c. 1965; Serge Bouder, in: *Le tunnel de Drancy*, documentary film by Claudine Drame, 1993.
33. Author's interview with Sonja Wagenaar-van Dam in Groningen on 18 May 2008.
34. Rudolf Schmitz, cited in: Schreiber, *Stille Rebellen*, p. 189 f.
35. Prowizur-Szyper, *Conte à rebours*, p. 106; Maurice Kubowitzki, 83 – 22 septembre 1943. Extraits de mes souvenirs, Cegesoma, mic 122 (original in YVA O3/1048).
36. Jaak Spitz, cited in: Bolle, '*Ich weiß, dieser Brief*', p. 124.
37. Interview with Claire Prowizur-Szyper in Tel Aviv on 6 September 2009; see also Prowizur-Szyper, *Conte à rebours*, p. 135 ff.
38. Interview with Régine Krochmal in Brussels on 23 January 2009.
39. Joseph Silber, cited in: Schreiber, *Stille Rebellen*, p. 266.

40. Unlike my findings, Simone Gigliotti suggests that escapes were not a gender-specific act. Gigliotti, *The train journey*, p. 117.
41. Clara Asscher-Pinkhof, *Sternkinder*, Hamburg 2012, p. 160 f.
42. Author's interview with Shaul Sagiv (formerly Paul Siegel) in the Yakum kibbutz near Tel Aviv on 3 October 2009.
43. Revital Ludewig-Kedmi, *Moraldilemmata jüdischer Funktionshäftlinge in der Shoah*, Gießen 2001, p. 10.
44. Ibid., p. 53.

Concluding Observations

The freight wagon has become a defining image of the Holocaust. In many places, wagons symbolize the deportations to the extermination camps.[1] Primo Levi writes:

> There is no diary and no report among the many we have written or told, in which the train does not appear, the sealed wagon that turns a means of transport for goods into a rolling prison or even a method of killing people.[2]

'Appear' is indeed an apt verb, for like something that 'appears' out of the fog, many autobiographical descriptions of deportation experiences are equally indistinct. Only few Holocaust survivors used clear words to describe the despair of the deportees and death in the wagons.

The extremely stressful situations in the wagons and the shocking experiences of being transported in such humiliating circumstances seem to have caused many descriptions of deportations to be made rather short or roundabout. Escapes are a part of the terrible experiences in the deportation trains and generally involved moral and ethical dilemmas. This is a possible reason why escapes have only rarely been discussed. Many survivors clearly found it difficult to report on the events and continue to do so. Abraham Kszepicki writes: 'it is impossible to describe the tragic situation in our airless, closed freight car. It was one big toilet'.[3] Ruth Klüger briefly described the deportations as follows: 'This experience cannot be discussed in respectable society'.[4] Simone Gigliotti interprets the deportation as a phenomenon that, unlike other fields such as the pre-war period, ghettos, camp internment and liberation, cannot be assimilated into the narrative cycle of the Holocaust.[5] Meike Herrmann proposes that for most survivors, only the period of camp internment that is regarded as a public experience is worth recounting.[6] It is possible that camp imprisonment is more suited for narrative as it is possible to create a strong descriptive dichotomy in the relationship between the guards and the prisoners, and because the period of camp internment was longer than the duration of the deportation.[7]

Due to the selection process carried out on arrival, the camp was for many people the place where they saw their loved ones for the last time. Terrible, traumatic events were connected to the physical location of the camp. This is different from the 'mobile' situation in the wagon. Perhaps deportations were regarded more as a transfer, an interim situation. The unprecedented horror at the destination probably outweighed everything that had been experienced before. Certainly, the camp is a social space with more recognizable contours and structures than the situation in the wagon. Despite the arbitrary events and terror in the camp, there was a structured daily routine: wake-up, roll call, bed making, labour shift and sleeping at night. Perhaps this can be described more easily than the anomic situation in the wagons.

Presumably, the physical conflicts and sometimes stark competition for resources, as well as the struggle to impose one's own interpretation of events, was perceived as a shameful coarsening of interaction between the prisoners. Many surviving deportation escapees undoubtedly carried the moral burden of having dared to flee and thereby having abandoned and endangered others. Claire Prowizur-Szyper reports that she suffered greatly for decades knowing that she had left her dying father behind in the wagon, until she learned that he had regained consciousness and had received the news of his daughter's escape with relief.[8] Equally, people in the wagon who prevented possibly life-saving escape attempts also suffered under the moral burden.

Outlook

Further research is feasible on the basis of this study. It would be especially fruitful to carry out further individual or comparative studies in and with Eastern Europe. As many sources suggest, a study of escapes and attempted escapes for instance in the Generalgouvernement would almost certainly show that there were many more escapes from deportation trains there than from those in the Western countries examined in this study, as the people in those trains knew for certain that they were travelling to their deaths.[9]

A rewarding overriding question is the integration of the phenomenon of escapes from deportation trains in the debate on Jewish resistance. The escapee Joseph Silber describes his flight as a 'Jewish revolt against deportation'.[10] If one applies the definition of resistance provided by H. G. Adler, which includes preventing 'access to Jews by the RSHA and its helpers',[11] then escapes from trains are undoubtedly acts of resistance. Nevertheless, at present, they neither form part of the debate on Jewish resistance nor are they an element of commemorative cultural and historical-political debate. The term 'Rettungswiderstand' ('rescue resistance')[12] has managed to establish itself in academic discourse, leading to a broader grasp of the term 'resistance'. It may also be possible to discuss the introduction of a further term, namely 'escape resistance'.

Notes

1. Alfred Gottwaldt, 'Der deutsche "Viehwaggon" als symbolisches Objekt in KZ-Gedenkstätten', Part 1, in: *GedenkstättenRundbrief* (2007) 139; idem, 'Der deutsche "Viehwaggon" als symbolisches Objekt in KZ-Gedenkstätten', Part 2: 'Standorte der Wagen in acht Ländern', in: *GedenkstättenRundbrief* (2007) 140.
2. Primo Levi, *Die Untergegangenen und die Geretteten*, Munich/Vienna 1990, p. 109.
3. Abraham Kszepicki, cited in: Yitzahk Arad, *Bełżec, Sobibór, Treblinka. The operation Reinhard death camps*, Bloomington, IN 1987, p. 63; see also Friedhelm Boll, *Sprechen als Last und Befreiung. Holocaust-Überlebende und politisch Verfolgte zweier Diktaturen*, Bonn 2003, p. 43 ff.
4. Ruth Klüger, *Weiter leben. Eine Jugend*, Munich 1999, p. 110.
5. Simone Gigliotti, '"Cattle Car Complexes": A Correspondence with Historical Captivity and Post-Holocaust Witnesses', in: *Holocaust and Genocide Studies* 20 (Fall 2006) 2, p. 267; Boll, *Sprechen als Last*, p. 43 ff.
6. Meike Herrmann, 'Historische Quelle, Sachbericht und autobiographische Literatur. Berichte von Überlebenden der Konzentrationslager als populäre Geschichtsschreibung? (1946–1964)', in: Wolfgang Hartwig and Erhard Schütz (Eds), *Geschichte für Leser. Populäre Geschichtsschreibung in Deutschland im 20. Jahrhundert*, Stuttgart 2005, p. 139.
7. Ibid.
8. Author's interview with Claire Prowizur-Szyper in Tel Aviv on 6 September 2009; see also Prowizur-Szyper, *Conte à rebours*, p. 137 f.
9. Ainsztein, *Jüdischer Widerstand*, p. 80; Zwi Fenster, Bericht über die Vernichtung (Juli 1941–April 1944), 2 August 1968, 1.2.7.8, ID 82188140 and ID 82188141, ITS Digitales Archiv; Serge Knabel, Escape from the gas-chamber, 20 October 1954, Wiener Library, Testaments of the Holocaust, 054-EA-0994; interview with Jurek Kestenberg by David Boder in Fontenay-aux-Roses, Frankreich on 31 July 1946, Voices of the Holocaust, http://voices.iit.edu/interviewee?doc=kestenbergJ (accessed 13 December 2013).
10. Joseph Silber, cited in: Schreiber, *Stille Rebellen*, p. 266.
11. H. G. Adler, *Der Kampf gegen die 'Endlösung der Judenfrage'*, Bonn 1958, p. 47.
12. For example, Peter Steinkamp, 'Rettungswiderstand: Helfer in Uniform', in: Johannes Tuchel (Ed.), *Der vergessene Widerstand. Zu Realgeschichte und Wahrnehmung des Kampfes gegen die NS-Diktatur*, Göttingen 2005, pp. 140–57.

Sources and Bibliography

Sources

Archiv Breendonk Memorial (NGFB), Breendonk
   Various documents
Archiv der KZ-Gedenkstätte Mauthausen, Vienna
   E/13/9/3 Eingangsregister
   Y/36 Register der Politischen Abteilung
   Y/46 Sterbebuch KZ Mauthausen
   Y/50 Veränderungsmeldungen, Zugangslisten
Archiv Redaktion Zeitgeschichte im ZDF, Mainz
   Interview with Philippe Kohn, raw material for the programme 'Brennt Paris?', Cassette Nr. 16, Prod. Nr. 437/00276
Archives départementales de la Meuse, Bar-le-Duc
   209 W 2 Rapports hebdomadaires (1943)
   209 W 3 Rapports mensuels (1941-1944)
Behörde für die Unterlagen des Staatssicherheitsdienstes der ehemaligen Deutschen Demokratischen Republik (BStU), Berlin
   MfS AKK, 2076/75 Ermittlungsbericht zu Jean Franklemon
Bundesarchiv (BArch) Berlin
   R 19 Ordnungspolizei
   R 58 Reichssicherheitshauptamt
   R 70 Niederlande
   Bestände des ehemaligen Berlin Document Center:
      NSDAP-Zentralkartei
      SSO SS-Offiziersakten
Bundesarchiv (BArch) Freiburg
   RW 36 Militärbefehlshaber in Belgien und Nordfrankreich
Bundesarchiv (BArch) Ludwigsburg
   B 162 Unterlagen der Zentralen Stelle der Landesjustizverwaltungen zur Aufklärung nationalsozialistischer Verbrechen
Centre d'Études et de Documentation Guerre et Sociétés contemporaines/Studie – en Documentatiecentrum Oorlog en Hedendaagse Maatschappij (Cegesoma), Brussels

Sources and Bibliography

AA 377 Verklaringen van getuigen en beschuldigden tijdens het proces Kurt Asche voor het Landgericht Kiel, 1980

AA 556 Correspondentie van de Abteilung IV B 3 (Gestapo, jodensectie) an de Beauftragte des Chefs der Sipo-SD für den Bereich des Militärbefehlshabers in Belgien und Nordfrankreich mit de Reichsführer SS-SD, Befehlshaber Sipo-SD Paris, MIlitärverwaltungschef Reeder en de Aussendienststelle Lille betr. de ‚Abschiebung' an joden van Belgische en Franse nationaliteit en de ‚Aktion Iltis' (oppakken van Belgische Joden), 06/1943-09/1943

AA 588 Correspondentie van de Beauftragte des Chefs der Sicherheitspolizei u. des SD in Belgien u. Nordfrankreich, Dienststelle Brüssel met de Reichsführer SS-SD, Gestapo Düsseldorf en Aachen en RSHA Amt I (Personal) betr. personeel van en voor Sipo-SD in België, in het bijzonder in Brussel, 1940-1944 (Overwegend 1940)

AA 1593 Plusieurs témoins (20ème convoi)

AA 1665 Dossier concernant la mise au travail

BA 50.506 ASLB La Mémoire de Dannes-Camier, Du permis de séjour à la déportation

BA L 13.1/11 Archives et documents du gouvernement militaire allemand, d'institutions allemandes civiles et concernant la Wehrmacht

BG microfiche 183 Le Flambeau

D 120 Commission des Crimes de Guerre de Belgique

mic 122 Témoignages des juifs belges (testimonies from Yad Vashem)

Centre de documentation juive contemporaine (CDJC), Paris

Various documents

Various testimonies, mainly produced during the project 'La Résistance Juive en France' by Anny Latour

Collège des Procureurs, Conseil de Guerre Bruxelles, Brussels

Cour Militaire Antwerpen, Berufungsverfahren Felix Lauterborn Sipo Brüssel, Vol. 10

Dokumentationsarchiv des Österreichischen Widerstands (DÖW), Vienna

MA12 Opferfürsorge Akt Moritz Margulies

Gedenkstätte und Museum Sachsenhausen, Oranienburg

Database of prisoners, personal data queries

Herinneringscentrum Kamp Westerbork, Westerbork

Various documents

Various interview manuscripts

Instituut voor Oorlogs-, Holocaust- en Genocidestudies (NIOD), Amsterdam

77 Generalkommissariat für das Sicherheitswesen (Höherer SS- und Polizeiführer Nord-West)

250 i Collectie Gevangenissen en Kampen Westerbork, Judendurchgangslager

270 g Proces W. Harster, W. Zöpf en G. Slotke

296 A Groep Westerweel

429 B Mechelen, Kamp

614 A Palestina Pioniers

International Tracing Service (ITS Arolsen), Bad Arolsen

1.1.0.4 Vernichtungspolitik (Bürokratie)

1.1.5.3 Individuelle Unterlagen Männer Buchenwald

1.1.5.3 Konzentrationslager Buchenwald, Individuelle Unterlagen Frauen

1.1.6.2 Individuelle Unterlagen Dachau

1.1.9.1 Listenmaterial des B.d.S. Frankreich
1.1.12.2 Individuelle Unterlagen Konzentrationslager Herzogenbusch-Vught
1.1.24.1 Listenmaterial Malines
1.1.26.3 Globale Findmittel
1.2.3.3. Kartei Gestapo Koblenz
1.2.4.2 Holland Kriegszeitkartei der Juden
1.2.7.8 Verfolgungsmaßnahmen 'Generalgouvernement'/Distrikt Galizien (Teilbezirk des damaligen Polen)
1.2.7.18 Verfolgungsmaßnahmen Frankreich und Monaco
2.3.3.3 Kartei der verstorbenen Verfolgten (überwiegend französische Zone, auch Franzosen in anderen Zonen)
2.3.5.1 Belgischer Katalog über Konzentrations- und Zwangsarbeiterlager in Deutschland und den besetzten Gebieten
2.3.6.1 Niederländischer Katalog über Konzentrationslager- und Zwangsarbeiterlager in Deutschland und besetzten Gebieten
3.1.1.3 Liste von zurückgekehrten Juden nach Süd-Limburg
Joods Museum van Deportatie en Verzet (JMDV), Mechelen
Convoi XX, Evadés + Sonderliste
Database Kazerne Dossin, Laurence Schram
Interviewsammlung Johannes Blum
Reliques Apfeldorfer, Simon
Reliques Baum, Jacheta
Reliques Beck, Israel
Reliques Bonheim, Alice
Reliques Goldsteinas, Mendelis
Reliques Imerglik, Szymon
Reliques Kleinmann, Salomon
Reliques Steinberg, Israel
Reliques Vistinezki, Hinda
Reliques Weber, Emil
Reliques Weisz, Sandor
Kreispolizeibehörde Recklinghausen, Recklinghausen
Personalakte Walter Kantim
Landesarchiv Nordrhein-Westfalen, Abteilung Westfalen (LAV NRW W), Münster
Q 223 Staatsanwaltschaft Dortmund, Az. 45Js 4/64
Q 225 Staatsanwaltschaft Münster, Nr. 249
Landesarchiv Nordrhein-Westfalen, Abteilung Rheinland, (LAV NRW R), Düsseldorf
Entnazierungsakten
Gerichte Rep. 158 Ermittlungsverfahren Endlösung der Judenfrage in Frankreich
Gerichte Rep. 230 Ermittlungsverfahren gegen Dr. Ganzenmüller, Generalstaatsanwaltschaft Düsseldorf, Prozeß gegen Dr. A. Ganzenmüller
Gerichte Rep. 372 Verfahren gegen Angehörige der Gestapoleitstelle Düdo Beihilfe zum Mord durch Verhängung von Schutzhaft und Deportation jüdischer Personen im Regierungsbezirk Düsseldorf
RW 58 Staatspolizeileitstelle Düsseldorf/Personalakten
Mahn- und Gedenkstätte der Landeshauptstadt Düsseldorf, Düsseldorf
Sammlung Mahn- und Gedenkstätte Düsseldorf

Politisches Archiv des Auswärtigen Amts (PA AA), Berlin
  R 99.406 Inland II A/B, Judenfrage in Belgien (1939–1944)
  R 99.417 Referat D/Abteilung Inland, Juden in Frankreich (1942–1943)
  R 99.429 Inland II A/B, Juden in den Niederlanden
  R 100.862 Inland II g, Judenfrage in Belgien (1939–1943)
  R 100.869 Inland II A/B, Juden in Frankreich
Direction générale Victimes de la Guerre, Directie-generaal Oorlogsslachtoffers (SVG),
    Brussels
  Dossier Apfeldorfer, Simon
  Dossier Altschuler, Michel
  Dossier Arari, David
  Dossier Aron, Walter Israel
  Dossier Aronowicz, Szulim
  Dossier Beck, Israel
  Dossier Berger, Kurt
  Dossier Blok, Reina
  Dossier Bonheim, Alice
  Dossier Cykiert, Majlych
  Dossier Dawid, Otto
  Dossier Fremder, Pinkus
  Dossier Keller, Lipa
  Dossier Keller, Ludwig
  Dossier Kleinmann, Salomon
Visual History Archive (VHA)
  Bretholz, Leo, Interview Code 8503
  Fraenkel, Alfred, Interview Code 17589
  Frank, Henry (formerly Heinz Frankl), Interview Code 1842
  Mendel, Günther, Interview Code 14173
  Mendel, Marie, Interview Code 14125
  Perl, Samuel, Interview Code 49097
  Rotnemer, Elie, Interview Code 32165
  Rueff, Georges, Interview Code 16236
  Wolder, Maurits, Interview Code 8590
Voices of the Holocaust
  Bertha Goldwasser
  Jurek Kestenberg
Wiener Library, Testaments of the Holocaust
  Various testimonies
Yad Vashem Archives (YVA), Jerusalem
  O.3 Various testimonies
  O.29 Belgium Collection
  YVA TR-10 835 Prozess gegen Dr. A. Ganzenmüller

Author's Interviews
  Jacques Altmann, Paris, 19 June 2008
  Simon Gronowski, Brussels, 24 January 2009
  Louis Handschuh, Paris, 28 September 2008

Rolf Joseph, Berlin, 27 August 2008
Régine Krochmal, Brussels, 23 January 2009
Jacques Lazarus, Paris, 19 October 2008
Claire Prowizur-Szyper, Tel Aviv, 6 October 2009
Fanny Rozelaar, Jerusalem, 7 October 2009
Shaul Sagiv (formerly Paul Siegel), Yakum kibbutz near Tel Aviv, 3 October 2009
Sonja Wagenaar-van Dam, Groningen, 18 May 2008
Frida Wattenberg, Paris, 24 September 2008

Conversations with and written statements by witnesses
Leo Bretholz, 3 November 2008
Josep Cajfinger, 29 November 2009
Simon Gronowski, Wuppertal, 27 January 2006
Philippe Kohn, Paris, 26 June 2008
Truus Menger, Haarlem, 29 October 2006
Jules Schelvis, Westerbork, 28 October 2006
Frida Wattenberg, Paris, 18 November 2012

Films
Aufschub, by Harun Farocki, 2007
Drancy. Dernière étape avant l'abime, documentary film by Cécile Clairval, 2002
L'évasion du convoi N° 62, in the series 'Au Rendez-vous de Souvenirs', by Mariana Grey, Jacques Muller, Monette le Boucher, c. 1965
Mit dem Mut der Verzweifelten. Jüdischer Widerstand im zweiten Weltkrieg, documentary film by Rena and Thomas Giefer, 2006
Premier convoi, documentary film by Pierre Oscar Lévy, 1992
Le tunnel de Drancy, documentary film by Claudine Drame, 1993

Radio programme
'Auschwitz Convoy Escape, Witness', BBC World Service, 18 April 2012

Daily and weekly newspapers
L'Aisne Nouvelle
L'Arche
De Telegraaf
De Waarheid
Der Spiegel
Est-Republicain
The Independent

Periodicals
1999. Zeitschrift für Sozialgeschichte des 20. und 21. Jahrhunderts
Drancy bulletin municipal
Einsicht. Bulletin des Fritz Bauer Instituts
International Journal of Social Research
Journal of Genocide
Journal of Modern History
Kölner Zeitschrift für Soziologie und Sozialpsychologie
La Revue d'histoire de la Shoah
La terre retrouvée

Le Flambeau
Le monde juif. La revue du Centre de documentation juive contemporaine (seit 1997 umbenannt in: La Revue d'histoire de la Shoah)
Le patriote resistante
Les Cahiers de la Mémoire contemporaine, Bijdragen tot de eigentijdse Herinnering
Mitteilungen aus dem Bundesarchiv
Social Forces
Westerbork Cahiers
Yad Vashem Studies on the European Jewish Catastrophe and Resistance

Bibliography

Aarebrot, Frank H., and Bakka, Pal H. 'Die vergleichende Methode in der Politikwissenschaft', in: Dirk Berg-Schlosser and Ferdinand Müller-Rommel (Eds), *Vergleichende Politikwissenschaft*, 4th ed., Opladen 2003, pp. 49–66.

Abuys, Guido, and Mulder, Dirk. 'Een gat in het prikkeldraad. Kamp Westerbork – ontsnappingen en verzet', in: *Westerbork Cahiers* (2003) 10.

Adler, H. G. *Der Kampf gegen die 'Endlösung der Judenfrage'*, Bonn 1958.

Adler, H. G. *Theresienstadt. Das Antlitz einer Zwangsgemeinschaft*, 2nd ed., Tübingen 1960.

Adler, H. G. *Der verwaltete Mensch. Studien zur Deportation der Juden aus Deutschland*, Tübingen 1974.

Adriaens, Ward, et al. (Eds). *Mecheln-Auschwitz 1942–1944. De vernietiging van de Joden en zigeuners van België. La destruction des Juifs et des Tsiganes de Belgique. The Destruction of the Jews and Gypsies from Belgium*, Vols. 1–4, Brussels 2009.

Ainsztein, Reuben. *Jüdischer Widerstand im deutschbesetzten Osteuropa während des Zweiten Weltkrieges*, Oldenburg 1993.

Akten zur deutschen auswärtigen Politik 1918–1945. Aus dem Archiv des Auswärtigen Amts, Serie E: 1941–1945, Bd. I, 12. Dezember 1941 bis 28. Februar 1942, Göttingen 1969; *Bd. III, 16. Juni bis 30. September 1942*, Göttingen 1974; *Bd. IV, 1. Oktober bis 31. Dezember 1942*, Göttingen 1975.

Altbeker Cyprys, Ruth. *A Jump for Life. A Survivor's Journal from Nazi-Occupied Poland*, London 1997.

Améry, Jean. *Jenseits von Schuld und Sühne. Bewältigungsversuche eines Überwältigten*, Stuttgart 1997.

Anckar, Carsten. 'On the Applicability of the Most Similar Systems Design and the Most Different Systems Design in Comparative Research', in: *International Journal of Social Research* 11 (2008) 5, pp. 389–401.

Arad, Yitzahk. *Bełżec, Sobibór, Treblinka. The Operation Reinhard Death camps*, Bloomington, IN 1987.

Arntz, Hans-Dieter. *Judenverfolgung und Fluchthilfe im deutsch-belgischen Grenzgebiet: Kreisgebiet Schleiden, Euskirchen, Monschau, Aachen und Eupen/Malmedy*, Euskirchen 1990.

As, Aad van, in: Willy Lindwer, *Kamp van hoop en wanhoop. Getuigen van Westerbork, 1939–1945*, Amsterdam 1990.

Asscher-Pinkhof, Clara. *Sternkinder*, Hamburg 2012.

Avni, Haim. 'The Zionist Underground in Holland and France and the Escape to Spain', in: Yisrael Gutman and Efraim Zuroff, *Rescue Attempts during the Holocaust*, Jerusalem 1977, pp. 555–90.

Bargatzky, Walter. *Hotel Majestic. Ein Deutscher im besetzten Frankreich*, Freiburg 1987.

Barnavi, Élie, and Frydman, Jean. *Tableaux d'une vie. Pour servir à l'histoire de notre temps*, Paris 2008.

Bauer, Yehuda. 'Forms of Jewish Resistance during the Holocaust', in: Michael R. Marrus (Ed.), *Jewish Resistance to the Holocaust*, London 1989, pp. 34–48.

Benbassa, Esther. *Geschichte der Juden in Frankreich*, Berlin/Vienna 2000.

Benz, Wolfgang. 'Typologie der Herrschaftsformen in den Gebieten unter deutschem Einfluß', in: Wolfgang Benz, Johannes Houwink ten Cate and Gerhard Otto (Eds), *Die Bürokratie der Okkupation. Strukturen der Herrschaft und Verwaltung im besetzten Europa*, Berlin 1998, pp. 11–25.

Benz, Wolfgang. 'Okkupation und Repression. Zur deutschen Besatzungsherrschaft in den Benelux-Ländern', in: Wolfgang Benz and Barbara Distel, *Terror im Westen. Nationalsozialistische Lager in den Niederlanden, Belgien und Luxemburg 1940–1945*, Berlin 2004.

Berler, Willy. *Durch die Hölle. Monowitz, Auschwitz, Groß-Rosen, Buchenwald*, Berlin 2003.

Birn, Ruth Bettina. *Die Höheren SS- und Polizeiführer. Himmlers Vertreter im Reich und in den besetzten Gebieten*, Düsseldorf 1986.

Blom, J. C. H. 'The Persecution of the Jews in the Netherlands in a Comparative International Perspective', in: Jozeph Michman (Ed.), *Dutch Jewish History. Proceedings of the Fourth Symposium on the History of the Jews in the Netherlands 7–10 December – Tel Aviv, Jerusalem, 1986, Volume II*, Jerusalem 1989.

Boll, Friedhelm. *Sprechen als Last und Befreiung. Holocaust-Überlebende und politisch Verfolgte zweier Diktaturen*, Bonn 2003.

Bolle, Mirjam, *'Ich weiß, dieser Brief wird Dich nie erreichen'. Tagebuchbriefe aus Amsterdam, Westerbork und Bergen-Belsen*, Frankfurt 2006.

Brandt, Harm-Hinrich. 'Nationalsozialismus und Bürokratie. Überlegungen zur Rolle der Eisenbahn bei der Vernichtung der europäischen Juden', in: Eisenbahnjahr Ausstellungsgesellschaft mbH Nürnberg (Ed.), *Zug der Zeit – Zeit der Züge*, Vol. 2, Berlin 1985, pp. 692–701.

Bretholz, Leo, and Olesker, Michael. *Flucht in die Dunkelheit*, Vienna 2005.

Bringmann, Fritz. *Kindermord am Bullenhuserdamm. SS-Verbrechen in Hamburg 1945: Menschenversuche an Kindern*, Frankfurt am Main 1978.

Broad, Pery, testimony, in: Staatliches Auschwitz-Museum, *Auschwitz in den Augen der SS. Rudolf Höß, Pery Broad, Johann Paul Kremer*, Warsaw 1992.

Broder, Pierre. *Des Juifs debout contre le nazisme*, Brussels 1994.

Browning, Christopher R. *Ganz normale Männer. Das Reserve-Polizeibataillon 101 und die 'Endlösung' in Polen*, Reinbek 1999.

Brunner, Bernhard. *Der Frankreich-Komplex. Die nationalsozialistischen Verbrechen in Frankreich und die Justiz der Bundesrepublik Deutschland*, Göttingen 2004.

Buchheim, Hans, et al. *Anatomie des SS-Staates*, Munich 1994.

Buggeln, Marc. 'Hannover-Mühlenberg', in: Wolfgang Benz and Barbara Distel (Eds), *Der Ort des Terrors. Geschichte der nationalsozialistischen Konzentrationslager*. Vol. 5: *Hinzert, Auschwitz, Neuengamme*, Munich 2007, pp. 440–43.

Cahen, Bob. *Brieven uit de trein Westerbork-Auschwitz (enkele reis)*, Haarlem 1996.

Caruth, Cathy. 'Trauma als historische Erfahrung: Die Vergangenheit einholen', in: Ulrich Baer (Ed.), *'Niemand zeugt für den Zeugen'. Erinnerungskultur nach der Shoah*, Frankfurt am Main 2000, pp. 84–98.

Catz, Hans. *The Eye of the Needle. A Story from World War II*, [self-published], Huizen 1999.

Chaigneau, Jean-François. *Le dernier wagon*, Paris 1981.

Claudi, Marianne, and Claudi Reinhard. *Die wir verloren haben. Lebensgeschichten Emder Juden*, Aurich 1991.

Cohen, Elie A. *The Abyss. A Confession*, New York 1973.

Comite de Defense des Juifs - C. D. J., *Groupement de résistance reconnu à la date du 1-3-1948. (Moniteur Belge), Affilie au 'Front de l'independance', Temoignages et documents recueillis entre 1947 et 1951 par René De Lathouwer, Liquidateur du C. D. J. au statut de la Résistance Civile.*

Commission Shoah du Consistoire de Paris. *Les derniers témoins. Paroles de déportés. Recueillies par Jean-Pierre Allali, Adolphe Fuchs. Les copains d'abord*, 2005.

Conze, Eckart, et al. *Das Amt und die Vergangenheit. Deutsche Diplomaten im Dritten Reich und in der Bundesrepublik*, Munich 2010.

Coupechoux, Patrick. *Mémoires de déportés. Histoires singulières de la déportation*, Paris 2003.

Courtois, Stéphane. 'Que savait la presse communiste?', in: Stéphane Courtois and Adam Rayski, *Qui savait quoi? L'extermination des Juifs 1941–1945*, Paris 1987.

Courtois, Stéphane, Peschanski, Denis, and Rayski, Adam. *L'Affiche Rouge. Immigranten und Juden in der französischen Résistance*, Berlin 1994.

Croes, Marnix. 'Gentiles and the Survival Chances of Jews in the Netherlands 1940–1945. A Closer Look', in: Beate Kosmala and Feliks Tych (Eds), *Facing the Nazi Genocide: Non-Jews and Jews in Europe*, Berlin 2004, pp. 41–72.

Croes, Marnix. 'The Holocaust in the Netherlands and the Rate of Jewish Survival', in: *Holocaust and Genocide Studies* (2006) 3, pp. 474–99.

Curilla, Wolfgang. *Die deutsche Ordnungspolizei und der Holocaust im Baltikum und in Weißrußland 1941–1944*, Paderborn et al. 2006.

Curilla, Wolfgang. *Der Judenmord in Polen und die deutsche Ordnungspolizei 1939–1945*, Paderborn 2011.

Dawidowicz, Lucy S. *Der Krieg gegen die Juden 1933–1945*, Wiesbaden 1979.

De Jong, Sytske. 'Die jüdischen Arbeitslager in den Niederlanden', in: Wolfgang Benz and Barbara Distel (Eds), *Terror im Westen. Nationalsozialistische Lager in den Niederlanden, Belgien und Luxemburg 1940–1945*, Berlin 2004, pp. 131–48.

De Kinderen van Gewapende joodse Partizanen van Belgïe (Ed.). *Gewapende Joodse Partizanen van Belgïe*, Getuigenissen 1997.

De Vries, Hans. 'Das Konzentrationslager Herzogenbusch bei Vught: "streng und gerecht"?', in: Wolfgang Benz and Barbara Distel (Eds), *Terror im Westen. Nationalsozialistische Lager in den Niederlanden, Belgien und Luxemburg 1940–1945*, Berlin 2004, pp. 197–216.

De Vries, Hans. 'Herzogenbusch (Vught) – Stammlager', in: Wolfgang Benz and Barbara Distel, *Der Ort des Terrors. Geschichte der nationalsozialistischen Konzentrationslager*, Vol. 7, Munich 2008, pp. 133–50.

De Wever, Bruno. 'Benelux-Staaten: Integration und Opposition', in: Wolfgang Benz, Johannes Houwink ten Cate and Gerhard Otto (Eds), *Anpassung, Kollaboration, Widerstand. Kollektive Reaktionen auf die Okkupation*, Berlin 1996, pp. 69–115.

Dierl, Florian. 'Das Hauptamt Ordnungspolizei 1936 bis 1945. Führungsspitze und die Befehlshaber in den Wehrkreisen', in: Alfons Kenkmann and Christoph Spieker (Eds), *Im Auftrag. Polizei, Verwaltung und Verantwortung*, Essen 2001, pp. 159–75.

Distel, Barbara. 'Frankreich', in: Wolfgang Benz and Barbara Distel (Eds), *Der Ort des Terrors. Geschichte der nationalsozialistischen Konzentrationslager*, Vol. 9, Munich 2009, pp. 273–91.

Doerry, Janine. 'Das Lager Drancy und die Deportation der Juden aus Frankreich', in: Akim Jah et al. (Eds), *Nationalsozialistische Lager. Neue Beiträge zur NS-Verfolgungs- und Vernichtungspolitik und zur Gedenkstättenpädagogik*, Münster 2006, pp. 166–84.

Doorslaer, Rudi van, et al. (Eds). *La Belgique docile. Les autorités belges et la persécution des Juifs en Belgique durant la Seconde Guerre mondiale*, Brussels 2006.

Durin, Jacques. *Drancy 1941–1944*, Paris 1988.

Eck, Nathan. 'The Rescue of Jews with the Aid of Passports and Citizenship Papers of Latin American States', in: *Yad Vashem Studies on the European Jewish Catastrophe and Resistance* I (1957), pp. 12–152.

Eggers, Christian. *Unerwünschte Ausländer. Juden aus Deutschland und Mitteleuropa in französischen Internierungslagern 1940–1942*, Berlin 2002.

Europa unterm Hakenkreuz. Belgien, Luxemburg, Niederlande. Dokumentenedition. Dokumentenauswahl und Einleitung von Ludwig Nestler. Unter Mitarbeit von Heidi Böhme u. a., Berlin 1990.

Europa unterm Hakenkreuz. Frankreich. Dokumentenedition. Dokumentenauswahl und Einleitung von Ludwig Nestler. Unter Mitarbeit von Friedel Schulz, Berlin 1990.

Evans, Mandy R. *Lest We Forget*. Berrien Springs, MI 1991.

Fein, Helen. *Accounting for Genocide. National Responses and Jewish Victimization during the Holocaust*, New York 1979.

Felsmann, Barbara and Prümm, Karl. *Kurt Gerron – Gefeiert und gejagt. 1897–1944. Das Schicksal eines deutschen Unterhaltungskünstlers. Berlin, Amsterdam, Theresienstadt, Auschwitz*, Berlin 1992.

Fénelon, Fania. *Das Mädchenorchester in Auschwitz*, Munich 1981.

Feuchtwanger, Lion. *Der Teufel in Frankreich*, Frankfurt am Main 1986.

Finger, Jürgen, and Keller, Sven. 'Täter und Opfer – Gedanken zu Quellenkritik und Aussagekontext', in: Jürgen Finger and Andreas Wirsching (Eds), *Vom Recht zur Geschichte. Akten aus NS-Prozessen als Quellen der Zeitgeschichte*, Göttingen 2009, pp. 114–31.

Finger, Jürgen, Keller, Sven, and Wirsching, Andreas (Eds), *Vom Recht zur Geschichte. Akten aus NS-Prozessen als Quellen der Zeitgeschichte*, Göttingen 2009.

Flim, Bert Jan. 'Opportunities for Dutch Jews to Hide from the Nazis 1942–1945', in: Chaya Brasz and Yosef Kaplan (Eds), *Dutch Jews as Perceived by Themselves and by Others: Proceedings of the Eighth International Symposium on the History of the Jews in the Netherlands*, Leiden/Boston/Cologne 2001, pp. 289–305.

Flörsheim, Chanan Hans. *Über die Pyrenäen in die Freiheit. Von Rotenburg an der Fulda über Leipzig nach Amsterdam und durch Frankreich und Spanien nach Israel 1923–1944*, Konstanz 2008.

Fondation pour la Mémoire de la Deportation. *Livre-mémorial des déportés de France arrêtés par mesure de répression et dans certains cas par mesure de persécution 1940–1945*, Vol. 3, Paris 2004.

Fransecky, Tanja von. *Sie wollten mich umbringen, dazu mussten sie mich erst haben. Hilfe für verfolgte Juden in den deutsch besetzten Niederlanden*, Berlin 2016.
Fransecky, Tanja von. *Bis ans Maul der Bestie. Nelly Klein - Eine österreichische Jüdin im belgischen Widerstand*, Berlin 2019.
Frei, Norbert. *Vergangenheitspolitik. Die Anfänge der Bundesrepublik und die NS-Vergangenheit*, Munich 1999.
Friedländer, Saul. *Die Jahre der Vernichtung. Das Dritte Reich und die Juden 1939–1945*, Munich 2006.
Frijtag Drabbe Künzel, Geraldien von. 'Das Gefängnislager Amersfoort', in: Wolfgang Benz and Barbara Distel (Eds), *Terror im Westen. Nationalsozialistische Lager in den Niederlanden, Belgien und Luxemburg 1940–1945*, Berlin 2004, pp. 73–100.
Fritz, Ulrich. 'Chemnitz', in: Wolfgang Benz and Barbara Distel (Eds), *Das Konzentrationslager Flossenbürg und seine Außenlager*, Munich 2007, pp. 74–76.
Galen Last, Dick van, and Wolfswinkel, Rolf. *Anne Frank and After. Dutch Holocaust Literature in Historical Perspective*, Amsterdam 1996.
Gallin, Isabel. 'Machtstrukturen im Reichskommissariat Niederlande', in: Robert Bohn (Ed.), *Die deutsche Herrschaft in den 'germanischen' Ländern 1940–1945*, Stuttgart 1997.
Gigliotti, Simone. '"Cattle Car Complexes": A Correspondence with Historical Captivity and Post-Holocaust Witnesses', in: *Holocaust and Genocide Studies* 20 (Fall 2006) 2, pp. 256–77.
Gigliotti, Simone. *The Train Journey. Transit, Captivity, and Witnessing the Holocaust*, New York/Oxford 2009.
Gottwaldt, Alfred. 'Der deutsche "Viehwaggon" als symbolisches Objekt in KZ-Gedenkstätten', Part 1, in: *GedenkstättenRundbrief* (2007) 139.
Gottwaldt, Alfred, 'Der deutsche "Viehwaggon" als symbolisches Objekt in KZ-Gedenkstätten', Part 2, in: *GedenkstättenRundbrief* (2007) 140.
Granzow, Jonny. *Der Ausbruch aus dem Geheimgefängnis in Castres. Eine historische Reportage*, Berlin 2012.
Greve, Michael. *Der justitielle und rechtspolitische Umgang mit den NS-Gewaltverbrechen in den sechziger Jahren*, Frankfurt am Main et al. 2001.
Gronowski, Simon. *Le petit évadé. L'Enfant du 20e Convoi*, Brussels.
Gross, Michael L. 'Jewish Rescue in Holland and France during the Second World War: Moral Cognition and Collective Action', in: *Social Forces* (1994) 2, pp. 463–96.
Grynberg, Anne. *Les camps de la honte. Les internés juifs des camps français 1939–1944*, Paris 1999.
Gueta, Anat. *Ha ṣaba' hayhwdiy bṢarpat qwrwteyha šel maḥteret ṣiywniyt lwḥemet* (The Jewish Army, the History of the Jewish Armed Underground in France), Israel 2001.
Gutmacher, F. 'Aus dem Lager Malines nach Auschwitz', in: Peter Longerich, *Die Ermordung der europäischen Juden*, Munich 1989.
Gutman, Yisrael, and Zuroff, Efraim. *Rescue Attempts during the Holocaust*, Jerusalem 1977.
H., Georg. 'Der Traum von Israel', in: Volker Jakob and Anne van der Voort (Eds), *Anne Frank war nicht allein*, Berlin/Bonn 1988.
Hafner, Georg M., and Schapira, Esther. *Die Akte Alois Brunner. Warum einer der größten Naziverbrecher noch immer auf freiem Fuß ist*. Frankfurt am Main 2000.

Hajkova, Anna. 'The Making of a Zentralstelle: Die Eichmann-Männer in Amsterdam', in: *Theresienstädter Studien und Dokumente* 10 (2003), pp. 353–81.
Hajkova, Anna. 'Das Polizeiliche Durchgangslager Westerbork', in: Wolfgang Benz and Barbara Distel (Eds), *Terror im Westen. Nationalsozialistische Lager in den Niederlanden, Belgien und Luxemburg 1940–1945*, Berlin 2004, pp. 217–48.
Henneboel, Jupp. 'Ich konnte nicht anders', in: Christoph Spieker (Ed.), *Freund oder Vijand? Een groene politieman in het Nederlandse verzet. Ein 'Grüner Polizist' im niederländischen Widerstand*, Münster 2004, pp. 147–232.
Herbert, Ulrich. *Best. Biographische Studien über Radikalismus, Weltanschauung und Vernunft 1903–1989*, Bonn 2001.
Herbst, Fabian, et al. *Ich muss weitermachen. Die Geschichte des Herrn Joseph*, [published by the author], Berlin 2008.
Herrmann, Meike. 'Historische Quelle, Sachbericht und autobiographische Literatur. Berichte von Überlebenden der Konzentrationslager als populäre Geschichtsschreibung? (1946–1964)', in: Wolfgang Hartwig and Erhard Schütz (Eds), *Geschichte für Leser. Populäre Geschichtsschreibung in Deutschland im 20. Jahrhundert*, Stuttgart 2005.
Hilberg, Raul. *Sonderzüge nach Auschwitz*, Mainz 1981.
Hilberg, Raul. *Die Vernichtung der europäischen Juden*, Vol. 2, Frankfurt am Main 1997.
Hilberg, Raul. *Die Quellen des Holocaust: Entschlüsseln und interpretieren*, Frankfurt am Main 2002.
Hillesum, Etty. 'Die Nacht vor dem Transport', in: Gerhard Schoenberner (Ed.), *Wir haben es gesehen. Augenzeugenberichte über die Judenverfolgung im Dritten Reich*, Wiesbaden 1981, pp. 222–31.
Hillesum, Etty. *Das denkende Herz. Die Tagebücher von Etty Hillesum 1941–1943*, Reinbek 1988.
Hirschfeld, Gerhard. 'Niederlande', in: Wolfgang Benz (Ed.), *Dimension des Völkermords. Die Zahl der jüdischen Opfer des Nationalsozialismus*, Munich 1991, pp. 137–66.
Hirschfeld, Gerhard. 'Kollaboration in Frankreich – Einführung', in: Gerhard Hirschfeld and Patrick Marsh (Eds), *Kollaboration in Frankreich. Politik, Wirtschaft und Kultur während der nationalsozialistischen Besatzung 1940–1944*, Frankfurt am Main 1991, pp. 7–22.
Hirschfeld, Gerhard. 'Die Verfolgung und Vernichtung der Juden in den Niederlanden', in: Joachim Castan (Ed.), *Hans Calmeyer und die Judenrettung in den Niederlanden*, Osnabrück 2003, pp. 102–15.
Hirschfeld, Gerhard. 'Kollaboration in Hitlers Europa als ein historisches Tabu: Vichy-Frankreich und die Niederlande', in: Nicole Colin, Matthias N. Lorenz and Joachim Umlauf (Eds), *Täter und Tabu. Grenzen der Toleranz in deutschen und niederländischen Geschichtsdebatten*, Essen 2011, pp. 49–59.
Hoffmann, Friedrich. *Die Verfolgung der nationalsozialistischen Gewaltverbrechen in Hessen*, Baden-Baden 2001.
Houwink ten Cate, Johannes. 'Der Befehlshaber der Sipo und des SD in den besetzten niederländischen Gebieten und die Deportation der Juden 1942–1943', in: Wolfgang Benz, Johannes Houwink ten Cate and Gerhard Otto (Eds), *Die Bürokratie der Okkupation: Strukturen der Herrschaft und Verwaltung im besetzten Europa*, Berlin 1998, pp. 197–223.

Houwink ten Cate, Johannes. 'Mangelnde Solidarität gegenüber Juden in den besetzten niederländischen Gebieten?', in: Wolfgang Benz and Juliane Wetzel (Eds), *Solidarität und Hilfe für Juden während der NS-Zeit. Dänemark, Niederlande, Spanien, Portugal, Ungarn, Albanien, Weißrußland. Regionalstudien 3*, Berlin 1999, pp. 87–133.

Houwink ten Cate, Johannes, and Kenkmann, Alfons (Eds). *Deutsche und holländische Polizei in den niederländischen Gebieten. Dokumentation einer Arbeitstagung*, Münster 2002.

In't Veld, Nanno. 'Höhere SS- und Polizeiführer und Volkstumspolitik: ein Vergleich zwischen Belgien und den Niederlanden', in: Wolfgang Benz, Johannes Houwink ten Cate and Gerhard Otto (Eds), *Die Bürokratie der Okkupation. Strukturen der Herrschaft und Verwaltung im besetzten Europa*, Berlin 1998, pp. 121–38.

Jakob, Volker and van der Voort, Anne (Eds). *Anne Frank war nicht allein*, Berlin/Bonn 1988.

Joods Historisch Museum Amsterdam. *Documents of the Persecution of the Dutch Jewry 1940–1945*, Amsterdam 1979.

Joods Museum van deportatie en verzet. *De Belgische tentoonstelling in Auschwitz. Het book. L'exposition belge à Auschwitz. Le livre*, 2006.

Joseph, Rolf and Joseph, Alfred. 'Rags, Picklocks and Pliers', in: Eric H. Boehm, *We Survived. Fourteen Histories of the Hidden and Hunted of Nazi Germany*, Santa Barbara 1966.

Kaminsky, Sarah. *Adolfo Kaminsky. Ein Fälscherleben*, Munich 2011.

Kapel, René S. *Un rabbin dans la tourmente (1940–1944). Dans les camps d'internement et au sein de l'Organisation juive de combat*, Paris 1986.

Kaufmann, Sylvain. *Le livre de la mémoire. Au-delà de l'enfer*, [Paris] 1992.

Kasten, Bernd. 'Zwischen Pragmatismus und exzessiver Gewalt. Die Gestapo in Frankreich 1940–1944', in: Gerhard Paul and Klaus-Michael Mallmann (Eds), *Die Gestapo im Zweiten Weltkrieg. 'Heimatfront' und besetztes Europa*, Darmstadt 2000, pp. 362–82.

Katzenelson, Jizchak. *Oh mein Volk! Mein Volk . . . Aufzeichnungen aus dem Internierungslager Vittel*, Berlin 1999.

Klarsfeld, Serge (Ed.). *Die Endlösung der Judenfrage in Frankreich. Deutsche Dokumente. Dokumentationszentrum für Jüdische Zeitgeschichte CDJC Paris. 1941–1944*, Paris 1977.

Klarsfeld, Serge, and Steinberg, Maxime (Eds). *Die Endlösung der Judenfrage in Belgien. Dokumente*, New York 1980.

Klarsfeld, Serge. *Transport No. 20 du 17. 8. 1942, 530 enfants de moins de 16 ans*, Paris [c. 1980].

Klarsfeld, Serge, and Steinberg, Maxime. *Mémorial de la Déportation des Juifs de Belgique*, Brussels 1982.

Klarsfeld, Serge. *Memorial to the Jews Deported from France 1942–1944. Documentation of the Deportation of the Victims of the Final Solution in France*, New York 1983.

Klarsfeld, Serge. *Le Calendrier de la persécution des Juifs en France 1940–1944*, Paris 1993.

Klarsfeld, Serge. 'L'acheminement des Juifs de province vers Drancy et les déportations', in: *Une Entreprise publique dans la guerre: La SNCF 1939–1945. Actes du Ville Colloque de l'Association pour l'histoire des chemins de fer en France*, Paris 2001.

Klarsfeld, Serge. *Vichy-Auschwitz. Die 'Endlösung der Judenfrage' in Frankreich*, Darmstadt 2007.

Klee, Ernst, Dreßen, Willi, and Rieß, Volker. *'Schöne Zeiten'. Judenmord aus der Sicht der Täter und Gaffer*, Frankfurt am Main 1998.

Klemp, Stefan. *Freispruch für das 'Mord-Bataillon'. Die NS-Ordnungspolizei und die Nachkriegsjustiz*, Münster 1998.

Klemp, Stefan, and Reinke, Herbert. 'Kölner Polizeibataillone in den Niederlanden während des Zweiten Weltkrieges', in: Harald Buhlan and Werner Jung (Eds), *Wessen Freund und wessen Helfer? Die Kölner Polizei im Nationalsozialismus*, Cologne 2000, pp. 263–76.

Klemp, Stefan. 'Einsatz im Westen – Deutsche Polizeibataillone in Holland 1940 bis 1945', in: Johannes Houwink ten Cate and Alfons Kenkmann (Eds), *Deutsche und holländische Polizei in den besetzten niederländischen Gebieten. Dokumentation einer Arbeitstagung*, Münster 2002, pp. 29–66.

Klemp, Stefan. *'Nicht ermittelt'. Polizeibataillone und die Nachkriegsjustiz. Ein Handbuch*, Essen 2005.

Klüger, Ruth. *Weiter leben. Eine Jugend*, Munich 1999.

Knigge, Volkhard, and Hoffmann, Detlef. 'Die südfranzösischen Lager', in: Volkhard Knigge and Detlef Hoffmann (Eds), *Das Gedächtnis der Dinge. KZ-Relikte und KZ-Denkmäler 1945–1995*, Frankfurt/New York 1998, pp. 208–22.

Knopp, Guido. *Die Befreiung. Kriegsende im Westen*, Berlin 2004.

Knout, David. *Contribution à l'histoire de la Résistance juive en France, 1940–1944*, Paris 1947.

Kochba, Adina. 'Joachim-Yachin Simon (Shushu)', in: Mirjam Pinkhof (Ed.), *De jeugdalijah van het Paviljoen Loosdrechtsche Rade 1939–1945*, Hilversum/Verloren 1998.

Kogon, Eugen. *Der SS-Staat. Das System der deutschen Konzentrationslager*, Reinbek 1974.

Kohlhaas, Elisabeth. 'Gertrud Slottke. Angestellte im niederländischen Judenreferat der Sicherheitspolizei', in: Klaus-Michael Mallmann and Gerhard Paul (Eds), *Karrieren der Gewalt. Nationalsozialistische Täterbiographien*, Darmstadt 2004, pp. 207–18.

Kolb, Eberhard. *Bergen-Belsen. Vom Aufenthaltslager zum Konzentrationslager 1943 bis 1945*, Göttingen 1996.

Koselleck, Reinhart. 'Vom Sinn und Unsinn der Geschichte', in: Klaus E. Müller and Jörn Rüsen (Eds), *Historische Sinnbildung. Problemstellungen, Zeitkonzepte, Wahrnehmungshorizonte, Darstellungsstrategien*, Reinbek 1997, pp. 79–97.

Kramer, Alan. '"Greueltaten". Zum Problem der deutschen Kriegsverbrechen in Belgien und Frankreich 1914', in: Gerhard Hirschfeld, Gerd Krumeich, and Irina Renz (Eds), *'Keiner fühlt sich hier mehr als Mensch . . .'. Erlebnis und Wirkung des Ersten Weltkriegs*, Essen 1993, pp. 85–114.

Kreutzmüller, Christoph. 'Die Erfassung der Juden im Reichskommissariat der besetzten niederländischen Gebiete', in: Johannes Hürter and Jürgen Zarusky (Eds), *Besatzung, Kollaboration, Holocaust. Neue Studien zur Verfolgung und Ermordung der europäischen Juden*, Munich 2008, pp. 21–44.

Kunz, Andreas. 'Justizakten aus NSG-Verfahren. Eine quellenkundliche Handreichung für Archivbenutzer', in: *Die Außenstelle Ludwigsburg, Mitteilungen aus dem Bundesarchiv* (2008).

Kwiet, Konrad. '"Mussert Juden" und die "Lösung der Judenfrage" in den Niederlanden', in: Hermann Graml, Angelika Königseder and Juliane Wetzel (Eds), *Vorurteil und Rassenhaß. Antisemitismus in den faschistischen Bewegungen Europas*, Berlin 2001, pp. 151–68.

Kwiet, Konrad and Eschwege, Helmut. *Selbstbehauptung und Widerstand. Deutsche Juden im Kampf um Existenz und Menschenwürde 1933–1945*, Hamburg 1984.

Lang, Hans-Joachim. *Die Namen der Nummern. Wie es gelang, die 86 Opfer eines NS-Verbrechens zu identifizieren*, Hamburg 2004.

Latour, Anny. *La résistance juive en France (1940–1944)*, Paris 1970.

Laub, Dori. 'Zeugnis ablegen oder Die Schwierigkeiten des Zuhörens', in: Ulrich Baer (Ed.), *'Niemand zeugt für den Zeugen'. Erinnerungskultur nach der Shoah*, Frankfurt am Main 2000, pp. 68–83.

Lazare, Lucien. *La résistance Juive en France*, Paris 1987.

Lazare, Lucien. *Dictionnaire des Justes de France (titres décernés de 1962 à 1999)*, Jerusalem/Paris 2003.

Lazare, Lucien, 'Introduction: Les combattants de la résistance juive à vocation communitaire', in: Les Anciens de la Résistance juive en France, *Organisation Juive de Combat. Résistance/sauvtage, France 1940–1945*, 2006, pp. 19–36.

Lazarus, Jacques. 'Dans le dernier wagon qui quitta Drancy', in: *La terre retrouvée* I (September 1944), 18.

Lazarus, Jacques. 'Dans le dernier wagon qui quitta Drancy', in: *La terre retrouvée* II (November 1944), 1.

Lazarus, Jacques. *Combattants de la liberté*, Paris 1995.

Lazarus, Jacques. ‚L'enfant martyr du dernier wagon de déportation', in: *L'Arche* (January 2001) 515.

Leo, Gerhard. *Frühzug nach Toulouse*, Berlin 1988.

Les Anciens de la Résistance juive en France. *Organisation Juive de Combat. Résistance/sauvtage. France 1940–1945*, 2006.

Lessing, Theodor. *Geschichte als Sinngebung des Sinnlosen. Oder die Geburt der Geschichte aus dem Mythos*, Hamburg 1962.

Levi, Primo. *Die Untergegangenen und die Geretteten*, Munich/Vienna 1990.

Liempt, Ad van. *Kopfgeld. Bezahlte Denunziation von Juden in den besetzten Niederlanden*, Munich 2005.

Lindeman, Yehudi. 'All or Nothing: The Rescue Mission of Joop Westerweel', in: David Scrase, Wolfgang Mieder and Katherine Quimby Johnson, *Making a Difference. Rescue and Assistance during the Holocaust*, Burlington 2004, pp. 241–65.

Lindwer, Willy. *Kamp van hoop en wanhoop. Getuigen van Westerbork. 1939–1945*, Amsterdam 1990.

Lotfi, Gabriele. *KZ der Gestapo. Arbeitserziehungslager im Dritten Reich*, Frankfurt am Main 2003.

Lublin, Aron. 'L'organisation juive de combat (OJC)', in: *Le Monde Juif. Revue d'histoire de la Shoah* (1994) 152.

Ludewig-Kedmi, Revital. *Moraldilemmata jüdischer Funktionshäftlinge in der Shoah*. Gießen 2001.

Lustiger, Arno. *Zum Kampf auf Leben und Tod! Vom Widerstand der Juden 1933–1945*. Cologne 1994.

Mageen, Nathan. *Zwischen Abend und Morgenrot. Eine Geschichte aus dem niederländischen Widerstand*, Düsseldorf 2005.
Majerus, Benoît. 'Belgien: Der Widerstand gegen die NS-Okkupation 1940-1945', in: Gerd R. Ueberschär (Ed.), *Handbuch zum Widerstand gegen den Nationalsozialismus und Faschismus in Europa 1933/39 bis 1945*, Berlin/New York 2011, pp. 125-35.
Mall, Volker, and Roth, Harald. *Jeder Mensch hat einen Namen. Gedenkbuch für die 600 jüdischen Häftlinge des KZ-Außenlagers Hailfingen/Tailfingen*, Berlin 2009.
Mallmann, Klaus-Michael. 'Vom Fußvolk der "Endlösung". Ordnungspolizei, Ostkrieg und Judenmord', in: *Tel Aviver Jahrbuch für deutsche Geschichte* 26 (1997), pp. 355-91.
Mallmann, Klaus-Michael. 'Frankreichs fremde Patrioten. Deutsche in der Résistance', in: *Internationales Jahrbuch für Exilforschung* 15 (1997): Exil und Widerstand, pp. 33-65.
Margulies, Hans. 'Hans Margulies', in: *Willy Lindwer, Kamp van hoop en wanhoop. Getuigen van Westerbork. 1939-1945*, Amsterdam 1990.
Marrus, Michael R., and Paxton, Robert O. 'The Nazis and the Jews in Occupied Western Europe 1940-44', in: *Journal of Modern History* 54 (1982) 4, pp. 687-714.
Marrus, Michael R., and Paxton Robert O. *Vichy France and the Jews*, Stanford 1995.
Martens, Stefan (Ed.). *Frankreich und Belgien unter deutscher Besatzung 1940-1944. Die Bestände des Bundesarchiv-Militärarchivs Freiburg*. Revised by Sebastian Remus, Stuttgart 2002.
Matthäus, Jürgen. 'An vorderster Front. Voraussetzungen für die Beteiligung der Ordnungspolizei an der Shoah', in: Gerhard Paul (Ed.), *Die Täter der Shoah. Fanatische Nationalsozialisten oder ganz normale Deutsche?*, Göttingen 2002, pp. 137-67.
Matthäus, Jürgen, and Georg Heuser. 'Routinier des sicherheitspolizeilichen Osteinsatzes', in: Klaus-Michael Mallmann and Gerhard Paul (Eds), *Karrieren der Gewalt. Nationalsozialistische Täterbiographien*, Darmstadt 2011, pp. 115-25.
Mechanicus, Philip. *Im Depot. Tagebuch aus Westerbork*, Berlin 1993.
Meckl, Markus. 'Unter zweifacher Hoheit: Das Auffanglager Breendonk zwischen Militärverwaltung und SD', in: Wolfgang Benz and Barbara Distel (Eds), *Terror im Westen. Nationalsozialistische Lager in den Niederlanden, Belgien und Luxemburg 1940-1945*, Berlin 2004, pp. 25-38.
Meershoek, Guus. 'Machtentfaltung und Scheitern. Sicherheitspolizei und SD in den Niederlanden', in: Gerhard Paul and Klaus-Michael Mallmann (Eds), *Die Gestapo im Zweiten Weltkrieg. 'Heimatfront' und besetztes Europa*, Darmstadt 2000, pp. 383-402.
Meinen, Insa. 'Die Deportation der Juden aus Belgien und das Devisenschutzcommando', in: Johannes Hürter and Jürgen Zarusky (Eds), *Besatzung, Kollaboration, Holocaust. Neue Studien zur Verfolgung und Ermordung der europäischen Juden*, Munich 2008, pp. 45-79.
Meinen, Insa. *Die Shoah in Belgien*, Darmstadt 2009.
Meinen, Insa, and Meyer, Ahlrich. 'Le XXIe convoi: études biographiques (Première partie)', in: *Les Cahiers de la Mémoire contemporaine, Bijdragen tot de eigentijdse Herinnering* 7 (2006-2007), p. 77.
Meinen, Insa, and Meyer, Ahlrich. 'Le XXIe convoi: études biographiques (Deuxième partie)', in: *Les Cahiers de la Mémoire contemporaine, Bijdragen tot de eigentijdse Herinnering*, 2008.

Meinen, Insa, and Meyer, Ahlrich. *Verfolgt von Land zu Land. Jüdische Flüchtlinge in Westeuropa 1938–1944*, Paderborn 2013.

Meyer, Ahlrich. '"Fremde Elemente." Die osteuropäisch-jüdische Immigration, die "Endlösung der Judenfrage" und die Anfänge der Widerstandsbewegung in Frankreich', in: *Arbeitsmigration und Flucht. Vertreibung und Arbeitskräfteregulierung im Zwischenkriegseuropa, Beiträge zur nationalsozialistischen Gesundheits- und Sozialpolitik*, Vol. 11, Berlin/Göttingen 1993, pp. 82–129.

Meyer, Ahlrich. *Die deutsche Besatzung in Frankreich 1940–1944. Widerstandsbekämpfung und Judenverfolgung*, Darmstadt 2000.

Meyer, Ahlrich. *Täter im Verhör. Die 'Endlösung der Judenfrage' in Frankreich 1940–1944*, Darmstadt 2005.

Meyer, Ahlrich. *Das Wissen um Auschwitz. Täter und Opfer der 'Endlösung' in Westeuropa*, Paderborn 2010.t

Micheels, Louis J. *Doctor #117641. A Holocaust Memoir*, New Haven/London 1989.

Michman, Dan. 'Die jüdische Emigration und die niederländische Reaktion zwischen 1933 und 1940', in: Kathinka Dittrich and Hans Würzner (Eds), *Die Niederlande und das deutsche Exil 1933–1940*, Königstein 1982, pp. 93–108.

Michman, Dan. 'Zionist Youth Movements in Holland and Belgium and Their Activities during the Shoah', in: Asher Cohen and Yehoyakim Cochavi (Eds), *Zionist Youth Movements during the Shoah*, New York et al. 1995, pp. 145–71.

Miquel, Marc von. *Ahnden oder amnestieren? Westdeutsche Justiz und Vergangenheitspolitik in den sechziger Jahren*, Göttingen 2004.

Moll, Martin. *'Führer-Erlasse' 1939–1945*, Stuttgart 1997.

Moore, Bob. *Refugees from Nazi Germany in the Netherlands 1933–1940*, Dordrecht 1986.

Moore, Bob. 'The Rescue of Jews from Nazi Persecution: A Western European Perspective', in: *Journal of Genocide Research* (June 2003) 2, pp. 293–308.

Moore, Bob. *Survivors. Jewish Self-Help and Rescue in Nazi-Occupied Western Europe*, Oxford/New York 2010.

Moore, Bob. 'Niederlande: Anpassung – Opposition – Widerstand', in: Gerd R. Ueberschär (Ed.), *Handbuch zum Widerstand gegen den Nationalsozialismus und Faschismus in Europa 1933/39 bis 1945*, Berlin/New York 2011, pp. 111–23.

Pätzold, Kurt, and Schwarz, Erika. *'Auschwitz war für mich nur ein Bahnhof'. Franz Novak – der Transportoffizier Adolf Eichmanns*, Berlin 1994.

Piper, Franciszek. 'Die Rolle des Lagers Auschwitz bei der Verwirklichung der nationalsozialistischen Ausrottungspolitik. Die doppelte Funktion von Auschwitz als Konzentrationslager und als Zentrum der Judenvernichtung', in: Ulrich Herbert, Karin Orth, and Christoph Dieckmann (Eds), *Die nationalsozialistischen Konzentrationslager. Entwicklung und Struktur*, Vol. I, Göttingen 1998, pp. 390–414.

Pohl, Dieter. 'Vernichtungskrieg. Der Feldzug gegen die Sowjetunion 1941–1944 im globalen Kontext', in: *Einsicht. Bulletin des Fritz Bauer Instituts* (2011) 6, pp. 16–31.

Pollak, Michael. *Die Grenzen des Sagbaren. Lebensgeschichten von KZ-Überlebenden als Augenzeugenberichte und als Identitätsarbeit*, Frankfurt am Main/New York 1988.

Prauser, Steffen. 'Frankreich: Résistance gegen Kollaboration und Besatzungsmacht 1940–1944', in: Gerd R. Ueberschär (Ed.), *Handbuch zum Widerstand gegen den Nationalsozialismus und Faschismus in Europa 1933/39 bis 1945*, Berlin/New York 2011.

Presser, Jacques. *Ashes in the Wind. The Destruction of Dutch Jewry*, Detroit 1988.
Prowizur-Szyper, Claire. *Conte à rebours: Une résistante juive sous l'occupation*, Brussels 1982.
Prowizur-Szyper, Claire. *Instantanés d'ici et d'ailleurs*, Brussels 1982.
Przeworski, Adam, and Teune, Henry. *The Logic of Comparative Social Inquiry*, New York et al. 1970.
Rajsfus, Maurice. *Drancy. Un camp de concentration très ordinaire*, Paris 1996.
Rayski, Adam. 'Face à l'extermination et au secret', in: Stéphane Courtois and Adam Rayski, *Qui savait quoi? L'extermination des Juifs, 1941–1945*, Paris 1987.
Rayski, Adam. 'Le combat contre le grand secret', in: Stéphane Courtois and Adam Rayski, *Qui savait quoi? L'extermination des Juifs, 1941–1945*, Paris 1987.
Röhr, Werner. 'System oder organisiertes Chaos? Fragen einer Typologie der deutschen Okkupationsregime im Zweiten Weltkrieg', in: Robert Bohn (Ed.), *Die deutsche Herrschaft in den 'germanischen' Ländern 1940–1945*, Stuttgart 1997, pp. 11–46.
Romijn, Peter. 'Die Nazifizierung der lokalen Verwaltung in den besetzten Niederlanden als Instrument bürokratischer Kontrolle', in: Wolfgang Benz, Johannes Houwink ten Cate, and Gerhard Otto (Eds), *Die Bürokratie der Okkupation. Strukturen der Herrschaft und Verwaltung im besetzten Europa*, Berlin 1998, pp. 93–121.
Romijn, Peter. 'Kein Raum für Ambivalenzen. Der Chef der niederländischen inneren Verwaltung K. J. Frederiks', in: Gerhard Hirschfeld and Tobias Jersak (Eds), *Karrieren im Nationalsozialismus. Funktionseliten zwischen Mitwirkung und Distanz*, Frankfurt am Main 2004, pp. 147–71.
Rood, Coen. *'Wenn ich es nicht erzählen kann, muß ich weinen'. Als Zwangsarbeiter in der Rüstungsindustrie*, Frankfurt am Main 2002.
Rousso, Henry. *Vichy. Frankreich unter deutscher Besatzung 1940–1944*, Munich 2009.
Rudorff, Andrea. 'Laurahütte (Siemianowice Śląskie)', in: Wolfgang Benz and Barbara Distel (Eds), *Der Ort des Terrors. Geschichte der nationalsozialistischen Konzentrationslager. Bd. 5: Hinzert, Auschwitz, Neuengamme*, Munich 2007, pp. 270–73.
Rudorff, Andrea. 'Neu-Dachs (Jaworzno)', in: Wolfgang Benz and Barbara Distel (Eds), *Der Ort des Terrors. Geschichte der nationalsozialistischen Konzentrationslager. Bd. 5: Hinzert, Auschwitz, Neuengamme*, Munich 2007, pp. 284–89.
Rudorff, Andrea. 'Das Lagersystem der "Organisation Schmelt" in Schlesien', in: Wolfgang Benz and Barbara Distel (Eds), *Der Ort des Terrors. Geschichte der nationalsozialistischen Konzentrationslager. Vol. 9: Arbeitserziehungslager, Ghettos, Jungendschutzlager, Polizeihaftlager, Sonderlager, Zigeunerlager, Zwangsarbeitslager*, Munich 2009, pp. 155–60.
Rüter, C. F., and Mildt, D. W. de (Eds). *Justiz und NS-Verbrechen. Die deutschen Strafverfahren wegen nationalsozialistischer Tötungsverbrechen*, Vol. XLVII, Amsterdam 2011.
Rutkowski, Adam. 'Les évasions des Juifs de trains de déportation de France', in: *Le Monde Juif. La Revue du Centre de Documentation juive contemporaine*, Paris, January–March 1974.
Saerens, Lieven. *Vreemdelingen in een wereldstad. Een geschiedenis van Antwerpen en zijn joods bevolking (1880–1944)*, Tielt 2000.
Saerens, Lieven. 'Die Hilfe für Juden in Belgien', in: Wolfgang Benz and Juliane Wetzel (Eds), *Solidarität und Hilfe für Juden während der NS-Zeit. Slowakei, Bulgarien,*

Serbien, Kroatien mit Bosnien und Herzegowina, Belgien, Italien. Regionalstudien 4, Berlin 2004, pp. 193–280.

Safrian, Hans. *Eichmann und seine Gehilfen*, Frankfurt am Main 1997.

Santin, Tullia. *Der Holocaust in den Zeugnissen griechischer Jüdinnen und Juden*, Berlin 2003.

Schelvis, Jules. *Vernichtungslager Sobibór*, Hamburg/Münster 2003.

Schmalz, Florian, 'Die Gaskammer im Konzentrationslager Natzweiler. Experimentenanlage der Chemiewaffenforschung und Instrument des Massenmords für den Aufbau einer anatomischen Skelettsammlung', in: Günter Morsch and Bertrand Perz (Eds), *Neue Studien zu nationalsozialistischen Massentötungen durch Giftgas*, Berlin 2011.

Schmorak, Dov B. *Sieben sagen aus. Zeugen im Eichmann-Prozeß*, Berlin 1962.

Schneider, Karl. *Auswärts eingesetzt. Bremer Polizeibataillone und der Holocaust*, Essen 2011.

Schnur Harry C. 'Flucht aus Holland', in: Gerhard Schoenberner, *Wir haben es gesehen. Augenzeugenberichte über die Judenverfolgung im Dritten Reich*, Wiesbaden 1981.

Schoenberner, Gerhard (Ed.). *Wir haben es gesehen. Augenzeugenberichte über die Judenverfolgung im Dritten Reich*, Wiesbaden 1981.

Schoenberner, Gerhard. *Zeugen sagen aus. Berichte und Dokumente über die Judenverfolgung im 'Dritten Reich'*, Berlin 1998.

Schram, Laurence. 'Les déportés du vingtième transport de Malines à Auschwitz', in: Maxime Steinberg and Laurence Schram, *Transport XX. Malines-Auschwitz*, Brussels 2008.

Schreiber, Jean-Philippe. *L'immigration juive en Belgique du moyen âge à la première guerre mondiale*, Brussels 1996.

Schreiber, Jean-Philippe. *Dictionnaire biographique des Juifs de Belgique. Figures du judaïsme belge XIXe–XXe siècles*, Brussels 2002.

Schreiber, Marion. *Stille Rebellen. Der Überfall auf den 20. Deportationszug nach Auschwitz*, Berlin 2002.

Schwarberg, Günther. *Der SS-Arzt und die Kinder. Bericht über den Mord vom Bullenhuser Damm*, Göttingen 1989.

Schwarz, Fred. *Züge auf falschem Gleis*, Vienna 1996.

Seibel, Wolfgang, and Raab, Jörg. 'Verfolgungsnetzwerke. Zur Messung von Arbeitsteilung und Machtdifferenzierung in den Verfolgungsapparaten des Holocaust', in: *Kölner Zeitschrift für Soziologie und Sozialpsychologie* (2003) 2, pp. 197–230.

Seidel, Irmgard. 'Jüdische Frauen in den Außenkommandos des KZ Buchenwald', in: Gisela Bock (Ed.), *Genozid und Geschlecht*, Frankfurt am Main/New York 2005, pp. 149–68.

Semprun, Jorge. *Die große Reise*, Stuttgart 1981.

Siegel, Paul. *In ungleichem Kampf – Von Köln nach Holland durch Westerbork über Frankreich und Spanien nach Israel 1924–1947. Christlich-jüdische Hilfsaktion der Westerweel-Gruppe*, Konstanz 2001.

Sofsky, Wolfgang. *Die Ordnung des Terrors: Das Konzentrationslager*, Frankfurt am Main 1997.

Spieker, Christoph. 'Von der Germanisierung zur Repression: Funktion und Politik der deutschen Ordnungspolizei in den Niederlanden 1943', in: Norbert Fasse, Johannes Houwink ten Cate, and Horst Lademacher (Eds), *Nationalsozialistische*

Herrschaft und Besatzungszeit. Historische Erfahrung und Verarbeitung aus niederländischer und deutscher Sicht, Münster 2000, pp. 179–90.

Spieker, Christoph. 'Enttäuschte Liebe: Funktionswandel der Ordnungspolizei in den Niederlanden', in: Johannes Houwink ten Cate and Alfons Kenkmann (Eds), *Deutsche und holländische Polizei in den besetzten niederländischen Gebieten. Dokumentation einer Arbeitstagung*, Münster 2002, pp. 67–95.

Spritzer, Jenny. *Ich war Nr. 10291. Tatsachenbericht einer Schreiberin der politischen Abteilung aus dem Konzentrationslager Auschwitz*, Darmstadt 1980.

Steinberg, Lucien. 'Un aspect peu connu de la résistance juive: le sauvetage à main armée', in: *Le Monde Juif* (1968) 52.

Steinberg, Lucien. *Le Comité de défense des Juifs en Belgique 1942–1944*, Brussels 1973.

Steinberg, Maxime. *Dossier Bruxelles-Auschwitz. La police SS et l'extermination des Juifs de Belgique*, Brussels 1980.

Steinberg, Maxime. *1942. Les cent jours de la déportation des Juifs de Belgique*, Brussels 1984.

Steinberg, Maxime. *L'Étoile et le fusil. La traque des Juifs 1942–1944*, Vol. I, Brussels 1986.

Steinberg, Maxime. *L'Étoile et le fusil. La traque des Juifs 1942–1944*, Vol. II, Brussels 1986.

Steinberg, Maxime. *Un pays occupé et ses Juifs. Belgique entre France et Pays-Bas*, Gerpinnes 1998.

Steinberg, Maxime. *La Persecution des Juifs en Belgique (1940–1945)*, Brussels 2004.

Steinberg, Maxime. 'Le Bulgare Théodore Angheloff et ses partisans juifs de la MOI à Bruxelles (1942–1943)', in: Maxime Steinberg and José Gotovitch, *Otages de la terreur nazie. Le Bulgare Angheloff et son groupe de Partisans juifs Bruxelles, 1940–1943*, Brussels 2007.

Steinberg, Maxime. 'L'exeption du vingtième transport', in: Maxime Steinberg and Laurence Schram, *Transport XX. Malines-Auschwitz*, Brussels 2008.

Steinberg, Maxime, and Schram, Laurence. *Transport XX. Malines-Auschwitz*, Brussels 2008.

Steinberg, Maxime, and Schram, Laurence. 'Mecheln-Auschwitz: The Destruction of the Jews and Gypsies from Belgium 1942–1944', in: Ward Adriaens et al. (Eds), *Mecheln-Auschwitz 1942–1944. De vernietiging van de Joden en zigeuners van België. La destruction des Juifs et des Tsiganes de Belgique. The destruction of the Jews and Gypsies from Belgium*, Vol. 1, Brussels 2009.

Steinberg, Maxime, and Schram, Laurence. 'Transport XVIII', in: Ward Adriaens et al. (Eds), *Mecheln-Auschwitz. Gezichten van gedeporteerden: transporten 14–26. Visages des déportés: transports 14–26. Faces of the Deportees: Transports 14–26*, Vol. 3, Brussels 2009.

Steinberg, Maxime, and Schram, Laurence. 'Transport XIX', in: Ward Adriaens et al. (Eds), *Mecheln-Auschwitz. Gezichten van gedeporteerden: transporten 14–26. Visages des déportés: transports 14–26. Faces of the Deportees: Transports 14–26*, Vol. 3, Brussels 2009.

Steiner, Hugues. 'Le témoignage de Hugues Steiner', in: Henry Bulawko (Ed.), *Les Jeux de la mort et de l'espoir. Auschwitz/Jaworzno. Auschwitz – 50 ans après*, Paris 1993.

Steinkamp, Peter. 'Rettungswiderstand: Helfer in Uniform', in: Johannes Tuchel (Ed.), *Der vergessene Widerstand. Zu Realgeschichte und Wahrnehmung des Kampfes gegen die NS-Diktatur*, Göttingen 2005, pp. 140–57.

Steur, Claudia. *Theodor Dannecker. Ein Funktionär der 'Endlösung'*, Essen 1997.
Strobl, Ingrid. *'Sag nie, du gehst den letzten Weg'. Frauen im bewaffneten Widerstand gegen Faschismus und deutsche Besatzung*, Frankfurt am Main 1989.
Strobl, Ingrid. *Die Angst kam erst danach. Jüdische Frauen im Widerstand in Europa 1939–1945*, Frankfurt am Main 1998.
't Hart-Velt, W. S. *Ik zou in mijn tranen willen wegzwemmen. Ontvluchtingen van Kamp Westerbork 1940–1945*, unpublished dissertation, 2003.
Thalhofer, Elisabeth. *Entgrenzung der Gewalt. Gestapo-Lager in der Endphase des Dritten Reiches*, Paderborn 2010.
Thiel, Jens. *Menschenbassin Belgien. Anwerbung, Deportation und Zwangsarbeit im Ersten Weltkrieg*, Essen 2007.
Thorpe, Janet. *Nous n'irons pas à Pitchipoï. Le tunnel du camp de Drancy*, Paris 2004.
Tuchel, Johannes, and Schattenfroh, Reinold. *Zentrale des Terrors. Prinz-Albrecht-Straße 8: Hauptquartier der Gestapo*, Berlin 1987.
Veen, Egbert J. van der. 'Yaagje naar de vrijheid. De sprong naar het leven van Sonja Wagenaar-van Dam', in: *Westerbork Cahiers* 6 (1998).
Vered, Yael. *Là où il n'y a pas d'hommes tâche d'être un homme . . .* , Paris 2006.
Von zur Mühlen, Patrik. *Fluchtweg Spanien – Portugal. Die deutsche Emigration und der Exodus aus Europa 1933–1945*, Bonn 1992.
Vrba, Rudolf, and Bestic, Alan. *Ich kann nicht vergeben*, Munich 1964.
Wegner, Bernd. *Hitlers politische Soldaten: Die Waffen-SS 1933–1945. Leitbild, Struktur und Funktion einer nationalsozialistischen Elite*, Paderborn 1999.
Weinhauer, Klaus. 'NS-Vergangenheit und struktureller Wandel der Schutzpolizei der 1950/60er Jahre', in: Wolfgang Schulte (Ed.), *Die Polizei im NS-Staat. Beiträge eines internationalen Symposiums an der Deutschen Hochschule der Polizei in Münster*, Frankfurt am Main 2009, pp. 139–58.
Weinke, Annette. *Eine Gesellschaft ermittelt gegen sich selbst. Die Geschichte der Zentralen Stelle Ludwigsburg 1958–2008*, Darmstadt 2008.
Weinmann, Martin (Ed.). *Das nationalsozialistische Lagersystem*, Frankfurt am Main. 1990.
Weinstock, Rolf. *Das wahre Gesicht Hitler-Deutschlands. Dachau-Auschwitz-Buchenwald. Häftling Nr. 59 000 erzählt von dem Schicksal der 10 000 Juden aus Baden, aus der Pfalz und aus dem Saargebiet in den Höllen von Dachau, Gurs-Drancy, Auschwitz, Jawischowitz, Buchenwald*, Singen 1948.
Wellers, Georges. *De Drancy à Auschwitz*, Paris 1946.
West- und Nordeuropa 1940 – Juni 1942, Die Verfolgung und Ermordung der europäischen Juden durch das nationalsozialistische Deutschland 1933–1945, Vol. 5, edited by Katja Happe, Michael Mayer, Maja Peers, collaboration: Jean-Marc-Dreyfus, Munich 2012.
Wijnperle, Nathan. *Zou ik het willen overdoen? Het levensverhaal van een joodse overlevende*, Sittard 1996.
Wildt, Michael. *Generation der Unbedingten. Das Führungskorps des Reichssicherheitshauptamtes*, Hamburg 2003.
Wouters, Nico. 'La chasse aux Juifs, 1942–1944', in: Rudi van Doorslaer et al. (Eds), *La Belgique docile. Les autorités belges et la persécution des Juifs en Belgique durant la Seconde Guerre mondiale*, Brussels 2006.
Wouters, Nico. 'Völkermord vor belgischen Militärtribunalen am Beispiel der ge-

richtlichen Ahndung von Verbrechen an Juden und Jüdinnen (1944–1951)', in: Heimo Halbrainer and Claudia Kuretsidis-Haider (Eds), *Kriegsverbrechen, NS-Gewaltverbrechen und die europäische Strafjustiz von Nürnberg bis Den Haag*, Graz 2007, pp. 171–91.

Yigael, Benjamin. *They Were Our Friends. A Memorial for the Members of the Hachsharot and the Hehalutz Underground in Holland Murdered in the Holocaust*, Tel Aviv 1990.

Zaich, Katja B. 'Das Sammellager Hollandsche Schouwburg in Amsterdam', in: Wolfgang Benz and Barbara Distel (Eds), *Terror im Westen. Nationalsozialistische Lager in den Niederlanden, Belgien und Luxemburg 1940–1945*, Berlin 2004, pp. 181–96.

Zee, Nanda van der. *'Um Schlimmeres zu verhindern'. Die Ermordung der niederländischen Juden: Kollaboration und Widerstand*, Munich/Vienna 1999.

Zeller, Ron, and Griffioen, Pim. 'Judenverfolgung in den Niederlanden und in Belgien während des Zweiten Weltkriegs: eine vergleichende Analyse', Part 1, in: *1999. Zeitschrift für Sozialgeschichte des 20. und 21. Jahrhunderts* (1996) 3, pp. 30–54.

Zeller, Ron, and Griffioen, Pim. 'Judenverfolgung in den Niederlanden und in Belgien während des Zweiten Weltkriegs: eine vergleichende Analyse', Part 2, in: *1999. Zeitschrift für Sozialgeschichte des 20. und 21. Jahrhunderts* (1997) 1, pp. 29–48.

Zuccotti, Susan. *The Holocaust, the French, and the Jews*, New York 1993.

Index of Places

This index lists places where people lived, fled, and were persecuted, imprisoned and interned.

Aachen, 102, 149, 152, 176, 186
Amersfoort, 230, 241, 249
Amsterdam, 8, 34, 78, 102, 117, 122, 128, 159, 208–210, 214–216, 219, 224–6, 228, 230, 232, 234–236, 239–244, 246, 259
Angers, 48
Annemasse, 99
Antwerp, 24, 34, 61, 129, 133, 136–138, 140, 143, 146, 151–152, 159, 178, 184–186, 188, 191, 199–200
Apeldoorn, 212
Arnhem, 212, 222, 228–229
Assen, 213
Auschwitz (Auschwitz I), 1–3, 13–14, 18, 20, 22–25, 27–29, 33–35, 45, 48, 50, 52–53, 55–57, 60, 63, 68, 71, 75, 89, 90, 92, 100, 105, 110, 114–124, 126, 129, 142–143, 146, 148–158, 160, 162–163, 166, 169, 172, 175, 179, 181–187, 189–201, 212–213, 216–227, 232, 234, 236, 238–239, 242–245, 248, 250–251, 261
Auschwitz-Birkenau (Auschwitz II), 21, 110, 153, 155, 194
Auschwitz-Blechhammer. *See* Blechhammer
Auschwitz-Jawischowitz. *See* Jawischowitz
Auschwitz-Jaworzno (Neu-Dachs). *See* Jaworzno
Auschwitz-Laurahütte. *See* Laurahütte
Auschwitz-Monowitz (Auschwitz III), 155–156, 183, 194, 199
Auschwitz-Neu Dachs. *See* Jaworzno

Bar-le-Duc, 67, 73, 81, 96
Barneveld, 228
Bastogne, 155
Beaune-la-Rolande, 43, 46, 48, 50, 84
Beilen, 234
Bełżec, 13, 35
Bergen-Belsen, 23, 110–111, 143, 161, 212, 218, 221–222, 231–232, 243, 245, 249
Berlin, 13, 15, 23, 30, 32–33, 35–36, 75, 89, 102, 113, 116, 119, 124–126, 130, 137, 145, 147, 151, 154, 156, 175, 186–190, 195, 199, 232, 239, 241–243, 246, 254
Besançon, 61
Birkenau. *See* Auschwitz-Birkenau
Blechhammer, 90
Bobigny, 48, 92, 104, 117
Bolzano, 64
Boortmeerbeek, 165
Borgloon, 174
Bottrop, 31, 36
Boulogne-sur-Mer, 155
Boutersem, 159, 163
Brätz, 77, 122
Breendonk, 143, 152, 165, 168, 178, 189, 193, 197–199

Bremen, 14, 26, 28, 35, 148, 216, 222, 224
Brummen, 229
Brussels, 3, 7, 8, 13–14, 24, 128, 135–137, 139, 140–141, 143–147, 149, 151–152, 155–158, 160, 162, 166–170, 173–178, 180, 182–189, 191, 193, 197–198, 259, 261
Brussels-Etterbeek, 156
Brussels-Forest, 163, 166, 178, 185
Brussels-Molenbeek, 157
Brussels-Saint-Gilles, 157–158, 162, 168, 176, 178, 182, 185
Buchenwald, 48, 60, 77, 102, 106, 109–11, 118, 127, 130–131, 143, 153, 162, 166, 175, 179, 189, 194, 197–199
Buchenwald-Langenstein. See Langenstein
Buchenwald-Lippstadt. See Lippstadt
Buchenwald-Mittelbau-Dora. See Mittelbau-Dora
Buchenwald-Raghun. See Raghun
Buchenwald-Witten-Annen. See Witten-Annen
Budapest, 94
Bussum, 234

Calais, 185
Casteau, 156
Castres, 128
Cattovice, 178
Châlons-sur-Marne, 69, 117
Cham, 110
Changis-sur-Marne, 80
Charleroi, 136
Chaumont, 73
Chełm (Russian: Cholm), 75–76, 82, 100
Chemnitz, 185, 201
Colmar, 59
Cologne, 31, 36, 115, 147, 149, 161, 163, 228, 244
Commercy, 73
Compiègne, 48–50, 57–58, 73, 78, 93
Cosel (Kozle), 18, 24, 60, 129, 146, 151, 216, 223

Cracow, 75, 178

Dachau, 89–90, 110, 116, 124, 175, 183
Dachau-Karlsfeld. See Karlsfeld
Dachau-Mühldorf. See Mühldorf
Dammartin-en-Goële, 106
Dannenberg, 124
Dannes-Camiers, 136, 154–155
Darmstadt, 13–14, 36, 83, 87–89, 114, 118
Dieren, 227
Dijon, 61
Dornheim, 87
Dossinkaserne. See Mechelen
Drancy, 21–22, 24, 33, 43, 46, 48–53, 55, 57–59, 61–62, 64–65, 68–72, 74–79, 82–84, 90, 92–94, 97–101, 104–105, 116–117, 119–126, 128–129, 156, 254–255, 261
Dresden, 89
Düsseldorf, 32, 115, 117, 149, 161, 175–176

Ebensee, 225
Ellecom, 230
Épernay, 51, 82–83, 85, 86, 91
Ernecourt, 73
Erneville-aux-Bois, 73
Essen, 14, 34–35, 114, 137, 183, 187, 242
Eupen, 135, 186
Euskirchen, 137, 186, 194

Fléron, 155
Flossenbürg, 110, 185, 201
Flossenbürg-Chemnitz. See Chemnitz
Forest. See Brussels-Forest
Fort Breendonk. See Breendonk
Frankfurt (Main), 13, 15, 30, 32–33, 35–37, 53, 82, 87–89, 99, 113–115, 122, 124–125, 131, 241, 243
Frankfurt (Oder), 77
Fréjus, 78
Fresnes, 102, 104
Friesland, 235, 238

Geneva, 152

Gleiwitz, 239
Gouda, 102
Groningen, 184, 218, 250–251
Gross-Gerau, 87–88
Gross-Rosen, 60, 179, 199
Gurs, 12, 63, 75–77, 116, 151–152, 156
Gusen, 90, 124, 161

Haarlem, 210, 242, 245
Halle, 178, 183
Hamburg, 14, 15, 76, 110, 114, 124, 131, 186, 245, 262
Hamm, 149
Hanover, 161
Hanover-Mühlenberg, 161, 196
Haren, 225
Hasselt, 154, 181
Hechtel, 157
Heidenheim, 221
Herzogenbusch. *See* Vught
Heydebrecht, 216
Hollandsche Schouwburg, 214, 224, 244
Hooghalen, 216
Hoyerswerda, 216
Huy, 176

Jawischowitz, 116, 152–153
Jaworzno (Neu-Dachs), 123, 157, 195
Juvisy-sur-Orge, 84

Kaiserslautern, 86
Karlsfeld, 89
Kassel, 89
Kasselbach, 87
Kiel, 181, 192
Kleinmachnow, 166
Koblenz, 158, 195
Kohlfurt, 218
Kovno, 48, 64
Krefeld, 183, 200

Langenstein, 60
Laon, 106
Laurahütte, 160–161, 196
Lausanne, 152
Le Bourget, 48, 68, 72, 76, 79, 82

Lérouville, 91–92
Les Milles, 152
Leuven, 147, 155, 159, 161, 168, 177
Liège, 63, 111, 154–159, 161–162, 172, 178–179, 183, 194–195
Liegnitz, 182
Limbourg, 151, 157
Limoges, 98
Lippstadt, 110
Litzmannstadt, 123, 176
Łódź, 100, 155, 176
London, 13, 22, 126, 245
Longeville-en-Barrois, 97
Longwy, 63
Loosdrecht, 102
Loxéville, 73
Lublin, 18, 32, 75–76, 83, 115, 119, 122, 128
Ludwigsburg, 11, 15, 30, 32, 36
Ludwigshafen, 86
Lviv, 64
Lyon, 48, 58, 75, 122

Magdeburg, 216
Majdanek, 48, 76–77
Malines. *See* Mechelen
Malmedy, 135, 186
Margival, 106
Marseille, 77–79, 123, 178
Mauthausen, 23, 90, 124, 186, 196, 208–9, 225, 248
Mauthausen-Ebensee. *See* Ebensee
Mauthausen-Siebenhirten. *See* Siebenhirten
Mechelen, 1, 8, 24, 138, 141–145, 147–192, 235, 255, 257–9
Memel, 178
Meppel, 236–237
Merksplas, 178, 199
Metz, 33, 55, 57, 75–76, 83, 85–86, 120, 122
Mittelbau-Dora, 111, 131, 166
Molenbeek. *See* Brussels-Molenbeek
Momalle, 157
Monowitz. *See* Auschwitz-Monowitz
Montpellier, 46
Moosburg, 63–64, 83

Morcourt, 130
Mühldorf, 89–90
Muizen, 153
Mülhausen, 55
Munich, 20, 32–33, 35, 37 63, 114, 127, 187, 190, 195, 201, 239, 240, 265
Münster, 26, 35, 37, 55, 116, 123, 240, 245–246
Mussy, 68

Namur, 160
Nançois-sur-Ornain, 73
Nancy, 67, 72, 121
Natzweiler-Struthof, 89
Neuburg an der Mosel, 51, 54, 57, 68–69, 71–73, 75–77, 81, 90–92, 121, 123
Neu-Dachs. *See* Jaworzno
Neuenburg, 118
Neuengamme, 110, 161, 195
Neuengamme-Hanover-Mühlenberg. *See* Hanover-Mühlenberg
Neustadt, 163
Nice, 58, 95–96, 255
Nieuweschans, 216
Nieuwleusen, 238
Novéant-sur-Moselle. *See* Neuburg an der Mosel

Ostrava, 18

Paris, 7, 8, 14, 26, 30, 33, 39–61, 65, 68, 70, 75–76, 83–84, 87–90, 92, 94–96, 98, 101–104, 108–109, 114–131, 178, 180, 185, 254, 261
Petit Château, 178
Pilsen, 185
Pithiviers, 43, 48, 50, 60, 156
Plauen, 89
Prague, 185, 208
Pyskowice, 24

Raghun, 110
Ravensbrück, 143, 163
Recklinghausen, 31, 36–37
Reims, 57–58

Rekem, 178
Reval, 48
Rivesaltes, 65, 156
Rotterdam, 60, 102

Saarbrücken, 62
Sachsenhausen, 78, 166, 183, 197
Seraing, 157
Siebenhirten, 156
Sobibór, 20, 30, 35, 48, 75–76, 78, 82–83, 93, 212, 220, 234, 245, 248, 265
Spoleto, 63
Stalingrad, 171, 212, 255
St. Cyprien, 64, 104, 156, 158
Stoumont, 155
St. Quentin, 108–109
Strasbourg, 89, 101, 119
St. Trond, 159–160
Stuttgart, 26, 55, 102, 144–115, 126, 178, 189, 240, 265

Tarn, 103, 111
Tel Aviv, 14, 34, 127–129, 173, 198, 232, 246, 248, 261–262, 265
Tergnier, 106
The Hague, 186, 206, 222, 232
Theresienstadt, 13, 15, 20, 23, 33, 131, 218–219, 241, 243, 245–246, 250, 261
Tienen, 158
Tilbourg, 221
Tilsit, 121
Tirlemont, 159, 181
Tittmoning-Laufen, 100
Tongeren, 154
Toulouse, 48, 103, 108, 128, 195
Treblinka, 100, 265
Trier, 64
Tronville-en-Barrois, 73

Vélodrome d'Hiver (Paris), 46
Vichy, 26, 41–44, 49–50, 55, 114–119, 121–123, 126, 206, 242
Vienna, 32–33, 64–65, 83, 102, 111, 113, 117, 124, 128, 152, 158, 169, 178, 206, 240, 254, 265

Vilnius, 178
Visé, 152, 162
Vittel, 100, 126
Vught (Herzogenbusch, 's Hertogenbosch), 8, 213–214, 226, 233, 243, 248

Warsaw, 33, 100, 156–157

Weimar, 89, 109, 130–131
Westerbork, 3, 8, 14, 22–23, 27, 34, 103, 127, 204–206, 210, 212–220, 223–224, 226, 229–231, 233–237, 240, 242–251, 255, 258, 261
Witten-Annen, 109–110

Zwolle, 144, 216, 234, 236, 238–239

Index of Names

Abetz, Otto, 42, 44, 47, 116, 135
Abramowicz, Fanny, 160
Achenbach, Ernst, 30, 42
Adler, H. G., 1, 10, 12, 14–15, 19, 33–34, 191, 261, 264
Aerts, Jean, 174–175
Ahnert, Horst, 78, 115, 118
Ainsztein, Reuben, 2, 12, 265
Alberts, Johann, 27, 35, 223–224, 247
Althusser, Arthur, 97
Altmann, Jacques, 117–118
Altschuler, Michel, 183, 200
Amar, André, 102, 107
Améry, Jean. *See* Mayer, Hans
Angheloff, Théodore, 140, 189, 195, 199
Apfeldorfer, Simon, 185–186
Appenzeller, Ernest, 102, 104, 107, 112, 127
Ardati, René, 123
Aron, Claude, 94
Aron, Walter, 151, 193, 260
Aronowicz, Szulim, 155–156, 194–195
As, Aad van, 27, 35
Asche, Kurt, 2, 135, 141, 146–147, 149, 161, 191–192, 195–196
Aschermann, Julius, 26, 35, 233, 247
Asscher, Abraham, 216, 262
Asser, Kurt, 76–77, 122

Bach, 167
Badinter, Simon, 86
Bardian, Alfred, 88

Bargen, Werner von, 135, 137, 145, 187–190
Bauer, Fritz, 14, 30
Bauer, Yehuda, 2, 13
Baum, Jacheta, 156, 157, 196
Beck, Israel, 154, 194
Beeckmans, Pierre, 139
Behrens, Friedrich, 224, 247
Bene, Otto, 135, 206, 212, 215, 243–244
Benkiel, Josek Majer, 181–182
Bercovici, 58
Berger, Julius, 137, 154
Berger, Kurt, 161, 188, 196
Berger, Leopold, 160
Berler, Willy, 178–179, 199
Bernard, René, 97
Best, Werner, 42–45
Billerbeck, Claudius, 149
Bina, Chaj, 181
Bloch, Marcel, 104, 106–107, 112
Blok, Reina, 104–105, 200–201
Blom, J. C., 34, 211, 242
Blum, Léon, 41
Blum, Robert, 93–94
Boden, Max Hermann, 24, 33, 143, 145, 180, 190–192, 199
Boder, David, 59, 119, 265
Böhlich, Ernst, 150, 192–193, 247
Bolle, Maurits, 164–165
Bonheim, Alice, (Annaliese) 182, 200
Borchardt, Werner, 135
Bouder, Serge, 93–97, 125–126, 258, 261

Bousquet, René, 46, 78
Bradfisch, Otto 150
Bradt, Marianne, 142
Brandes-Brilleslijper, Janny, 220, 246
Brandt, Harm-Hinrich, 17, 32
Braunschweig, Pierre, 87–89
Breslerman, Ludwig, 88–89
Bretholz, Leo, 33, 64–68, 177, 120, 254, 260–261
Broad, Pery, 20, 27, 33, 35
Browning, Christopher, 14, 25, 34–35, 246
Brückler, Ernst, 95, 104–106
Brudasch, Joseph, 83
Brunner, Alois, 22, 49–52, 55, 95, 101, 104–106, 125
Brunner, Menasche Maximilian, 180, 191–192, 199
Busch, Gottlob, 35, 52, 55–56, 117–119
Buys, Max, 234–238, 250

Cahen-Salvador, Jean, 94
Cajfinger, Joseph, 97, 126
Canaris, Constantin, 135
Cats, 227
Catz, Hans, 60–63, 116, 117, 120, 258
Catz, Theo, 60–63, 258
Chaigneau, Jean-François 128–131
Chamay, César, 102, 104–107, 112, 127–131, 261
Clément, Albert, 171
Clercq, Staf de, 134
Cohen, David, 215
Cohen, Elie A., 22, 34, 116, 217, 220, 243, 245–246, 257, 261
Cohen, Ru, 230, 249
Coors, Ludwig Walter, 36, 236, 245, 247
Craushaar, Harry von, 149, 189
Cukier, Schaja, 184
Cykiert, Majlych, 154, 194
Cykiert, Maurice, 154, 194

Daigfuss, Franz-Ludwig, 31, 36, 81–82, 123
Daluege, Kurt, 42

Dannecker, Theodor, 18–19, 32–33, 42, 44, 46, 49, 52, 54, 57–58, 84, 114, 116–119
Dawid, Anna (née Salzmann), 153
Dawid, Otto, 152–153, 193
Degeler, Friedrich, 221
Degrelle, Léon, 134
De Metz, Henri, 61–63
De Metz, Jacques Marcel, 61–63
Derenthal, Meinolph, 35, 224, 247 309
De Roeck, Camille, 157
Domice (married couple), 97
Dreyfus, Robert, 94
Dubost, Lucian, 87
Dumon, 164

Eck, Nathan, 100–101, 109
Ehlers, Ernst, 135
Eichmann, Adolf, 33, 41, 47, 50, 52, 57, 68, 71, 75, 78, 114, 116–117, 120, 123, 125, 192, 241
Ekart, Lolly, 102–103
Engels, Wilhelm, 224, 247
Erdmann, Fritz, 135
Eschwege, Helmut, 2, 14

Falke, Heinrich, 222, 247
Falkenhausen, Alexander von, 135, 205
Fastag, Eva, 34, 144, 179, 190, 192
Fein, Helen, 4, 14
Fénelon, Fania, 22, 33
Fischböck, Hans, 205
Fogel, Paul, 84–86, 88, 90, 124
Fogel, Robert, 84–86, 88, 90, 124
Fouckmann, Leon, 88
Fraenkel, Alfred, 102–103, 105, 107–110, 112–113, 127, 129–131, 231–232, 249
François, Jean, 79
Frank, Gerhard Johannes, 143–144, 147–149, 190, 192
Franklemon, Jean, 165–166
Frei, Norbert, 32, 37
Fremder, Pinkus, 156–157, 195
Friedländer, Saul 2, 13, 242
Frijtag Drabbe Künzel, Geraldien von, 206, 241, 249

Fritz, Hans, 158, 195
Fritz, Monika, 158
Frydman, Jean, 106–107, 126, 128–130
Fuchs, Adolphe, 60, 120, 257
Fünten, Ferdinand Hugo aus der, 33–34, 207–208, 216
Furck, Herbert, 221

Galitzine, Olga, 104, 107
Gansel, Hermann, 28
Ganzenmüller, Albert, 32
Gehring, Otto, 56, 119
Gemmeker, Albert Konrad, 213, 217–219, 230, 234, 242, 245
Gerritsen, Frans, 232, 249
Gerschel, Georges, 94–97, 258
Gerschel, Roger, 94–98, 126
Gigliotti, Simone, 3, 14, 262–263, 265
Glogowski, Icek (gros Jacques), 193
Goebbels, Joseph, 228
Goldschmidt, Félix, 96–99, 126
Goldsteinas, Mendelis Judelis, 33, 166, 198
Goldwasser, Bertha, 58–60, 119
Goldwurm, Léopold, 24
Grabiner, Charles 184
Griffioen, Pim, 34, 145, 189–190, 206, 211, 241–242
Groenteman, Abraham, 236–238, 250–251
Gronowski, Simon, 1, 13, 173–175, 198
Guérin, Paul. *See* Breslerman, Ludwig
Gueta, Anat 105, 113, 129, 131
Günther, Rolf, 33, 57, 116–119
Gutmann, Simon, 59, 148

H., Georg, 246
Haberkorn, Alfons, 119
Hakker, Joseph, 159, 191
Handschuh, Eugène, 33, 93–96
Handschuh, Louis, 94, 96, 116, 125–126, 261
Handschuh, Oscar, 93–94, 96–97, 126
Harlan, Thomas, 30, 36
Harster, Wilhelm, 34, 206–208, 213, 215–216, 241–245
Hatker, Karin, 183

Heerbrandt, 110
Heißmeyer, Kurt, 110
Hellenbroich, Heinz, 87–89, 124
Helwes, Hans, 26, 28–29, 35, 222, 224, 247
Henke, Alfred, 223, 247
Henneicke, 209
Herbert, Ulrich, 32–37, 42, 44, 114–115, 195
Herbst, Toni, 183
Hermann, Susi, 102
Hershkowitz, Albert, 66–67, 120
Herskovic, William, 24
Herskoviez, Abram. *See* Hershkowitz, Albert
Herszaft, David, 156–157
Hespe, Hans, 28, 35
Heydrich, Reinhard, 25, 41, 42, 188, 206
Hilberg, Raul, 2, 13, 15, 25, 33, 35, 115
Hillesum, Etty, 22, 34, 213, 220, 243, 246
Himmler, Heinrich, 18, 25, 41, 44, 77, 89, 115, 123, 135, 143, 146, 215–216, 244
Hirsch, Ernst, 102–103, 110–113, 131
Hirschfeld, Benita, 144, 190
Hirschfeld, Gerhard, 15, 114, 187, 216, 239–244, 246
Hitler, Adolf, 40, 45, 116–118, 140, 183, 205, 209, 228, 240, 242, 261
Holdhoff, Wilhelm, 223, 247
Holzinger, Robert, 141
Honig, Ignac, 105, 129
Horn, Edgar, 233
Horn, Leon, 233
Höß, Rudolf, 33, 68
Houwink ten Cate, Johannes, 34, 36, 186–188, 206, 239–244, 246
Humpert, Viktor, 135

Iest, Henk van der, 228–229
Imerglik, Joël Fiszel, 158
Imerglik, Szymon 157, 195
Israel, Walter, 193, 260
Italiaander, Hermann 230–232

Jospa, Ghert, 164, 189, 197
Jospa, Yvonne, 164
Jung, Albert, 137, 154–155, 194
Just-Dahlmann, Barbara, 32, 37

Kalifat, Maurice, 93, 94, 96
Kantim, Walter, 30–31, 36, 80
Kapel, René, 101–102, 104, 107–109, 111–115, 127–131
Kapelovitz, Sami. *See* Kapel, René
Käsewieter, Alfred, 221–222
Kassel, Walter, 70–71, 76, 82, 85, 90, 121, 123
Katzenelson, Jizchak, 100, 126
Kaufmann, Paula, 102–104, 107–113, 126–132
Kaufmann, Sylvain, 83–90, 116
Keller, Lipa Abraham, 151, 193
Keller, Ludwig, 151
Kessler, Paul, 108, 112
Kibel, Rosa, 163
Klarsfeld, Serge, 2, 13–14, 33–34, 75–76, 114–126, 129, 188–193, 195, 200, 261
Kleinmann, Salomon, 182–183, 200
Klemp, Stefan, 29, 34–36, 123, 246–247
Klüger, Ruth, 263, 265
Knochen, Helmut, 41–42, 44, 47, 50, 100, 115–117, 119
Koffman, Gilbert, 88
Kohn, Antoinette, 106
Kohn, Armand, 104–111, 131
Kohn, Marie-Jeanne, 110
Kohn, Philippe, 109–110, 129–131
Kohn, Robert, 83
Kohn, Rose-Marie, 104–110
Kohn, Suzanne, 104–110
Köhnlein, Friedrich 52, 92–93, 100, 117–119, 125, 261
Kolk-Cohen, Lisa van de, 237, 250
König, 81
Köpf, Ludwig, 149–150
Kotälla, Josef Johann, 235
Kotz, Jean, 88–89
Kounio, Heinz Salvator, 10, 15
Krämer, Theodor, 27–28, 35, 244

Kreutzmüller, Christoph, 207, 239, 240–241, 243
Krochmal, Régine, 166–168, 198, 254, 258–259, 261
Krull, Erich, 160
Kszepicki, Abraham, 263, 265
Kubowitzki, Maurice, 182, 184, 200, 261
Küchler, 204
Kunz, Andreas, 11, 15
Kuper, Arja, 156–157
Küver, 75–76, 122
Kwiet, Konrad, 2, 14, 239, 242

Lachman, Icek, 35
Lachmann, Rudi, 157
Lande, Meta, 111, 113, 131
Lazarus, Jacques, 101–104, 107, 111–113, 127–131
Lebeau, Lucien, 109, 130
Leeuwe, Sal de, 76, 122
Leguay, Jean, 78, 115
Leipziger, 152
Leopold III., King of Belgium, 134
Lessing, Theodor, 10, 15
Lessner, Rosa, 154
Levi, Primo, 263, 265
Liebehenschel, Arthur, 100, 126
Lienke, Gerhard, 149, 192
Liennewiel, Joseph, 111
Lischka, Kurt, 54, 116–118, 123
Livchitz, Alexander, 162, 165
Livchitz, Youra (Georges), 165–166
Loeb, 229
Loebenberg, Maurice, 102
Lovenwirth, Émile, 180
Lüdeke, Georg, 222, 247
Luther, 137, 187, 188, 242

Mager, Charles, 97–98, 126
Magier, Margareta, 158
Magier, Szlama, 158
Maintz, Twan, 227–228
Mainzhausen, Karl, 162
Maistriau, Robert, 165–166, 198
Mannheim, Betty, 234, 250
Margulies, Abraham, 22, 33, 261

Margulies, Hans, 23, 243, 245
Margulies, Maurice. *See* Margulies, Moritz
Margulies, Moritz, 104–109, 128, 130, 260
Matarasso, Albert, 76
Matthäus, Jürgen, 25, 35–36
Mayer, Hans (later Jean Améry), 142
Meershoek, Guus, 206, 241–243
Meinen, Insa, 3, 14, 181, 186–188, 190–191, 193, 195, 199, 200
Meinshausen, Karl, 24, 144
Melkman, Herman, 234–236, 238, 250
Mendel, Günther, 175–177
Mendel, Marie. *See* Neufeld, Marie
Mengele, Josef, 89
Menger, Truus, 210, 242
Meyer, Ahlrich, 2, 13–14, 23–24, 33, 118, 186, 211
Meyer, Walter, 222
Micheels, Louis J., 13, 168–169, 198, 240, 254, 261
Micka, H., 137
Moore, Bob, 199, 239–240, 242–243, 253, 260
Moschkovitch, Henri, 91, 124
Moses, Gustel, 249
Muni, Paul, 163
Mussert, Anton Adriaan, 203, 209, 239–240, 242

Nabet, Alfred, 89
Nebe, Arthur, 150
Neufeld, Marie (later married name Mendel), 175–177, 254
Niemann, 73, 212–122
Novak, Franz, 19, 32, 57
Novitch, Miriam, 100–101
Nowak, Willi, 32, 56, 68–69, 71–73, 119, 121

Oberg, Carl Albrecht, 45, 78, 115
Ott, 75
Ottenstein, Hans, 218, 244–245

Pageot, Raoul, 69, 121
Perelsztejn, Samuel, 83

Perl, Samuel, 159–162, 188, 191, 195–196
Pétain, Philippe, 41, 78
Philbert (family), 98
Philip, Justus, 239, 251
Pinkhof, Menachem, 102, 127, 262
Pirlot, Jean, 155–156, 194–195
Poche, Oswald, 87, 124
Pohoryles, Henri, 101, 104–105, 107, 109, 111–112, 115, 127–128, 130–131
Pollak, Michael, 10, 15
Posener, Kurt Friedrich, 156
Posener, Ludwig, 156
Posno, Jacques, 234–238
Possicelsky, Jacques, 94
Praag, Roger van, 164
Presser, Jacques, 3, 14, 128, 218, 240, 243–245, 249
Prowizur (later Prowizur-Szyper), Claire, 13, 140, 169–173, 198, 259, 261, 264–265
Prowizur, Klara. *See* Prowizur, Claire
Puls, Abraham, 226

R., Erwin, 150
Rackwitz, Helmut, 223, 247
Rajakowitsch, Erich, 207
Rauter, Hanns Albin, 205–206, 208, 212, 215, 240, 244
Reeder, Eggert, 135–137, 146, 187–188
Reilinger, Kurt, 102–103, 110–113, 131
Reymann, Jacob, 88
Rodd, Hans, 183
Rodenbüsch, Hans, 149, 190–192
Romsée, Gerard, 136
Rondor, Maurice, 258, 261
Rosenthal, Heinrich, 61
Roth, Ernst, 119
Röthke, Heinz, 46–47, 49–52, 65, 68, 70–71, 73–76, 78–79, 89–92, 100, 115–118, 120–125, 129, 261
Rozenberg, Bernard, 88
Rueff, Georges, 57–58, 116, 119, 257, 261
Rutkowski, Adam, 2, 13

Saerens, Lieven, 138, 141, 186–190
Sagiv, Shaul. *See* Siegel, Paul
Salomon, Chaïm, 105, 129
Schaft, Hannie, 210
Schandalow, Roger, 94–95, 125
Schelvis, Jules, 220, 245–246
Schlesinger, Kurt, 234
Schmelt, Albrecht, 18, 32, 146
Schmidt, Fritz, 205
Schmidt, Georges, 104
Schmitt, Philipp, 143–144
Schmitz, Rudolf, 161–162, 196–197, 258, 261
Schneider, Karl, 14, 235–36, 247
Schoellen, Anne, 97
Schoellen, Ernest, 97
Schouns, 165
Schram, Laurence, 3, 13, 141, 150, 153, 181–182, 186–187, 189–191, 193–197, 199–201, 160
Schramm, 55
Schreiber, Marion, 3, 13–14, 33, 196–197, 199, 261, 265
Schwartz, Henri, 94–95
Schwarz, Fred, 218
Schwarzbaum, Aron, 151–152
Schweblin, Jacques, 57
Serignan, 70, 74, 121–122
Seyß-Inquart, Arthur, 205–206, 215, 240
Siegel, Margot, 229
Siegel, Paul, 127–128, 131, 228–232, 240, 242–243, 245, 248–249, 260, 262
Siegel, Ruth, 229
Siegel, Salomon, 228
Siesel, Fritz, 231–232, 249
Siesskind-Zimmels, Lore, 249
Silber, Jakob, 74–76, 122
Silber, Joseph, 258–259, 261, 264–265
Silberwasser, Manfred, 64–68, 254
Simon, Albert, 164
Simon, Joachim, 102–103, 127
Slottke, Gertrud, 34, 208, 219, 241, 245–246
Sluijzer, Levie, 220, 246
Sluijzer, Moses, 220

Smit, Jan, 232
Speer, Albert, 157
Spitz, Jaak, 259, 261
Steinberg, Lucien, 2
Steinberg, Maxime, 2–3, 13–14, 34, 139, 141, 153, 182, 186–201, 241, 260
Steiner, Hugues, 83–88, 90, 123–124
Stoppelman, Gerard, 236–239, 250–251
Stoppelman, Isidor. *See* Stoppelman, Gerard
Strubel, Léon, 97
Stülpnagel, Carl-Heinrich, 45
Stülpnagel, Otto von, 41–45
Szolom, Jakob, 154–155
Sztejnberg, Izrael, 176
Szyper, Philippe, 169–173

Tabakman, Meyer, 162–164, 185, 197, 255, 259, 261
Tabakman, Szrul-Israël, 163
Taittinger, Pierre, 109
Telghuis, Ciska (née Rine) 234–239, 250
Terfve, Jean, 164
Thomas, Alfred, 139
Thomas, Max, 135
Toff, Jehuda (Juda) Arnold, 224–225, 247
Trautz, Ernst, 119
Trèves, Raymond, 95
Trumpeldor, J., 127, 249
Tulard, André, 57
Tulp, Sybren, 209

Uffenheimer, Martin, 228, 231–232
Uhlemann, Hermann, 30, 36, 79–81, 90, 123
Urban, 90–91, 117–118, 124

Van Dam, Sera Jeannette. *See* Wagenaar-van Dam, Sonja
Van der Iest, Henk, 228–229
Visscher, 229
Vistinezki, Hinda, 166, 198
Vogel, Georg Friedrich, 30, 36

Wagenaar-van Dam, Sonja (née Sera Jeannette van Dam), 235–239, 242, 250–251, 257, 261
Wahrhaftig-Siesel, Lottie, 232, 249
Wajnberg, Ryla, 151–152
Walter, Kurt, 232
Wand, Wolf, 154–155, 194
Wannenmacher, Karl, 52, 55
Wattenberg, Frida, 103, 128
Weber, Emil, 186, 201
Weichselbaum, Abraham, 99–100, 126
Weidmann, Fritz, 135
Weil, Léo, 113
Weinhauer, Klaus, 32, 37
Weinstock, Rolf, 53–54, 116–118, 261
Weisz, Sandor, 179–180, 199
Wellers, Georges, 21, 33, 116–117, 125–126
Westerweel, Johan Gerard (a.k.a Joop), 101–103, 105, 107, 110–113, 127–128, 131, 210, 232, 245, 249
Westerweel, Wilhelmina, 102
Wiegand, 81
Wiewerich, Heinrich, 223, 247
Wijnperle, Elsa, 225–228
Wijnperle, Manus, 225, 228
Wijnperle, Nathan, 226–228, 240, 248
Wilhelmina, Queen, 204
Wimmer, Friedrich, 205
Windmüller, Max, 102–103, 110, 112–113, 131
Winkelman, 204
Wolder, Maurits, 224–225, 247–248
Woll, 81
Wouters, Nico, 139, 187–188, 190

Zeitschel, Carltheo, 42, 47, 116
Zeller, Ron, 34, 146, 206, 211, 242
Zoepf, Wilhelm, 33, 206, 219, 232, 245–246, 249, 256, 261
Zuschneid, Gustav, 56, 69, 71–73, 90, 118–119, 121, 124

Index of Organizations

Ainheit, 133
Armée belge des Partisans, 156
Armée Juive (AJ), 46, 101, 111, 113
Armée Secrete, 157
Association des Juifs en Belgique/ Jodenvereeniging in België (AJB/ JVB), 23, 136, 140–141, 143, 145, 148, 254

Belgian Communist Party (PCB), 140, 157
Belgian Legion (*later*: Armée Secrète/ Geheim Leger), 140
Bund, 43, 133

Combat, 93
Comité Amelot, 43
Comité de défense des Juifs (CDJ), 142, 164–165, 180, 253–254

Deloncle, 44
Duitsch-Vlaamsche Arbeidsgemeenschap (DeVlag), 138

Eclaireurs Israélites de France (EIF), 46
Ezra, 64

Faucons Rouges/ Rode Valken, 133, 169
Forces françaises de l'intérieur (FFI), 59
Francs-tireurs et partisans (FTP). *See* Main-d'œuvre immigrée (MOI)
Francs-tireurs et partisans français (FTPF), 45
Freies Österreich, 108

Friends of Nature, 96
Front de l'Indépendence/ Onafhankelijkheidsfront, 140, 142, 185, 253
Fürsorgedienst, 230–231

Groupe G, 164–165

Hashomer Hatzaïr, 133
Hechaluz, 102, 229, 230, 232
Hitachdut, 100

International Brigades, 42, 140, 167, 180

Jeune Garde Socialiste Unifiée, 133
Jewish Committee (Comité d'Assistance aux Réfugiés juifs), 177
Joodse arbeiders sportklub, 133
Joodse Raad, 211, 215–216, 227, 230
Judenrat. *See* Union générale des Israélites de France (UGIF) (France); Association des Juifs en Belgique/ Jodenvereeniging in België (AJB/ JVB) (Belgium); Joodse Raad (Netherlands)

Kolonne Henneicke, 209

La Sixième, 68
Le mouvement de la jeunesse sioniste, 46

M 7, 111

Main-d'œuvre étrangère (MOE), 40
Main-d'œuvre immigrée (MOI), later also FTP-MOI or FTP, 40, 43, 45–46, 60, 93, 101, 106, 108, 111–112, 140–141, 157, 180, 254
Mobile Corps des Partisans, 140, 180
Mouvement National Belge (MNB), 180

Nationaal Socialistische Beweging (NSB), 203, 208–209, 228
Nederlandse Zionistenbond, 203

Ordnungsdienst (OD), 23, 214, 234
Organisation juive de combat (OJC), 46
Organisation Spéciale (OS), 45
Organisation Todt, 9, 12, 103, 136, 150, 153–154, 156–157, 253

Paalei Zion 203
Parti Communiste français (PCF), 40, 45, 106

Poale Zion, 133, 140, 142, 162

Radio Oranje, 22
Red Cross, 9, 109, 111, 148
Rex, 134, 138, 185

Travail allemand (TA), 142, 167, 180

Union générale des Israélites de France (UGIF), 50

Vereniging tot Vakopleiding van Palestina (Deventer Vereniging, 229
Vlaamsch Nationaal Verbond (VNV), 134, 136, 138
Volksverwering, 134, 138, 139

Weer Afdeling, 208
Westerweel Group, 101–103, 105, 107, 110–113, 210, 232

Index of Escapes and Escape Attempts

Entries are listed by country and in chronological order.

France, 57
- 1st transport, 27 March 1942, Rueff, Georges, 57–58
- Unknown date, Goldwasser, Bertha, 58–60
- 35th transport, 21 September 1942, Fuchs, Adolphe, 60
- 40th transport, 3 November 1942, Catz, Hans and Theo, 60–64
- 42nd transport, 6 November 1942, Bretholz, Leo; Silberwasser, Manfred, 64–68
- 46th transport, 9 February 1943, 68–70
- 47th transport, 11 February 1943, 70–71
- 48th transport, 13 February 1943, 71–74
- 50th transport, 4 March 1943, 74–76
- 51st transport, 6 March 1943, 76–77
- 52nd transport, 23 March 1943, 77–82
- 53rd transport, 25 March 1943, 82–90
- 55th transport, 23 June 1943, 90–92
- 62nd transport, 20 November 1943, Drancy tunnel diggers, 92–100
- 72nd transport, 29 April 1944, Eck, Nathan, 100–101
- 79th transport, 17 August 1944, 101–113

Belgium, 150
- 12th/13th transport, 10 October 1942, Aron, Walter; Keller, Lipa A. and Ludwig, 151
- 14th/15th transport, 24 October 1942, Wajnberg, Ryla; Sschwarzbaum, Aron, 151–152
- 14th transport, 24 October 1942, Dawid, Otto, 152–153
- 16th and 21st transports, 31 October 1942/31 July 1943, Beck, Israel, 154
- 16th transport, 31 October/1 November 1942, Cykiert, Majlych and Maruice; Szolom, Jakob, Wand, Wolf, 154–155
- 16th transport, November 1942, Aronowicz, Szulim, 155–156
- 16th transport, 31 October/1 November 1942, Posener, Ludwig; Fremder, Pinkus; Kuper, Arja; Herszaft, David; Baum, Jacheta, 156–158
- 18th/19th transport, 15 January 1943, Fritz, Monika and Hans; Magier, Margareta, 158
- 18th transport, 15 January 1943, Hakker, Joseph, 159
- 18th/19th transport, 15 January 1943, and 20th transport, 19 April 1943, Perl, Samuel, 159–160
- 18th/19th transport, 15 January 1943, Abramowicz, Fanny; Berger, Leopold and Kurt, 160–161

18th/19th transport, 15 January 1943, Schmitz, Rudolf, 161–162
19th and 20th transports, 15 January 1943/19 April 1943, Tabakman, Meyer, 162–166
20th transport, 19 April 1943, Vistinezki, Hinda; Goldsteinas, Mendelis J., 166
20th transport, 19 April 1943, Krochmal, Régine, 166–168
20th transport, 19 April 1943, Micheels, Louis J., 168–169
20th transport, 19 April 1943, Prowizur, Claire; Szyper, Philippe, 169–173
20th transport, 19 April 1943, Gronowski, Simon, 173–175
20th transport, 19 April 1943, Neufeld, Marie; Mendel, Günther, 175–177
20th transport, 19 April 1943, Sztejnberg, Izrael, 178
20th transport, 19 April 1943, Berler, Willy, 178–179
20th transport, 19 April 1943, Weisz, Sandor et al., 179–180
21st transport, 31 July 1943, Bina, Chaj; Benkiel, Josek M., 181–182
22nd transport (A), 20 September 1943, Bonheim, Alice (Annaliese); Kleinmann, Salomon, 182–183
22nd transport (B), 20 September 1943, Altschuler, Michel, 183
22nd transport (B), 20 September 1943, Grabiner, Charles, 184
23rd transport, 15 January 1944, Cukier, Schaja, 184
23rd transport, 15 January 1944, Blok, Reina, 184–185
23rd transport, 15 January 1944, Apfeldorfer, Simon, 185–186
24th transport, 4/5 April 1944, Weber, Emil, 186

The Netherlands, 224
11 January 1943, Toff, Juda A.; Wolder, Maurits, 224–225
29 January 1943, Wijnperle, Elsa and Nathan, 225–228
1 February 1944, Siegel, Paul; Uffenheimer, Martin, 228–232
Unknown Date, 1943, Levy, Max M., 232–234
1944, unnamed girl, 234
4 September 1944, various prisoners, 234–239

www.ingramcontent.com/pod-product-compliance
Lightning Source LLC
Chambersburg PA
CBHW050207130526
44590CB00043B/3052